A. E. Burns

MAJOR GENERAL

AMBROSE E. BURNSIDE

AND THE

NINTH ARMY CORPS:

A NARRATIVE OF CAMPAIGNS IN

NORTH CAROLINA, MARYLAND, VIRGINIA, OHIO, KENTUCKY, MISSISSIPPI AND TENNESSEE, DURING THE WAR FOR THE PRESERVATION OF THE REPUBLIC,

BY

AUGUSTUS WOODBURY.

ILLUSTRATED WITH PORTRAITS AND MAPS.

PROVIDENCE:
SIDNEY S. RIDER & BROTHER.
1867.

PRESS OF KNOWLES, ANTHONY & CO., PROVIDENCE.

TO THE

OFFICERS AND MEN

OF THE

Ninth Army Corps:

TO THE

WELL WON RENOWN OF THE

LIVING,

AND TO THE TENDER AND SACRED MEMORY OF THE

DEAD,

THE AUTHOR DEDICATES THIS BOOK.

PREFACE.

FOR the volume which is here given to the public, no more is claimed than that which appears upon the title page. It is a simple narrative—in the four distinct parts into which the subject naturally divided itself—of the actions and events in which the soldiers of the Ninth Army Corps and their principal commander participated. No corps in the army, with the exception of those which made the grand march from Atlanta to the coast and up through the Carolinas, has performed more arduous service, or marched or fought over a wider territory than the Ninth. The soldiers used to speak of themselves as composing "the first class in geography." It can hardly be expected that, in traversing so extensive a field, I have succeeded in avoiding all mistakes. One or two errors have already been detected, but unfortunately not till after the sheets had been printed, when it was impossible to rectify them. In general, however, I think it will be found that the story is as truthfully told as it could well have been by one, who was not an eye witness of the scenes which he describes. I shall be very grateful to any person who will point out to me any errors into which I have unwittingly fallen. My design has simply been to tell a plain, unvarnished tale. I have sought to extenuate nothing, and I am sure that I have set down nothing in malice. I have sought to narrate actual occurrences, rather than to express opinions. If, in some instances, the statements which here appear are somewhat different from those which others have made, all that I wish to insist upon is, that they are the statements of facts, and not of prejudice or fancy.

One mistake, which no one regrets more than myself, occurs upon page 253, where the 9th New Hampshire regiment is spoken of, as though it had been separated from the Corps for a time, and then returned to it. Such was not the fact. The 9th New Hampshire was connected with the Corps from the beginning unto the end. It joined the Corps in the latter part of August, 1862, having then just arrived from home, and was assigned to General Sturgis's division. It immediately entered into active service, was very creditably engaged at South Mountain, Antietam and Fredericksburg, went West, was in the Mississippi campaign, was on garrison duty in Kentucky, gaining deserved honor by its good discipline, returned to the East with the Corps, and shared in all the operations of the summer of 1864 and around Petersburg, until the close of the war. Everywhere the regiment performed manful and soldierly service, and won for itself and its State, in its earliest days as in its last, an honorable fame. Its officers were brave and able, and its enlisted men, at its original organization, were drawn from the ranks of the intelligent yeomanry of the Granite State. My regret, for the occurrence of the error respecting its career, is lessened by the satisfaction which I feel in giving this particular notice of its faithful service.

My grateful acknowledgments are due to the officers of the Ninth Corps for acts of consideration and confidence, and for the readiness with which they have entrusted to me many of their cherished papers and documents. I wish expressly to declare my obligations to Generals Burnside, Parke, Willcox, Cox, Potter and Ferrero, for repeated kindnesses; to General S. G. Griffin, for the use of his manuscript notes; to General Loring, for many excellent suggestions and much indispensable information; to Lieutenant Colonel Larned, for constant and laborious coöperation, and to Alexander Farnum, Esq., of Providence, for most important assistance.

I thus send forth my book, hoping for it, from the general public, a kindly reception, and trusting that the officers and men of the Ninth Corps will look upon it with considerate favor, as an appreciative, though imperfect story of their patriotism and valor.

A. W.

Providence, R. I., December, 1866.

CONTENTS.

THE EXPEDITION TO NORTH CAROLINA.

THE ARMY OF THE POTOMAC.

THE DELIVERANCE OF EAST TENNESSEE.

THE LAST YEAR OF THE REBELLION.

MAPS.

ILLUSTRATIONS.

THE EXPEDITION

TO

NORTH CAROLINA.

THE EXPEDITION

TO

NORTH CAROLINA.

CHAPTER I.

THE FIRST COMMANDER OF THE NINTH CORPS.

BY a singular good fortune, not paralleled by any other corps in the Army of the United States, the relations of the Ninth Corps with its leading officers were unchanged during the continuance of the War of the Rebellion. General Ambrose Everett Burnside was its first commander, and from the date of the organization of the Corps until his retirement from the service, General Burnside's history was identified with its own. Many of the officers and men who composed it were those who fought the battles of Roanoke Island and Newbern. They were with their General at South Mountain and Antietam. They were a part of the Army of the Potomac when the heights of Fredericksburg were assailed. They followed their leader to the deliverance of East Tennessee. They again became a portion of the Army of the Potomac in the closing campaign of the war, and the ensanguined fields of the Wilderness, Spottsylvania, Cold Harbor, and Petersburg bore witness to their united valor. The career of the Corps and its story are inseparable from those of him who, in the early days of the war, led the First Rhode Island Regiment to the relief of Washington. Several of the privates and officers of that regiment were afterwards officers in the Corps. They followed the fortunes of the man whom they had learned to love, from the first to the last, and with undeviating fidelity. It becomes necessary, therefore, before entering upon the history of the Ninth Corps, as a distinct organization, to sketch, in the preliminary chapters of this volume, the early life of General Burnside, and to give some account of the operations which he conducted in Virginia and North Carolina.

In the year 1813, a party of friends from South Carolina joined the great caravan of emigrants that were rapidly filling the great fields of the west. Belonging to this party were a Mr. Edgehill Burnside and Miss Pamelia Brown, with others of their acquaintances and neighbors. The emigrants settled in what was then Indiana Territory, in that section which afterwards became Union County. In the veins of Mr. Burnside flowed the blood of those heroic men who, at Bannockburn and Flodden Field and on many a well fought field in both hemispheres, have proved that the Scotch are among the best soldiers in the world. His parents were born in Scotland, and, removing to America in the latter part of the last century, settled in South Carolina. Here their son was born and educated. Here he remained until the tide of emigration bore him away upon its surface to the West. Having decided to fix his residence in Indiana, he selected a fine place near what is now the town of Liberty, and there proceeded to establish his home. There, soon after his arrival, he was married to Miss Brown. His subsequent success in gaining the confidence and esteem of his fellow citizens, attests a character industrious, faithful and trustworthy. Following the profession of the law, he acquired a respectable reputation as a counsellor, was largely employed in the administration of estates, and enjoyed an extensive and lucrative practice. He is found afterwards and for several years, honorably and creditably filling the offices of clerk and judge of the county Probate Court.

Into this family, Ambrose—the fifth child—was born on the 23d day of May, 1824. He was carefully nurtured, and received his elementary education in the best schools of the neighborhood. There are glimpses of a boyhood ardent, affectionate and adventurous—of high hopes, of generous ambition, of honorable spirit—early evincing a love for military sports and studies, and for any enterprise that had the spice of romance or danger. As he grew up, other children were added to the family—a son and daughter. The farm had become cultivated and comfortable. The family had grown to be one of the most prominent and respected in Eastern Indiana. Mr. Burnside had received abundant testimonials from his neighbors and friends of their confidence and regard. The children were enjoying that training which would fit them for future usefulness and honor.

But as the older sons and daughters were entering upon an active course of life, misfortunes came. Mr. Burnside lost his property in some unprofitable business transaction, and it almost seemed as though the days which had been so bright and prosperous were to end in poverty. But if material possessions were lost, there were resources of character which could not fail. The children—both girls and boys—at once set themselves to work to help their father out of his pecuniary troubles. Ambrose engaged himself to a trader in the town, who carried on a country store, held the office of postmaster, and also followed the business of a tailor. But young Burnside was not destined for a long continuance in this situation.

His father had already desired that one of his sons should be educated at West Point, and Ambrose was selected for the position. It is a pleasing evidence of the esteem in which Mr. Burnside was held, that all the members of the Legislature of Indiana united in a recommendation to Hon. Caleb B. Smith, the member of Congress having the appointment, to give young Burnside the coveted privilege. Mr. Smith accordingly acceded to the request, and at the commencement of the academical year 1842, Ambrose Everett Burnside was enrolled among the cadets in the military service of the United States.

His life at West Point was similar to that of his fellow students. He numbered among his classmates Orlando B. Willcox, Ambrose P. Hill, Romeyn B. Ayres, Otis H. Tillinghast, Charles Griffin, and Henry Heth, all of whom have won distinction upon one side or the other in the course of the war. Among the other classes are found the names of Ulysses S. Grant, Fitz John Porter, Charles P. Stone, Barnard E. Bee, Wm. L. Crittenden, Geo. B. McClellan, Thomas J. Jackson, Geo. F. Evans, John G. Foster, Darius N. Couch, John G. Parke, and Jesse L. Reno. Upon the academic staff were Professor Mahan, Wm. S. Rosecrans, Israel Vogdes, Joseph G. Totten, and E. D. Keyes. The friendships then formed continued until later life, and helped to enhance the enjoyment of a soldier's life in the camps of the Union army, and to mitigate the pains of hostile encounter with those whom the civil war made temporary enemies. During the term of study, the war with Mexico broke out, and the young men partook of the general excitement of the nation. In 1847, young Burnside graduated in the artillery—the eighteenth in rank in a class of thirty-eight members. His commission, as brevet Second Lieutenant in the 2d Artillery, was dated July 1, 1847, and on the 8th of September, 1847, he was promoted to a full second lieutenancy, and assigned to the 3d Artillery.

Immediately upon his graduation, Lieutenant Burnside proceeded to the seat of war. On his arrival at Vera Cruz, he was put in command of an escort to a baggage train, and sent into the interior. Although the route was in the nominal possession of the United States Army, the Mexicans, by a species of guerilla warfare for which they are famous, had succeeded in disabling and cutting off several trains that had previously been sent out. The duty was hazardous, and the post responsible. But the young officer handled his command with great address and skill, carried it safely through, and won the hearty commendation of his superiors. Before he reached the Capital, however, the battles in front of the city of Mexico had been fought, and the war was virtually at an end. He was thus deprived of the opportunity which he wished of engaging, to any great extent, in the active operations of the armies in the field. When peace was proclaimed, and the army had returned home, Lieutenant Burnside was ordered to Fort Adams, Newport, R. I., where, by his eminently social qualities, and his frank, urbane, and honorable bearing, he gained many friends, and laid the foundation of that remarkable esteem with which he has long been regarded in the State of Rhode Island.

In the year 1849, Lieutenant Burnside was transferred from the agreeable duty of the post at Fort Adams and ordered to New Mexico, to join Bragg's famous battery, of which he was now appointed First Lieutenant. It was found that the country was not favorable for the operations of light artillery. Bragg's command was reorganized as cavalry, and Lieutenant Burnside, as second in command to Capt. H. B. Judd, was assigned to the duty of mail escort upon the Plains. The service was very perilous and exciting, but the young officer bore himself with so much coolness and bravery as to elicit warm encomiums for his conduct. He reached New Mexico on the 1st of August, and immediately entered into active service. On the 21st of that month, while stationed near Los Vegas with a force of twenty-nine men, he came in contact with a company of Indian warriors more than double his own command in number, drawn up at the head of a ravine to dispute his progress. He immediately determined to attack them ; and, after a single discharge of their rifles, his men, led by their gallant commander, charged with sabres, and swept the Apaches like chaff before them. In this brief and brilliant engagement, eighteen Indians were killed, nine were taken prisoners, forty horses and all the supplies of the band were captured, and the whole party was completely dispersed. The commander of the post, Capt. Judd, warmly complimented Burnside in despatches, and recommended him for promotion.

In the winter of 1850–51, Lieutenant Burnside acceptably filled the office of Quartermaster of the Boundary Commission, then engaged in running the line between the United States and Mexico, as established by the treaty of peace negotiated by the two nations. In September, 1851, he was ordered from the Gila River, where the Commission was then encamped, to proceed across the vast plains of the West to Washington, as bearer of despatches to the government of the United States. It was a duty which required the utmost vigilance, prudence, and persistence. It was necessary that the despatches should reach Washington at the earliest possible moment. With an escort of three men—one of whom was his faithful negro servant, whom he had found in New Mexico, and who has since followed his fortunes with a singular devotion—he started on his difficult enterprise. Twelve hundred miles of wilderness, occupied by wild beasts and Indians, many of whom were hostile, lay between him and civilization. He accomplished the distance in seventeen days, meeting with many adventures and hair-breadth escapes upon the way. At one time, a party of Indians was upon his trail for more than twenty-four hours, and he only escaped by taking advantage of the darkness of the night to double upon his pursuers. He fully attained the object of his mission, and was commended by the authorities for his fidelity and success.

During his time of service in New Mexico, Lieutenant Burnside had ascertained that the carbine then generally in use among our mounted soldiers, was wholly unsuitable and inadequate for the peculiar warfare of that region. While upon his journey to Washington, he occupied his mind with an attempt to supply the deficiency. He revolved the subject in his thoughts, and when further opportunities were given him, elaborated his plans, until, as the result of his reflection and study, he was enabled to produce a new arm. He invented a breech-loading rifle, which was vastly superior to any arm of the kind then in the service. It was distinguished for the facility with which it could be loaded, discharged, and cleansed, for its endurance as a serviceable weapon, its accuracy of aim, and its length of range. Other breech-loading rifles have been invented since that time, the excellences of which have somewhat obscured the merit of this arm. But at the time of its invention, it was beyond question the best of its kind. The inventor was especially desirous that his own country should receive the benefit of his labors, and that our soldiers upon the frontiers should enjoy the protection which a really superior weapon would afford. He offered to contract with the Government for the manufacture of the rifle, and was encouraged by the War Department to feel that his offers would be accepted. Meanwhile, he returned to his former post at Newport. While here, on the 27th of April, 1852, he was married to Miss Mary Richmond Bishop, of Providence.

The expectation of a contract for the manufacture of the newly invented weapon, and the flattering encouragement which he received from the War Department and the authorities at Washington, his marriage, and the peaceful state of the country induced Lieutenant Burnside to leave the service, and accordingly, on the 1st of November, 1853, he resigned his commission. Removing to Bristol, Rhode Island, he built a large manufactory, entered into business arrangements with some of the leading capitalists of the State, and prepared to complete his negotiations with the National Government. Unfortunately for him, the contract was not consummated, and after a few years of struggle and loss, Mr. Burnside became so deeply involved as to prevent any further progress in his adopted occupation. He was still more embarrassed by the action of John B. Floyd, who became Secretary of War in 1857, and who held out promises, encouragements, and inducements, only to disappoint their object. Mr. Burnside therefore soon found himself compelled to withdraw entirely from the manufacture of arms. With characteristic high mindedness and honorable feeling, he gave up everything which he

2

possessed, including his patent, to his creditors; and, selling even his uniform and sword, sought to retrieve his fortunes at the West.

The city of Chicago invited the efforts of the embarassed but still hopeful young man. His old friend and schoolmate, Captain George B. McClellan, had resigned his commission, and now occupied an honorable position in that place as Vice President of the Illinois Central Railroad. Mr. Burnside went to Chicago in the latter part of April, 1858, and there met Mr. William H. Osborn, the President of the road, who proved himself a fast and valued friend. Upon Mr. Osborn's recommendation, Mr. Burnside obtained the situation of cashier in the Land Department of the road. He made his quarters with Captain McClellan, and around a common fireside the two friends renewed the intimacy of former days. Mr. Burnside, limiting his expenses to a certain amount, devoted the remainder of his salary to the payment of his debts; and, when afterwards he was enabled to free himself entirely from the claims of his creditors, his unblemished integrity in business was as conspicuous as his fidelity in the field. In June, 1860, he had won the confidence of the Directors of the Railroad Company to such an extent as to receive the appointment of Treasurer of the Corporation.

By these vicissitudes of fortune, thus hastily sketched, was the early character of General Burnside trained. He had known what it was to struggle against poverty, disappointment, and failure. He had so conducted himself—he had manifested such courage and persistence through all the contest as to attract attention to his true and manly qualities. The people of Rhode Island had made him the Major General of their State Militia. He had also stood through one political canvass as a candidate for a seat in Congress, and was defeated only by his connection with an unpopular party. In Chicago, he had been widely and favorably known for his energy and his skill in affairs, his geniality in social intercourse, his high sense of honor, and his honest simplicity. By the proper exercise of such qualities he had won his way through all difficulties, till at last he had secured an honorable and lucrative position. Always patriotic, he could not endure the idea of the secession of the Southern States, which had begun to be seriously discussed in the latter part of President Buchanan's administration.

A few months before the war broke out, Mr. Burnside happened to be in New Orleans, and of course the conversation among those he met turned upon the all-absorbing question. "There will be no war," said his friends. "Northern men will not fight. The South will separate herself from the Union, will set up an independent government, and will draw to her the Middle and Western States. We shall do whatever we please, and give laws and government to the continent. The North will not fight, and the South will have an easy triumph."

"You entirely mistake the character of the Northern people," said Burnside. "They will fight. They never will allow the Union to be broken, and a free government to be thus destroyed without a contest. If you persist in your purpose of secession, there will be war, a bloody and cruel war. Not only will the North fight, but she will also triumph. The experiment of secession will fail, and the South, in ruin and desolation, will bitterly repent the day when she attempted to overthrow a wise and beneficent government. Why do you seek redress for what you call your wrongs, in civil war? The first gun that you fire will unite us all—whatever our political opinions may be—in opposition to your attempt. The government will be sustained, and you will suffer a disastrous defeat."

He spoke in sadness, for he deplored war. But he spoke earnestly, for he was thoroughly loyal, and he knew, better than his Southern friends, the spirit of the North. He little thought, at that time, of the extent and severity of the struggle, nor did he expect to become one of the most conspicuous actors in its scenes.

CHAPTER II.

THE FIRST RHODE ISLAND REGIMENT.

THE memorable 13th of April came upon the country not unawares. Fort Sumter was bombarded by South Carolina troops, and the whole North—as Mr. Burnside had predicted—was aroused to arms. Preceding events had prepared the country, in some degree, for the struggle. But it was hardly supposed that the challenge which the South had offered would be so promptly accepted, or that the gage of battle which it had thrown down would be so readily taken up. The North was peaceful. Northern men were engaged in industrial pursuits, and did not seek the excitement, the danger, or the glory of war. But throughout the North there was a deep-seated sentiment of loyalty to free institutions, and a determination that such institutions should not be rudely and needlessly overthrown. Northern men were not pusillanimous, as the South had supposed. They were not, and never have been, quarrelsome. But they had a reverence for order and law, and though they might not at times be willing to resent a personal injury, they would not permit the national integrity to be assailed with impunity. A personal enemy they might not punish. But a public enemy would meet with no favor at their hands.

Mr. Burnside shared in the general feeling. His ardent temperament and his devotion to a principle of duty led him to adopt, with the whole force of his nature, the cause of the government as his own. He was not, politically, a friend of the administration of Mr. Lincoln. But he was a lover of his country. Mr. Lincoln was the constitutionally elected President of the United States. The secessionists of the South became, by the act of war, rebels and traitors against a free government. As such, they must be opposed to the death. It was no question of parties. It was a question of patriotism, and no one, who knew Mr. Burnside, could mistake as to the course which he would pursue. His country had given him an education, and he must now make return for her generosity by devoting himself to her service. Inclination agreed with duty, for, though averse to arms, he loved an active and laborious life. There was, indeed, great danger, but the sentiment of patriotism was stronger than the regard for bodily safety. He loved his home. But the obligation to his country was more imperative than his affection for family and friends. He was not a rich man. He had but little income beyond the salary of his office. But the claims of the nation, in her hour of peril, surpassed all others, and he was ready to sacrifice fortune, happiness, and life in her behalf.

On Monday, the 15th of April, 1861, Mr. Burnside was sitting in his office in the city of New York, when a telegraphic despatch was handed to him. It was dated at Providence, was from William Sprague, then Governor of Rhode Island, and was to the following purport: "A regiment of Rhode Island troops will go to Washington this week. How soon can you come on and take command?" The reply was very brief and to the point. Two words expressed it: "At once." The next morning he was in Providence, received his commission as Colonel of the First Regiment Rhode Island Detached Militia, immediately appointed his staff, and commenced the work of organization and equipment. The Governor and the other State authorities co-operated with him in a very efficient and creditable manner. The people of the State forgot their political differences, and were filled with enthusiasm for the impending enterprise. More men offered their services for the campaign than could be accepted. So promptly and effectively did the work proceed, that, on Thursday, April 18th, a light battery of six rifled pieces, fully furnished with horses, equipage, and men, left Providence, and on Saturday, the 20th, the first detachment of five hundred men and forty-four officers, completely armed, uniformed, equipped, and provisioned for a three weeks' campaign, and accompanied by the Governor of the State with members of his staff, embarked for the seat of war. The second detachment, of equal force, followed in the course of the next few days. The first detachment landed at Annapolis, Md., on the afternoon of the 24th, and marched the next morning for Annapolis Junction. The troops reached that place on the morning of the 26th, and took cars for Washington, arriving about noon. The 6th Massachusetts had reached there on the 19th, the 7th New York and the 8th Massachusetts on the 25th. But it is due to the First Rhode Island to say, that it was the first regiment that had arrived fully prepared, independently of the aid of the General Government, to take the field immediately. It could have started, for a week or fortnight's march into hostile territory, on the very evening of its arrival in Washington.

Colonel Burnside at once put his regiment under drill. A site for an encampment was found about two miles out from the heart of the city, near the Bladensburg turnpike. The camp soon became a favorite place of resort. The comfort, the cleanliness, the fine bearing, the excellent discipline of the Rhode Island troops were themes for commendation upon every tongue. Their dress parade at sunset was one of the acknowledged "sights" of Washington. Hundreds of spectators, among whom were not infrequently President Lincoln, the members of the Cabinet, and the most distinguished men of the country, daily assembled to witness the parade and to participate in the religious services that usually concluded it. The scene was of great impressiveness and beauty. Colonel Burnside was everywhere recognized as a skillful and admirable soldier. The regiment joined General Patterson's column, for a week or two in June, in a demonstration against Harper's Ferry, then held by the rebel troops under General J. E.

Johnston, and then returned to Washington to take part in more serious and important movements.

On the 21st of July was fought the first battle of Bull Run. The troops marched out from Washington on the 16th. Colonel Burnside was put in command of a brigade, consisting of his own and three other regiments — the 2d Rhode Island, the 2d New Hampshire, and the 71st New York — and Captain (afterwards Lieutenant Colonel) Reynolds' Rhode Island Battery.* This brigade belonged to a division under Colonel (afterwards Major General) David Hunter, and took the advance of the movement upon Fairfax Court House, by way of Annandale. The army, under General McDowell, occupied Centreville on the 18th. A reconnoissance on the same day developed the fact that the enemy, hitherto retreating, was determined to make a stand upon the south side of Bull Run and around his intrenchments at Manassas Junction. Here, on the 19th and 20th, while General McDowell was resting at Centreville, General Johnston from the Shenandoah Valley joined General Beauregard, and the enemy judged himself in sufficient strength to deliver battle, which he was preparing to do when he was informed that General McDowell was on the march.

General McDowell decided to attack on the 21st, and at two o'clock A. M. of that day, the troops were silently moved out of their encampments and put upon the march. The plan was for Colonel Hunter's division to make a flank movement to the right as far as Sudley Ford, then cross Bull Run, and marching down the south bank of that stream, unite with two other divisions, under the command of General David Tyler and Colonel (afterwards Major General) Heintzelman, which were to cross at lower fords and the Stone Bridge on the turnpike, and then offer battle to the enemy. After considerable delay in starting, on the part of the leading division, (General Tyler's,)

---

*Afterwards known as Battery A, 1st R. I. L. A., and distinguished throughout the war for most gallant and effective service.

the flank movement was made, with Colonel Burnside's brigade in advance. The route lay along the Warrenton Turnpike as far as a point just beyond Cub Run, when it turned to the right towards Sudley Ford. General Tyler's division was to continue on the turnpike and cross Stone Bridge. Colonel Heintzelman's was to follow Colonel Hunter for a short distance, and then go down to the run and cross at a ford above the bridge. The road was scarcely more than a wood path, across which many trees had fallen. Delayed by the removal of these obstructions, the column was occupied five or six hours in doing the work of three.

It was half past nine o'clock when the skirmishers of the 2d Rhode Island in advance crossed Sudley Ford, and immediately after, the enemy, who had been forewarned and had gathered a considerable force, opened upon the head of the column with round shot and shell. Our troops responded briskly, Colonel Burnside soon formed his brigade in line of battle, and advanced to meet the foe. The battle raged with great fury in this quarter for two or three hours. The enemy concentrated at this point all his forces, with the exception of two brigades, near Union Mills and Blackburn's Ford, and was determined to break our lines if possible. But our leading brigade firmly held its ground until its supports had come up, and even succeeded in driving the enemy from his strong position. Colonel (afterwards Lieutenant General) Wm. T. Sherman came on from Stone Bridge with his brigade, crossing his troops by a ford above the bridge. Colonel Heintzelman, with his division, followed Hunter, not having been able to find the ford at which he was to cross the run, and participated gallantly in the conflict on the extreme right of our line.

By two o'clock, the enemy was beaten back at all points. Several of his best officers had been killed or wounded. By three, a part of his forces were retreating, broken and demoralized, towards Manassas. Colonel (afterwards Lieutenant General) T. J. Jackson, with a fine brigade of Virginia troops, seemed to be the only man in the rebel army who was determined to hold his ground at all hazards, and all our attacks upon him were unavailing. "See how like a stone wall Jackson's troops stand," cried some one,—and the sobriquet of "Stonewall" was thenceforward fixed upon the gallant soldier.

At half past three o'clock, fresh reënforcements for the enemy, under General W. Kirby Smith, arrived from the Shenandoah Valley, and attacked our lines upon the right flank with great energy. Heintzelman's division was at once broken. Two batteries of our artillery—Griffin's and Ricketts'—were overpowered, their supports fled, and the pieces fell into the enemy's hands.* Captain Reynolds succeeded in drawing his guns off from the field unharmed, but both Captains Griffin and Ricketts lost all their pieces. Colonel Orlando B. Willcox, in command of a brigade in Heintzelman's division, and other officers were taken prisoners. Colonels Slocum of Rhode Island, Cameron of Pennsylvania, and a considerable number of officers of a lower grade were killed or mortally wounded. The army was somewhat disorganized. The troops, though without food, and suffering much from the heat, had marched well and fought well; but they were not able to stand against the unexpected onset of the enemy's reënforcements. General McDowell, seeing that the battle was going against him, ordered a retreat. It proved to be the worst possible order for volunteer troops in their first engagement. The fortunes of the day were immediately and irremediably changed. Had our troops been directed to rally after their first surprise, and to hold their ground, they could easily have repulsed the last rebel attack, and have sent the enemy panic-stricken beyond Manassas. But the word "retreat" had then an ominous sound.

* The loss of these pieces, which decided the issue of the action, is said to have been caused by the mistake of Colonel W. F. Barry, Chief of Artillery, who, standing by Captain Griffin's battery at the time of the enemy's advance, supposed that the new troops were our own and would not permit our artillerists to open on them. The guns were turned away, the enemy coolly deployed at short range, opened a volley of musketry, made a sudden rush, scattered the infantry support, and captured the battery.

The army soon fell into utter disorder, and the broken and disorganized mass poured along the roads in disgraceful flight. The retreat soon became a rout. Colonel Burnside rallied his brigade just across the run, and, with the aid of Captain Arnold's battery and Major Sykes's battalion of regulars, covered the retreat along the forest road, and saved the army from utter destruction. General Tyler's division had already retreated along the turnpike. The army reached Centreville soon after dark, but in such a demoralized condition that it could not be held, and the entire command was ordered to Washington.

Colonel Burnside's brigade rested in its camp at Centreville for three or four hours, marched during the remainder of the night, was gathered near Long Bridge in the morning, and the several regiments of which it was composed returned to their encampments in Washington during the forenoon of the 22d.

The battle of Bull Run has given rise to much discussion. It was the first battle of the war, and attracted great attention. It is universally conceded that General McDowell planned the movement skilfully. Had it been carried out according to the order, we should have won a great success. But several circumstances occurred to prevent. The importance of punctuality has never been recognized at any time during the war. It certainly was not considered on the morning of the 21st of July. The leading division ought to have been across Cub Run at the time it was moving out of its camp. The two hours' delay was fatal. Another unfortunate circumstance was Colonel Heintzelman's inability to reach the ford at which he was ordered to cross. Still another was the order in which our troops were sent into the battle, not by brigades but regiment by regiment. Still another was the distance of our reserves from the field of battle, and their inactivity. But most of all was the failure of General Patterson to hold General Johnston in the Shenandoah Valley, while General McDowell forced General Beauregard out of Manassas, as could easily have been done. This entire subject has been considered in another volume, to which the reader curious in such matters is referred.*

The First Rhode Island Regiment, a few days after the battle, was ordered to Providence, where it arrived on the 28th, and was received with unprecedented enthusiasm. Colonel Burnside and his command received the thanks of the General Assembly of Rhode Island, and, on the 2d of August, the regiment was mustered out of the United States service, having won for itself and its Colonel a proud name in the annals of the war.

---

* Campaign of the First Rhode Island Regiment, pp. 74 and following.

CHAPTER III.

HATTERAS INLET.

THE issue of the battle of Bull Run had demonstrated the necessity of a complete organization of the forces, which a patriotic but impatient country was placing in the field. To arm, to equip, and to organize five hundred thousand men, who had just been drawn from peaceful pursuits, from farm, workshop and counting room, and to make of them an effective military force, was a task of no small magnitude. It was felt that more energetic counsels should prevail at Washington than had thus far characterized the conduct of the war. A younger man was needed to invigorate the army. General Scott, an old and highly meritorious soldier, was thought to be—and thought himself to be—incapacitated for so arduous a service as would naturally devolve upon a General-in-Chief. The most prominent of our younger officers, at that time, was General George B. McClellan, who had won distinction in a rapid and brilliant campaign in Western Virginia. He was called to Washington, placed in command of the Army of the Potomac, and immediately engaged in the work of putting that army into a condition fit for successful operations. The rebel army had gradually extended its posts from Manassas to the neighborhood of Washington, till its advance was encamped within sight of the Capitol. Our own army was encamped around the city, and a cordon of forts was projected and put in process of construction.

Most of the superior officers engaged in the battle of Bull Run had been promoted. Among these, Colonel Burnside had been conspicuous, and he was accordingly appointed a Brigadier

General of Volunteers, his commission dating August 6, 1861. General McClellan desired his services in aiding him to organize the army, and for a month or two, General Burnside was employed in that important work. But it soon became evident that General McClellan's policy was one of inaction, so far as his own army was concerned, while the enemy was to be harassed by expeditions sent out to make a lodgment at different points upon the southern coast. These points were to become the bases for future operations, when a simultaneous advance would be made upon the enemy, and the rebellion would be crushed by overwhelming pressure upon all sides. Some of the islands off the coast of South Carolina had already been secured. The coast of North Carolina was selected as another section to be occupied. An expedition was projected to secure that important result, and the duty of arranging and carrying this to a successful end was intrusted to General Burnside.

General Burnside at once entered upon the discharge of his duties. His headquarters were established in New York city, and the months of November and December were occupied in contracting for transportation, in organizing the troops assigned to him, in procuring arms, ammunition, supplies and material of war of all kinds. The entire land force concentrated at Annapolis, Md. The naval coöperating force assembled at Hampton Roads. General Burnside's personal staff was composed of Captain Lewis Richmond, Assistant Adjutant General, Captain Herman Biggs, Division Quartermaster, Captains T. C. Slaight and Charles G. Loring, Jr., Assistant Quartermasters, Captain E. R. Gooodrich, Commissary of Subsistence, Captains James F. De Wolf and William Cutting, Assistant Commissaries, Lieutenant D. H. Flagler, Ordnance Officer, Dr. W. H. Church, Division Surgeon, Lieutenants Duncan A. Pell and George Fearing, Aides de Camp.

The land force was divided into three brigades. The first was composed of the 23d, 24th, 25th, 27th Massachusetts, and 10th Connecticut regiments of infantry, and was under the command of Brigadier General John G. Foster. The second was composed of the 6th New Hampshire, 9th New Jersey, 21st Massachusetts, 51st New York, and 51st Pennsylvania regiments of infantry, and was under the command of Brigadier General Jesse L. Reno. The third was composed of the 4th Rhode Island, 8th and 11th Connecticut, 53d and 89th New York regiments of infantry, a battalion of the 5th Rhode Island infantry, and Battery F, 1st Rhode Island Light Artillery, and was under the command of Brigadier General John G. Parke. A naval brigade, recruited in New York by the name of the Volunteer Marine Artillery, under the command of Colonel Howard, was also specially organized for this expedition. The regiments were full, and the command numbered twelve thousand strong. For the transportation of the troops and their materiel, forty-six vessels were employed, eleven of which were steamers. To these were added nine armed propellers to act as gun-boats, and five barges fitted and armed as floating batteries, carrying altogether forty-seven guns, mostly of small calibre. These formed the army division of the fleet, and were commanded by Commander Samuel F. Hazard. A fleet of twenty vessels, of different sizes—mostly of light draft, for the navigation of the Albemarle and Pamlico Sounds, but carrying a heavy armament of fifty-five guns—accompanied the expedition, under the command of Flag Officer Louis M. Goldsborough.*

* The names of the vessels composing the army division were as follows: Picket, 4, Captain Thomas P. Ives; Hussar, 4, Captain Frederick Crocker; Pioneer, 4, Captain Charles E. Baker; Vidette, 3, Captain John L. Foster; Ranger 4, Captain Samuel Emerson; Lancer, 4, Captain U. B. Morley; Chasseur, 4, Captain John West, Zouave, 4, Captain William Hunt; Sentinel, 4, Captain Joshua Couillard. The barges were the Rocket, 3, Master's Mate James Lake; Grenade, 3, Master's Mate Wm. B. Avery; Bombshell, 2, Master's Mate Downey; Grapeshot, 2, Master's Mate N. B. McKean; Shrapnel, 2, Master's Mate Ernest Staples. The gunboats of the naval division were the Philadelphia, (flag ship,) Acting Master Silas Reynolds; Stars and Stripes, 5, Lieutenant Reed Werden; Louisiana, 5, Lieutenant A. Murray; Hetzel, 2, Lieutenant H. K. Davenport; Underwriter, 4, Lieutenant William N. Jeffers; Delaware, 3, Lieutenant S. P. Quackenbush; Commodore Perry, 4, Lieutenant Charles W. Flusser; Valley City, 5, Lieutenant J. C. Chaplin; Commodore Barney, 4, Acting Lieutenant R. T. Renshaw; Hunchback, 4, Acting Volun-

On the 19th of December General Burnside broke up his headquarters at New York, and proceeded to Annapolis. On the morning of the 5th of January, 1862, the troops commenced embarking, and by the morning of the 8th all were on board the transports. General Burnside selected the gunboat Picket as the flag ship of the expedition. She was under the command of Captain Thomas P. Ives. On the 9th and 10th, the fleet of transports dropped down Chesapeake Bay and anchored in Hampton Roads. On the morning of the 11th, the Picket came into the roads and cast her anchor under the guns of Fortress Monroe. During the subsequent night, most of the vessels of the expedition went to sea, and at 10 o'clock on the morning of the 12th General Burnside himself sailed. For the next ten days no intelligence of the movements of the fleet was made public.

But on the 23d of January, the public mind at the North was wonderfully excited by reports of shipwreck and disaster. It was supposed at one time, that the entire movement had proved a failure, and that a useless expenditure of materiel, money, and men had been made. As more trustworthy accounts reached the public ear, it became evident that, although there had been extreme peril, yet there had been no serious calamity, and that the officer in charge of the expedition was to be relied upon for success by an expectant country. Through storm and darkness, he had ever remained calm, collected, and hopeful, and by his perseverance had won a victory over the elements, which presaged a brilliant and triumphant result.

The entire fleet had been ordered to rendezvous at Hatteras

---

teer Lieutenant E. R. Colhoun; Southfield, 4, Acting Volunteer Lieutenant C. F. W. Behm; Morse, 2, Acting Master Peter Hayes; Whitehead, 1, Acting Master Charles A. French; I. N. Seymour, 2, Acting Master G. W. Graves; Shawsheen, 2, Acting Master Thomas G. Woodward; Lockwood, 3, Acting Master C. L. Graves; Ceres, 2, Acting Master John McDiarmid; General Putnam, 1, Acting Master W. J. Hotchkiss; Henry Brinker, 1, Acting Master John E. Giddings; Granite, 1, Acting Master's Mate E. Boomer. The naval division was under the general command of Commander S. C. Rowan, second to the Flag Officer. Most, if not all these vessels were improvised men-of-war, fitted from ferry boats, propellers, river steamboats, canal boats, &c.

Inlet, preparatory to its subsequent operations. When it left Hampton Roads, the weather was fine. But after getting clear of the capes of Virginia, it became dull and foggy. There was much delay in consequence. The steamers could make but slow progress in towing the sailing vessels and barges, and it was not till the 14th, that the fleet was off Cape Hatteras. This dread of mariners, the abode of storms, was true to its former repute. It seemed as though a tempest had been lurking behind this fearful point, ready to dash out and sweep to ruin any adventurous vessel that should dare approach. A few steamers with their convoy succeeded in passing safely, and, making the inlet, crossed the bar, and came to anchor in the comparatively smooth waters of Pamlico Sound. But the remaining vessels of the fleet were caught by the rising storm, and were dispersed. By the 17th, most of the vessels had made a harbor, but it was not till more than a week later, that the expedition could be said to have escaped the perils of the sea.

For nearly two weeks a succession of storms beat upon the "dark-ribbed ships" and the heroic men who filled them. There was scarcely a lull of more than two or three hours in duration, and even then the sea was running very high, and a movement of any of the vessels was extremely dangerous to the rest. At times, the sea would break over the island itself, and the fort upon its southern point was completely isolated. One or two regiments managed to get on shore, and found a precarious shelter beneath their tents. One steamer, the City of New York, loaded with ammunition, and another, the Pocahontas, with horses on board, went ashore and were lost. One gunboat, the Zouave, dragged her anchors, and staving a hole in her bottom was wrecked. A floating battery, the Grapeshot, was swamped. One or two schooners loaded with forage and provisions were driven upon the beach. But fortunately, amid all the terrors of the storm, there was but little loss of life. Six men of the crew of one of the transports were drowned in attempting to reach the land, and the vessel was wrecked. Two officers of the army, Colonel J. W. Allen and Dr. F. S. Weller, both belonging to the 9th New Jersey infantry, were lost on the 15th, by the swamping of a boat in which they were returning from the flag ship of the commanding general to their transport. They had gone on board, in company with others, early in the morning, to consult with General Reno. After spending an hour or two very agreeably, they left the ship, went on board their boat, and put off towards their own vessel. But in moving through the surf, the boat was capsized, and the entire party, twelve in number, were thrown into the waves. They succeeded however in clinging to the boat, and for half an hour they were in this perilous position. At last, the steamer Highlander came within hailing distance, sent out her boats, and picked up the drenched and exhausted men. But no means availed to bring back to life the two insensible officers. They had passed away from earth. Colonel Allen was a native of Burlington County, in New Jersey, had been a member of the State Senate, and had acquired considerable reputation as a civil engineer. He resided in Bordentown, where he left a widow and several children. Dr. Weller was a resident of Paterson, where he was highly esteemed as a man and a physician.

The storm, which had well nigh proved the ruin of the expedition, was the severest which had visited that region for several years, and it burst upon the fleet at the very moment when it was capable of inflicting the greatest injury. Hatteras Inlet is a passage made by the sea breaking across the narrow spit of land which, in its bolder and more prominent point, is known as Cape Hatteras. The channel, if so it might be called, is simply the place where the water, for the time, happens to be deepest. Outside the island, at the entrance of the inlet from the ocean, is a bar, and just inside the island, where the waters of the inlet meet those of the Sound, there is another bar. The channel between the two, in the vernacular of that section, is called the "swash." As the bottom is loose and sandy, its depth varies, at different times, from five to nine feet, according to the force of the winds and the current. The tide rises but a few feet. The inlet is scarcely over a mile wide, and at the entrance of the Sound, is the bar or "bulk-head," on which the water, in the height of the tide, can be no more than six or eight feet deep*. Beyond the point, a slight curve in the shore makes a small harbor. In the Sound itself, there is sufficient water to float in safety vessels of considerable draft and tonnage. It is in general about twenty feet in depth, but abounds in shoals, which render its navigation somewhat difficult and dangerous. Into the narrow passage called Hatteras Inlet, and immediately beyond, the storm had driven over one hundred vessels of different sizes. Some were found too large and of too great draft of water to pass through the shallow channel. The anchorage was uncertain. Even before their arrival, the vessels had been considerably shaken by the heavy weather. They were, moreover, filled to their utmost capacity, with troops, many of whom had never before sailed a mile upon the ocean, and were overcome by seasickness. Crowded into this narrow and uncomfortable anchoring place, which could hardly be called a harbor except by an extreme stretch of courtesy, with no secure ground to catch the anchors, the vessels were forced about by the wind in a most uncomfortable and vexatious manner. It was no uncommon thing for hawsers to become entangled, for schooners, brigs, and steamboats to fall foul of each other, for the bowsprit of a sailing vessel to run itself unceremoniously through a steamer's saloon, or for a gunboat to come drifting along, threatening destruction to some poor defenceless shell of a transport. It was indeed providential that the inhospitable shores of Hatteras were not thickly strewn with the wrecks of vessels, the bodies of men, and the debris of an expedition which had been fitted out with a generous expenditure of money and with every material of war.

The officers of the navy, on their part, did all that could be

*"Scarcely an inch more than seven and a half feet," says Flag Officer Goldsborough.

reasonably expected. Commander Rowan was especially active in this respect. From the beginning of operations in North Carolina till the end, the most cordial relations existed between the army and the navy. The officers of each arm of the service seemed to vie with those of the other in doing all that could be done for the promotion of their country's cause. No feeling of jealousy ever showed itself, for none was provoked. The Flag Officer and his subordinates were ready to aid the transport fleet in this emergency to the extent of their power. But, of necessity, they could not accomplish a great deal. Their own vessels required their constant supervision and care. It is true, that they had none of that narrowness of opinion which sometimes induces one to feel that he has no responsibility beyond the strictest line of his own duty, and no inclination to go beyond the established routine of his life; but they were compelled, by the circumstances of the case, to pay more attention to their own ships than to the army transports. With the most willing disposition, the ability was lacking. Gunboats and transports were in equal peril, and demanded the vigilance and faithful service of every officer and man.

General Burnside, therefore, was obliged to act the part of Admiral as well as General, and to manage his great fleet of transports and supply-vessels as best he could. With no experience at sea, he suddenly found himself called upon to perform the duties of a skillful navigator at a time when the sailor is compelled to summon up all his resources. All accounts agree that General Burnside proved himself to be fully equal to the trying occasion, and was completely master of the situation. He was indefatigable, unwearied, ubiquitous. Generals Foster, Reno, and Parke gave him their ablest assistance, and were always ready with counsel and help. The commanders of regiments, and indeed all the officers and men behaved in a manner beyond all praise, and performed the duties and bore the extraordinary burdens of the time with great fidelity and fortitude. They saw in their commanding general an example of patience and hopefulness which they were glad to imitate.

A correspondent of the London News, who accompanied the expedition, published at the time a very graphic account of the storm off Hatteras and in the Inlet, and, in the course of his narrative, took occasion to speak of the commanding general in very warm terms of commendation. "Bravely we breasted on in our little boat," he wrote, "staggering beneath the giant blows of each successive sea, our decks swept fore and aft, and all on board reeling from side to side like drunken men. One figure stood immovable, grasping by the bitts, scanning the horizon for traces of ships, as we rose on each glittering mass of foam. It was the square, manly form of General Burnside, whose anxiety for the fate of his army was intense." After speaking of the manner in which the general bore himself in the storm, he adds: "He has performed all the duties of a harbor master, narrowly escaping being swamped on more than one occasion, and there is not a grade in his army that he has not filled during the last fortnight, so anxious is he for the well being and comfort of his troops."

This community of danger, and the courage and skill with which the emergency was met and its duties performed by all parties, endeared the officers and men to each other more closely than a well fought and victorious battle could have done. The troops gave to their commander their entire confidence, regard, and admiration, and they were ready to go with enthusiasm to meet any danger to which he led the way. It was with grateful hearts that, when on the 25th of January, the storm finally broke, and calm weather came again, they felt that they had a leader whose hopefulness and patience even the elements could not subdue, and whom they could implicitly trust. He also was glad to feel that he had a command willing, eager, and able to accomplish every result that he could reasonably wish. Fortunate was the storm in the revelation of character which it had so fully made!

CHAPTER IV.

ROANOKE ISLAND, AND ITS CAPTURE.

WHEN a coastwise expedition was first projected, General McClellan's plan was to operate with about ten thousand men, "in the inlets of Chesapeake Bay and the Potomac, in conjunction with a naval force operating against points on the sea coast." This expedition was to be composed mostly of New England regiments, as it was thought that the men of these regiments would be conversant with boat-service, the management of steamers and sailing vessels, barges, launches, floating batteries, and the like. These regiments were "to be uniformed and equipped as the Rhode Island" troops were—an expressive testimonial to the sagacity of General Burnside, who had first suggested the pattern of the Rhode Island uniform. The expedition thus prepared was to form an integral part of the Army of the Potomac. General Burnside was conversant with General McClellan's plan, and when he was first selected to lead the enterprise, it was with the understanding that the force would not pass beyond the Virginia capes. The plan was submitted to the War Department on the 6th of September. On the 1st of November, General Scott was relieved of his command, and General McClellan was appointed in his place as General-in-Chief of the Armies of the United States. After General Burnside had proceeded, to a considerable extent, in perfecting his arrangements, the plan of operations was very essentially changed. General McClellan, late in the autumn, decided to increase the force to be sent, and to order it to the coast of North Carolina. A change in the plan necessitated considerable delay. A larger naval force, an augmentation of supplies, more transportation became needful. Thus it happened that the remarkably fine weather that characterized the autumn and early winter of 1861, slipped away, and that the expedition did not start till so late a period as to be caught by the wintry storms which howl around the "ship-breaking" Hatteras. Escaped from these, General Burnside set himself to obey the further instructions of his general-in-chief.

Those instructions contemplated, in the first place, the formation of the Department of North Carolina, carrying with it, of course, the command of the garrison of Hatteras Island. Afterwards, General Burnside was to make Roanoke Island and its dependencies his first point of attack. It was presumed that the navy could reduce the batteries on the shore, and cover the landing of troops on the main island, by which, in connection with a rapid movement of the gunboats to the northern extremity, it was hoped that the entire garrison of the place would be captured. Roanoke Island was then to be fortified, and a sufficient force left to guard its defences. Immediately subsequent to these operations, the naval force coöperating, a descent was to be made upon Newbern, "having gained possession of which, and the railroad passing through it," General Burnside was "to throw a sufficient force upon Beaufort, and take the steps necessary to reduce Fort Macon and open that port." The railroad west of Newbern was also to be seized "as far west as Goldsborough, should circumstances favor such a movement." Raleigh was also to be threatened, if not occupied; but in this last named movement, "great caution" was advised. "Having accomplished the objects mentioned, the next point of interest would probably be Wilmington, the reduction of which" might require additional means. Surely here was work enough for a long campaign and a large number of troops. To penetrate to Goldsborough and Raleigh with a few thousand men, one battery of light artillery, and an amphibious kind of force of a few hundred men—the Marine Artillery—which had been added to the expedition, was madness. The rebels had large armies in the field, and Goldsborough was an important railroad junction. To support such a movement, it was General McClellan's intention to send an army, under General Buell, by rapid marches upon Cumberland Gap and Knoxville, in East Tennessee. General Butler was to reduce the forts on the lower Mississippi, capture, and occupy New Orleans. General T. W. Sherman was to bombard Fort Pulaski, compel its surrender, and "to study the problem" of capturing Fort Sumter and Charleston. Meanwhile, it was hoped that these movements would distract the attention of the rebel leaders, and scatter their forces in an attempt to prevent the occupation of the various points by our armies. Then the Army of the Potomac would move with overwhelming force upon Richmond. General McClellan was a man of large plans, but with little facility of execution. In connection with the movement upon Goldsborough and Raleigh, those upon Knoxville and Richmond were most important and necessary. General Buell was entrusted with the one, but succeeded only partially. A portion of his forces marched through Kentucky and seized Cumberland Gap. But the occupation of this point was only temporary, and no advance was made beyond it. The dispositions of the enemy during the summer of 1862, soon forced its evacuation. General McClellan undertook the other movement, and the Peninsular campaign of 1862 has become the synonym of delay and disaster. It is a curious fact in the history of the war, that, two years after the date of the present operations, upon General Burnside himself was devolved the duty of occupying Knoxville, and performing a movement which should have been cooperative with his campaign in North Carolina. Had as much zeal and energy been displayed in other quarters as in this, the year 1862 would have borne a glorious record of victory. But after the first temporary success, an unaccountable apathy seems to have vitiated the counsels and checked the action of government, army, and people. Was it that the defeat of our material forces was needed to prepare the country for the moral triumphs of the war?

Immediately upon the arrival of General Burnside at Hatteras Inlet, he issued an order assuming command of the newly constituted Department of North Carolina. General Thomas Williams had command of the troops at Hatteras, which had been stationed there to hold the point against the enemy's forces which had concentrated at Roanoke Island. The importance of General Butler and Flag Officer Stringham's operations during the preceding season had now appeared. Two regiments of infantry, the 9th New York and 48th Pennsylvania, and one company, C, of the 1st United States Artillery, occupied Forts Clark and Hatteras and the neighboring parts of the island. Beyond this, the Department of North Carolina was only upon the decks of the vessels which had cast their anchors in Pamlico Sound. General Burnside's first care was to enlarge the boundaries of his command, and establish himself securely upon the land. Losing not a moment, after getting his transports and gunboats through the swash and over the bulkhead, he prepared to obey his instructions, which contemplated an attack upon the enemy's works on Roanoke Island and the neighboring shore. There were known to be several forts on the island, both near the Sound and in the interior. It was also known that the enemy had a small fleet of gunboats in those waters, coöperating with his land forces in the defence of the island. To our navy was intrusted the work of reducing the shore batteries and scattering or destroying the rebel fleet, while the army should land, push into the interior of the island, and carry the enemy's works wherever they could be found.

How could the troops be landed? Where was the best point for debarkation? These were questions that demanded considerable thought and discussion. They were happily solved by an unexpected reënforcement of intelligence from Roanoke Island itself. A short time before the expedition arrived at the inlet, a negro boy, sixteen or seventeen years of

age, came into the camp of our troops at Hatteras. He proved to be a bright, intelligent lad, had escaped from his master, a Mr. Robinson who lived on Roanoke Island, and sought protection from our forces. His name, he said, was "Tom." General Williams chanced to hear of him, and, wishing for information, questioned him and ascertained that he had something of real value to communicate. When General Burnside arrived, General Williams sent Tom on board the flag ship. General Burnside had a long interview with the escaped slave. Tom knew all about Roanoke and the forts and forces there. There was one strong battery about in the centre of the island. There were two or three others at different points. There were infantry and artillery on the island. There were the "Overland Greys," "Yankee Killers," "Sons of Liberty," "Jackson Avengers," "O. K. Boys," from North Carolina, and some, with a more respectable name, from Virginia—altogether a pretty formidable array. Did Tom know of a good landing place? "Oh, yes; at Ashby's Harbor, about two miles below Pork Point." Tom knows all about it, has lived not far from the harbor, has been there many a time, and will gladly go there with the troops and show them the way. Up from the harbor is a pretty good road to the place where the rebel battery is. The troops will march up there, drive the enemy out, and take the shore batteries in reverse.

Here was an important auxiliary. Tom's information was particularly valuable. The boy was immediately taken care of, and made to feel that he was no longer a slave. Captain Richmond took charge of him, and found him, during the campaign, faithful and true in every respect. The very important facts which he imparted were of the greatest service, and most materially aided in accomplishing the success of the movement. He was a quick-witted and bright boy, and he was observed afterwards in the general's quarters at Falmouth, conning over a spelling-book of which he had possessed himself, and steadily engaged, at every leisure moment, in learning to read.

Roanoke Island, which was the object of General Burnside's

first attack, is an island about twelve miles long from north to south, and three miles broad, occupying a commanding position in the dividing waters between Pamlico and Albemarle Sounds. Of Pamlico, we were already in possession, and could, at any time, have occupied any of the towns upon its shores. But to do this, leaving Roanoke Island in our rear, would have manifestly been a useless and very dangerous work. Roanoke Island, moreover, commanded the approaches to Norfolk from the North Carolina side. It was an outpost of Norfolk, indeed, and had been fortified by the rebels with considerable care and skill. A long narrow spit of sand lies beyond Roanoke, breaking the waves of the Atlantic. Between this and the island is a narrow, shallow sound, not navigable by gunboats of any great size. Across this spit, at a point about opposite the middle of Roanoke Island, the sea had at some time broken through and formed an inlet, which had afterwards closed. A little hillock of sand, marking the place, is called Nag's Head. Further to the northern extremity, the sea had forced another passage, which is called Currituck Inlet. Beyond this was still another long, narrow neck of land, which, at the north, opens upon the main land, and thence to Norfolk the way was comparatively unobstructed. Roanoke Island was, then, a position of the utmost importance to the enemy. Its reduction and occupation would give us the undisputed command of Albemarle Sound, and would be a perpetual menace to Norfolk. The occupation of the debouches, and the entire line of the Dismal Swamp and Albemarle and Chesapeake Canals, which was contemplated by the instructions of General McClellan, would give to our army an easy communication with Hampton Roads.

To protect this important place, the enemy had erected no less than five earthworks of different size, and defended, for the most part, by heavy ordnance. Three of these were built at different points upon the western shore of the island most suitable for defence. One was built in the interior of the island upon rising land—the highest point—and was the key to the position. Upon the main land opposite, were other batteries, and in the channel of Croatan Sound, near the southernmost work, piles were driven and hulks were sunken, to form a barricade for the prevention of the near approach of any hostile fleet to the land. The position of the barricade was immediately within range of the heavy guns mounted upon the lower forts. The batteries on the shore were to be silenced by the navy, while the troops were landing. But the barricade might prove to be a very serious obstruction to the naval operations. Lurking behind the barricade in the channel, the enemy had a fleet of eight small steamers. The names of the earthworks, beginning with that on Pork Point—the first encountered—are mentioned as Forts Bartow, mounting ten guns, in casement; Blanchard, four guns, *en barbette;* Huger, at Weir's Point, about three miles above Bartow, thirteen guns, in embrasures; Shallowbag Bay Fort, a small earthwork, mounting two guns on pivot; the Centre Redoubt, commanding the causeway through the marshy land to the solid ground of the island, three guns, *en barbette*, and Fort Forrest, eight guns, at Redstone Point, on the main land of North Carolina. The barricade of piles and sunken vessels extended from Fort Bartow to Fort Forrest, entirely across the Sound. The forts were armed mostly with smooth bore 32-pounders. The island was held by three regiments, reënforced on the day of battle by two regiments and two battalions—among which was the company once famous in the annals of the Virginia Militia, as the "Richmond Blues," under the command of Captain O. Jennings Wise. The entire garrison was under the command of Brigadier General Henry A. Wise, with headquarters at Nag's Head, who acted under the orders of Major General B. C. Hill, commanding the Department. At the time of the action, General Wise was not upon the island, and the command devolved upon Colonel Henry M. Shaw, of the 8th North Carolina Volunteers. That the garrison was brave, even to desperation, was amply proved by the gallant but unavailing resistance which they made to our determined troops.

Early in February, signs of immediate action were visible. The 6th New Hampshire, the 11th Connecticut, and the Rhode Island battery had been landed on the 17th of January, and with the 48th Pennsylvania and the 9th New York, (Zouaves,) had formed the command of General Williams on Hatteras Island. Of these, the 9th New York, Colonel R. C. Hawkins, was selected to accompany the expedition to Roanoke. The others remained at Hatteras. The 53d New York Regiment (the D'Epineuil Zouaves) had been ordered back to Fortress Monroe, after the arrival of the expedition at Hatteras Inlet. With these exceptions, the force designed to attack Roanoke Island was the same that had sailed from Annapolis. On the evening of the 4th of February, General Burnside announced to Flag Officer Goldsborough that the army was ready to move, and orders were accordingly issued to the fleet to get under way on the following morning. All hearts beat high with expectation. A seven days' moon shone softly down upon the now placid waters of Pamlico, and the air was vocal with song and cheerful talk that passed from ship to ship as the vessels swung idly at their anchors. General Burnside with his brigade commanders sought the flagship, and in consultation with Flag Officer Goldsborough and his officers, arranged the details of the morrow's enterprise.

The morning of the 5th is clear, with a fresh, cold breeze from the north. At seven o'clock, the army transports begin to move, and by eleven o'clock, after considerable manœuvering for stations, the entire armada is on its way. Disaster, shipwreck, and storm are left behind, the sun shines brightly, flags, pennants, signals are floating gaily on the morning air, hope animates every heart, and victory, glory and a nation's gratitude are in the near and now brilliant prospect. During that day, the fleet slowly makes it way along through the waters of Pamlico, until, in the middle of the afternoon, it approaches the narrow channel of Croatan Sound. At half past four o'clock, the outline of Roanoke Island is in sight, and soon after five, the fleet anchors at the appointed rendezvous, about five miles below the "Marshes." All the arrangements of the day have thus far been carried out with complete success, and the leading officers of the expedition meet and exchange congratulations. A boat's crew went on shore upon the main land during the night, and brought off a pilot for the Philadelphia.

The work assigned for the 6th was the engagement of the navy with the rebel batteries, and the landing of the army. The entire force started early in the morning to work up towards the shore. But the sky was clouded, and though, at nine o'clock, the weather cleared a little, there was but little prospect for a fair day. At half past ten, rain set in, and the wind rose. No great progress was made, the fleet came to anchor, and in the afternoon, a heavy gale blew for several hours. The morning of the 7th opened with better signs, and at nine o'clock, the sky had cleared, and the sun was shining. The Flag Officer within the next quarter of an hour signalled to get under way, and ran up the inspiring motto: "The country expects every man to do his duty." The gunboats immediately dashed forward to their appointed work. The leading vessels threaded the narrow channel of the Marshes, and passing beyond into the more open waters of Croatan Sound, approached the shores of Roanoke. The heavy armed gunboats closed up around the flagship after passing the Marshes, prepared for a strong attack. At eleven o'clock, the Underwriter reconnoitered the shore near Sandy Point, just above Ashby's Harbor, threw a shot or two on shore without drawing a response, and Lieutenant Jeffers signalled "No battery on Sandy Point." The enemy's fleet, under the command of Captain W. F. Lynch, drawn up behind the barricade, was now observed to be preparing for action, and to fire a signal gun to notify the troops on shore that the hour for action had come.

At half past ten o'clock, the army division of gunboats—the Picket, Huzzar, Pioneer, Vidette, Ranger, Lancer, and Chasseur—under Commander Hazard, opened the battle by engaging the enemy's fleet and Forts Bartow and Forrest. By noon, all the vessels had come up, and the action became very lively and general. The barracks in the rear of the earthwork on the shore of the island were set on fire, the enemy's fleet driven off beyond the range of our heavy guns, and the enemy's guns on shore silenced. Just before sunset, Forts Bartow and Blanchard opened once more, and the enemy's fleet ventured forth again and put in a few shots. But in forty minutes, the vessels had been driven off a second time, one of them in a sinking condition, another disabled, and the guns from the forts slackened a little in their fire. As the darkness came on, our fleet ceased firing. The garrison on shore had made a very creditable resistance. The forts had maintained a fierce contest, and showed no signs of surrender. Above the parapets, the rebel flag still flew defiantly. The navy had done a good day's work, but the island was not yet in our possession. The casualties had not been very great on either side. The Louisiana had been struck by an 80-pound rifled projectile, which had exploded in the fore hold, and set the vessel on fire. But no one was injured, and the flames were soon extinguished. On board the Hetzel, one of our own 80-pound rifles burst, and wounded six men. The magazine was set on fire, but was extinguished in time to prevent an explosion, by the intrepidity of Lieutenant Charles L. Franklin. Master's Mate Charles Harris, a gallant officer, was killed by a fragment of an exploded shell from one of the enemy's vessels. The Valley City was struck in the foremast. The Hunchback was hit eight times, but without injury to her crew. The Southfield had a shot through her upper works. The Morse was struck several times, and lost one man killed. The Ceres received a shot from the enemy which passed through the upper and lower decks. The Commodore Perry was hit seven times, but suffered no material injury. The Seymour had one man killed and one wounded. The Delaware and Picket covered the landing of the troops. The Flag Officer sent ashore a party, composed of officers and men selected from different vessels of the fleet, from the Naval Brigade—or more properly the Union Coast Guard — and the 9th New Jersey, to assist the army in holding the road from the harbor. The party filled six launches carrying six howitzers, and was under the command of Midshipman Benjamin H. Porter, of the Hunchback.

In the meantime, the army was busily engaged in preparing to land and occupy the shore of the harbor and the road into the interior. The transports were anchored off the mouth of the cove, and the soldiers were rapidly transferred to boats and light draft steamers—one of which, the Cadet, drew but two feet of water. About ten o'clock P. M., a boat load of volunteers from the 5th Rhode Island battalion, guided by Tom, and under the command of Lieutenant Andrews, detailed from the 9th New York to act as Engineer on General Burnside's staff, was sent up the harbor to take soundings and reconnoitre the landing place. The duty was performed with great coolness and intrepidity by the party. The men landed and remained a short time. Just as they were leaving, they were fired upon, and one man was seriously wounded. At a little past four o'clock in the afternoon, all being ready, the signal to land was given. The steamers started, each towing several boats filled with men. The landing was effected in a most gallant and brilliant manner. The scene was animated and striking beyond description. The boats dashed up to the shore, each vieing with the other, the men jumped overboard as the boats grounded, waded to the land, and, amid cheers of exultation, planted the stars and stripes on Roanoke Island. A detachment of General Foster's brigade had the advance, and the 25th Massachusetts was the first regiment to land. By five o'clock, four thousand men were put on shore. Midshipman Porter's battery was dragged up through the mire, and out on the road, and posted in advance. Two pieces were placed at a fork of the roads, a short distance from the landing. Two pieces were posted about half a mile in advance on the left fork, and two about the same distance on the right. Detachments from the brigades of Generals Reno and Parke followed that of General Foster so rapidly, that the landing was almost simultaneous. As soon as the troops reached the land, they marched up the island through the swamps and along the causeway, pushing out on the double quick. The remainder of the command was put on shore before ten o'clock. As the night came on, those in the rear lighted their camp fires and made themselves comfortable. Those in front were not so fortunate. They were obliged to be very cautious, as it was not known how near the enemy was. Indeed General Foster had already discovered an armed party in the woods, and the Delaware and Picket had thrown a few shells for the purpose of dispersing them. The 21st Massachusetts, in support of the battery, passed a wearisome and disagreeable night. No fires could be built, and the discomfort was increased by a heavy rain which continued to fall at intervals through the gloomy hours.

A cold and dismal morning succeeded the cheerless night. But the troops were in the highest spirits, and when the word "Forward!" was given, every man sprang at once, and with the utmost alacrity, to the performance of his duty. General Foster's brigade led the way, and marched with steady step up the narrow causeway. Midshipman Porter's battery fell into the line of march, the men dragging the cannon, following immediately the rear of the 25th Massachusetts. The skirmishers of the advancing column soon came in close contact with the enemy's pickets, who promptly gave the alarm and retired before our approach. A mile and a half further on, the enemy's earthwork was discovered, completely covering and commanding the road, and flanked on either side by a morass, in which every standing place was covered with vines and briars. General Foster deployed his troops, posted his battery, and engaged the enemy with his musketry and howitzers. Little effect was produced, and it was deemed impossible to carry the enemy's battery without reënforcements. The enemy was strongly posted, his artillery was superior to our own, and his infantry had the advantage of fighting behind breastworks.

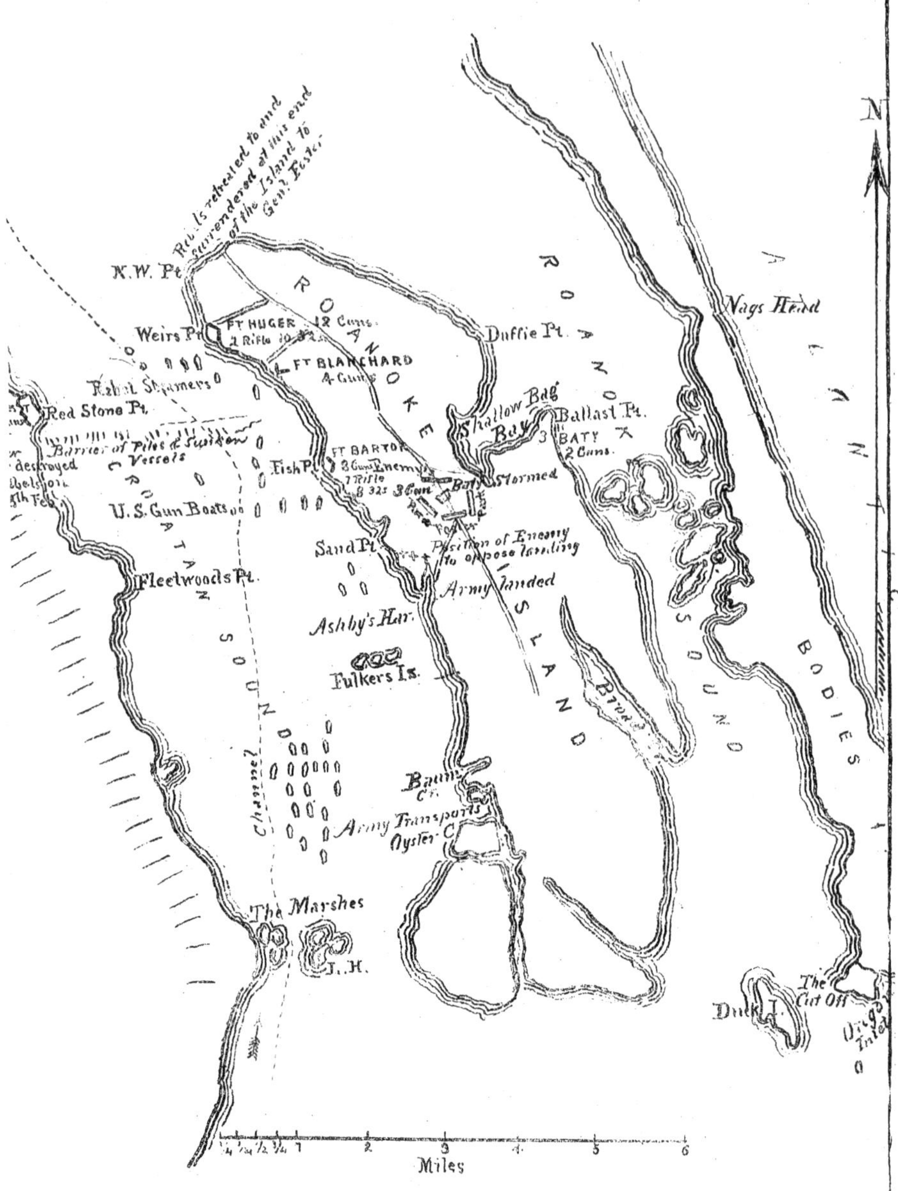

MAP OF OPERATIONS

OF THE ARMY UNDER

General Burnside

AT

ROANOKE ISLAND

1862.

His sharpshooters were scattered through the swamp, and did good execution. The 27th Massachusetts sought them out in their lurking places and dislodged them.

Meanwhile, General Reno, with all the ardor of his nature, was hurrying up his brigade. If there was any man who felt "the rapture of battle," it was the brave commander of the 2d Brigade. His men felt the influence of his enthusiastic spirit, and were eager to join the fray. General Reno ordered his troops to the left, with the intention of turning the right of the battery. The movement was accordingly made as well as it could be, considering the state of the ground. The troops found themselves entangled in a morass, where the water and mud were waist-deep, and in which almost the only firm places were the clumps of bushes, briars, and coarse grass that were scattered through the swamp. The advance in this difficult movement was taken by two companies of the 21st Massachusetts, led by Colonel Maggi and Adjutant Stearns, the latter of whom gives the following account of the attack: "General Reno came to Colonel Maggi, and, pointing to a dense, almost impenetrable cypress swamp, said: 'Colonel, you must flank the battery.' Colonel Maggi led the way, I followed, then Captain Foster leading his company. After an hour of almost superhuman effort, cutting bushes with our swords, and wading to our middle in bogs and water, two companies got on to the flank of the battery and began the fire." Three companies of the 51st New York, under Lieutenant Colonel Potter, followed this movement, and took position to the left of Colonel Maggi's force. The enemy, not anticipating the advance of our troops in this direction, was somewhat surprised at their appearance. It was but for a moment. He quickly trained his guns upon the men in the swamp and on the cleared ground immediately around his works. A fearful storm of grape and canister fell around our men. But they pushed steadily on, and finally reached a position where they could turn and possibly capture the battery, by a steady, well supported charge. General Reno coolly formed his line amid the heaviest of the enemy's fire. Colonel Ferrero brought up the remainder of the 51st, and formed on the left. Major Clark brought up the remainder of the 21st, and formed on the right, relieving the two companies that had been engaged in the unequal conflict with the enemy's battery. It was now about half past one o'clock in the afternoon. The troops had been struggling through the swampy ground for two or three hours, but were ready for the further duty of the day.

While these movements were making on our left, General Foster was occupying the attention of the enemy immediately in front. The troops had advanced within short range, the naval battery steadily keeping its place in the line. The 25th Massachusetts, which had suffered quite severely, was now withdrawn, and the 10th Connecticut took its place. The 23d and 27th Massachusetts skirmished through the woods and the morass upon the right, coming full upon a battalion of the enemy and forcing it back. The 51st Pennsylvania was held in reserve. The 24th Massachusetts, which arrived from Hatteras and landed during the forenoon, was hastened up from the landing to take part in the engagement. The 23d and 27th Massachusetts succeeded, after great exertion, in penetrating the swamp and woods on our right, and in reaching, with some loss, the cleared ground upon the enemy's left. The 9th New York, of General Parke's brigade, under Major Kimball, pushed its way slowly through the underbrush to the right, then deflecting towards the road again, advanced along the edge of the causeway.

General Burnside, at the landing, now sent forward General Parke's brigade to the support of the forces combining for the grand final attack. General Parke, immediately upon his arrival, ordered the 4th Rhode Island to follow the 23d and 27th Massachusetts in the demonstration upon the enemy's left. With the utmost toil, through mud and water half-leg deep—sometimes nearly waist-deep—the men struggled through the morass. The 8th Connecticut occupied the woods to the north and east of the landing, guarding the main road to prevent any movement of the enemy in our rear. The 5th Rhode Island guarded Ashby's house, now occupied as a hospital. Such was the state of affairs when General Reno prepared, soon after one o'clock in the afternoon, to charge the enemy's battery upon its right flank. It had required hard fighting and persistent struggling through a swamp and wood, that the enemy had considered impenetrable, to reach this point. The artillery of the enemy's battery had been well served, and his infantry had shown great pluck and determination. But our men had been gradually enveloping his position, attacking him in front and on both flanks, and his time had come.

General Reno, having got his brigade into position, ordered the charge. Away went the 21st Massachusetts and the 51st New York, followed closely by the remainder of the brigade. They advanced most gallantly and with great enthusiasm. The courage of veterans could not have been more conspicuous as these brave men rushed forward to storm "the deadly breach." Onward they went. Adjutant Stearns describes the charge as "magnificent." "As our noble men advanced with bayonets fixed, at a short quick step, a low, involuntary cry burst from their lips. It was no war cry; it was a cry of exultation, of joy, which came leaping from a thousand hearts, swelling into a perfect storm of cheers."* The troops moved rapidly over the ground in front, leaped down into the ditch, struggled through, clambered up the parapet, poured through the embrasures, drove out the enemy at the point of the bayonet, and, with thundering shouts of triumph, planted the colors of their respective regiments and the national flag upon the captured works. Generals Foster and Parke, observing from their position in front that the enemy was somewhat embarassed by General Reno's appearance upon his right flank, ordered the 9th New York to charge. Then almost at the same time the enemy was taken upon his front and flank. The Zouaves rushed forward with their peculiar cry of "Zou! Zou!"—their

* Adjutant Stearns, p. 92.

red caps filling the road—an exciting scene. They mounted the parapet and scattered the garrison. The two victorious columns met in the centre of the work and congratulated each other on the happy result. At the same time, the head of the column that had passed through the swamp upon our right appeared on the left of the enemy's position, and was received with hearty and exultant shouts. The 24th Massachusetts also came up the road to share in the general joy.

A halt of half an hour was allowed to refresh the men and to replenish the partially exhausted cartridge-boxes, and then the troops were once more put in motion to pursue the retreating enemy. General Reno with his brigade marched up the central road, and then down to the right upon the eastern shore of the island. General Foster pursued over the central road, and General Parke went to the left. As the troops advanced in pursuit, the evidences of the total rout of the enemy were observed on every side. The way was strewn with guns, bowie knives, blankets, canteens, knapsacks, and everything that could have impeded the flight of the defeated foe. The 21st Massachusetts was in advance, and as the troops, after marching about three miles, came out upon the beach, they descried a few boats filled with the enemy's wounded and other fugitives, attempting to cross the narrow channel to Nag's Head. A few well-directed shots brought to the rearmost boat, which returned to land. It had on board Captain O. Jennings Wise and another wounded officer, who had been among the bravest defenders of the enemy's battery. In a large farm house upon the beach, other wounded officers and soldiers were found. The troops scoured the beach right and left, and picked up numerous scattered parties of prisoners. General Foster had pushed on to the northern end of the island, and, after a march of four or five miles, the advanced companies of skirmishers were fired upon from a belt of woods. The line was immediately formed, and the men prepared for a charge. The enemy then sent forward a flag of truce. The officer bearing it, on being received and led to General Foster, asked what terms of capitulation would be allowed. General Foster replied that the surrender must be unconditional. There was no escape, and the officer, upon a further conference with his superior, returned with Colonel Henry M. Shaw, of the 8th North Carolina Volunteers, the commandant of the post, who surrendered all the forces on the island. The number of prisoners was two thousand six hundred and seventy-seven, fifty of whom were wounded. These were tenderly cared for, and with our own wounded, received every attention. Captain Wise was mortally wounded, but was defiant to the very last. He died on the next morning after the battle, expressing with his latest breath, his deep regret that he could not live longer to fight against the Union. The surrender to General Foster included all the defences and material of war on the island. General Parke, with the 4th Rhode Island and the 10th Connecticut, marched down to the Pork Point battery, found it abandoned, and at once occupied the work. The navy had engaged the attention of the garrison during the day by occasional firing. As soon as the central battery had fallen, the enemy had given up the contest, and sought only the means of escape.

The fruits of this splendid achievement, besides the prisoners captured, were "five forts, mounting thirty-two guns, winter quarters for some four thousand troops, three thousand stand of small arms, large hospital buildings, with a large amount of lumber, wheelbarrows, scows, pile drivers, a mud dredge, ladders, and various other appurtenances for military service."* The enemy had received a severe chastisement. Among the prisoners was a battalion of North Carolina Militia that had come over from Elizabeth City that morning to take part in the fight, but had been obliged to surrender without firing a gun. The names of the captured forts were changed, and received the names of the successful generals. Fort Bartow was called Fort Foster, Fort Blanchard received the name of Fort Parke,

---

* Burnside's Report.

and Fort Huger that of Fort Reno. Our losses amounted to forty-one killed and one hundred and eighty-one wounded. The enemy's loss was considerably less, as he fought behind defences.

Among our killed were several valuable officers. Captain Joseph J. Henry, of the 9th New Jersey, was a good officer and brave man, and fell gallantly fighting in front of the enemy. Second Lieutenants Stillman and John H. Goodwin, Jr., of the 10th Connecticut, were both steady and unflinching in the discharge of their duty, and willingly yielded their lives for its sake. The 10th Connecticut suffered a severe loss in the death of its Colonel, Charles L. Russell, who fell a short time before the final charge, while watching the progress of our men upon the left. Colonel Russell was a native of Northfield, Connecticut, and was thirty-three years of age at the time of his death. He left a wife and family of small children to mourn his death. He had long been associated with the militia of his native State, and had taken great interest in its welfare. Upon the breaking out of the war, he was commissioned as Adjutant in the 2d Connecticut regiment, and fought bravely at the battle of Bull Run. He was appointed Captain in the 8th, and afterwards to the command of the 10th, and marched with the latter to the seat of war in November, 1861. His regiment was distinguished for its soldierly bearing and discipline, and reflected great credit upon its brave and faithful commander. He died in the performance of his duty, and as a brave officer should, at the head of his troops. Lieutenant Colonel De Montiel remained, after his regiment had been ordered back to Fortress Monroe, and was permitted to join the Hawkins Zouaves as a volunteer. He was killed while charging with the regiment upon the enemy's battery. General Parke had offered him a position upon his staff for the day, but this he declined, preferring to take a rifle and fight by himself. He displayed conspicuous courage until picked off by one of the enemy's sharpshooters. General Burnside paid handsome tributes to the memory of these brave men in General Orders. In their honor, the enemy's captured work in the centre of the island was called Battery Russell, and one of those taken on the eastern shore Battery Monteil. One of the victims of the battle, though not shot in action, was Dr. Meinis, of the 48th Pennsylvania regiment. He was detached from his own regiment, and appointed to accompany the 9th New Jersey, then going into action. He lost his life by disease brought on by his untiring devotion to the wounded during and after the action of the 8th, and ending fatally on the 10th. "To his forgetfulness of self," says the commanding general in an order issued at the time, "which kept him at his post at the hospital, regardless of rest or sleep, the Department owes a debt of gratitude."

The casualties in the navy proper, during the engagement of the 7th, amounted to three killed and eleven wounded. One of the latter was a private of the 4th Rhode Island, who was serving temporarily on the Commodore Perry. In Midshipman Porter's battery, three men were killed, six wounded, and two were missing. They belonged to the Union Coast Guard and the 9th New Jersey infantry. On the 8th, the navy was engaged at intervals with the shore batteries, the Flag Officer governing his action according to the condition of things on shore. During the afternoon of the 8th, the barricade across Croatan Sound was removed sufficiently to allow a free access to our naval forces into the waters where the enemy's fleet had sought escape. Of this fleet, one vessel, the Curlew, had been disabled on the previous day, had been reduced to an almost sinking condition, had retreated under the guns of Fort Forrest, and was now set on fire and blown up to prevent her falling into our hands. The fort itself also shared her fate. Captain Lynch, with his seven remaining vessels, steamed away for Elizabeth City. Thither the Flag Officer directed Commander Rowan to proceed, and capture or destroy the enemy's vessels. A flotilla of fourteen vessels, mounting thirty-four guns, was placed under his command. With this force, Commander Rowan left the anchorage off Roanoke Island on the afternoon of the 9th, and making directly for the mouth of the Pasquotank river, entered and steamed slowly up to a point about fourteen miles below Elizabeth City, where, at eight o'clock in the evening, the flotilla came to anchor. Ten miles above, was Cobb's Point, where the enemy had a four gun battery. Opposite to this was anchored a schooner—the Black Warrior—armed with two heavy guns. At daylight the next morning, the vesels moved up in order, the Underwriter in advance, and at half past eight o'clock, the enemy's fleet was descried drawn up in the rear of the batteries, in line of battle, "diagonally across and up the river."* As our vessels came within long range, the enemy commenced firing. Our own vessels did not reply, but continued silently and steadily to advance. When within three-fourths of a mile of the rebel fleet, Commander Rowan signalled "Dash at the enemy!" The order was enthusiastically received and eagerly obeyed. The vessels were at once put to the top of their speed, pressed up the river, ran past the batteries, and immediately engaged the enemy. The onset was daring and desperate. The fight was short and decisive. The Commodore Perry made for the enemy's flag ship, the Sea Bird, ran her down and sank her. The Ceres lay alongside the Ellis and captured her. The Underwriter and Shawsheen chased the Beaufort and another steamer up the river and canal, but could not overtake them. The Lockwood made for the Black Warrior, which the enemy soon deserted, first setting her on fire. The Shawsheen attacked the Fanny, which the enemy also set on fire and abandoned. The Forrest, which was lying near the wharf of the city, repairing injuries suffered in the fight at Roanoke, and a new gunboat not quite completed, were destroyed. The battery was deserted, and the guns captured. In fifteen minutes, the entire action was finished, and in half an hour, the fleet was lying quietly at anchor off Elizabeth City. The garrison and crews that escaped, in flying through the town, set it on fire in several places. In this engagement a notable incident took

* Commander Rowan's Report.

place, which was very creditable to a quarter-gunner on board the Valley City, by the name of John Davis. A shot from the enemy had passed through the Valley City's magazine and exploded in a locker beyond. Lieutenant Chaplin went into the exposed part of the ship to provide for extinguishing the flames, and found Mr. Davis coolly seated on an open barrel of powder, covering it with his person as the only means of keeping out the fire.* Secretary Welles recognized the importance of the service, and at once appointed Davis acting gunner in the navy of the United States. Commander Rowan, on the 11th, sent Lieutenant Murray with the Louisiana, Commodore Perry, Underwriter, and Lockwood, to Edenton, where our forces destroyed eight cannon and a vessel on the stocks, and captured two schooners. Immediately on the return of this expedition, another was sent, under the same officer, to obstruct the Currituck canal. Lieutenant Murray effectually accomplished this important duty.

In the coöperative movements of the army and navy, the signal corps attached to the expedition was found to be of great service. This corps was composed of twenty officers and fifty men, under the instruction and command of First Lieutenant Joseph Fricker, of the 8th Pennsylvania. Twenty-four Second Lieutenants, selected mostly from Massachusetts regiments, formed the complement of officers. Two officers and four men were assigned to each brigade, army and naval division headquarters, and their services were gratefully acknowledged by the officers of both arms.

The intelligence of the brilliant victories won by our land and naval forces was received at the North with feelings of grateful exultation. The winter had been one of inaction and almost despondency. The disasters at Hatteras Inlet had not conduced to raise the public mind. News of the most cheering character had been received from the West of the movement of Flag Officer Foote upon Fort Henry, and of General

* Commander Rowan's Report.

Grant upon Fort Donelson. But in the East nothing had been done as yet in the campaign of 1862, to arouse the public enthusiasm, and the victory of General Burnside and Flag Officer Goldsborough was accordingly welcomed as the beginning of a splendidly successful campaign. Appreciative letters were sent from the President and the War and Navy Departments to the triumphant leaders. The Mayor of the city of New York issued a proclamation of congratulation. The Legislatures of Massachusetts and Ohio passed votes of felicitation. The General Assembly of Rhode Island, upon the recommendation of Governor Sprague, voted its thanks and a sword to General Burnside. Salutes were fired in the principal northern cities. The successes of our arms were accepted as the auguries of future and more decisive triumphs.

CHAPTER V.

NEWBERN AND FORT MACON.

THE second part of General Burnside's instructions contemplated the occupation of Newbern. As soon as affairs were sufficiently settled at Roanoke Island, and the necessary preparations had been made, it was the commanding general's intention to proceed at once to the main land. Not a long time was required for either labor. In the course of a week or two, the forts on Roanoke Island were put in proper order and condition for defence, and the 51st Pennsylvania and 5th Rhode Island regiments were detailed for a temporary garrison. These regiments were relieved, early in March, by the 9th New York and 6th New Hampshire, and Colonel Hawkins was appointed Post Commandant. Expeditions were sent out during the month of February, to reconnoitre the neighboring country. One or two regiments were sent over to Elizabeth City, and remained there for a short time. Winton, on the Chowan river, was examined on the 18th, and Old Currituck Inlet on the 19th. At these places, some public property and artillery were found and destroyed or captured. But these excursions were simply designed to distract the attention of the enemy, and to afford occupation to the troops while preparations were making to strike the heaviest blow of all. General Burnside was also engaged in administering the oath of allegiance to the inhabitants of the island and others who desired to renew their political relations with the United States. On the 18th, the commanding general, jointly with Flag Officer Goldsborough, issued a proclamation to the people of North Carolina, disabusing their minds of the false impressions which the rebel government had sought to make respecting the objects of the war, and inviting them to return to their allegiance.* But the loyal sentiment of the people was not particularly strong, and the well-meant measures of reconciliation had but little effect. General Burnside was also occupied, during the month of February, in disposing of the prisoners that had fallen into his hands. He could not spare the transports which would be required to carry them North. He could not leave a large body of his troops on the island to guard them. He remembered the prisoners that had fallen into the hands of the enemy at the battle of Bull Run, and as he recalled the story of their sufferings, he resolved that he would leave no pretext to the enemy for a deferral of an exchange. Good policy and humanity alike dictated liberal terms to the vanquished. He determined, therefore, to parole his prisoners and release them. Lieutenant Colonel Osborne, of the 24th Massachusetts, was sent to Elizabeth City to confer with the enemy's officers near that point upon the subject. The result of the consultation was that the prisoners in our hands should be released, upon signing a parole not to take up arms against the United States, nor to give any information respecting our forces until regularly exchanged. In the meantime, the enemy was to make arrangements in good faith to exchange the prisoners in his hands, according to rank, or with certain equivalents, according to the rules of war. The prisoners were conveyed to Elizabeth City on the 20th, and there released. Lieutenant Colonel Osborne performed his duty with great acceptance, and General Burnside had the satisfaction of feeling that proper measures had been inaugurated for releasing from the enemy's hands our unfortunate men. His action was approved by the Secretary of War.

On the 26th of February, the troops—with the exception of the garrison at Roanoke—were ordered to be in readiness to embark. But it was not till the 6th of March that they commenced going on board the transports, and it was not till the

* See Appendix.

9th that all were in readiness to move. The last regiment to embark was the 4th Rhode Island, of General Parke's brigade. At ten o'clock on the evening of the 11th, the fleet anchored off the mouth of Hatteras Inlet, in Pamlico Sound, and on the morning of the 12th, the commanding general issued a general order, notifying his troops that they were on the eve of an important movement, which would greatly demoralize the enemy, and assist the Army of the Potomac in its contemplated operations against Richmond. It was a bright, warm, and beautiful day, and the expedition had every promise of success.

At this time, events were taking place in Hampton Roads which demanded the presence at that point of the Flag Officer of the North Atlantic Blockading Squadron. The enemy's iron clad ship, called by the rebels the "Virginia"—fitted from the United States ship Merrimac, abandoned by us at the time of the evacuation of the Norfolk Navy Yard—ran out of the harbor of Norfolk, and approached our naval station near the Fortress. Several wooden tenders or consorts accompanied the iron clad. The particulars of the remarkable and disastrous naval battle that ensued are well known, and need not be repeated here. The powerlessness of our wooden ships to contend with the foe; the sinking of the Cumberland, her crew fighting her guns till the very last, and going down with the vessel with the flag still flying; the burning of the Congress; the disabling of the Minnesota by running aground; the timely arrival of the Monitor and the effectual punishing which she gave the audacious enemy, are familiar facts. The fear which such an almost invulnerable and invincible monster was liable to produce; the mischief which she might do, if she should succeed in getting out to sea, in dominating Chesapeake Bay and even the entire coast, and laying Washington, Baltimore, Philadelphia, New York and other northern cities under contribution, and the necessity of guarding against such a contingency, all required extraordinary vigilance. As it was, the enemy's ship came near neutralizing General McClellan's plan for a movement upon the Peninsula. One can readily imagine what destruction she might cause among a fleet of transports. The duty of providing for the preservation of our fleet and our army must be committed to no inferior. Flag Officer Goldsborough accordingly left the waters of North Carolina, and did not appear in that quarter again during the war. He had cordially coöperated with General Burnside while the two officers were together, and had rendered most efficient service to the country. His administration of naval affairs had been judicious, and he had acted the part of a gallant and patriotic sailor. He had been especially fortunate in his subordinates, chief among whom Commander Rowan and Lieutenant Flusser had already given promise of the distinction which they afterwards acquired. Commander Rowan was left in command of the coöperative fleet.

Before proceeding to Newbern, General Burnside had made himself somewhat acquainted with the enemy's force and means of defence. His scouts had visited the town and the fortifications, and had brought back full reports. It was known that the enemy had batteries planted along the west bank of the Neuse, and that extensive fortifications were built upon or near the railroad connecting Beaufort with Newbern, a mile or two south of the Trent river, and extending west from the Neuse a distance of three miles. On the river bank, a large fort was constructed, mounting thirteen guns, and completely commanding the river channel on the one side and the line of works on the other. From this fort, the works extended to the centre, defended by a moat in front, and terminating in a bastion. Beyond was the railroad, which was itself fortified, and beyond that was a sytem of redoubts, thirteen in number and a mile in length, erected upon six little mounds or hills which rose conveniently to the main work, furnishing admirable sites for defensive works.* Along this fortified line were mounted forty-six guns of different calibres, some of which were field

* These last named works, however, were not known to the scouts or to our officers. They were doubtless hastily thrown up in the interval between the report of the scouting party and the day of battle.

artillery. Three miles below these works was a shore battery, Fort Ellis, mounting eight guns, and two miles below this was Fort Dixie, garrisoned by light artillery. From these two works extended lines of defences running across the road and into the country in the rear. About three miles in the rear of the main line ran the river Trent, spanned by a railroad and a turnpike bridge, of seven hundred feet or more in length, which connected the adjacent country with the city of Newbern. General Burnside's scouts had at one time attempted to burn these bridges, but with indifferent success. Against the formidable works of the enemy, garrisoned by eight thousand men, under the command of General L. O'B. Branch, General Burnside was to lead his infantry regiments, supported only by eight small naval howitzers for artillery, and by the gunboats in the river.

On the morning of March 12th, the fleet of transports, escorted by a fleet of fourteen gunboats under the command of Commander S. C. Rowan,* got under way from Hatteras and sailed across the placid waters of Pamlico Sound, heading for the mouth of the Neuse river. The Sound was as smooth as a mirror. Scarcely a ripple stole over its bosom. The light winds that were blowing from the North could barely flutter the ensigns and pennants. The sun was shining, and the command was hopeful of victory. At noon, the sky began to be clouded, and when the fleet, after pushing up the Neuse, anchored at nightfall off the mouth of Slocum's Creek, about fifteen miles below Newbern, the heavens were dark with portents of rain and storm. The signs were not deceptive, and the next morning opened cheerless and rainy enough to dispirit men of ordinary courage. But at eight o'clock, the clouds broke, the sun shone out once more, and the troops in high spirits prepared to

* The naval vessels in this expedition were the Philadelphia, Stars and Stripes, Louisiana, Hetzel, Delaware, Commodore Perry, Valley City, Underwriter, Commodore Barney, Hunchback, Southfield, Morse, Brinker, and Lockwood. They were commanded by the same officers as when in the movement against Roanoke Island, with the exception of the Underwriter, which was now under the command of Lieutenant A. Hopkins.

disembark. At nine o'clock, they were in the launches, and soon after, the flag was planted on the shore by a detail of a sergeant and three men belonging to the 51st New York regiment. The boats, obeying the signal, dashed away for the landing. Unfortunately, the water was very shallow, and the men were obliged to wade a considerable distance to the firm earth. The sun was again shut in, and the rain began to fall. But wet as the troops were, they commenced their march with undiminished vigor, and fully merited the confidence which General Burnside had already expressed. It was a long, wearisome, and muddy march, through sand, through mud and water, over fallow land, along forest paths. The gunboats flanked the column, maintaining a position a little in advance, shelling the shore to disperse any hostile force that might be disposed to dispute our progress. The men trudged on along the muddy roads, cheering each other with joke and song and laugh, as best they could. A few officers were mounted, but most were on foot, sharing the labors of the men. Each carried his own baggage. The gunboats had furnished a battery of six howitzers, each of which was dragged by twelve sailors, commanded by naval officers detailed for the purpose, and led by Lieutenant R. S. McCook, of the gunboat Stars and Stripes. Two Wiard 12-pounders, manned by sailors from the transports, were commanded by Captains Bennett, of the Cossack, and Dayton, of the Highlander. The skirmishers of the 24th Massachusetts led the advance, and the 11th Connecticut brought up the rear. Through the afternoon the troops toiled forward, and soon after dusk, bivouacked at a point nine miles distant from the landing, and about a mile from the enemy's defences. Nothing of great interest had happened during the march, except the discovery that the enemy had abandoned the two lower lines of earthworks and camps. General Reno's brigade marched along the railroad; the other troops occupied the county or turnpike road. One prisoner was captured, who communicated the welcome intelligence of the evacuation of Manassas and the advance of General McClellan from around the fortifica-

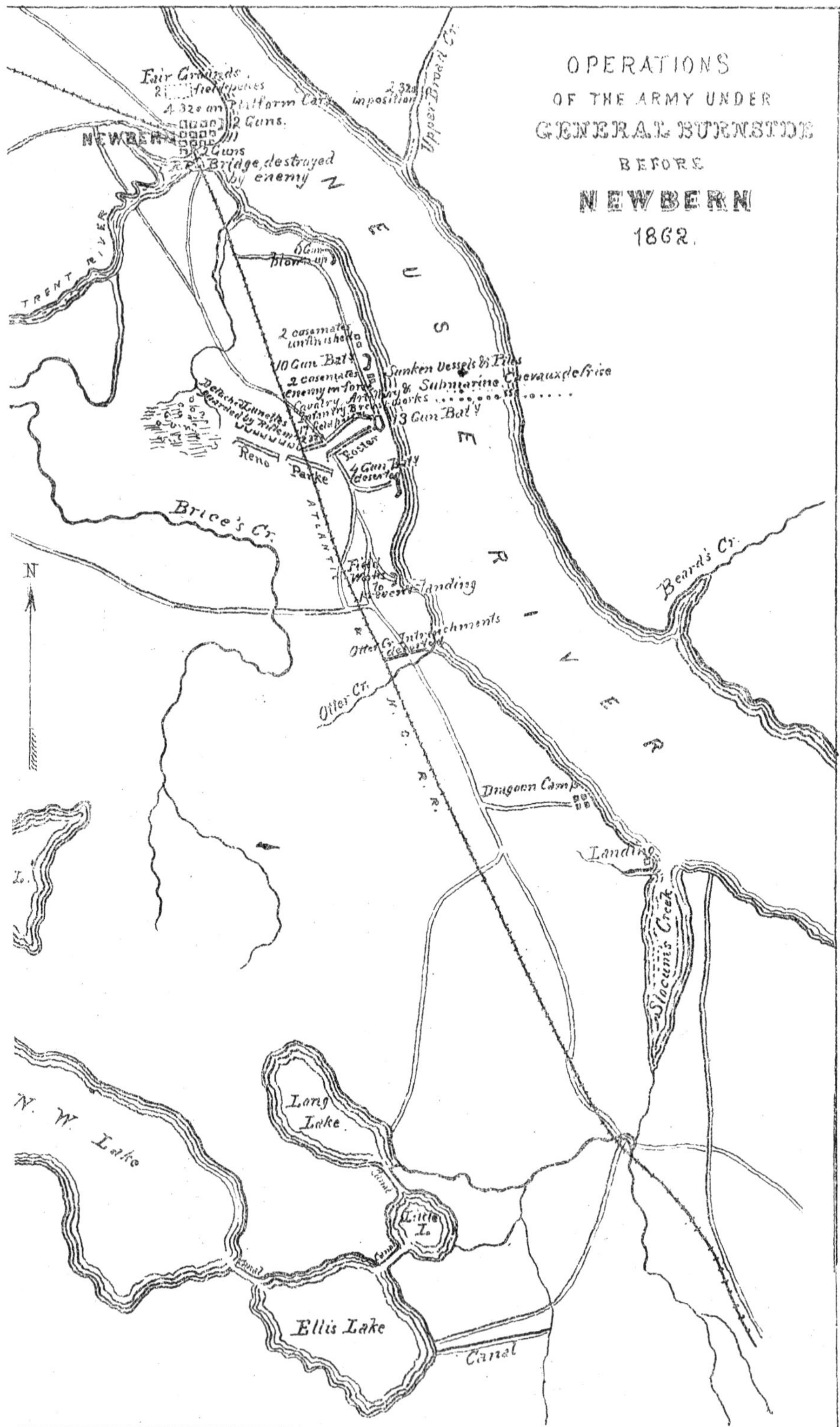

OPERATIONS
OF THE ARMY UNDER
GENERAL BURNSIDE
BEFORE
NEWBERN
1862.
Fair Grounds
NEWBERN
Bridge, destroyed by enemy
TRENT RIVER
N E U S E R I V E R
Upper Broad Cr.
10 Gun Bat'y
Sunken Vessels & Piles
3 Gun Bat'y
Reno
Parke
Foster
Brice's Cr.
Otter Cr.
Dragoon Camp
Landing
Beard's Cr.
Slocum's Creek
Long Lake
N. W. Lake
Ellis Lake
Canal
N

tions of Washington. Tired, wet, and hungry, the men were glad to halt and seek what rest might be found in the mud around the camp fires.

Occasional showers fell during the night, and when the morning of the 14th dawned, clouds of fog enveloped the army itself and all surrounding objects. The troops were early awake and ready for the day's work. Much of the ammunition had been spoiled by the excessive moisture, and during the subsequent action many of the men had nothing but the bayonet to rely upon for either offensive or defensive operations. But there was no murmuring, and the discipline and good order of the army prevailed over every unfavorable circumstance. The plan of the attack was very simple. The position of the enemy admitted of little or no manœuvering of the troops. The works to be assailed must be captured by downright fighting. They could not be turned. They would have to be stormed. The large work on the river, Fort Thompson by name, had four guns bearing on a party advancing by land. The breastwork to the railroad was fully manned and armed. The small redans upon the enemy's right beyond the railroad were filled with men, and prevented any flanking movement on our part. The enemy's right rested upon an almost impenetrable morass. It was simply a question of unflinching bravery. Would our men march steadily up to works blazing with artillery, and enter them in the face of every opposition? General Burnside believed that they would. It was an audacious enterprise. But its very audacity contributed to its success. The simple plan was to "move on the enemy's works" and capture them.

The line of battle was formed with General Foster's brigade on the right, General Reno's on the left, and General Parke's on the right centre, ready to render assistance to either wing as the occasion might demand. General Foster formed his brigade by posting the 25th Massachusetts on the extreme right, followed in order by the 24th Massachusetts in line of battle, with the left resting on the county road. Immediately on the left of the road the Highlander's howitzer was placed, under command of Captain Dayton, supported by the 27th Massachusetts. Lieutenant McCook's battery of boat howitzers was posted on the left of Captain Dayton's gun, and the 23d Massachusetts regiment was placed in support on the left of the 27th. The 10th Connecticut coming up, was formed on the left of the 23d Massachusetts. These dispositions were made by eight o'clock and the battle opened. The firing on both sides was very heavy and at short range, but from the bad condition of our ammunition, our men could do but little execution. The enemy's fire was hot and somewhat destructive. The ammunition of the 27th Massachusetts was soon expended, and these troops were obliged to retire from their dangerous position. Their place was supplied by the 11th Connecticut, of General Parke's brigade, which had been sent round by General Burnside for that purpose. The ammunition of the naval howitzers giving out, the 25th Massachusetts was marched by the flank to their support, leaving the 24th Massachusetts on the extreme right. Here this regiment was exposed to a hot fire from Fort Thompson, which was partially kept down by the deliberate and accurate fire of our own men and by the guns of the fleet. The entire line of breastwork was alive with men, and furnished but little opportunity for any execution, except as the enemy exposed himself above the parapet. Our men were compelled to seek shelter by lying down in the hollows of the ground, and directing thence their fire upon the foe. But, with such a trial of endurance and courage, the New England brigade manfully held its ground and kept up a well directed and continuous fusilade. The enemy was fully occupied until the time came for the final advance of the entire line. The attack in all parts by General Foster's brigade was exceedingly well sustained, and afforded great assistance to the more decisive operations on the left.

General Reno, at an early hour in the morning, put his brigade in motion along the railroad, with the 21st Massachusetts in advance, followed in order by the 51st New York, 9th New Jersey, and 51st Pennsylvania. At about the same time that

General Foster became engaged, the skirmishers of the 21st, proceeding cautiously but rapidly through a belt of woods along the left of the railroad track, descried a locomotive battery coming down the track. A few well directed shots sent it back within the defences, and soon after the head of the column struck the right flank of a battery, that rested at this point upon a deep cut in the railroad and a cleared brick yard, containing several buildings and brick stacks. The air was filled with mist and the smoke of the battle which was raging on the right. But little could be seen, and one company of the 21st was sent forward to reconnoitre, while the remainder of the regiment was formed in line for attack. General Reno, with characteristic gallantry, was with the extreme front of his brigade—at one time just saved from death by Colonel Sinclair of the rebel service, who desired to capture rather than kill him*—and immediately ordered the regiment to charge and take the brick yard. The enemy retired at the approach of our troops, and took a position immediately in the rear of the yard, and in a trench upon the opposite side of the railroad, from which they poured in a very destructive fire upon our advancing lines. While this movement was going forward, the 51st New York and 9th New Jersey came up and formed on the left of the 21st Massachusetts—the 51st Pennsylvania being held in reserve on the extreme left. As soon as General Reno could understand the position of affairs and could penetrate the mist, he found that he had not reached the enemy's right, but that the redans on the hills extended far beyond his own lines. His safety consisted in attacking in front, and he moved his brigade as nearly as possible towards the enemy's works, ordering the men to pick off the enemy's gunners—meanwhile vigilantly watching for an opportunity to advance. The 21st Massachusetts found that opportunity and gallantly improved it.

*Colonel Sinclair's command, as the men saw General Reno approach, prepared to fire upon him, but were peremptorily forbidden to do so. For this act of humanity Colonel Sinclair was accused of treachery to the rebel cause, and was obliged to leave the service.

Lieutenant Colonel Maggi had resigned the command of the regiment while at Roanoke Island, and Major W. S. Clark promoted to Lieutenant Colonel, was now its commanding officer.* General Reno ordered him to charge upon the enemy's position, intending to support him immediately with the rest of the brigade and sweep the hostile lines, but found that he could not do so. Lieutenant Colonel Clark started forward with four companies of his men in the midst of a most galling fire, pressed vigorously on, planted the flag within the enemy's intrenchments, rallied his men around it, and made a second charge. He was opposed by a six gun battery, which he immediately attacked with great fury. So vigorous was the assault, that the enemy retired with precipitation, and the guns fell into the hands of the brave men of the 21st. But the supporting regiments could not come up, and Lieutenant Colonel Clark, with his little band of brave men, was in danger of being himself cut off and captured. The enemy, recovering from his first surprise, and perceiving the smallness of the force that had driven him out, returned to the attack in overwhelming numbers. Lieutenant Colonel Clark, with difficulty, but with great skill, extricated his command and retired to the railroad. It was a brave attempt, and had General Reno been able to bring up the remainder of his brigade from under the fire of the redans upon his left, it would have been a magnificent success. But it was reserved for General Parke to strike the decisive blow with the 4th Rhode Island regiment.

General Parke, soon after daylight, formed his brigade and moved in rear of General Foster upon the county road. The 4th Rhode Island was in advance, followed by the 8th Connecticut and the 5th Rhode Island battalion. The 11th Connecticut, of this brigade, had been assigned to General Foster's command to support the howitzer battery, as has already been stated. Upon General Foster's opening of the battle, General Parke was ordered to file to the left and take such position as

*Colonel Augustus Morse of the 21st had been detached at Annapolis and placed in command of the depot of supplies at that place.

would enable him to support either General Reno or General Foster, as the vicissitudes of the fight might require. General Parke moved to a point about midway between the two wings, a little in the rear, and halted. The ground in front, so far as it could be observed, was discovered to be quite difficult, abounding in swampy places and broken with hollows and ridges of a slight elevation. Among these ridges the men found some shelter from the missiles of the enemy, which were now flying thick and fast among them. Colonel Rodman, of the 4th Rhode Island, finding his position too much exposed, moved forward to the railroad and rested his men near the embankment, which afforded good cover. It was now about eleven o'clock in the forenoon. While here, Colonel Rodman noticed the gallant but ineffectual charge of Lieutenant Colonel Clark and his subsequent retirement. He put his men on the alert, and meeting Lieutenant Colonel Clark, was informed of the situation of affairs and the feasibility of renewing the attack. Colonel Rodman immediately assumed the responsibility of assaulting, ordered his men to the charge, sending intelligence to General Parke of the movement which he designed to make. General Parke at once sent an aide to ascertain the real condition of the troops and the enemy, and upon his report of the practicability of the movement, approved the action of Colonel Rodman and advanced the rest of his brigade in support. Colonel Rodman pressed forward with his regiment, entered the works which Lieutenant Colonel Clark had left, and fought his way along gun by gun, until he had swept the enemy's lines for some distance to the right, and captured nine pieces of artillery. The 8th Connecticut followed closely upon the steps of the 4th Rhode Island, and the 5th Rhode Island brought up the rear, turning the enemy completely out of the works which he had so well defended. General Foster, observing the progress made by General Parke's brigade, ordered an advance along his entire front. His troops charged cheering, and the 11th Connecticut soon stood side by side with its old comrades. But the enemy, now thoroughly shaken and demoralized, did not wait for the attack. He hurriedly retreated from his intrenchments, and Fort Thompson and the whole line of breastwork from the railroad to the river fell into the hands of our victorious troops. The action on the left was not yet over. General Reno's brigade was still hotly engaged. Sending out the 8th Connecticut and the 5th Rhode Island battalion as skirmishers to ascertain what the enemy was doing, General Parke ascertained that the rifle pits and redoubts on the left of the railroad were still occupied, and that our troops were exposed to a galling fire. Again he called upon the 4th Rhode Island to charge the enemy. Again did Colonel Rodman lead his men through a heavy and severe fire to victory. They charged gallantly through the storm of shot and shell, took the enemy's line in flank, rolled it up and swept it away. General Reno pressed his brigade forward, leading on his troops with impetuous daring. They quickly cleared the rifle pits, they stormed the redoubts, they carried everything away before them. The day was bravely and brilliantly won, and as General Burnside rode into the captured works, he was received with enthusiastic cheers. The victorious army was immediately put upon the track of the retreating rebels. But the flying foe was too quick in his movements. A train of cars was in waiting on the track in rear of the enemy's lines, and the defeated troops at once filled it and were carried across to Newbern. Others fled across the railroad and turnpike bridges, setting the former on fire and destroying the draw of the latter. Not stopping at Newbern longer than to apply the torch to several of its buildings, the enemy's commanding general pushed on into the country in the rear, and scarcely felt himself secure till at Kinston he had placed another river between himself and General Burnside's army. But, devoid of cavalry as we were, our troops could make no pursuit. They marched rapidly to the river Trent—finding other abandoned works on the way—and were there stopped by the burning bridge. Later in the afternoon, General Foster's brigade was carried across to the city, and encamped in and about the place. The next day was occupied in posting the troops in and around the city. On Saturday night, the commanding general—having ordered Divine Service for the morrow—had the satisfaction of knowing that the week had ended well. His second great victory had been won, and the shores of Albemarle and Pamlico Sounds were now in undisputed possession of our arms. It was certainly an occasion of gratitude to the Almighty, who had given the success.

The battle of Newbern was a peculiar conflict. It may be doubted whether another such was fought during the war. It was a bold attack upon a strongly fortified position, heavily armed and abundantly manned, made by an infantry force without siege guns or any artillery, in fact, except a few howitzers. It was a fight in a fog. Our officers did not really know the extent of the works to be assaulted, till the army was immediately under their guns. It would seem that the existence of the redoubts upon the enemy's extreme right was hardly suspected until General Reno found his brigade suffering from their fire, and was unable, in consequence, to support Lieutenant Colonel Clark's movement as he had at first intended. But, on the other hand, the enemy was laboring under the disadvantage of not knowing the number of the forces that were attacking him. He knew that there were men in his front, but how many, and with what engines of destruction, he did not know. The unexpected appearance of Lieutenant Colonel Clark's battalion of four companies in the midst of his intrenchments disconcerted him for the moment, and he yielded the battery which they attacked without fully understanding by how small a force it had been captured. His right wing fought better than his left, and continued the contest with great gallantry, even after the fortune of the day had been decided. As it happened, Lieutenant Colonel Clark's charge was an act of great temerity. But General Reno, when he ordered it, intended to follow immediately with the remainder of his brigade. As it resulted, it proved a great benefit; for it revealed the weak places of the enemy's line. Colonel Rodman, with a fine soldierly instinct, perceived that the enemy's line could there be successfully pierced, and his prompt and daring spirit suggested that, without losing time in waiting for orders, he should take advantage of the opportunity so fortunately offered. General Parke, had he been a martinet in discipline, might have recalled his subordinate from his perilous enterprise. But he had sufficient sense and sagacity to perceive that Colonel Rodman was acting for the best, though upon his own responsibility. He accordingly followed up the attack with his remaining force, and, effectually and successfully piercing the enemy's centre, broke up his line and threw his troops into confusion and dismay.* In this battle, moreover, every man was engaged. There were no reserves, properly so called. Every regiment was under fire from the start, and was put into the action whenever and wherever it could most effectively do its required work. General Burnside was along the line at every point where his presence was most required, repairing a mistake here, pushing an advantage there. His subordinate officers were thoroughly brave and skilful soldiers, and his men were flushed with victory and inspired with unlimited confidence in their commander. The enemy was shaken by the defeat on Roanoke Island, the Commanding General Branch was not distinguished for any remarkable soldierly qualities, and the impression which the valor of Burnside's troops, already tried and proved, had made, was not encouraging for any prolonged resistance. On both sides, the number of assailants and defenders was about equal, but the advantage clearly lay with the enemy, who was emboldened by his sense of security behind his defences. The contest, therefore, was somewhat stubborn, though not of long duration, and the victory that was gained reflected great credit upon our arms; for it demonstrated beyond all cavil the fearlessness of our soldiers and the skill and bravery of their officers. The fruits of the victory

* When General Burnside was told that the 4th Rhode Island was in the rebel works, as he saw the flag moving rapidly along, he exclaimed, "I knew it. It was no more than I expected. Thank God, the day is won!"

were the possession of the North Carolina coast washed by the two Sounds, the occupation of the city of Newbern, which proved to be an invaluable accession, the capture of about two hundred prisoners, sixty-six guns, a great amount of forage, supplies and naval stores, tents and barracks for ten thousand men, and large quantities of small arms, equipments, accoutrements, and horses abandoned by the flying enemy. It was a very damaging blow to the enemy in that quarter, and it spread a wholesome idea of the power and the prowess of the army of the Union among the people of North Carolina.

The casualties among our troops in the battle of Newbern amounted to eighty-eight killed and three hundred and fifty-two wounded. The 21st Massachusetts, from its exposed position and the daring of its officers and men, suffered the greatest loss. Among the wounded was Lieutenant Colonel Robert B. Potter of the 51st New York. He received his injury early in the action, but, bandaging the wound as well as he could at the time, he continued with his regiment till the close of the engagement, and rendered great service. Major Stevenson of the 24th Massachusetts, received a severe wound while exhibiting great gallantry before the enemy's works. Captain Frazer of the 21st Massachusetts, was taken prisoner at the time the charge was made upon the enemy's position. But upon the retreat of the enemy, he managed to keep in the rear, and, drawing his revolver, captured and brought in the three men left to guard him. The abandoned earthworks which were discovered upon the march to the field were found by Captain R. S. Williamson, of the Topographical Engineers, who made several daring reconnaissances, accompanied by Captain Potter and Lieutenants Pell, Fearing, Strong, Reno, Morris, and other staff officers.

Among the killed were numbered several excellent officers. Rev. O. N. Benton, Chaplain of the 51st New York, was mortally wounded, and died soon after the action. He was a most useful man in the regiment, and exercised a very beneficial influence by the exemplary Christian character which he illustrated in word and deed. He was struck while encouraging and cheering on the men in the midst of the severest part of the engagement. Lieutenant Colonel Henry Merritt of the 23d Massachusetts was killed early in the engagement, while bravely urging his men into line in a most exposed position. He was from Salem, Mass., was a very promising officer and an estimable man. He is mentioned by the commanding officer of his regiment as of kindest heart and of great gallantry in action. He had gathered in a large measure of confidence and friendship, and his loss was severely felt by all who knew him. Captain Charles Tillinghast of the 4th Rhode Island was killed, while gallantly leading his company forward in the charge upon the enemy's works. He was a faithful officer—"frank, manly, courteous and kind"—and rendered excellent service in council, camp, and field. His last words, addressed to his Lieutenant, were: "If I fall, press on with the men." Lieutenant Henry R. Pierce, of the 5th Rhode Island battalion, was killed in the second charge upon the enemy's lines. He was a teacher by profession, had applied for and accepted his commission in the finest spirit of duty. He was a man of very estimable and worthy character, of scholarly attainments, and of manly principles. He stood in the very front rank of his profession in the State of Rhode Island, and his death was felt as a public calamity by many who were beyond the immediate circle of his personal friendship.

But among those who gave up their lives in their country's service upon this field of sacrifice and victory, the most interesting and striking character was that of Adjutant Frazar Augustus Stearns. His extreme youth, (he was not quite twenty-two years of age when he fell,) his high tone and spirit, his gallant and daring behavior when in action, his faithful and dutiful conduct in camp, and his earnest, affectionate and religious disposition at all times had endeared him to his comrades and attracted the warm regard of his superior officers. He was the son of President Stearns of Amherst College, Mass., had been tenderly reared, carefully nurtured, and thoroughly trained in habits of study. He was a student in Amherst College at the outbreak of the war. But the quiet and secluded life of a student did not suit the thoughts or desires of one who felt that the call for men which was made after the battle of Bull Run was meant especially for him. "There is a call for Frazar A. Stearns," he said, and after much deliberation and discussion, gained the consent of his father and friends, and gave himself to his country. He was commissioned First Lieutenant in the 21st Massachusetts Regiment in the summer of 1861, and was ordered, with his regiment, to Washington on the twenty-first of August. The regiment was soon after stationed at Annapolis, and became a part of the Expedition to North Carolina. General Reno desired to have the young officer upon his staff, but Lieutenant Stearns preferred remaining with his regiment, of which he was now Adjutant. His bravery was conspicuous on the battle field of Roanoke Island, where he received two wounds. His ardent and impulsive temperament urged him into the thickest of the conflict, while his firm Christian faith kept him cool and composed in the midst of all dangers. He received his death wound early in the battle, while his regiment was charging gallantly into the enemy's works near the brick yard. He was the first to fall, receiving a bullet in his right breast, and uttering a short ejaculation he breathed forth his spirit, supported in the arms of one of his soldiers. It was a pure and beautiful life sacrificed with a willing devotion to duty, freedom, and God. A Memoir, written by his father, and published by the Massachusetts Sabbath School Society, is a warm and graceful tribute to his memory as a man, a soldier and a Christian. General Burnside directed, in special orders dated March 16th, 1862, that "the six-pounder brass gun taken in the battery where Adjutant Stearns, of the 21st Massachusetts Volunteers, met his death while gallantly fighting at the battle of Newbern, be presented to his regiment as a monument to the memory of a brave man." The regiment voted to present the piece to Amherst College. General Reno expressed, in his official report of the battle, his admiration of young Stearns as "one of the most accomplished and gallant officers in the army." His death was the occasion of numerous kind and cordial expressions of sympathy from officers and soldiers, and from many friends and acquaintances who had been attracted to him by his generous and affectionate nature.

In the battle of Newbern, the navy rendered efficient service, by bombarding the enemy's earth works, by defending the right flank of our army, by crossing the troops to the city and holding it in connection with the land forces. General Burnside, in his official report, mentions the conduct of the naval officers in terms of high commendation. Captain Thomas P. Ives, in command of the Picket, is declared to have rendered marked service here, as at Roanoke and elsewhere. The fleet under Commander Rowan was always ready for any service which General Burnside desired. The naval battery, that was sent on shore under Lieutenant McCook, was most handsomely and efficiently handled. It suffered a loss of two men of the Union Coast Guard killed, and two officers, five men of the Guard and four seamen wounded. Near the close of the action, the battery captured Colonel Avery and a portion of the 25th North Carolina, who had been driven out of the rifle pits and were endeavoring to escape, when encountered by Lieutenant McCook and his command. Commander Rowan speaks of the obstructions in the river as "very formidable, and prepared with great care." "The lower barrier was composed of a series of piling driven securely into the bottom and cut off below the water. Added to this was another row of iron-capped and pointed piles, inclined at an angle of about forty-five degrees down the stream. Near this was a row of thirty torpedoes, with trigger lines attached to the pointed piles." A second barrier "consisted of a line of sunken vessels closely massed and chevaux de frise," leaving open only a narrow passage directly under the guns of Fort Thompson. In passing the barrier, the Commodore Barney and the Stars and Stripes were somewhat injured. The Commodore Perry struck one of the iron stakes and carried off with her its head sticking in her bottom. The torpedoes did not explode. The Delaware ran up to the city and captured one schooner, two steamers, and a large amount of naval stores sufficient to load nine vessels. Thus brilliantly and without serious casualty did Commander Rowan and his sailors do their part of the work.

The next point in General Burnside's instructions was to secure the towns of Beaufort and Morehead City, and to reduce Fort Macon. Not a moment was lost in proceeding to this task. As soon as the captures at Newbern could be properly cared for, and the necessary business of closing up the affairs, which a battle of this kind always carries in its train, had been transacted, General Burnside made his preparations for investing Fort Macon. The storage of supplies, the paroling of prisoners, the communications with the enemy respecting the late contest, the settlement of affairs in the city and the inauguration of a new order of things occupied considerable time. The position required to be fortified to some extent, to guard against any attempt of the enemy to reöccupy it. It was feared at the North, that a portion of the enemy's forces, which had just evacuated Manassas and its neighborhood, might have been sent to North Carolina to drive our troops away from that point. The battle of Newbern demonstrated the ability of General Burnside and his troops to take care of themselves against an ordinary or equal force of the enemy. But it was yet barely possible, that an overwhelming number of the enemy might attack them. Newbern was open to such attack, and must consequently be fortified, so that it could be easily defended even against superior forces. Happily its situation at the confluence of the rivers Neuse and Trent was such that fortifications could be speedily thrown up, and a canal dug between the two rivers, which when filled with water, would entirely insulate the city, and thus render it when defended by a resolute garrison, almost impregnable. It was also necessary to destroy the railroad leading westward towards Goldsboro' for a considerable distance. General Burnside initiated these two undertakings and then gave his attention to Fort Macon.

The first act was to take possession and occupy the railroad leading from Newbern to Beaufort, by gradually extending our outposts towards the latter city. General Parke's brigade was selected for this movement, and the navy, at the proper moment, was to go round by sea and assist in the reduction of the fort. The distance from Newbern to Beaufort is about forty miles, and the country between is a series of morasses, traversed by the railroad and the common highway. Our forces could use both these roads in marching. But the destruction of the bridge at Newbern prevented the use of the railroad for purposes of transportation. Still our troops were in the rear of the desired points, and no resistance was anticipated except immediately under the guns of the fort. No resistance was made. The first movement was a reconnaissance down the railroad for about fifteen miles, made by General Burnside and Lieutenant Williamson, engineer officer, on the 18th of March. It was found that a force could be transported by water to Slocum's Creek, there land, and march thence by way of the highway and railroad. Hand cars on the railroad were used for carrying supplies. On the 20th, this movement was made, and a part of the command proceeded as far as Havelock Station, about a mile from the landing, where one company of the 5th Rhode Island Battalion remained until the 23d as guard of the post. Captain Arnold, who was in command, found near his camp an abandoned grist mill, the machinery of which the rebels had attempted to destroy, when they abandoned the neighborhood. The mechanics of the 5th, under the intelligent direction of their captain, soon put it in order again, and the mill was found to be very serviceable to the comfort and subsistence of the troops. The rest of the command marched on well into the night, and finally reached and occupied some barracks which had been previously built and used by the enemy's troops. On the 21st, the advance proceeded as far as Carolina City, a village containing from fifty to one hundred inhabitants, a few respectable dwellings and the ruins of a large hotel — a place of considerable summer resort. The hotel had been burnt by the enemy a few days before the arrival of our troops. Opposite the town across a narrow channel was Bogue Island, on the eastern extremity of which was Fort Macon. On the 22d two companies of the 4th Rhode Island were sent to Morehead City, and on the night of the 25th another detachment of the same regiment, supported by one company of the 8th Connecticut, occupied Beaufort. On the night of the 23d the command was closed up, the 5th Rhode Island occupying Newport. Here a railroad bridge had been destroyed by the enemy, which Major Wright was directed to rebuild. He commenced work on the 24th, and by the night of the 29th he and his command had constructed a bridge of one hundred and eighty feet in length, capable of bearing a train of the weight of fifty tons.

General Parke made his headquarters at Carolina City and summoned the fort. Its commandant, Colonel Moses J. White, declined to surrender his post. He was even disposed at one time to bombard the towns occupied by our forces, but happily refrained from such an unwarrantable proceeding. The citizens seemed to be about equally divided in their sentiments of loyalty. In some instances our troops were welcomed with great cordiality. It was remarked at the time, as an encouraging fact, that on the Sunday following the occupation of Beaufort, prayers for the President of the United States were read in the Episcopal church of the town and responded to with marked earnestness.

Fort Macon itself is a small, but strong stone, casemated work, mounting sixty-seven guns at the time, and was then garrisoned by a battalion of about five hundred men. Its commandant was a brave and resolute officer, and though entirely isolated, was determined to hold his position till the last moment. He had made preparations for defence by procuring supplies, by levelling the ground for the sweep of his guns, by undermining and overthrowing the neighboring light-house, and was evidently resolved to give an attacking party a warm reception. General Burnside therefore decided to make a complete investment of the fort, and, by a combined attack by land and sea, force its surrender. General Parke was an accomplished engineer, and to him the work of besieging the fort by land was entrusted. It could not have been committed to better hands. Assisted by Captain Williamson and Lieutenant Flagler, General Parke began his task. On the 29th, he threw a part of his brigade upon the island and prepared to construct his batteries. The operations for investing the fort were materially assisted by the configuration of the island. General Parke found here what General Gillmore afterwards found on Morris and James Islands near Charleston—long, low ridges of sand, behind which the troops could work almost unmolested by the enemy's fire. These ridges are doubtless formed by the wind, and like the sands of Cape Cod, and other exposed places upon our seaboard, change their situation and form according to the force of the gale to which they are opened. Some delay had been experienced by the destruction of the railroad bridge. But immediately upon its completion, large quantities of ordnance stores and siege material began to arrive from Newbern. Trenches were dug, mortar beds formed, and the mortars mounted, some heavy Parrott guns placed in position and the number of troops on the island increased. Nearly a month was occupied in these important operations. General Parke was vigilant and indefatigable. General Burnside was as frequently at Beaufort and Carolina City as affairs at Newbern permitted his presence, and the siege was pushed on as rapidly as the circumstances of the case would allow. The fort was hemmed in on every side. The blockading squadron, consisting of steamers Daylight, State of Georgia and Chippewa and the bark Gemsbok, all under the command of Commander Samuel Lockwood, kept a sharp look out at sea. Our soldiers picketed the island in all directions. A few small sailing boats that had been found at Beaufort were made extremely convenient by our officers for parties of duty and pleasure, and considerable information and an occasional prisoner were picked up from time to time. The siege was by no means devoid of variety, and our officers enjoyed the opportunity of making acquaintances among the former adherents of Jefferson Davis, some of whom did not hesitate to profess an amount of original "Unionism" which was absolutely suspicious. There were two English vessels lying in the harbor of Beaufort when our forces occupied the town, the officers and crews of which displayed a somewhat unfriendly spirit. It had been supposed that the noted rebel privateer and blockade runner, the Nashville, was lying at Morehead City. But she had run out to sea immediately after the battle of Newbern, and succeeded in eluding our blockading fleet.

The month of April was drawing to a close. At last, on the 23rd, General Parke reported himself ready. Under his intelligent direction every preparation had been thoroughly made and there was no hope for the devoted fort. No shot had as yet been fired by our men. But so complete had been the arrangements, that General Burnside, who was now present and desired to prevent a loss of life, again summoned Colonel White to surrender, offering generous terms. Colonel White again declined in the fewest possible words. Nothing more was to be done than to open our batteries. Commander Lockwood, ever ready to coöperate, stationed his vessels near the point on which the fort was built, with the expectation of taking part in the bombardment. But, unfortunately, the weather was boisterous, the sea was rough, and on the day of battle, the naval forces could accomplish but little. They had a smart engagement with the fort of about an hour's duration. The Daylight was struck once and had one officer wounded.

On the morning of the 25th, General Parke opened his guns on the fort. He had prepared three siege batteries, one of three thirty-pound guns, under the command of Captain L. O. Morris, one of four eight-inch mortars, under the command of Lieutenant D. W. Flagler, one of four ten-inch mortars, under the command of Second Lieutenant M. F. Prouty, of the 25th Massachusetts. From these the fire was accurate and destructive. The bombardment continued through that day, the fort replying vigorously. But the commandant saw that his case was desperate. For ten hours our missiles of destruction rained down upon the work. Our heavy guns made breaches in its walls, our shells exploded within its enclosures. The ramparts were swept clean of men. Seventeen guns were disabled and dismounted. The face of the fort showed the marks of many an indentation. The garrison was too small to make a prolonged existence without exhaustion. On the morning of the 26th, therefore, Colonel White hung out the white flag, obtained honorable terms of capitulation, marched out his command, and surrendered to General Parke the fort which he had so persistently defended. The 5th Rhode Island battalion at once marched in, took possession, and the flag of the United States once more floated over the recovered work. This was the second of the forts which had been "reoccupied and repossessed" by our forces by process of siege, Fort Pulaski having surrendered to General Gillmore, after a fierce bombardment, on the eleventh of April. The fall of Fort Macon, so creditably accomplished by General Parke, gave us possession of a new base of supplies and of operations, and relieved that portion of the blockading fleet which had been lying off the harbor of Beaufort. Not many supplies were found in the fort, as the length of the siege had depleted the store houses. The armament and the fort itself had been considerably injured by our attack. Much of the artillery, however, was in good condition as it fell into our hands. The losses on both sides were inconsiderable. Upon our part, but one man was killed and five wounded. The enemy lost eight killed and twenty wounded. The interior of the fort is said to have been "literally covered with fragments of bombs and shells."*

---

* Commander Lockwood's Report.

But one stronghold of the enemy on the coast of North Carolina now remained unconquered—that of Wilmington, which was heavily fortified and well defended. But it was not permitted to General Burnside to add the capture of this important place to his series of victories. He had already done enough to deserve the commendations of his grateful countrymen, but he would have been glad to complete the occupation of the North Carolina shores. He received the most flattering testimonials from the authorities at Washington of the appreciation of the service which he had already rendered. The Secretary of War expressed his gratitude in the following terms: "The report of the late brilliant successes of the United States forces under your command at Newbern has afforded the highest satisfaction to the President, to this Department, and to the whole nation, and thanks for distinguished services are again tendered to you and the officers and soldiers under your command."* These expressions of approval were not mere empty words. General Burnside was promoted to Major General of Volunteers, his commission dating March 18th. Generals Foster, Reno, and Parke were also promoted to the same grade, dating from the fall of Fort Macon, April 26th. Colonel Rodman received a deserved advancement to the rank of Brigadier General, dating from the 28th of April. Flag Officer Goldsborough and Commander Rowan also received the thanks of Congress for their services at Roanoke Island and Newbern, and were duly promoted to a superior rank. Thus did a grateful country manifest its approval of patriotic and heroic deeds.

---

* Mr. Stanton's Letter, as quoted in General Order No. 23.

CHAPTER VI.

THE DEPARTMENT OF NORTH CAROLINA.

THE boundaries of General Burnside's jurisdiction as commander of the Department of North Carolina, were necessarily defined by the limits of the conquests which our arms should make. After the battle of Newbern, the pursuit of the flying foe into the interior would have been an easy task, had the victorious army been appointed and equipped for an aggressive campaign of such importance. But General Burnside had no cavalry. He had also no reserves. All his forces had been put into the battle after a wearisome march, and they were too much exhausted to do more than drive the enemy out of his defences. The orders for the expedition pointed to the immediate reduction of Fort Macon. General Burnside, therefore, was obliged to content himself with the administration of affairs, and with strengthening Newbern and putting it in condition for defence, that it might become a suitable base for future military operations. His instructions contemplated no movement at present beyond the reoccupation of Fort Macon. On Sunday, March 16th, public services of Thanksgiving to God for the victories of our arms were held in the churches of Newbern, and on Monday, the serious civil work of the Department began.

General Burnside found that he had by no means an easy task to perform. While the siege of Fort Macon was in progress, affairs at Newbern demanded almost constant personal supervision. There were questions of property to settle, the employment and care of large numbers of "contrabands" who had been abandoned by their masters, the subsistence of many poor persons who had no visible means of support, and a thousand other matters of greater or less importance, which required perpetual attention. The Department had been constituted upon the arrival of the expedition at Hatteras Inlet. While it included within its boundaries only Hatteras Inlet and its neighborhood, its civic duties were not arduous. But as its limits enlarged, its labors increased. It had been supposed that North Carolina was a State which had been reluctantly dragged out of the Union. There must be a strong loyal sentiment somewhere latent among the people. It was not the least of General Burnside's duties to seek, to find and to develope this sentiment. Could it be done best by diplomacy or by arms? General Burnside did not think that, while the rebels had a large army in the field, any State could be allured from its subjection to the rebel government. It would be useless for any number of people to declare themselves independent of the authority at Richmond, while that authority could command the arms of half a million of soldiers. A State must be conquered, or its professed allegiance was of small value. It was the duty of the Commander of a Department to show to all the people within the boundaries of his authority, that the government which he served was more powerful than the usurping government, and that he had ample means for protecting those persons who would renounce their allegiance to the enemy and declare themselves loyal to the Union. The policy of the United States was not only to conciliate, but to subdue and to defend. If there should be any considerable numbers of loyal persons on the shores of North Carolina, it would be cruel to leave them exposed to the hatred and hostility of their enemies. As a military movement, it was also necessary to hold certain points upon the coast, to manifest the supreme authority of the government of the United States, and to prove that the attempts making to restore that authority all over the South were made earnestly and with an eye to success.

With some such object in view, General Burnside sent out

detachments of his troops to visit, examine, and, if thought necessary, to occupy certain portions of the coast. While General Parke's brigade was busy at Beaufort and Fort Macon, the command at Newbern was not suffered to lack employment. Colonel Hartranft, with the 51st Pennsylvania Regiment, made a reconnaissance into the interior of the coast counties, acquiring considerable valuable information, and picking up a few prisoners.

A somewhat important expedition, under the command of General Foster, was sent to Washington, at the head of the Pamlico river. On the 19th of March, eight companies of the 24th Massachusetts, under Colonel Stevenson, were embarked on board the steam transport Guide, and on the 20th, they sailed, under convoy of the gunboats Louisiana, Delaware, and Commodore Perry. The steamers anchored in the Pamlico river the same night, and on the 21st, proceeded up the river. At a distance of five miles below the place, obstructions were found in the channel, to prevent the ingress of any hostile force. One or two deserted batteries were observed upon the shore. The gunboats broke through the obstructions, but owing to the shallowness of the water, the transport could not approach the town. Two companies were transferred to a boat of lighter draft, were landed, and marched into the place without hindrance.

An account of the occupation given by the correspondent of the Boston Journal, presents a very good view of the expedition and its results : "Washington is a village of twenty-five hundred inhabitants, some two-thirds of whom have seen fit to leave for the interior. It is a pleasant, inviting locality. Our troops landed at a wharf, and visited the village about two o'clock in the afternoon, where they were received by the remaining inhabitants with every expression of welcome. In passing through the streets, one lady appeared at her door and displayed the stars and stripes, which she had long kept secreted from the rebels. She seemed overjoyed at the sight of our troops. The line of march extended to the Court House, where was a flag staff, and upon this was run up the national flag. The people gathered wonderingly about, and seemed to enjoy the sight, though they refrained from any strong expression of their feelings. It was ascertained that the principal portion of the rebel force here had left immediately after Newbern was taken, and that a squad of cavalry, which lingered behind, had recently left the place." Our naval forces found that two gunboats had been building at this place. One of them, pierced for six guns, was launched and carried up the river a short time before the arrival of our forces. It was burnt on the night of the 20th, by the enemy's hands. The other boat was not yet completed, and was destroyed by our seamen, assisted by some of the inhabitants of the town. After a short stay, our troops were reëmbarked, and on the next day returned to Newbern. Other small bodies of troops were sent into the country upon reconnoitering expeditions. They returned with reports of a not very encouraging nature. The loyal sentiment of the people of North Carolina was not so strong as had been supposed. The people had at first, doubtless, beeen overawed by the superior power of the rebel government. But they had also, to a very great extent, willingly entered into the war against the Federal Government. North Carolina had also profited largely, and was destined to profit still more by the blockade-running, for which Wilmington afforded unusual facilities. The people were not yet ready to break away from the yoke of the insurgent power. They had not felt its heavy burden as they were destined to feel it a later period. Still, our own government did not despair of bringing the State back to its allegiance.

Roanoke Island was also the base of some operations which kept the troops employed, though they accomplished no extraordinary results. Before the army had started for Newbern, on the 8th of March, a force of six companies of the 6th New Hampshire had been sent to Columbia in search of a regiment of rebels which was said to be gathering recruits at that place. General Foster led the expedition. The troops landed, marched into the village, but could find no enemy. The population of that section of the State was so sparse, that the game was not worth the candle. The village was very small, and the inhabitants of slight account as to either character or courage. Nothing more formidable than the public whipping post was found, and that was speedily destroyed.

A rather more brilliant affair was conducted by Lieutenant Colonel Griffin of the 6th New Hampshire with four companies of his own regiment and two companies of the 9th New Jersey, about six hundred men in all. Receiving information that a rebel camp was pitched for recruiting purposes near Elizabeth City, Colonel Griffin proceeded thither under convoy of the gunboats Virginia, Ceres, General Putnam, Commodore Perry, and Stars and Stripes, on the night of the 7th of April. Colonel Griffin landed his forces the next morning near the designated place. The two companies of the 9th New Jersey disembarked at Elizabeth. The 6th New Hampshire proceeded about three miles above the city to cut off the enemy's retreat. The attack was gallantly made. The camp was surprised, one of the enemy killed, two wounded and seventy-four captured. The remainder took to the woods, leaving three wounded and fifty stands of arms and a considerable quantity of ammunition and public stores to fall into the hands of our victorious troops. The command returned to Roanoke Island without loss.

An expedition on a somewhat larger scale than any that had yet been undertaken, was sent to Camden County for the purpose of ascertaining what force of the enemy, if any there were, had become established in the neighborhood of the Albemarle and Chesapeake Canal, and what opportunity existed for obstructing the canal itself. The troops engaged in the enterprise were the 21st Massachusetts, Lieutenant Colonel Clark, 51st Pennsylvania, Major Schall, the 9th New York, Lieutenant Colonel Kimball, 89th New York, Colonel H. S. Fairchild, and 6th New Hampshire, Lieutenant Colonel Griffin. The 9th New York had with them two howitzers, and two other pieces of artillery manned by the Marines and commanded by Colonel Howard, accompanied the expedition. The first two regiments and Colonel Howard's command were from Newbern and formed a brigade under Lieutenant Colonel Bell. The remainder of the troops were from Roanoke Island and formed a brigade under Colonel Hawkins. The gunboats Commodore Perry, Delaware, Lockwood, Picket, Southfield, Stars and Stripes, Underwriter, General Putnam and Whitehead escorted the expedition. The land forces were under the command of General Reno. The work of disembarkation at a point about four miles below Elizabeth City commenced about midnight of the 18th of April. Colonel Hawkins had his command landed about two o'clock A. M. on the 19th. The other troops were delayed by the transports getting aground and did not reach the shore until about seven o'clock. Colonel Hawkins was ordered to march his brigade to South Mills, where was a bridge which the enemy would be obliged to cross in retreating. The guides which he had were either incompetent or treacherous, and led him in a long, circuitous march through the country, but not into the enemy's rear. He came out upon the road upon which General Reno was leading the remainder of the command, about twelve miles from the landing place, and there about noon the two columns made a junction. This was not precisely according to General Reno's instructions and somewhat disturbed his arrangements. The only thing to be done, however, was to push forward as rapidly as possible.

The march had told very severely upon all the troops, particularly upon Colonel Hawkins's brigade. The day was very hot; the roads were very dry and dusty. The men had had little or no experience in marching and sensibly felt the debilitating influence of the weather. Many suffered from slight sun strokes and fell out from the line of march exhausted by the unaccustomed hardship. The surgeons and chaplains in the rear were obliged to impress wagons and other vehicles, with mules and horses that were found in the barns along the road, to relieve the weary soldiers.

About three o'clock in the afternoon, at a point near Camden, about twenty miles distant from the landing, the enemy was discovered posted in a strong position with infantry and artillery and a few cavalry. In front was a plain broken and cut by ditches, in the rear a forest, and on the left an "open piney wood." Our howitzers, that were in advance, first received the enemy's fire from his field pieces. Colonel Howard put his own pieces in position and returned the fire with spirit. General Reno quickly made his dispositions. He sent the 21st Massachusetts and 51st Pennsylvania of Lieutenant Colonel Bell's brigade, through the woods upon the enemy's left to turn that flank of the position. He deployed the 9th and 89th New York to the right to support Lieutenant Colonel Bell's attack, and held the 6th New Hampshire upon the left of the road in reserve. The leading brigade slowly made its way through the wood while the troops in front occupied the attention of the enemy. The engagement now became sharp and even bloody. Our troops, wearied as they were, stood well up to the work. The enemy was obstinate in holding his ground. General Reno, becoming impatient for the development of the attack upon the right, rode over to that part of the line to hasten forward the movement. Meanwhile, Colonel Hawkins, ambitious to repeat the success of the attack at Roanoke Island, ordered the New York regiments to charge the enemy's line. It was gallantly but ineffectually done. Across the broken plain the men went with their wonted enthusiasm. But the ditches, with the enemy's fire, proved a serious obstruction. Men fell, officers were unhorsed, Colonel Hawkins was wounded. Some were killed. The troops were broken and compelled to retire. But now the regiments on the right had entered into the action and delivered their fire vigorously. At the same time, the 6th New Hampshire advanced silently till within short musket range, when, at the word of command, the men poured in a terrific and destructive volley, still advancing. Elated at the prospect of success our men charged furiously forward, and the enemy, pressed in front and flank, at once gave way, broke and fled up the road, carrying with him his artillery. He had received a severe chastisement and had been made to believe that the entire "Burnside Expedition was marching upon Norfolk." A thunder storm that had been gathering during the fight now burst forth, and amid peals and flashes from above and torrents of rain the battle ended. The opposition with which General Reno had been met, though not altogether unexpected, was yet more severe than had been anticipated. It was thought at the time that the enemy had retired to a new and stronger position a few miles in the rear, where he had defensive works. The advantage had clearly been on our side, and a decisive defeat had been inflicted upon the enemy's troops. But General Reno decided not to follow up his success. His orders distinctly were not to risk a disaster, and as the greater part of the object of the movement had been accomplished, he thought it best to return to his transports. The troops were allowed till night to rest, the dead were buried, the slightly wounded were put into the extemporized ambulances, and the severely wounded were left in charge of Chaplain T. W. Conway of the 9th New York, and Dr. Warren, Assistant Surgeon of the 21st Massachusetts, under a flag of truce. The line of retreat was taken at ten o'clock, P. M.—leaving camp fires burning brightly—the troops arrived at the landing early the next morning, and the expedition returned to Roanoke Island and Newbern. The entire loss was fourteen killed, ninety-six wounded and two missing. Among the former was Lieutenant Chas. A. Gadsden, Adjutant of the 9th New York, who fell during the charge at the head of his regiment. "He was a kind, considerate man," says Colonel Hawkins in his report of the battle, "and a most excellent soldier, and died greatly lamented by all his companions." He had been but five days in the service, having just arrived from New York as the expedition was preparing.

It was afterwards ascertained that the enemy was more badly defeated than was at first supposed. Had General Reno's men been more fresh, and had the design of the movement been to go further towards Norfolk, there is no doubt that the road was laid open by the enemy's hasty retreat. He had even abandoned a formidable battery a few miles beyond the scene of the engagement, and had made the best of his way to the neighborhood of the defences of Norfolk. A naval expedition under Lieutenant Flusser, with the gunboats Lockwood, Whitehead and General Putnam, succeeded a few days afterwards in obstructing the mouth of the Canal.

During the month of April, reënforcements, to the number of four regiments and two batteries of light artillery, arrived from the North. The need of cavalry had been sorely felt. It could only be supplied by using the horses of the Rhode Island battery, which had been brought over to Newbern after the capture of that place. Scouting and patrolling were done by the members of the battery, and were sometimes the occasion of covert attacks from the lurking videttes of the enemy. Among the reënforcements now arriving, was the 3d New York cavalry, under Colonel S. H. Mix, an excellent officer. The 17th Massachusetts, Colonel Thomas J. C. Amory, 103d New York, Colonel F. W. Von Egloffstein, and 2d Maryland regiments of Infantry, and two batteries of New York Light Artillery completed the contingent.

The arrival of these troops induced a change in the organization of the command, which was effected early in May. The promotions of the brigade commanders would necessarily imply an increased command. Their brigades were accordingly subdivided, and, with the additions of the reënforcements, formed three divisions. General Foster's division was organized in two brigades, the first under the command of Colonel Thomas G. Stevenson, of the 24th Massachusetts; the second under the command of Colonel T. J. C. Amory, of the 17th Massachusetts. General Reno's two brigades were under the command of Colonel Edward Ferrero, of the 51st New York, and Colonel James Nagle, of the 48th Pennsylvania. General Parke's division was not so compact a command as that of his brother officers. The garrison of Beaufort, Fort Macon and neighborhood was brigaded under General Rodman. The garrison of Roanoke Island was similarly organized, under

Colonel Hawkins. General Williams retained command at Hatteras.

Thus organized, General Burnside was prepared to hold Newbern against any force which the enemy might bring. Indeed, the enemy was even rash enough to believe that he could reoccupy the place. Having fled as far as Kinston after the battle of Newbern, and finding that he was not pursued, he began to take heart again. Concentrating a considerable number—some reports mentioned fifteen thousand men—in the neighborhood of Kinston, he began to make threatening demonstrations upon General Burnside's position. But he soon ascertained that it was too strong to be forced by direct attack, and that General Burnside was too wary an antagonist to be surprised. All that he could do, therefore, was to place an army for the purpose of observing the movements of our forces, without making any serious attempt to dislodge them. The defences of Newbern were perfected, and its commander prepared to carry out the residue of his original instructions.

But the movements contemplated by those instructions depended upon certain other movements which were then making in a different quarter of the vast field of action. The capture of Wilmington would unquestionably have been a very serious blow to the rebel cause. The city is situated upon the Cape Fear river, and its approaches were then defended by formidable works. Through it passed the important line of seaboard communications uniting Virginia with the Gulf States. It was the most difficult port on the coast to blockade, and it thus became the enemy's greatest entrepot for smuggled goods. Were our troops in possession of that point, the enemy's communication with the extreme South would be severed, and his supplies stopped. Its importance was clearly appreciated by the rebel government, and a garrison held the defences sufficiently numerous to make an obstinate resistance. The enemy also held all the interior, and could thus, in a short time, transport such reënforcements to the threatened point as would make an attempt to capture it a very doubtful, as well as hazardous experiment. Naval coöperation was also a decided desideratum. But, at that time, no vessels could be spared for an attack upon the fortifications along the banks of Cape Fear river. The iron-clad monster that lay in the harbor of Norfolk effectually neutralized any independent naval operations along the North Atlantic coast. The fear of its emergence a second time from its retreat, to scatter devastation and ruin along Hampton Roads and the entrance of Chesapeake Bay, and the imperative necessity of guarding that avenue of communication and supplies for General McClellan's army, then operating on the peninsula, prevented the Flag Officer of the North Atlantic Squadron from detaching any of his vessels. The gunboats already in the North Carolina waters were not armed heavily enough for an encounter with the works that protected Wilmington. The forces that General Burnside had at his command were not more than large enough to reduce the place, even if the help of the navy could be assured. Without the aid of the fleet, nothing could be done. Wilmington, therefore, could not at that time be added to the territory within the jurisdiction of the Department of North Carolina.

Was it possible to penetrate into the interior of the State, and, moving upon Goldsborough and Raleigh, cut the enemy's communications at either or both of those points? It was possible under certain conditions, but not otherwise. If those conditions did not exist, a movement into the interior was hazardous, even to the extent of foolhardiness. One condition was that General Buell should operate towards Knoxville and East Tennessee. But General Buell at that time was needed to reënforce General Grant, struggling desperately forward towards Corinth and West Tennessee, by way of Fort Donelson and Pittsburg Landing. Another condition was the triumphant advance of the Army of the Potomac up the Peninsula between the James and York rivers. But General McClellan, in command of that army, had encountered obstacles which rendered his advance anything but triumphant. The season was especially unpropitious. The route chosen was through swamps and muddy plains, rendered almost impassable by the continuous rain. The enemy was sullen and defiant even in retreat, giving back only step by step, and under the pressure of superior numbers. General McClellan proved himself to be slow and unready in all his enterprises, preferring to fight defensive battles, instead of pushing the enemy away from his front by determined attacks. Even in success, he did not seem to understand the proper method of pressing an advantage. Another condition was the occupation of the enemy's attention at Charleston and in its neighborhood. But in the Department of South Carolina, little was doing towards a speedy termination of the attempt upon the stronghold of secession. In fact, the movement of our armies on the Atlantic seaboard seemed to depend altogether upon the success of General McClellan's movements. The plan of the commanding general of the Army of the Potomac evidently was to have the armies at Newbern and Pôrt Royal set in motion to cut off the enemy's retreat, when he should be driven out from Richmond. Until that most desirable consummation should be reached, the other movements were not to be expected. General McClellan and the Secretary of War had already written to General Burnside from Yorktown, that no offensive movement was to be made into the interior of North Carolina until the issue of the operations on the lower peninsula had been determined. When Yorktown was abandoned by the enemy, General McClellan hoped that the way would be opened to Richmond, and that he would have to fight but one decisive battle in front of the coveted point. The sharply contested fight at Williamsburg showed him that the enterprise was more difficult than he had supposed. He then began to feel that there were largely superior forces before him, and that they must be beaten before any successful operations could be made farther to the South. The most that could by any means be done would be simply a diversion, and the authorities in the field and at headquarters were undecided as to whether Winton, Weldon, or Goldsborough should be the objective point. In fact, the irresolution and delay which prevailed in regard to affairs in Virginia, had their natural effect upon affairs in North Carolina, and General Burnside was in consequence restricted within the narrow limits of his conquests along the coast. But the chief condition of moving into the interior was a supply of transportation and cavalry for a march of sixty miles. General Burnside had thus far marched his troops and fought his battles without baggage or cavalry. There was scarcely a wagon in the Department, and, without means of transportation for his supplies and his sick and wounded soldiers, the march to Goldsborough could not be made. Colonel Mix's cavalry relieved the mounted artillery men in their picket duty, and supplied the deficiency which had previously existed in that arm of the service. It was not till nearly the middle of May, that cavalry, wagons, ambulances, cars and locomotives arrived in the Department for the purposes of a long campaign.

On the tenth of May, General Wool, stimulated by the presence of the President and the Secretaries of the Treasury and War, advanced from Fortress Monroe on Norfolk. The city surrendered, the rebel General Huger having withdrawn his command. On the eleventh, the rebels set fire to the Merrimac, and she was blown up and sunk near Sewall's Point. This event opened the James River as far as Drury's Bluff, the Elizabeth River and the canals between North Carolina and Norfolk to the undisputed possession of our naval and military forces. Had General McClellan immediately transferred his base of operations from the York River to the James and made an attack upon Petersburg, he would have changed the entire character of his campaign and indeed of the whole record of the summer of 1862 in Virginia. The perils of the Chickahominy swamps, the disastrous and bloody battles around Richmond, and the terrible scenes of the retreat to Harrison's Landing would have been avoided. Then General Burnside could have made a successful demonstration on Goldsborough, and it is safe to presume that the most brilliant and satisfactory results would have followed. Indeed, while General McClellan was at Harrison's Landing, General Burnside suggested an attempt upon Petersburg. But then the opportunity had passed, and the baffled Army of the Potomac was not equal to such a movement.

During the military operations in North Carolina the Government had steadily kept in view the political pacification of the State. With this end, communications had passed between the authorities at Washington and the Hon. Edward Stanley, once a member of Congress from North Carolina, and a popular and influential man there, but at this time resident in California. The correspondence culminated in his appointment as Military Governor of North Carolina. He arrived at Newbern on the 26th day of May, and General Burnside at once turned over to him the jurisdiction of all civil and political affairs, assuring him of the most cordial coöperation on the part of the military officers. It was a manifest relief to the commanding general, and whatever was the subsequent success of the experiment, it had the merit of having originated in a humane spirit and was conducted with good and patriotic intentions.

With the exception of Governor Stanley's arrival, the month of May was a comparatively quiet season in the Department. On the 14th the naval expedition visited Plymouth. The newly arrived troops were engaged in short expeditions into the neighboring country, in which Colonel Mix's cavalry bore a conspicuous part. The enemy made occasional dashes upon our outposts with indifferent results upon either side. Political events were of unimportant significance. The life of the camp was somewhat monotonous and dull. The most pleasing event of the month was the release of several hundred Union prisoners, in accordance with the cartel at Roanoke Island. Among these, General Burnside was glad to recognize and welcome several members of his old command, the First Rhode Island. The great exploits that were performing elsewhere—at New Orleans, on the Mississippi, in Tennessee—had no parallel on the Atlantic seaboard. Finally "Stonewall" Jackson's discomfiture and pursuit of General Banks down the Shenandoah valley and across the Potomac disturbed the plans of General McClellan to such an extent, as to make the Peninsula campaign a decided and manifest failure. General Jackson's movements threatened Washington, caused considerable consternation at the War Office, shook General McDowell's position at Fredericksburg, and, at a later period, recoiled on General McClellan with disastrous effect. Our officers in North Carolina awaited the course of events—since they could do nothing more—with as much patience as was compatible with the circumstances of the case.

Another month of inaction followed. The monotony of life in North Carolina was somewhat varied by a smart engagement which took place at Tranter's Creek about ten miles from Washington on the 5th of June. Eight companies of the 24th Massachusetts under Lieutenant Colonel F. A. Osborn, a squadron of Colonel Mix's cavalry and a battery of two steel Wiard guns under Lieutenant William B. Avery, manned by twenty-five men of the Marines, constituted our force. The enemy had cavalry and infantry, was attacked boldly and received a severe punishment. The affair was of short duration but was very creditable to the officers and men engaged in it. On the 10th, General Burnside visited General McClellan at his headquarters in front of Richmond. This visit gave to General Burnside some explanation of the inactivity of the Army of the Potomac. One cause at least existed in the condition of that section of the country. The roads were found to be in horrible condition. The almost continuous rains of the preceding months had made almost the entire Peninsula like a vast morass. Even an enterprising general would have found it difficult, amid such circumstances, to satisfy the hopes of the country.

Another event of more personal than general interest was the presentation of the sword, voted by the General Assembly of Rhode Island, to General Burnside in recognition of the services rendered by him at the commencement of his campaign. The weapon and its appurtenances were exceedingly elegant in design and finish, and happily illustrated the good taste of the manufacturer and the generosity of the State. Adjutant General E. C. Mauran was designated by the Governor of Rhode Island to present the sword, and he, in company with Captain Henry Bedlow, left Providence on the 2d day of June for Newbern. The presentation was made on the 20th, and the pageant is described by those who witnessed it in enthusiastic terms. The garrison of Newbern, all the Rhode Island troops in the Department and others that could readily be spared from their posts, were concentrated at Newbern. About eight thousand were in attendance. A grand review took place; and amidst the waving of banners, the inspiriting notes of martial music, and in the presence of a large multitude of spectators, the ceremony of presentation was performed. Congratulatory and very felicitous addresses were gracefully and eloquently pronounced on both sides, and a banquet, attended by all the officers present in the city, closed the festivities of the day. The honor, thus worthily conferred and modestly received, found readiest response in the hearts of the officers and men of the army in North Carolina, who attested, by long continued cheering and other demonstrations of joy, their appreciation of the compliment thus paid to their beloved commander.

But this concentration and review of troops had other purposes than those of display and compliment. General Burnside, weary of his long enforced quiet, had determined upon a movement into the interior. His supplies had been collected, his means of transportation prepared, his cavalry well trained for service, and his troops eager for marching orders. He proposed to strike at Goldsboro'. The most encouraging accounts had been received of General McClellan's operations towards Richmond, and hopes were entertained of the triumphant close of the campaign—and the war. With the communications cut, and the line of retreat obstructed, it was expected that the rebel Army of Northern Virginia would fall an easy prey to the victorious Army of the Potomac. The last days of June therefore were devoted to the work of final preparation, and, on the 30th, orders were issued for the immediate movement of the troops. But the next morning, an order was received to reënforce General McClellan without delay. The order occasioned some surprise and considerable apprehension for the safety of the Army of the Potomac. It was immediately obeyed, and the troops were embarked. But now came another sudden turn of affairs. Colonel Hawkins at Roanoke Island had heard, through certain sources of information which he deemed trustworthy, that General McClellan had achieved a magnificent success, had driven out the enemy from Richmond and had occupied that city with his army. On the 2d of July, this information was transmitted from Colonel Hawkins to General Burnside, who at once stopped his contemplated voyage to the James River, expecting to receive orders to resume his land movements.

The information received, however, had no foundation in fact. Colonel Hawkins had been deceived. What was really true was, that General Lee's entire army had fallen upon General McClellan with great fury, and had forced him from his position in front of Richmond. The army of the Potomac was struggling in the memorable and disastrous "seven days' fight," and at last succeeded, on the night of the 3d of July, in reaching Harrison's Landing. Vague reports of these disastrous days reached General Burnside on the 4th. The enemy was careful to put them in exaggerated and discouraging forms. But General Burnside, still hopeful, was not willing to believe that the brave Army of the Potomac was yet annihilated. He knew that that could not be, and he did not entirely credit the intelligence even of the enemy's decisive victory. What he did believe is best expressed in the language which he used, in addressing the Secretary of War, on the 5th: "We have Richmond papers giving information, or rather their version of the events up to ten o'clock of the night of the 1st. After making due allowance for the exaggerations, we are led to believe that General McClellan has made a successful retreat to some point on the James River nearly opposite City Point, thereby securing a new and better base of operations, in which case he can, I imagine, after resting his army and receiving proper reënforcements, work his way up the James to Richmond." In this communication to the Secretary, General Burnside submits three propositions for the disposal of his own command, which sufficiently indicate his ideas of the situation: "First, we can move with 7,000 Infantry (which were started the other day for the James River) at once;—at the same time holding with tolerable security all the points now in our possession, together with the railroad from this place to Beaufort. Second, or we can send 8,000 Infantry and hold all these points, but cannot protect either the railroad or Beaufort. The latter, however, can be protected by the navy, while we hold Fort Macon. This move will require two days' notice. Third, or we can move from here with from three to five days' notice with the entire command, except the garrisons for Hatteras Inlet, Fort Macon and Roanoke Island, placing our sick at the latter place and leaving this place to be protected by the navy. This would involve the dismantling of the two very strong forts on the outskirts of the city. We can thus add to the Army of the Potomac a force of 11,500 Infantry, one regiment of Cavalry, 20 pieces of light Artillery, and, if necessary one hundred wagons and a supply of ambulances, all in good condition. All these propositions presuppose that the rebel army at Richmond is still occupied at that place by the establishment of the Army of the Potomac at some point on James River near City Point. If such is the case, General McClellan would, I imagine, cut off the enemy's communications with North Carolina by taking Petersburg, thus rendering it unnecessary for the present to cut the two lines in the interior of the State."

The first proposition was evidently that which seemed most feasible to General Burnside himself, and also to the Secretary of War; for on the very day upon which the communication above referred to was dated, the troops—eight thousand in number—began to leave Newbern for the James River. They all arrived and were landed at Newport News on the 8th. In the course of the next two weeks, this force was joined by a small division from Hilton Head and its neighborhood, under the command of Brigadier General Isaac I. Stevens. Not far from twelve thousand men were thus collected at Newport News, available for a reënforcement of the Army of the Potomac, and for further operations against Richmond, if such were deemed advisable by the Government. But this force was without cavalry, artillery, wagons, or teams, and had for means of transportation by land only a few ambulances and the officers' horses. General Burnside's headquarters were on board the small steamer Alice Price.

This departure from Newbern terminated, in effect, General Burnside's connection with military operations in North Carolina. He still retained a nominal authority there, but he never returned to a personal supervision of affairs in that quarter. He finally relinquished all jurisdiction in the Department on the 26th of August, and General Foster succeeded to the vacant command. General Burnside's farewell order was dated from Fredericksburg, and bore witness to the harmony and reciprocal good will which had so eminently characterized the conduct of affairs in North Carolina, and which had contributed so fully to the brilliant successes which had been there achieved.

Major General John G. Foster, who succeeded General Burnside in the command of the Department of North Carolina, had already won for himself a brilliant reputation. He had been for a considerable time in the service of the country, and had always been found to be a faithful and skilful officer. He was born in New Hampshire, in the year 1824, and was appointed from that State to the United States Military Academy at West Point. He graduated from the Academy in 1846, the fourth in rank in a class of fifty-nine. Among his classmates were McClellan, Reno, Seymour, Sturgis and Stoneman, of the loyal service, and "Stonewall" Jackson, Wilcox and Pickett, of the rebel army. He was commissioned as brevet

Second Lieutenant in the corps of Engineers, July 1, 1846. He bore a very active and distinguished part in the Mexican war, and his record of promotion is a sufficient testimony to his bravery and merit. "Brevet First Lieutenant, August 20, 1847, 'for gallant and meritorious conduct in the battles of Contreras and Churubusco;' severely wounded in the battle of Molino del Rey, September 8, 1847; Brevet Captain from that date, 'for gallant and meritorious conduct in the battle of Molino del Rey;' Second Lieutenant, May 24, 1848." Such is the honorable record of his first two years of service. His gallant conduct and his proficiency in military knowledge attracted the attention of the authorities, and in 1854, promoted to First Lieutenant on the first of April of that year, we find him Assistant Professor of Engineering in the Military Academy at West Point. He was appointed in charge of the fortifications in North and South Carolina, April 28, 1858, and there acquired a knowledge that became serviceable for subsequent operations. He was commissioned as Captain in the Engineers, July 1, 1860, and was brevetted Major on the 26th of December of the same year. During the eventful winter of 1860–'61, and the following spring, he was stationed at Charleston, South Carolina, and was one of the officers under Major Anderson in the defence of Fort Sumter. His loyal and fearless bearing on the occasion of the bombardment of Sumter, is fresh in the recollection of all. Returning North after the surrender, he was employed on the fortifications of New York. On the 23d of October, 1861, he was commissioned as Brigadier General of Volunteers, and was in command of the rendezvous at Annapolis previous to the arrival of General Burnside. After he assumed command of the Department of North Carolina, he was engaged in conspicuous services in his own Department and in the neighborhood of Charleston. Subsequently, as will be hereafter mentioned, he commanded the Department of the Ohio. After the surrender of General Lee, he was for a time in command at Tallahassee, Florida, and now enjoys the rank of Major in the Corps of

Engineers, and Brevet Major General in the Army of the United States. As a genial companion, a skilful officer, and an honorable and brave man, General Foster holds a high place in the affections of his friends and the esteem of his fellow countrymen.

It must be with feelings of more than ordinary satisfaction, that General Burnside and his friends can look back upon the record of his campaign and his administration in North Carolina. From the moment of the inception of the plan until the time of departure from Newbern, the story is one of uninterrupted success. The terrible storm at Hatteras Inlet, which, at the outset, threatened the destruction of the expedition, could not appal the heart or lessen the hope of the earnest leader. The battle of Roanoke Island, so skilfully projected and so gallantly executed, was not only a source of grateful pride to the commanding general; it also gave new courage and satisfaction to the country, that had longed for some decisive success in the East. The battle of Newbern, following swiftly, and ending in the victorious assault upon a very strong and well-chosen position of the enemy, justified the expectations of those who had perceived the promise of the soldier whose reputation was now fairly won and firmly established. The reduction of Fort Macon added to the public joy and the public estimation of the officer under whose superintendence it had been accomplished. The undisputed occupation of the North Carolina coast and waters north of Wilmington, resulting from these achievements, was a gain to the cause of the Union not easily to be estimated. That it was not followed up by the capture of Wilmington and the occupation of Raleigh, was certainly due to other causes than those which had their seat within the limits of General Burnside's Department.

But what was most especially gratifying to all concerned, was the extreme cordiality and even affection which existed among all ranks of the service—among all the officers and men towards one another and their commanding general. Jealousy, that bane of military service, was unknown. A hearty,

Eng.d by A.H. Ritchie.

GEN. JOHN G. FOSTER.

coöperative spirit everywhere prevailed. Each one was proud of the other's success and good fortune. "It was like a well-ordered and affectionate family at Newbern," said a visitor on his return from North Carolina: "nothing like it has been known among us during the war." It is possible that this was an overstatement of the case. But the spirit of mutual confidence and concord so fully prevailed, as to put out of sight all minor differences, and to impress all witnesses that, in the Department of North Carolina, discord, envy and ill-will were altogether unknown! General Burnside attributes his success to the prevalence in his command of the kindly and cordial feeling for which it was distinguished, and at all times bears the heartiest testimony to the gallantry, good conduct, and co-operative zeal of the officers and soldiers with whom he was associated.

THE ARMY

OF

THE POTOMAC.

THE ARMY

OF

THE POTOMAC.

CHAPTER I.

THE ORGANIZATION OF THE NINTH CORPS.

GENERAL BURNSIDE'S first care after landing his troops, and seeing them comfortably bestowed, was to ascertain the condition of the Army of the Potomac, and to consult with General McClellan in regard to future operations. He found the army at Harrison's Landing in a somewhat broken condition after the severities of the campaign. He found the officers almost unanimous for the evacuation of the Peninsula, and the concentration of all the forces operating in Virginia in the neighborhood of Washington. He also found, that the best of feeling did not prevail at headquarters between General McClellan and General Halleck who had been appointed to the chief command of all the armies of the United States on the 11th of July. The correspondence between General McClellan and the Secretary of War was not conducted in the most friendly spirit, though there was no open breach. Of course, in such a state of affairs, a certain degree of partizanship prevailed in the army itself. The officers and men took sides—some for, some against their commanding general. The policy of the campaign had been somewhat freely discussed around the camp fires and at the Corps and Division headquarters. While some were enthusiastic in their support of their general, others were ready to go as far as the rules of the service would permit in condemnation of the plans and methods of the campaign. Coming from the harmony and concord of the Department of North Caroliua, General Burnside was as much pained as surprised, to perceive the existence of this spirit of petty jealousy and discord. He still indulged the hope, that the differences between General McClellan and the Secretary of War might be composed, that better counsels might prevail and that a blow might be struck against General Lee and his army, if not in the direction of Petersburg, then immediately towards Richmond itself. He did not wholly agree with the policy of evacuation. But, after long and anxious consultation with General McClellan at his headquarters, in company with Generals Halleck and Meigs, he found that General Halleck had determined upon the measure and was not to be moved from it. In the early part of August the step was finally resolved upon. It was about this time, that the offer of the command of the army of the Potomac was made to General Burnside, and was by him declined. He thought that General McClellan had hardly had a fair chance. The season had been one of extraordinary severity, as regarded the movements of troops. The heat had been intense, the rains almost constant. Terrible battles had been fought, and great losses had been suffered by disease. The plans of the campaign had been very seriously deranged by the diversion of General McDowell's corps in pursuit of General Jackson. The armies in Virginia had thus been separated, and General Lee taking advantage of the fact, attacked the right and rear of the Army of the Potomac with such violence as to force it from its base to the James river. Had General McDowell, instead of marching to Front Royal and its neighborhood, left General Fremont to take care of General Jackson, and hastened to Richmond, forming a junction with General McClellan and attacking

General Lee, the result might have been different. The place to defeat Jackson was not among the Bull Run mountains but in front of Richmond. Had the Secretary of War, who was then acting as general-in-chief, taken advantage of Jackson's diversion, and vigorously pushed McDowell forward, there can be but little question, that the raid down the Shenandoah would have been a most serious misfortune to the rebel army. As it happened, it was the defeat of all the plans and operations of our own generals. To give General McClellan his due, it certainly was not his fault, that General McDowell was not forced into the gap, and the rebel lines pierced, broken and destroyed. Thus reasoning, General Burnside pleaded that another opportunity might be given to the unfortunate commander of the Army of the Potomac, and General McClellan was accordingly retained.

But General Lee's movements now began to make the evacuation of the Peninsula a necessity. Major General John Pope on the 14th of July was put in command of our forces in Virginia north of General McClellan's position. He concentrated his army, to which was given the name of the Army of Virginia, and pushed boldly southward, declaring his intention to subsist upon the country through which he marched. He reached as far as Cedar Mountain, in Culpepper County, on the 9th of August, and had a sharp engagement with General Jackson without decisive results. General Lee was feeling our position. Contented to have forced General McClellan to the James, and leaving a small force in the intrenchments around Richmond, the commander of the Rebel army began a counter movement against Washington, which was now defended only by General Pope's Army of Virginia. To save that army and the capital itself, a junction must somehow be formed between the separate forces. It was decided to move General Burnside's command to Aquia Creek and Fredericksburg, and the Army of the Potomac to Aquia Creek and Alexandria, as seemed most convenient at the time. As soon as the forces joined, all the troops south of the Potomac were to be placed under the command of General Pope. The consolidation would in effect, deprive General McClellan of a command in the field, and place General Burnside under the orders of his inferior in rank. But General Burnside knew no duty but obedience to the Government when his country was in peril, and cheerfully waived his own rank to assist General Pope in the extremely arduous campaign that was now opening before him.

Congress, in the last days of the session of 1861–'62, had passed a law authorizing the President "to establish and organize army corps at his discretion," and prescribing that the staff of the commander of each army corps should be "one assistant adjutant general, one quartermaster, one commissary of subsistence, and one assistant inspector general who should bear respectively the rank of lieutenant colonel; also three aides de camp—one to bear the rank of major and two to bear the rank of captain." This act was approved by the President and became a law, July 17, 1862. General Burnside on the 18th of July received authority to organize his command upon such a basis, and on the 22nd the organization was made and the NINTH ARMY CORPS took its place in the history of the war—a place unsullied by a single act of dishonor! Of the staff, Captain already promoted to Major Richmond, Captains Goodrich and Biggs were advanced to the rank of Lieutenant Colonel. Captain Loring was appointed Assistant Inspector General with the same rank, and Captain Cutting was appointed Aide de Camp, with the rank of Major, their commissions dating from the day of the organization of the Corps. Three divisions were formed, under the command respectively of Generals Reno, Parke and Stevens. On the 26th General Burnside again visited General McClellan in company with General Halleck, and on his return made a flying journey to New York, where he remained for a single day and received a most cordial and enthusiastic reception. On the 30th he was at Washington, and on the next day he returned to Newport News, prepared to carry out his part of the contemplated movements with all needful promptitude. On the 2d of August, the Ninth Corps, numbering now nearly thirteen thousand men, embarked at Newport News, and on the night of the 3d landed at Aquia Creek, and proceeded immediately to Fredericksburg. General King's division of General McDowell's corps, that had been stationed there, was at once relieved and joined the Army of Virginia in the field. The Ninth Corps was engaged in holding Fredericksburg, and guarding the line of the Rappahannock, while General Pope was operating in the neighborhood of Culpepper Court House, and in the direction of Gordonsville. General Burnside's transports were immediately returned to the James River, to facilitate the removal of the Army of the Potomac. In the course of the ensuing week, five batteries of artillery and one regiment of cavalry were sent to Aquia Creek, as reënforcements to the troops on the Rappahannock, where the enemy was beginning to appear in force.

On the 3d of August, General Halleck ordered General McClellan to withdraw from the Peninsula. But the latter officer now began to make excuses and protests and to find occasions for delay. At one time there was no sufficient transportation. At another time there were great difficulties in removing the sick and wounded. Again, the army was not in condition to move. General Halleck became impatient, and at the same time somewhat alarmed. His dispatches breathed an acrimonious spirit, which vexed General McClellan and did not certainly dispose him to any extraordinary exertions. Meanwhile General Pope was embarrassed by the rapid movements of General Jackson's corps, and pressed by the constantly accumulating forces of the enemy. The timely arrival of the Ninth Corps at Fredericksburg doubtless saved his left flank from being turned and his entire army from being cut off from its communications with the Potomac.

General Burnside returned to the Peninsula to assist General McClellan in expediting matters, and, by the night of the 15th, two corps were on the march for Yorktown, while other troops were embarking at Harrison's Landing. On the afternoon of the 16th, "the last man had disappeared from the deserted camps,"* and the Army of the Potomac had left the scene of its unavailing struggles and its patient endurance. On the 20th, the army was ready to embark at Yorktown, Newport News and Fortress Monroe. General Keyes's Corps was left at Yorktown to garrison that point. It was not however till the 28th that General Sumner's corps, which had been the last to embark, was landed at Alexandria. General Burnside was stationed at Fredericksburg, to direct the movements of troops in that quarter and to hasten them forward to General Pope, who was now sorely pressed by the enemy. General McClellan repaired to Alexandria.

The month of August was the gloomiest month of the gloomy summer of 1862. The campaigns that had been so brilliantly commenced by Grant and Foote in the West, Burnside and Goldsborough in the East, and Butler and Farragut in the South, seemed in danger of ending in disaster and defeat. The interest of the country centered upon the movements that were making in Virginia. General Lee, released from the necessity of defending Richmond, was hurling his entire army upon General Pope, who with forty thousand men was endeavoring to hold the line of the Rappahannock. With the aid of the Ninth Corps, he succeeded, with admirable persistence, in sustaining himself until reënforcements began to arrive from the Peninsula.

Perhaps there has not been, in the history of the war, such confused, and, at the same time, such sanguinary fighting as marked the retreat of General Pope from the Rapidan to the defences of Washington. On the part of the enemy, General Jackson seemed ubiquitous, and harassed our troops almost beyond measure. On our own side, some of the officers of the Army of the Potomac, somewhat sore from their failure on the Peninsula and in a measure dispirited, appeared to be content with doggedly preventing an utter defeat, without any de-

*McClellan's Report, p. 165.

sire to achieve a victory. General Pope, in his report, particularly complains of the want of zeal and even of subordination on the part of General Fitz John Porter, whom he accuses of "flagrant disregard of orders."* General Heintzelman's corps rendered very efficient service. The corps of Generals Franklin and Sumner reached the scene of operations only in time to cover the retreat and receive the broken and defeated remains of the Army of Virginia.

But whatever may be said of other parts of General Pope's command, that portion of the Ninth Corps which came under his direction did its whole duty, in the most gallant and praiseworthy manner. General Reno, who commanded the corps in the field, is warmly eulogized by General Pope. "I cannot express myself too highly," says the commander of the army, "of the zealous, gallant and cheerful manner in which General Reno deported himself from the beginning to the end of the operations. Ever prompt, earnest, and soldierly, he was the model of an accomplished soldier, and a gallant gentleman."† The Ninth Corps, under his command, had most important tasks to perform. In the early part of the movement, it was the guard of the left flank of General Pope's army, and watched the fords of the Rappahannock above Fredericksburg with the utmost vigilance. At the last, it was the guard of the right flank as the army fell back, and fought a sharp and sanguinary battle, scattering the enemy and forcing him away from the line of retreat.

On the 12th of August, General Reno, with his command, joined General McDowell near Cedar Mountain, and on the north bank of the Rapidan, holding the high ground on this side of that river and watching the fords below. On the 18th, information was received to the effect that the enemy was massing his forces below the ridge upon the south bank, with a view to crossing the Rapidan at Raccoon Ford, and getting between our main body and the Potomac. It be-

* Pope's Report, p. 27. † Ibid., p. 28.

came necessary for our army to fall back to the north bank of the Rappahannock. The Ninth Corps was to return by the road up which it had marched a few days before. The movement was executed with entire success, during the night of the 18th and through the day of the 19th. The enemy crossed the Rapidan, but was too late. When he arrived at the Rappahannock, and attempted a crossing, he found that Kelly's Ford, his most available crossing-place, was guarded by the Ninth Corps, which was ready to dispute his passage. Compelled by this manœuvre to give up his scheme of cutting our communications, the enemy seemed disposed to change the plan of his operations. He could do nothing upon our left. He decided to attempt the turning of our right. Almost the entire force of his army, which had been concentrated below and had been baffled, traversed our front behind the woods upon the south bank of the Rappahannock. His heavy columns were plainly to be discovered by our lookouts, and clouds of dust rising above the trees of the forest indicated his line of march towards our right. General Pope resolved to attack this moving column on the morning of the 23d, and gave orders to that effect to General McDowell, in command at the river. But much rain had fallen on the night previous, the river became suddenly swollen, the fords were rendered impracticable, the trestle bridge, which had been built for the passage of the troops, was swept away and the railroad bridge was threatened with destruction. The attack could not be made, and the forces under General McDowell were moved up the north bank of the river to intercept the enemy as he crossed at Sulphur Springs. But the enemy had been too rapid in his movements, and our army, leaving the river, marched in the direction of Warrenton and on the 24th occupied that town. On the 25th the line of the entire army was formed, reaching from Warrenton to Kelly's Ford. At the latter place, upon the extreme left was stationed General Reno with the Ninth Corps, who was ordered to keep open the communication with the forces below him on the river. On the 26th, however, General

Reno was at Warrenton, and on the 27th, at Fayetteville. The enemy's movements had not yet been developed. After crossing the Rappahannock at Sulphur Springs he had returned to the river, and, pushing rapidly forward beyond our right, had disappeared from our immediate front.

But General Pope was not long in doubt respecting his intentions. On the night of the 26th, our scouts brought in the intelligence that the advance of the enemy's column under Jackson had passed through Thoroughfare Gap, and was directed upon our depot at Manassas Junction. General Pope threw General Hooker's division of General Heintzelman's corps against the leading division of the enemy, which happened to be General Ewell's, and on the afternoon of the 27th a smart engagement took place near Bristow Station. General Ewell was steadily forced back, leaving his dead, many of his wounded, and much of his baggage on the field. During the same day General Reno moved his corps to Greenwich, to communicate with General McDowell, who was marching on Gainesville.*

On the night of the 27th, the position of affairs seems to have been as follows: General Pope's army was distributed on the different roads leading to Manassas Junction from Gainesville on the west, from Warrenton and Greenwich on the southwest, and on the railroad below Bristow Station. The enemy, under Jackson, was at and around Manassas Junction. Both armies were cut off from their respective bases. General McDowell's corps was between Jackson and Thoroughfare Gap. General Jackson was between our army and Washton, but was isolated from the main body of the enemy's force, which was still beyond the Bull Run mountains. The enemy had made a most audacious movement, and one which should have insured his ruin. General Pope supposed, and with good

* On the 27th, Captain Pell, of General Burnside's staff, was taken prisoner by a party of the enemy, while engaged in some perilous duty. He was released in the course of the following month and rejoined the Ninth Corps soon after the battle of Antietam.

reason, that Jackson's force would either be captured entire or would be crippled so badly as to prevent any further aggressive movement on the part of General Lee. Jackson could not retreat directly from Manassas. He did not venture to attack our forces at Bristow. He determined to retreat to Centreville, thence retiring northwards to Leesburg or through the northerly gaps of the Bull Run mountains, or west, by way of Sudley's Springs and Groveton, trusting to the chances of beating back our attack, or of turning our left flank, or of being joined by an advancing column from General Lee's main body.

On the 28th General Jackson retreated from Manassas Junction to Centreville, and not an hour had elapsed when the advance of the Ninth Corps had reached the vacated position, and, with the divisions of Generals Hooker and Kearney, pushed forward in pursuit of the enemy. In the afternoon General Kearney drove the enemy's rearguard out of Centreville. In the meantime, a part of General McDowell's force, marching upon Centreville from the west, came in contact with the enemy not far from the old battle field of Bull Run, and a pretty severe engagement ensued, lasting from six o'clock in the afternoon till dark. Thus far everything was working well, and General Pope was sanguine of success. If his entire command could be concentrated, his forces would be superior to those of the enemy. But it would appear that some of the corps commanders operated mostly at their own discretion, and paid but little attention to the orders of the commanding general. General Sigel, instead of marching from Gainesville at daylight on the 28th, as ordered, was still lingering there till the day had considerably advanced. General Fitz John Porter, who had been ordered up from Warrenton Junction on the 27th, had left there one division of his corps at least, as late as daylight on the 28th, and had proceeded only as far as Bristow by the night of the latter day. General McDowell had detached one division of his corps to proceed to the neighborhood of Thoroughfare Gap, by which his means of defence against Jackson were sensibly weakened. General King's division of the same corps was thus compelled to fall back towards Manassas Junction, leaving the road open to the enemy's retreat. On the morning of the 29th, therefore, affairs did not look so promising as on the day previous. The issue on either side was doubtful. If General Porter's comparatively fresh corps could be got into action, the enemy was in imminent danger. If General Longstreet's corps could make a junction with Jackson, the enemy could not only secure a retreat from his present perilous position, but would also be ready to take the aggressive at some more favorable point. General Porter was moving up from Bristow, but very slowly, as the roads were encumbered with baggage trains and artillery.

On the 29th, the enemy stood at bay, occupying a position near Sudley's Springs, not far from the lines which our own forces held at the first battle of Bull Run. General Kearney had kept close to him during the night, to prevent his retreat, and in the morning General Sigel, who had come down from Gainesville during the preceding day, attacked with considerable vigor. General Jackson fell back a short distance, but still showed a defiant front. General Sigel was reënforced by Generals Reno, Hooker and Kearney, and the battle raged with fury until noon, neither party gaining a decisive advantage. Our line of battle extended from a point a short distance west of the Sudley's Springs road, to a point south of the Warrenton turnpike. General Heintzelman's corps occupied the right, General Reno the right centre, with four regiments in reserve, General Sigel the left centre, and General Reynolds' division the extreme left. During the afternoon until four o'clock, but little fighting was done, except when the enemy attempted to draw off, which became the occasion of several severe skirmishes. General Pope, in the meantime, had sent orders to Generals McDowell and Porter, who were near Manassas Junction, to bring up their corps to unite with the remainder of the army. General McDowell put his corps in motion, and began to close with the main body not far from five o'clock.

General Porter's command was halted within sound of the battle, and did not join during the day. At half past five, Generals Heintzelman and Reno were ordered to fall upon the enemy's left. With such spirit was the order executed, that, by seven o'clock, the enemy's flank was doubled back upon his centre, despite all his efforts to withstand the attack. If General Porter had now come up, all would have been well. But it was General Longstreet that made the junction with the enemy's force, and at eight o'clock, after a hard fight of two hours and more, in which Heintzelman and Reno had swept the enemy from the greater part of the field, leaving his dead and wounded in their hands, both parties ceased the struggle. The first brigade of General Reno's own division, composed of the 48th Pennsylvania, 6th New Hampshire and 2d Maryland, was conspicuous on this day for the persistence with which it held its ground when assailed, and the gallantry with which it advanced to the attack.

The day had been very warm, the troops were exhausted, and supplies were very short. But we had forced the enemy away from our line of communications, had foiled his attempts to get between us and Washington, except for a single day, and had secured the Capital from attack. During the night of the 29th the enemy was largely reënforced, and by noon on the 30th the superiority of numbers was clearly on his side. General Pope had expected to be reënforced from Alexandria by the corps of Generals Franklin and Sumner. But they had moved out only for a short distance, and the Army of Virginia could now expect nothing more than to withdraw to the defences of Washington with as little loss as possible. General Pope conceived that the best method to secure his retreat was by attacking the enemy. General Porter's corps was now up, and on the afternoon of the 30th the battle was renewed, and soon became as severe as on the previous day. General Reno and the Ninth Corps were again conspicuous for their gallantry, and fought with determined valor. Colonel Ferrero's brigade, composed of the 51st Pennsylvania, the 21st Massachusetts, and the 51st New York regiments, did especially good service in saving the left wing of the army from utter defeat. It was posted on a hill, to the rear of the left of our line, and with the aid of Graham's battery, succeed in checking the triumphant advance of the enemy. The enemy made three successive charges upon this position, and was very handsomely repulsed, till becoming convinced that further attempts would be ineffectual, he drew off in disorder. But it was useless for our army to contend with such fearful odds as the enemy was preparing to bring up, and soon after dark, having lost about three-fourths of a mile of the field and having suffered severely, General Pope decided to fall back to Centreville and place his exhausted troops within the intrenchments at that place. The withdrawal was made during the night, slowly and quietly, the enemy making no pursuit. The Ninth Corps covered the retreat. Generals Franklin and Sumner joined from Alexandria, General Banks, who had been guarding the trains, came in from Bristow, and on the 31st the entire army rested, after its unexampled fatigues, in and about the works at Centreville. The enemy contented himself with sending a reconnoitering party of cavalry to observe our position at Cub Run.

On the 1st of September, a reconnaissance sent out by General Sumner developed the fact that General Lee had not yet given up his plan of forcing his army between our position at Centreville and the fortifications around Washington. A large body of the enemy's forces was observed moving towards Fairfax Court House. General Pope, though his army was much broken by fatigue and scarcity of supplies, promptly adopted measures to meet this new movement of the enemy. His troops were disposed along the different roads leading from Centreville to Fairfax Court House, with the Ninth Corps in advance and nearest the enemy at Chantilly, covering the main road, and supported by Generals McDowell, Hooker and Kearney. The disposition of troops was made by the afternoon of the 1st, and the enemy's movement towards Fairfax Court House was at once checked. He prepared for battle, and about six o'clock made a vigorous attack upon the Ninth Corps. A terrific thunder storm came on at the same time, and the artillery of Heaven mingled in the fray. The scene was sublime. The flashes and reports of our guns were answered by the vivid fires above and the loud reverberating peals that shook the skies. Our troops made fierce and furious charges against the foe, and by great exertions forced him from the field. The action terminated soon after dark, the enemy was beaten back, and our men, having cleared the road and rested for a few hours, pursued their march towards Fairfax, arriving at daybreak on the 2d of September. But the severe fight at Chantilly was signalized by the loss of two of the bravest and most skillful officers in our army—Major General Philip Kearny, and Brigadier General Isaac I. Stevens. General Kearny's gallantry is well known, and it is not necessary in these pages to record his worth, his dauntlessness of spirit, his manly generosity and his earnest loyalty to the country and the flag which he ardently loved.

The Ninth Corps mourned the death of General Stevens, as of one whose future was bright with unusual promise, whose past was illustrious with brave and brilliant deeds. He had but lately come into the Corps, but he had secured for himself a very large measure of esteem, confidence and affection. He was born in Andover, Mass., March 25th, 1817, and passed his boyhood much as others do, early manifesting a decided talent especially for mathematical studies. He attracted the observation of the leading men of his neighborhood, and was appointed to a cadetship in the Military Academy at West Point. He entered the Academy in 1835, and soon distinguished himself for scholarship and manliness of character. *Facile princeps*, he graduated in 1839 at the head of his class, distancing his fellow students, leaving his next competitor at least fifteen marks behind him. He was appointed second Lieutenant in the Corps of Engineers, July 1st, and was employed in superintending the erection of coastwise fortifications, especially attending to the construction of a fort near Bucksport, Maine. He was promoted to a first lieutenancy July 1st, 1840, and in the years 1847 and 1848 was adjutant of the corps to which he belonged. In the war with Mexico, he was actively engaged on the staff with General Scott and was held in the very highest esteem by that distinguished captain, who spoke of him as the most promising officer of his age in the country. He participated in all the battles on the plain of Mexico, and was particularly conspicuous for his daring, his utter insensibility to fear, his boldness in reconnaissance, his coolness in action and his accurate knowledge of the principles of the art of war. He was brevetted Captain for gallant and meritorious conduct at Contreras and Churubusco, Aug. 20, 1847, and promoted to Brevet Major Sept. 13, in the same year, for gallantry at Chapultepec and the San Cosmo gate of the city of Mexico. At the last fight he was severely wounded in the foot. Returning home, at the close of the war, he assisted in the Coast Survey and won great honor by his skill and abilities. When President Pierce came into power, he placed Major Stevens in charge of one portion of the Pacific Rail Road survey. He resigned his position in the army in 1853, and was appointed Governor of Washington Territory. His great energy and administrative power became at once manifest. He was occupied in developing the resources of the territory, and reducing the Indian inhabitants to a state of subjection and peace. These difficult affairs were conducted with great humanity and consummate skill. A wagon expedition, which he organized, commanded and led across the northern plains, made him famous. In 1857 he was elected delegate to Congress, and there as elsewhere made his mark. Opposed to Mr. Lincoln in politics, he became Chairman of the Executive Committee of the Breckenridge Democracy in the campaign of 1860, little supposing that his colleagues were plotting the ruin of the Republic. In the gloomy and anxious session of 1860–'61, he was in familiar communication with President Buchanan, and strenuously urged the dismissal of Messrs. Floyd and Thompson from the

Cabinet, and, moreover, gave his valuable counsel to General Scott in relation to the defence of the Capitol. At the close of the session he returned to Washington Territory, and there anxiously awaited further developments. The bombardment of Fort Sumter aroused his patriotic feeling to intense fervor. He hurried East, offered his services to the government, and was appointed soon after the battle of Bull Run to the command of the 79th (Highlander) Regiment of New York Volunteers, made vacant by the lamented death of Colonel Cameron. He was promoted to Brigadier General, Sept. 28, 1861, and was sent with his brigade upon the Port Royal expedition. He was selected to command a force sent out to dislodge the enemy at Port Royal Ferry, and met the rebel forces near that point on the 1st of Jannuary, 1862. When General McClellan was reënforced from the Department of the South, General Stevens was sent in command of the troops selected for that purpose. His division was incorporated with the Ninth Corps, took part in the campaign as already described and fought most gallantly in the battle of Chantilly, in which its beloved commander met his death. He had seized the colors of his old regiment, the 79th, and was leading on a desperate charge against the enemy, when he was shot directly through the head, immediately fell and expired without a groan or murmur. His son, the adjutant general of his division, emulating his father's bravery, fell wounded almost at the same time. General Stevens's remains were carried to Newport, Rhode Island, where his wife's family resided, and interred under the direction of the city authorities, Sept. 10, 1862. The tears of whole communities mingled with those of his family and friends in sympathy with their loss. The statesman, soldier, hero, lies at peace upon the shore of the sounding sea, that sings his requiem forever!

After the battle of Chantilly, the enemy made no further hostile movement, and on the afternoon of the 3d of September the Army of Virginia was withdrawn within the defences of Washington. General Pope on the 3d of September was relieved of his command at his own request, and General

McClellan resumed the control of the Army of the Potomac. General Burnside, having remained at Fredericksburg with a small force until all the reënforcements landed at Aquia Creek had passed through to General Pope, was directed to evacuate his position. In pursuance to orders from Washington, he destroyed machine shops, bridges and other material, and on the 4th of September he embarked a portion of his troops and proceeded to Washington. On the 7th the few soldiers that were left on guard at Aquia Creek were brought off, and the active operations of the army were transferred to other and more interesting scenes.

CHAPTER II.

THE CAMPAIGN IN MARYLAND.—SOUTH MOUNTAIN.

AFTER the retreat of General Pope's forces and their arrival at Washington or in its neighborhood, the enemy ceased all hostile demonstrations south of the Potomac. He drew off his troops and disappeared from our front. But although foiled in his attempt to capture or destroy the Army of Virginia, and thus secure possession of the Capital, he had by no means relinquished the object of the campaign. He was still resolved upon further and bolder enterprises. Passing through the gaps of the mountains into the Shenandoah Valley, the main body moved rapidly down towards the ford at Williamsport, while smaller and detached bodies moved towards Leesburg and threatened to cross the Potomac into Maryland at the neighboring fords. The confusion resulting from the untoward character of the operations of our forces in Virginia had not yet subsided, and the authorities at Washington seemed undecided as to the question of the command of the now consolidated army. General Burnside was called into consultation with the President and General Halleck, and the honorable but responsible post of command was again offered to him. It was again declined, and General Burnside used his best endeavors to induce a renewal of confidence in General McClellan. The President had always been well disposed towards the unfortunate chief, but it was very evident that no very friendly relations existed between General Halleck and the commanding general of the Army of the Potomac. The result of the consultation was that General McClellan was again entrusted with the direction of affairs. He at once disposed his garrisons for the occupation of the works around Washington, and put his army in motion to meet the enemy at the point of his new attack. His command consisted of the first corps, General Hooker; second, General Sumner; one division of the fourth, under General Couch; one division of the fifth, under General Sykes; the sixth, General Franklin; the Ninth, General Reno; and the twelfth, General Williams. The first and Ninth Corps formed the right wing, and were under the command of General Burnside who had the advance. The second and twelfth, with General Sykes's division, formed the centre, and were under the command of General Sumner. The sixth and the detached division of General Couch formed the left, and were under the command of General Franklin. As the enemy's plans were not yet developed, it was uncertain whether he intended by crossing the Potomac into Maryland, to turn Washington by a flank movement down the north bank, or march on Baltimore, or invade Pennsylvania. It became necessary, therefore, for General McClellan to move cautiously, keeping his left flank near the river, while the right pushed into the interior of Maryland to head off any offensive movement upon Baltimore. The enemy had the advantage of moving behind the Kittoctan and Blue Ridge Mountains in Virginia, and the South Mountain range in Maryland. In the latter State, the line of the Monocacy river gave him an additional means of defence in case of an attack from our troops.

On the 3d of September, the Ninth Corps moved out on the Seventh street road and encamped just outside the line of the defences of Washington. On the 6th, the Ninth and the first corps, now acting in conjunction, moved out to Leesboro'. On the 9th the two corps were at Brookville, and on the 11th at Newmarket. The enemy, after having occupied Frederick for a day or two, decided not to dispute the passage of the Monocacy with anything more than a mere show of resistance. Nor did he think it feasible to push on toward Baltimore. In fact, General Lee had ascertained that the people of Maryland were not disposed to give him so cordial a reception as he had anticipated. They had never cherished any very strong love for secession, and their southern proclivities had been in former years strengthened by the undue influence of Virginia. Separated from that State by a line of military posts, and left free to follow their interests, if not their real principles, they had early in the struggle developed a love for the Union, which had become more powerful as the war went on. In Western Maryland, particularly, the loyal sentiment was well pronounced and even conspicuous. General Lee, instead of an oppressed and down-trodden people who would welcome him as a deliverer from federal tyranny, found a people well contented with the federal rule, disposed to pay a willing obedience to the government at Washington, and regarding him and his army as intruders and invaders; more inclined, in short, to speed his departure than to hail his coming. On the other hand, our own troops were on familiar ground, among a people who, not sullenly, but gladly acquiesced in their presence. They derived inspiration and courage from the surrounding circumstances. The swamps of the Chickahominy had been left. The hardships of the Virginia campaign were over. They had recovered their strength in the more bracing air of the early autumn. They had rested from their unusual fatigues. They were in a region where they could be quickly reënforced and amply supplied. Moreover, they were advancing to meet the enemy in the open field, and at a distance from his base. It is more than probable that the two differing circumstances and influences operating upon the two armies were very effective in determining the result of the campaign.

On the 12th of September General Burnside entered Frederick with the advance of the Army of the Potomac. The rearguard of the enemy had left the place a few hours before, and our cavalry and infantry at the head of the column had a smart skirmish in the streets with the enemy's cavalry that was covering the withdrawal of his army. In this skirmish we lost two men killed and seven prisoners, among whom was

Colonel Moore, of the 30th Ohio, who led the charge. General Burnside's reception was especially enthusiastic. The people crowded around him, covered his horse and himself with flowers, saluted him with cheers and shouts of welcome and manifested their joy in every method of demonstration. General McClellan's reception, at a later hour, was equally cordial and demonstrative. The citizens of Frederick felt as though they had been delivered from a great affliction, and the Army of the Potomac had the opportunity of enjoying a new sensation. But there was little time for congratulations, and the army pressed forward upon the heels of the now retreating enemy.

General Lee, deciding not to defend the line of the Monocacy, retired through the passes of the South Mountain. But he had also determined, before quitting Maryland altogether, to strike a blow at Harper's Ferry. General McClellan's left flank had been drawn away from the river and was approaching the centre. General Lee, in leaving Frederick, after crossing the Kittoctan range, divided his army, sending General Jackson to Sharpsburg, across the Potomac to Martinsburg and thence to Harper's Ferry, General McLaws directly to Maryland Heights to attempt the capture of Harper's Ferry itself, and General Walker with a division across the Potomac to Loudon Heights. Generals Longstreet and D. H. Hill were halted at Boonesboro', and held that place and the passes of the South Mountain range in the vicinity. The portions detached were to return after accomplishing the tasks committed to them and join the main body in the neighborhood of Boonesboro', or, if that was impracticable, somewhere behind Antietam Creek. General Jackson, with his accustomed vigor, performed his allotted work so well as to compel the surrender of Harper's Ferry on the 15th, with its garrison, arms and stores.

Had Colonel Miles, in command at Harper's Ferry, been able to hold out a few hours longer, he would have been relieved by General Franklin, who with his corps supported by General Couch's division, had carried Crampton's Gap on the

16

14th, after a severe engagement, and bivouacked on the same night within six miles of the beleagured post. But on the next day, the enemy formed between General Franklin and the Potomac in line of battle, greatly outnumbering our forces and preventing any further progress in that direction. The loss of Harper's Ferry was very serious and effected considerable derangement in the movements of our troops. Whether the post could have been promptly relieved and saved is a question which it is not designed here to discuss. General McClellan wished Colonel Miles to evacuate the position as early as the 10th. But General Halleck thought otherwise and the post was held — and lost. A large number of prisoners and a great amount of property were captured by the enemy.

While the left wing was thus making its way painfully and slowly to Burkettsville, the main body of the army, having closed up its centre and joined it with the right, moved on the line of the retreating enemy, and the advance under General Reno bivouacked at Middletown on the night of the 13th. The enemy, under General Longstreeet, was disposed to dispute the passage of the mountain, and General Pleasonton's cavalry, which had been skirmishing through the day on the 13th, found the enemy in force at Turner's Gap. It became evident that a severe engagement must be fought before our forces could cross the mountain. General Burnside with his two corps hurried to the scene of the impending action, and on the morning of the 14th prepared to deliver battle. The Ninth Corps was now large and in admirably fighting trim. It was organized in four divisions, under command respectively of Generals Willcox, Sturgis, Rodman and Cox. As General Reno was in command of the Corps, his division had been assigned to General Sturgis. General Stevens's death had placed General Willcox in command. General Parke had been appointed Chief of Staff to General Burnside and his division was placed in charge of General Rodman — well remembered in the corps as the commander of the 4th Rhode Island regiment. He had taken the command at Fredericksburg about the middle of August. General Cox's division, which had belonged to the Western Virginia army, had been in the campaign with General Pope, and was now assigned to the Ninth Corps. It was known in the army as the "Kanawha Division."

The position which General Lee had determined to defend was naturally very strong, and he doubtless expected to hold General McClellan's army in check sufficiently long to enable his detachments to return and rejoin the main body. The South Mountain rises between the villages of Middletown and Boonesboro', and through Turner's Gap runs the turnpike road from Frederick to Hagerstown. Near the summit a road comes in upon the turnpike from the northerly side, called the "old Hagerstown road." Another road, called the "old Sharpsburg road," runs about half a mile distant from the turnpike on the left or southerly side, and nearly parallel to it as far as the crest, when it bends off to the left. They are both common country roads. On the turnpike, pleasantly situated near the crest of the mountain, stands a comfortable-looking inn, the Mountain House. The place is one of great natural beauty, and the view from the summit commands a wide and most picturesque landscape — the mountains of the Blue Ridge rising in graceful outline upon the western horizon. The road from Middletown winds up the mountain slope with a gentle ascent, and is commanded at several points on either side by the irregular summits of the mountain crest. Tracts of forest land, amid the trees of which companies of sharpshooters could find ready concealment, stretch along the sides of the mountain. Altogether it was a difficult place to carry. The enemy was in force on the three roads leading to the summit. But very little artillery could be brought into action for attack, and the contest must mainly be decided by infantry. General Burnside had marched over the mountain, while in command of the First Rhode Island regiment in the summer of 1861, and had then noted its military capabilities.

General Pleasonton, in his reconnaissance, succeeded early

in the morning of the 14th in placing Benjamin's battery of the Ninth corps in position on high ground left of the turnpike, and brought a well-directed fire to bear upon the enemy posted in the Gap. The first infantry to arrive on the field was General Cox's division, the first brigade of which reached the scene of action at nine o'clock, and marched up the old Sharpsburg road. It was immediately followed by the other brigade, the remainder of the corps, with the exception of General Sturgis's division, coming up early in the day. Of the Kanawha division Colonel Scammon's brigade, which had already done remarkably good service in the recent campaign, was in advance. It was deployed on the left side of the road among the brush, and, well covered by skirmishers, forced its way up the slope in despite of all obstacles. It first came into conflict with General Garland's brigade of the enemy's troops, whose commander was killed at the opening of the action. It gained the crest, notwithstanding the vigorous attempts of the enemy to check its career and the destructive fire of a battery which poured in canister and case shot upon its right flank.

General Crook's brigade followed in columns at supporting distance. A section of artillery was brought up with great difficulty, but was soon silenced by the enemy's infantry, with the loss of its commander Lieutenant Croome. Another section was brought up about two-thirds of the way and succeeded in maintaining its position. The troops of General Cox's division heroically maintained the position which they had won, and repeatedly repulsed the enemy, who endeavored to drive them away. General Willcox's division was sent up the same road and took a position upon its right commanding the turnpike. Two regiments were ordered up to the crest to support General Cox. A section of Cook's battery was brought into action near the turn of the road. But these dispositions were not made without great efforts on the part of the enemy to prevent them. At the moment of deploying the division, the enemy opened a very severe fire at short range enfilading the road, driving off Cook's cannoneers and throwing the line into a temporary confusion. Two regiments, the 79th New York and the 17th Michigan — a new regiment scarcely three weeks in the service, under the command of Colonel William H. Withington — rallied, changed front under a galling fire, moved forward in the most gallant manner and saved the guns. Order and confidence were soon restored by this timely movement, and the division deployed on the right of General Cox's division. The 17th Michigan was especially conspicuous on that day and won for itself great renown, by its steadiness under fire and its daring in the charge. It came out of the battle with a loss of twenty-seven killed and one hundred and fourteen wounded — a worthy attestation of its prowess. The 35th Massachusetts was also particularly distinguished for the bravery with which it entered into the battle and the steadiness with which it fought. It had but recently arrived at the seat of war and was thus early called to receive its baptism of blood. Its Colonel Edward A. Wild was very badly wounded, losing his right arm from the shoulder. The 45th Pennsylvania is mentioned by General Willcox in terms of high commendation, and the old regiments of Colonel Ferrero's brigade added new lustre to their well-won fame. The enemy was still stubbornly contesting our advance, but so fiercely was he pressed that he was obliged to draw reënforcements from the main body at Boonesboro'. General Longstreet came up and assisted General Hill in holding his position. Still our men were fighting bravely, and the entire aspect of affairs promised victory. The two divisions of Generals Cox and Willcox were promptly supported by Generals Rodman and Sturgis, with their entire commands with the exception of two regiments of the latter — the 2d Maryland and 6th New Hampshire — which were held in reserve upon or near the turnpike. General Rodman supported the extreme left with Colonel Fairchild's brigade, and with Colonel Harland's brigade held the extreme right of our line in this quarter. General Sturgis formed his division directly in the rear of General Willcox.

Up to one o'clock in the afternoon, the contest had been entirely carried on by the two divisions of the Ninth Corps under Generals Cox and Willcox. General Hooker's corps, which, with the Ninth, was under General Burnside's direction, arrived at the base of the mountain soon after noon, and was mainly sent up the road to the right. General Gibbon's brigade of General Hatch's division, with a battery of artillery, was detached for an advance up the turnpike itself. At two o'clock, General Meade's division of General Hooker's corps moved out on the old Hagerstown road, and began to climb the mountain. It was deployed on the right of the road, and was followed by General Hatch's division, which deployed on the left, and by General Ricketts' division, which brought up the rear. An attempt was made to get up some pieces of artillery, but the nature of the ground prevented. The road way was narrow, and the ground on either side was very difficult for the movement of troops. Stone walls, forest land, and fallen timber obstructed the progress of our men. But they gallantly and persistently went forward, and soon encountering the enemy, came into general action along the entire front. The enemy was steadily beaten back, and on his left was outflanked by the skilful manœuvering of General Seymour's brigade. On the left of General Hooker's line, General Hatch bravely urged his division forward, until he fell wounded, when General Doubleday took command, and the enemy's troops in that quarter were driven back by an impetuous charge of General Phelps's brigade.

By the continuous and steady forward movement of our troops, we had thus gained commanding positions on both sides of the turnpike, and the expulsion of the enemy was rendered certain. General Longstreet had now come up with reenforcements for the enemy's broken lines, and established his corps with Evans on the left, Hood in the centre, and Drayton on the right. But even these fresh troops could not prevent our victory. About five o'clock in the afternoon General Burnside ordered General Gibbon, with his brigade and one section of artillery, to move up the turnpike and demonstrate upon the enemy's centre. It was a very delicate and hazardous manœuvre, but the manner in which it was executed by General Gibbon elicited the highest commendation for its skill and success. General Gibbon "advanced a regiment on each side of the road, preceded by skirmishers and followed by the other two regiments in double column, the artillery moving on the road until within range of the enemy's guns, which were firing on the column from the gorge. The brigade advanced steadily, driving the enemy from his positions in the woods and behind stone walls."* It reached the top of the pass, received a heavy fire on the front and both flanks, but persistently held its own and repulsed the enemy's attack. General McClellan, coming on the field late in the day, approved the arrangements, dispositions and orders which General Burnside had made, and was in time to confirm the order already given by General Burnside for the entire line of the Ninth Corps to advance. The order was most gallantly obeyed under the personal direction of General Reno. The troops moved forward with enthusiasm, pushed the enemy from all his positions and sent him over the crest in confusion. He again rallied, again attempted to take the lost ground, again failed. Even the coming on of the evening did not deter him from the ineffectual endeavor. He continued firing, with occasional charges upon the position of the Ninth Corps, until nine o'clock, when, giving up the struggle, he retreated down the mountain, defeated along his whole line, and leaving his dead on the field, his wounded unattended, and fifteen hundred prisoners in our hands. It was a most gallant and well contested action, and reflected the highest credit upon the officers and men of the first and Ninth Corps. General Burnside fought it with great skill, moving his troops with consummate promptness, and, heartily sustained by his subordinates, carried a most difficult position and gained a victory which was a propitious presage of better things to come. It was the first of a series of conflicts

* McClellan's Report, p. 199.

with General Longstreet's corps of the rebel army in which the Ninth Corps was engaged on different fields. The forces engaged were nearly equal, with about thirty thousand men on each side. The enemy had greatly the advantage of position and was comparatively fresh. General Lee did not contemplate fighting a pitched battle at this point. The instructions to General D. H. Hill were "to hold the position at every hazard until he was notified of the success" of Jackson's movement. But our attack was so vigorous, that General Longstreet was hurried up to the field, and the engagement was much more severe than had been anticipated. The enemy confessed to a loss of "quite twenty-five hundred" killed and wounded. Our losses were three hundred and twelve killed, one thousand two hundred and thirty-four wounded, and twenty-two missing, of which were to be numbered in the Ninth Corps one hundred and forty-four killed and five hundred and forty-six wounded.

The greatest loss of all was that of General Reno. He was killed about sunset, while reconnoitering the position of the enemy. The firing had ceased, and it was supposed that the battle was over. General Reno, always fearless, was now particularly unmindful of danger. He exposed himself to the enemy's view and was instantly shot down. He fell, as he would have wished, in the extreme front. Jesse L. Reno was born in Virginia in 1825, but in early life removed to Pennsylvania. He was a boy of quick parts and impetuous disposition, ready at all times for a fight or a frolic. He soon showed decided proclivities for a military life, and succeeded in obtaining an appointment as cadet in the United States Military Academy at West Point. He entered in 1842, passed successfully and honorably through his curriculum, and graduated in 1846 in the Ordnance Department, eighth in a class of fifty-nine members. He received his commission as brevet Second Lieutenant, July 1, 1846. He was sent to Mexico and, serving temporarily in the Artillery, joined a battery at Vera Cruz. He was advanced to the full grade of Second

MAJ. GEN. JESSE L. RENO.

Lieutenant March 3, 1847. He accompanied the army in its triumphant march into the interior, and greatly distinguished himself for his gallantry at the battle of Cerro Gordo, April 18, 1847. For his conduct upon this occasion he was brevetted First Lieutenant, his commission dating from the day of the victory. He faithfully served through the summer campaign, and by his energy and intelligence attracted the favorable attention of his superior officers. At the storming of the castle of Chapultepec, September 13th, he was again prominent and was severely wounded in the course of the action. For his gallantry in this action, he was rewarded by a promotion to a brevet Captaincy. Returning home in 1848, he was appointed, January 9, 1849, Assistant Professor of Mathematics at West Point and held the position for six months, when he was selected as Secretary to a Board of Artillery officers. He was thus engaged for nearly two years in making experiments with heavy guns, which led to extremely interesting and valuable results. He also prepared a system of tactics for heavy artillery. He was subsequently detailed upon the Coast Survey, in which he served but a short time, when he was ordered to the Engineer Department, and proceeding to the West, superintended the construction of a military road from the Big Sioux river to St. Paul's, Minnesota. He was made a full First Lieutenant of Ordnance, March 3, 1853.

In the year 1854, General Reno was stationed at the Frankford Arsenal, Bridesburg, Pennsylvania. Here he served three years, when he accompanied General J. E. Johnston, in his expedition to Utah, as Chief of Ordnance. He returned in 1859, was on duty for a time at the Mount Vernon Arsenal in Alabama, and was subsequently sent to Fort Leavenworth, Kansas. On the 1st of July, 1860, he was promoted to a full Captaincy, was called to Washington in the early part of the war and was commissioned as Brigadier General of Volunteers, November 12, 1861. His distinguished gallantry at Roanoke Island and Newbern secured his promotion to Major General of Volunteers, April 26, 1862. His subsequent career, and the nature of his services to the date of his death, have been made sufficiently familiar to the reader of these pages. In all the acts of his life his fine and generous qualities of character were made manifest. He was quick and hasty in temper, thought, speech and act, and of great daring. Possibly he may have sometimes been impatient of results, and so may have exposed himself to unnecessary danger, thinking that his personal example might stimulate others to a more prompt and vigorous performance of duty. But he was always just, always ready to recognize and reward merit, if equally ready to condemn unfaithfulness. Warm-hearted, cordial, fearless, he was a thorough soldier, and fully deserved all that his superiors in command have said of him. General Pope's testimony in his behalf has already been adduced. "The loss of this brave and distinguished officer," says General McClellan, "tempered with sadness the exultations of triumph. An able general, endeared to his troops and associates, his death is felt to be an irreparable misfortune. He was a skilful soldier, a brave and honest man."* "I will not attempt, in a public report," says General Burnside in his report of the operations of his command in Maryland, "to express the deep sorrow which the death of the gallant Reno caused me. A long and intimate acquaintance, an extended service in the same field, and an intimate knowledge of his high and noble character had endeared him to me as well as to all with whom he had served. No more valuable life than his has been lost during this contest for our country's preservation." A brave and gallant gentleman, indeed, who knew no fear and suffered no reproach!

The officers of our army recognized his sterling qualities of head and heart. Even strangers and casual acquaintances perceived his worth, and felt the impression which the sense of his manliness and honor made upon them. The public journals throughout the loyal States bore witness to his fine nobility of character, and it was universally agreed that the

* McClellan's Report, p. 197.

loyal cause had lost one of its best, bravest and most trustworthy defenders. His remains were taken from the field where he fell, were carried to Boston, Massachusetts, where his family then resided, and were carefully and tenderly consigned to the earth. In person, General Reno was of middle stature, stout, well knit and compact in frame. His forehead was high and broad, his face wore a genial expression, his eye beamed upon his friends with rare and quick intelligence, or, kindled in the excitement of conflict, flashed out in brave defiance of the foe. He had a magnetic kind of enthusiasm, and when leading on his men, he seemed to inspire his followers and make them irresistible in action. A dauntless soldier, whose like we rarely see!

CHAPTER III.

THE BATTLE OF ANTIETAM.

FOR the battle of South Mountain which General Burnside fought,* General McClellan received the hearty thanks of the President. Mr. Lincoln, immediately upon hearing the gratifying intelligence of the victory, sent the following kind message: "God bless you and all with you; destroy the rebel army if possible." General McClellan, during the fight on the 14th, had massed his entire army, with the exception of General Franklin's command, in Middletown and its immediate vicinity. At early dawn on the 15th, the advance of the pickets revealed the fact that the enemy had retired during the night from the mountain and its neighborhood. General Mansfield had arrived at headquarters early in the morning after the battle, and immediately assumed command of the twelfth corps. That Corps, with those of Generals Sumner and Hooker, the latter of which had been detached from General Burnside's command, and General Pleasonton's cavalry, were ordered to pursue the enemy on the main road through Boonesboro'. General Franklin was ordered to move into Pleasant Valley, and occupy Rohrersville. General Burnside with the Ninth Corps, now under command of General Cox who had succeeded General Reno, and General Sykes's division, was directed to march by the old Sharpsburg road. But little occurred during the day, except a severe skirmish with the enemy's cavalry in the village of Boonesboro', which resulted in killing and wounding a number and capturing two guns and two hundred and

*General McClellan in his first dispatch transmitting intelligence of this battle made no mention whatever of General Burnside.

fifty prisoners from the retreating foe. The infantry followed promptly on the heels of General Lee's rear guard, but could not bring on an engagement. The enemy carefully retired, and passing throngh Boonesboro' and Keedysville, crossed Antietam Creek and took up a strong position upon the heights beyond. General Richardson's division of General Sumner's corps was in the advance on this road, and immediately upon approaching the enemy's position deployed between the turnpike and the old Sharpsburg road. General Sykes's division, which was in the advance of General Burnside's pursuit, reaching a point contiguous to General Richardson's position, deployed upon the left of the Sharpsburg road. The remaining troops occupied the two roads in columns. General McClellan states that he was desirous of engaging the enemy on the 15th. But the relative positions of the two armies forbade any such enterprise, and the commanding general was only able to post his batteries and mass his troops near and on both sides of the Sharpsburg road. The Ninth Corps occupied the extreme left close to the hills on the southeast side of the valley of the Antietam.*

Antietam creek at this point is a sluggish stream, with but few fords and those difficult of crossing. Above in the neighborhood of Funkstown, there are high banks, and the scenery up and down the river is quite picturesque. The battle, however, was confined to the region adjacent to the lower part of the stream. Here the creek is spanned by four substantial stone bridges,† the upper one on the Keedysville and Williamsport road; the second about two miles and a half below on the Keedysville and Sharpsburg turnpike; the third about a mile below the second on the Rohrersville and Sharpsburg road; and the fourth near the mouth of the creek, three miles below the third. Our army lay along the eastern bank of the creek not quite down to the bridges, but with the right wing commanding the two upper bridges and the roads towards Funks-

* Cox's Report. † McClellan's Report, p. 200.

town beyond. General Burnside — now in command upon the extreme left — was posted opposite the bridge upon the Rohrersville and Sharpsburg road, but at some distance from it. The enemy showed evident signs of standing to his defence. General Lee had carried his troops across the creek, had stationed them in a commanding position between that and the Potomac river, and was thus within easy communication with his detachments on the Virginia side near Harper's Ferry, and manifested every sign of making a severe fight. His campaign in Maryland had thus far been entirely fruitless with the exception of the capture of Harper's Ferry, and he could not endure to retire across the Potomac without making some endeavors to retrieve his ill-fortune. During the night of the 15th he changed his position and threw up some slight intrenchments. Through the same night General McClellan's army was occupied in getting into position on the hither side of the creek. General Franklin remained in camp near Crampton's Gap and did not come up till the day of the main battle. Two divisions of General Fitz John Porter's corps, to which General Sykes's division belonged, were on the way from Boonesboro' and Frederick, but were making slow progress on account of the crowded state of the roads. Supplies of provision and ammunition were not abundant, as the troops in advance had hurried forward with great celerity, leaving their baggage train to follow more leisurely. On the morning of the 16th General McClellan was not ready for offensive operations, and the enemy showed a decidedly threatening front.

The bridge in front of the Ninth Corps was a substantial structure difficult of approach on either side, when well guarded by a resolute enemy. Our line had been formed at some distance from the bridge, and it was thought best on the morning of the 16th that it should be moved to a nearer position, from which an assault could be made with greater assurance of success. General Burnside accordingly advanced his command to the immediate vicinity of the bridge, and proceeded to reconnoitre the approaches from his front. During the day his troops were placed in position, and bivouacked at night in line of battle. "The distribution of the forces was as follows:* On the crest of the hill, immediately in front of the bridge was Benjamin's battery of six 20-pounders with the remaining batteries in rear of the crest under partial cover. In rear of Benjamin's battery, on the extreme right, joining on to General Sykes's division was General Crook's brigade with General Sturgis's division in his rear. On the left and in rear of Benjamin's battery was General Rodman's division with Colonel Scammon's brigade in support. General Willcox's division was held in reserve." Nothing of especial moment occurred during the day in this part of our lines. The enemy dropped some shells in the midst of our troops at intervals, but did not succeed in doing much execution or causing much alarm. On the right the army was a little more busy, and there was considerable fighting before our formations were entirely completed.

As the enemy during the night of the 15th had contracted his lines, General McClellan decided to throw a portion of his forces across the creek on the 16th, and occupy the opposite bank and the ground adjoining, threatening the enemy's left. The morning was spent in making preparations for the intended movement, and in the afternoon our right was advanced. About two o'clock General Hooker took his corps over the creek by the upper bridge and a ford in the immediate neighborhood. The command struck the enemy's left soon after crossing and a spirited skirmish ensued. The enemy gradually gave way, and General Hooker's troops rested on their arms upon the ground which they had occupied. During the night General Mansfield's corps following General Hookers', crossed the creek, and bivouacked about a mile in his rear.

On the morning of the 17th, the lines of our army were formed as follows: Across the creek beyond the upper bridge were the two corps of General Hooker and General Mansfield,

---

*Burnside's Report.

the latter directly in rear of the former. On this side the creek, in support of the advanced line, was General Sumner's own corps*—the second—ready to move over as soon as its services were required. General Fitz John Porter's corps occupied the centre, and was posted upon the main turnpike leading to Sharpsburg. General McClellan considered this as the vital point, as it was the main avenue of communication to the rear and to the position of our supply and ammunition trains. General Franklin's corps was now upon the march from Crampton's Gap, heading directly for the scene of the impending engagement. The left was occupied by General Burnside, with the Ninth Corps in the position which has already been described. The enemy's position was extremely well chosen, and his lines were formed as follows: Two divisions of General Jackson's command, (commanded respectively by Generals J. R. Jones and Lawton,) which had reached the enemy's position on the morning of the 16th, were on the left flank formed in two lines. General D. H. Hill's corps occupied the centre; General Longstreet's the right. The batteries of Poague, Carpenter, Brockenbrough, Raine, Caskie and Wooding were posted on the left and centre. The divisions of Generals McLaws, R. H. Anderson and Walker came up on the morning of the 17th, and were posted in support of the centre and left. General Hood's command had been engaged on the previous evening with General Hooker's advance, and was relieved during the night by the brigades of Generals Lawton and Trimble, belonging to General Jackson's corps.† Hooker and Jackson were well matched in fighting qualities, and their troops now stood face to face ready for the impending death-struggle. The forces on either side were very nearly equal—not far from one hundred thousand men in each army being engaged during the day or within supporting distance.

General McClellan states that his plan of battle "was to attack the enemy's left with the corps of Generals Hooker and

---

*General Sumner was in command of the right wing. †Jackson's Report.

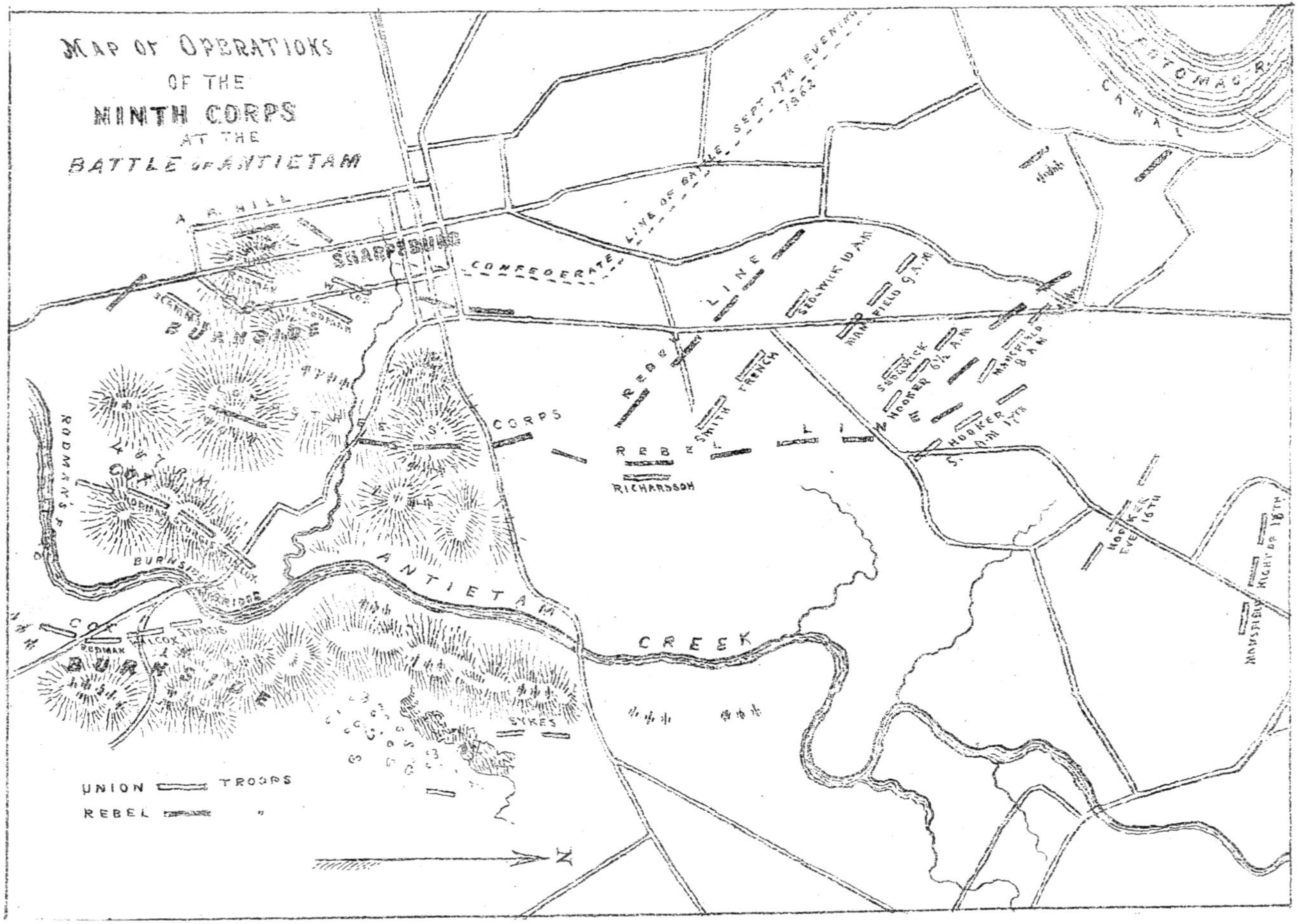

MAP OF OPERATIONS
OF THE
NINTH CORPS
AT THE
BATTLE OF ANTIETAM

A. P. HILL
SHARPSBURG
BURNSIDE
RODMAN
CONFEDERATE LINE OF BATTLE SEPT 17TH EVENING 1862
POTOMAC R.
CANAL
REBEL LINE
SEDGWICK 10 A.M.
MANSFIELD 9 A.M.
SEDGWICK
HOOKER 6½ A.M.
MANSFIELD 8 A.M.
HOOKER 5 A.M. 17TH
SMITH
FRENCH
CORPS
RICHARDSON
HOOKER EVE 16TH
MANSFIELD NIGHT OF 16TH
RODMAN'S FORD
BURNSIDE BRIDGE
STURGIS
ANTIETAM
CREEK
WILCOX
SYKES
BURNSIDE
UNION TROOPS
REBEL "
N

Mansfield, supported by General Sumner's and, if necessary, by General Franklin's; and as soon as matters looked favorably there, to move the corps of General Burnside against the enemy's extreme right upon the ridge running to the south and rear of Sharpsburg, and having carried that position, to press along the crest towards our right."* Whenever either of these flank movements should be successful, our centre was to be advanced with all the forces then disposable. To accomplish the first object, General McClellan had a force of fifty-six thousand one hundred and ninety-five men. To accomplish the second, General Burnside had at his disposal thirteen thousand eight hundred and nineteen men. For the third, there were nearly, if not quite, twenty thousand men. The main attack, of course, was to be made upon the enemy's left, for which purpose twenty-five thousand men—or to speak accurately, twenty-four thousand nine hundred and eighty-two—had already crossed the creek, and were eagerly awaiting, on the morning of the 17th, the signal to attack.

At daylight on Wednesday, September 17th, the great battle of Antietam was opened by the skirmishers of the Pennsylvania Reserves in General Meade's division of General Hooker's corps. From that time until the sun set and the darkness put an end to the conflict, the struggle went on with varying fortune. The opposing lines swayed to and fro in the writhings of the death-struggle. At the close of the day, the two armies occupied nearly the same position as in the morning, with the exception of the Ninth Corps, which had gallantly carried the bridge in its front, moved across the creek and occupied the heights beyond, securing, in spite of the enemy's most strenuous efforts, the most advanced position of any corps in the army. It was a desperate struggle, a bloody day. The two armies, whose blood had dyed the waters of the Chickahominy, again confronted each other along the banks of the Antietam, and fought with desperate valor another of those great battles

* McClellan's Report, p. 201.

which decided scarcely anything more than the equal courage, persistence and obstinacy of the combatants. A few guns and flags were left in our hands, and thirty thousand dead and wounded lay scattered over the fields of the sanguinary contest.

The main attack commenced from our right. The whole of General Hooker's corps was soon engaged, and, fighting with impetuous courage, was successful in forcing the enemy back from an open field in front of its position to a line of woods in his rear. As the battle became more general, it became more determined. The enemy hurried up his troops to counteract the temporary check which he had sustained. General Hooker pushed forward the supporting corps of General Mansfield to secure the advantage which he had already gained. The brave old soldier, General Mansfield, whose age might well have kept him from the field, but whose spirit was as ardent as the youngest soldier there, led his troops forward to the contest. Scarcely had he come within the line of fire, when a bullet struck him, and he fell, mortally wounded. General Williams took command of the corps once more and fought it through the remainder of the day. The piece of ground over which General Hooker was attempting to force the enemy was most obstinately contested. For two hours the battle raged with great fury, and without material advantage to either party. Finally, the enemy's line was driven back and our forces advanced into the woods. General Sumner's corps now began to arrive, General Sedgwick leading the command. The division in advance came on gallantly in three columns, deployed into three lines when near the enemy, advanced through the woods in front, and, passing through them, was met by a galling fire as it attempted to emerge into the open field. At the same time, the enemy coming up on the left, succeeded in turning the flank of General Sedgwick's division, and taking it in reverse threw the troops into a temporary confusion. They gave way towards the right and rear, but were soon rallied again by their officers, and prevented the enemy from securing any fruits from his momentary success. So fierce now became the resistance of our men, that the enemy found himself compelled to desist from his advance, and again retired into the woods from which he had previously been dislodged. During the assault General Sedgwick was twice wounded, but kept the field until faintness and exhaustion consequent from loss of blood compelled his withdrawal. About the same time, or just previously, General Hooker was severely wounded and was taken to the rear. General Meade succeeded to the command of the first corps. Our lines were rearranged and the prevailing confusion partially remedied.

In the meantime, the two remaining divisions of General Sumner's corps, under Generals French and Richardson, had crossed the creek in the rear of General Sedgwick, and facing to the left, advanced against the enemy, pushing on with great vigor through fields of corn, over fences, stone walls and other obstructions, and bravely entered into the fight. Pressing the enemy before them, they made their way very nearly to the crest of a range of small hills, where the rebel forces were posted in a sunken road and adjoining cornfields, from which issued a most destructive fire. The enemy made repeated attempts on both flanks and in front to drive our men back, but was as repeatedly repulsed with great slaughter. For four hours, these brave troops maintained their position, when, having exhausted their ammunition, they withdrew immediately below the crest, the enemy declining to follow. In the course of these movements and operations General Richardson was mortally wounded, while directing the fire of his artillery. General Franklin came up with his corps, between twelve and one o'clock, and was immediately sent over to the right to reenforce General Sumner, whose corps had suffered a loss of more than one-fourth of its men, so severe had been the contest with the enemy at General Sedgwick's and particularly General French's position. But after General Franklin had got into position, it was deemed advisable for him not to attack, but only to do little more than to relieve the troops who had been engaged, and to hold his men in readiness to repel any assault which the enemy might make. One brigade, under Colonel Irwin, was sent forward to check a force of the enemy which was advancing down the road, and succeeded, though with great loss, in accomplishing its object. Between nine thousand and ten thousand men had already been killed or disabled in the three corps engaged, and numbers of the remainder were badly scattered and demoralized. General Sumner, who was in immediate command upon the field across the creek, did not venture to risk another general attack with the only available corps on the right wing, and the enemy seemed to be equally averse to a recommencement of the severe fighting. By the middle of the afternoon all serious hostilities had ceased upon our right. General Jackson at one time made a movement to turn our right, but found our troops and our "numerous artillery so judiciously established" in our front, "as to render it inexpedient to hazard the attempt." Desultory firing was kept up until dark, and our troops rested upon the ground which General Hooker's corps had occupied on the previous night, and upon that which General French's division had gallantly won.

The centre of our line was held by the corps of General Fitz John Porter, the cavalry division of General Pleasonton and the Reserve Artillery. These troops were occupied during the day at different points, with the exception of portions of two divisions, which remained inactive. General Pleasonton, with the batteries of Captains Robertson, Tidball, Gibson, and Lieutenant Haines, supported by a battalion of infantry, advanced across the second bridge, and made a resolute and daring attack upon that portion of the enemy that was engaged with General Sumner's left. Tidball's battery especially did great execution. The boldness of the movement which this battery made excited the admiration of the enemy himself, for Captain Tidball showed great skill and daring in putting his guns in an advanced position, and in directing his case shot and canister upon the masses of the foe. An eye-witness on the enemy's side describes the great accuracy of our artillery fire and the suffering which it inflicted. "Dead and wounded men, horses and disabled caissons" were visible in every battery. By three o'clock in the afternoon, however, the storm of battle had lulled, and the artillery was withdrawn. Two brigades of General Porter's corps were held in reserve on the right centre, and one brigade occupied a position in the rear of General Burnside's command, on the hither side of the creek. The forces in the centre numbered a little over seventeen thousand, and suffered a loss during the day of one hundred and fifty-eight killed, wounded and missing.

The battle on the left, under General Burnside's direction, was very sanguinary and desperate. In the general plan, the work assigned to the Ninth Corps was to cross the stone bridge immediately in front of its position, dislodge the enemy and press up the creek upon the opposite bank, rolling in the enemy's flank upon his centre, if it were possible. That, however, was to depend in some measure upon the success of our right attack. If it were favorable, General Burnside's movement was to be vigorously made, with the hope of a complete victory. But the attack upon the right had not terminated so favorably as had been expected. The enemy still contested his ground there with great stubbornness. Nevertheless, General McClellan decided to put in the Ninth Corps, with the hope, doubtless, of creating a diversion and assisting our troops on the right to make a more successful advance.

About the time of General Hooker's attack, the enemy opened with artillery upon General Burnside's position, but without doing much damage. Our batteries returned the fire, and succeeded in silencing the enemy and blowing up two of his caissons. Agreeably to the order of General McClellan, General Burnside formed his corps and held his men in readiness to carry the enemy's position, but awaited further directions from headquarters. The dispositions of his troops were as follows: General Crook's brigade of the Kanawha division, and General Sturgis's division were formed immediately in front of the bridge and of a ford immediately above. Their front was covered by the 11th Connecticut regiment, Colonel T. H. W. Kingsbury, thrown out as skirmishers. General Rodman's division, with Colonel Scammon's brigade of the Kanawha division in support, was posted further to the left, opposite a ford about three-quarters of a mile below the bridge. General Willcox's division was formed in the woods in rear of the other lines. Of the artillery, Benjamin's battery occupied the position which it had taken on the previous day, Clark's and Durell's were posted on the right, Muhlenburg's, Cook's and McMullen's on the left, a little in advance of Benjamin. The batteries on the left overlooked the bridge and the heights above it. One section of Simms's battery was with General Crook's brigade, and one section with Benjamin. The battery of Dahlgren boat howitzers, attached to the 9th New York regiment, covered the ford opposite General Rodman's position.

At ten o'clock General Burnside received orders to attack, carry the bridge, move up the heights above, and advance upon Sharpsburg. The troops were immediately put in motion.

But the order could be given more easily than it could be executed. The enemy's position was most admirable for defence, and the part of his line which General Burnside's command was to assault was particularly strong. The valley of the Antietam, says a writer in the rebel army, who was present at this battle, "has not a level spot in it, but rolls into eminences of all dimensions, from the little knoll that your horse gallops easily over to the rather high hills that make him tug like a mule. Many of the depressions between these hills are dry and afford admirable cover for infantry against artillery. Others are watered by the deep, narrow and crooked Antietam, a stream that seems to observe no decorum in respect to its course, but has to be crossed every ten minutes ride which way you will. Sharpsburg lies on the western side of the valley, across which from the northeast runs the turnpike from Boonsboro'. Nearly every part of the valley is under cultivation, and the scene is thus varied into squares of nearly ripened corn, the deeper green of clover and the dull brown of newly ploughed fields. Towards the north are dense woods."* In the lower part of the valley, near the bridge which General Burnside was to carry, the hills thus described rise abruptly and the banks of the stream especially upon the western side are nearly precipitous. They effectually command the eastern approaches to the bridge. Part way down the slope is a stone wall running parallel with the stream. The road from the bridge, like other roads in a similar conformation of country, winds up the bank with several turnings. At each of these the enemy had constructed rifle pits and breastworks of rails, rocks and timber. The woods covering the slope were filled with the enemy's riflemen, and his batteries were posted so as to enfilade the bridge and sweep away with a storm of shot and shell every party that dared attempt its passage. The bridge itself is of no great width, built of stone with three stone arches and low stone parapets. Many brave men must breathe their last before a lodgment could be effected among the woods and on the heights beyond. Who should be selected as the forlorn hope?

General Burnside ordered General Cox, who had the immediate execution of all the commands on the field, to detail General Crook's brigade to make the assault, with Colonel Kingsbury's skirmishers in front and General Sturgis in support. At the same time, General Rodman was directed to cross his division at the lower ford, and join upon the left of the force that would be thrown across. General Crook bravely made the attempt to cross, but the enemy was very obstinate in disputing the passage. A brigade under General Jenkins, and two regiments of Georgia troops—the 2d and 20th—under Colonel Cummings, poured in a destructive fire. General Toombs's brigade posted near the bridge strenuously resisted our approach. The enemy's artillery under Major Garnett, admirably planted on the opposite heights, made rapid and

*Life of Stonewall Jackson by Daniels, p. 207.

effective discharges upon the advancing troops. The road occupied by our troops and along which they were to move goes down to the creek about three hundred yards below the bridge, then turns at right angles and continues along the bank, turning again at right angles to cross the bridge. The road was swept by the enemy's fire before which our men recoiled, were broken and retired. They could not make the passage. General Sturgis was ordered to make a detail from his division for the second attempt. The force selected this time was composed of two regiments, the 6th New Hampshire, Colonel S. G. Griffin, and the 2d Maryland, Lieutenant Colonel Duryea—good regiments both. Unfortunately their position at starting was not such as promised any great success. They charged from a point at a considerable distance below the bridge, were compelled to make their way through a narrow opening in "a firm chestnut fence, which there was no time to remove, and then run a long distance in the face of a well posted enemy."* They performed this part of their difficult and perilous duty in a most gallant and praiseworthy manner, but they could not cross the bridge. They were repulsed with considerable loss. Again they made the attempt, and again they were checked and prevented. It was now noon and the bridge had not yet been wrested from the tenacious hold of the enemy. General McClellan, not appreciating the difficulty of the position, seems to have exhibited an unreasonable amount of impatience, and sent repeated orders to General Burnside to carry the point at all hazards—which General Burnside was earnestly endeavoring to do.

Another attempt, more decisive and more successful as it eventuated, was now made. The batteries on our left concentrated their fire on the woods above the bridge, and General Sturgis was ordered to make a second detail. General Ferrero's† brigade—consisting of the 51st Pennsylvania, Colonel

*Colonel Griffin's Letter.

†General Ferrero received his commission as Brigadier General while on the field.

Hartranft, the 51st New York, Colonel Potter, the 21st Massachusetts, Colonel Clark, and the 35th Massachusetts, Lieutenant Colonel Carruth*—was chosen. The two leading regiments were formed in the rear of a spur fronting the bridge, which partially protected the men from the enemy's fire, and eagerly awaited the signal. They had not long to wait. They crowned the crest of the hill—the gallant Colonel Hartranft leading—they poured down the road to the river bank, disregarding the terrific storm of fire which sadly thinned their ranks, and charging impetuously with the bayonet, crossed and secured the bridge so long and so obstinately contested. The other regiments of the brigade followed closely upon the heels of their gallant comrades. The prize was at last won, though at great loss of life. Lieutenant Colonel Bell of the 51st Pennsylvania Regiment, a gallant soldier and amiable gentleman, was killed by a piece of shell, and at least two hundred other brave men from the two regiments in advance fell in this short, sharp struggle.

It was one o'clock when the bridge was finally carried. General Sturgis promptly brought up the residue of his division to complete the success which had been so bravely achieved. The regiments separated at the head of the bridge to the right and left, and with great intrepidity moved up the steep bank, crowning the height and driving the enemy everywhere before them. Again we met with great loss, the enemy being posted in his rifle pits and behind his barricades and thus enabled to bring an infernal fire upon our men at easy musket range. It was literally the jaws of death. Here Colonel Kingsbury fell, a most brave and excellent gentleman and soldier, the pride and flower of the class of 1861 at the Military Academy at West Point. He had been a ward of General Burnside, and his many manly qualities had endeared him to all who knew his worth. We had paid a great price for our success.

---

* Lieutenant Colonel Carruth was wounded in this battle and the regiment was badly cut up.

General Crook's brigade crossed immediately after General Sturgis's division and took position in its rear in support. General Rodman at the same time threw his division across the ford below, after a sharp fight in which the enemy was worsted. He formed his command upon the left of General Sturgis. Colonel Scammon's brigade followed across the ford, and took position in the rear in support. Clark's and Durell's batteries accompanied General Sturgis. General Willcox's division crossed by the bridge and took position on the extreme right of the line. Cook's battery accompanied General Willcox; Muhlenburg's and part of Simms's were already over with the troops of the Kanawha Division. General Cox in person directed the operations of the corps on the west side of the creek. These movements were made across a narrow bridge and a difficult ford, and in the face of a sullen and obstinate enemy, who contested every foot of ground. They occupied considerable time, and at three o'clock the entire corps stood arrayed upon the opposite bank of the Antietam, and began a further advance upon the enemy, making for the village of Sharpsburg. General Sturgis's division was held upon the heights in reserve, and our batteries on the hither side covered the forward movement of the corps.

The order to advance was received and obeyed by the troops with great enthusiasm. They pressed forward rapidly, cheering and exultant, as they had been accustomed to charge in North Carolina. For a time all went well. General Willcox with General Crook in support moved up the Sharpsburg road on both sides, and his advance even gained the outskirts of the town. General Rodman pushed on in his own fearless style and handsomely carried the heights on the left of the town. The 9th New York was again conspicuous for its daring. It made a heroic charge upon one of the most formidable of the enemy's batteries, and succeeded in capturing it, losing in the contest nearly half its men. Out of little more than five hundred men it lost, during the afternoon, two hundred and fifty of whom ninety-five were killed. This battery, it would seem, belonged to the brigade of General Toombs who was highly incensed at its capture. The story told by one of the southern writers is, that "the General, instantly dismounting from his horse, and placing himself at the head of his command, briefly told his men in his effective way that the battery must be retaken, if it cost the life of every man in his brigade, and then ordered them to follow him. Follow him they did into what seemed the very jaws of destruction, and after a short but fierce struggle they had the satisfaction of recapturing the prize."* Doubtless there was some rhodomontade of this description on the part of General Toombs. But the recapture was due to something more than the gallantry of this redoubtable brigade.

The enemy, now relieved from our attack upon his left, which had in effect ceased at three o'clock, hurried down reenforcements of infantry and artillery, hoping to overwhelm the Ninth Corps, isolated as it was from the rest of the army. General Lee felt assured that if General Burnside's command could be driven off, victory would rest with them. "It is certain," says Mr. Pollard in his history of the war, "that if we had had fresh troops to hurl against Burnside at the bridge of Antietam, the day would have been ours." The fresh troops came, but they did not retake the bridge. They were "hurled against Burnside" in vain. General A. P. Hill's light division of Jackson's corps, with fresh troops from Harper's Ferry, appeared upon our left about four o'clock and began a vigorous attack. Our lines were contracted and reformed to meet this new danger. General Rodman's division, which had been obliged, by the inequalities of the ground and other circumstances, to bear more to the left than was originally intended, had become outflanked and was hard pressed. It was recalled from its advanced position, and ordered to move more to the right to close up our lines in that quarter. The movement was made in the face of the enemy in a very steady manner, but it was fatal to the commanding general of the divison and

*Life of Stonewall Jackson.

his aide de camp, Lieutenant Robert H. Ives, Jr. General Rodman was struck by a minie ball, which penetrated his left lung, and knocked him from his horse. Lieutenant Ives was struck by a fragment of shell, which gave him a frightful wound in the thigh and killed his horse. Both officers were carried to the rear and received every attention, but their wounds proved mortal, and they died a few days after the battle. The division, now under the command of Colonel Hawkins of the 9th New York, completed its movement, but in the forced withdrawal of Colonel Harland's brigade, the captured battery was abandoned, and again fell into the hands of the enemy. The time was critical. Reënforcements of the enemy continued to press upon the field, and our left flank was in great danger of being turned and driven in. Colonel Scammon with commendable promptness "caused the 12th and 23d Ohio regiments of his brigade to execute a perpendicular change of front, which was done with precision and success, the other regiment, the 30th Ohio, maintaining its proper front."* This timely movement checked the enemy and protected our exposed flank.

General Burnside, observing the state of affairs, ordered General Sturgis forward to assist the advanced forces in their desperate struggle with the constantly increasing masses of the enemy. The division reëntered the fight with the greatest alacrity and enthusiasm and, though they were already somewhat exhausted and short of ammunition, they presented a bold front and with great courage held the enemy at bay. Numbers of troops came down from the enemy's left, where their presence was no longer needed, and, with the addition of General Hill's division, now on the ground and doing good service for the enemy, began to press us back. But the Ninth Corps as yet stood firmly, and could reënforcements have been sent from our side, would not only have made good its position in the neighborhood of Sharpsburg, but would have decisively

---

* Cox's Report of the Battle of Antietam.

beaten the enemy. General Burnside begged of General McClellan for help. But no help was to be obtained. General Franklin, with twelve thousand men, was thought to be needed upon the right. General Fitz John Porter, with thirteen thousand, could not be spared from the centre. At least so thought General McClellan, who, careful to guard points that were not in absolute peril, did not think it necessary to reënforce those which required aid. The rest of the army seemed to be waiting on their arms, while the Ninth Corps waged its unequal battle.

The day was now rapidly declining. As the enemy greatly outnumbered us and as no aid could be given, General Cox gradually withdrew the corps to the high banks of the creek in his rear, and there firmly held his ground. It had been hard work through this long September day, but it had been most nobly done. As the sun set and the evening shadows gathered, and the cessation of the firing on both sides proclaimed the end of the great battle, General Burnside was gratified to know that his command had gained the most advanced position of any portion of our army, and had attested its bravery in the most signal and distinguished manner. No duty had been left unperformed. No unnecessary delays had been made. No cessation of fighting had taken place. No part of its line had been broken. But everything that was possible to brave men had been done. A position well nigh impregnable had been dauntlessly carried. A steady advance had been made. The enemy had been pressed back, and had reënforcement met reënforcement, the day would have been most certainly our own. The enemy's account acknowledges that "the immense Yankee force crossed the river and made the dash against our line, which well nigh proved a success. The timely arrival of General A. P. Hill, however, with fresh troops, entirely changed the fortunes of the day, and after an obstinate contest, which lasted from five o'clock until dark, the enemy were driven"* back. It had been a day of most san-

* Life of Stonewall Jackson.

guinary fighting, and the commanding generals on both sides were not sorry to see the sun go down below the western horizon, and to know that the darkness prohibited any further carnage.

Our losses were large. The ground over which the great struggle of the morning had taken place, alternately in our own and the enemy's possession, was literally covered with the dead and wounded of both armies. General Sumner's corps of eighteen thousand eight hundred and thirteen men lost no less than five thousand two hundred and nine in killed, wounded and missing, of whom forty-one officers and eight hundred and nineteen men were killed, and four general and eighty-nine other commissioned officers, and three thousand seven hundred and eight men were wounded. General Hooker's corps of fourteen thousand eight hundred and fifty-six men lost three hundred and forty-eight killed, two thousand and sixteen wounded, and two hundred and fifty-five missing. General Mansfield's, afterwards General Williams's corps of ten thousand one hundred and twenty-six men lost two hundred and seventy-four killed, one thousand three hundred and eighty-four wounded, and eighty-five missing. General Franklin's corps of twelve thousand and three hundred men lost seventy killed, three hundred and thirty-five wounded, and thirty-three missing. General Fitz John Porter's corps of twelve thousand nine hundred and thirty men, and the reserve artillery, lost twenty-one killed, one hundred and seven wounded, and two missing. General Pleasonton's division of four thousand three hundred and twenty men lost five killed and twenty-three wounded.

The Ninth Corps numbered, on the morning of the battle, thirteen thousand eight hundred and nineteen officers and men. Its losses during the day were twenty-two officers and four hundred and ten enlisted men killed, ninety-six officers and one thousand six hundred and forty-five enlisted men wounded, and one hundred and twenty missing. The trophies of the entire campaign in Maryland captured from the enemy were thirteen guns, thirty-nine colors, fifteen thousand stands of small arms and more than six thousand prisoners. The Army of the Potomac lost neither a gun nor color. The enemy's losses were very severe. Generals Branch and Starke had been killed, General Jones disabled, General Lawton severely wounded. General Jackson, in his report of the battle, speaks of our fire as having been "well sustained and destructive." More than half of the brigades of Lawton and Hays were either killed or wounded, and more than a third of Trimble's, and all the regimental commanders in those brigades, except two, were killed or wounded. Thinned of their ranks and exhausted of their ammunition, Jackson's division and the brigades of Lawton, Hays and Trimble retired to the rear, and Hood, of Longstreet's command, again took the position from which he had been before relieved.* The enemy must have buried a portion of his dead, but he left more than two thousand five hundred upon the field to be buried by our troops. "The carnage," as General Jackson says, "on both sides was terrific."

Among our losses were those of officers whom we could ill afford to lose. Major General Joseph K. F. Mansfield, the commander of the twelfth corps, was one of the oldest officers in the army, having entered the service in 1822. He was unsurpassed for his skill and thoroughness as an engineer, and was remarkable for the manly simplicity and the bravery of his character. Highly esteemed by the army, his death was deeply lamented. But he died, as he would have desired, in the full possession of all his military faculties, and in the course of the faithful discharge of his duty. Major General Israel B. Richardson, of General Sumner's corps, mortally wounded at Antietam, died at Sharpsburg on the 3d of November. He was born in Vermont, educated at West Point and appointed Brigadier General of Volunteers, May 17, 1861. He was a brave officer, and his loss was severely felt by the officers and men under his command.

* Jackson's Report in Pollard's History of Second Year, p. 132.

In the Ninth Corps, the death of Colonel Kingsbury and Lieutenant Colonel Bell has already been appropriately noticed. Colonel Kingsbury lingered till the 18th, when he died amidst the sorrow of a multitude of friends. Lieutenant Robert H. Ives, Jr., of General Rodman's staff, was a young man of liberal education, a graduate of Brown University in Providence, Rhode Island, and the prospective heir to a very large fortune. With every comfort and even luxury of life at his command, he could not endure the thought that the sacred war for the Union should go on without his participation. He left a delightful home, an agreeable social circle in which he was a favorite, and entered the army as a volunteer aide to General Rodman, at the commencement of the Maryland campaign. He cheerfully endured every privation of the camp and bravely faced every danger of the battle field. He endeared himself to the whole command by his kindness and his readiness to share all hardships and perils. His conduct in battle, calm, cool and self-possessed, called forth the unqualified approbation of his superior officers. He lingered in great pain for several days after the battle, attended with the best surgical skill which could possibly be secured. But all means were unavailing, and he died at Hagerstown on the 27th day of September. Truly, he had left all and followed the command of duty, devoting a life of hope and promise to his country's welfare!

But the severest loss in the Ninth Corps was that caused by the death of General Rodman. His bravery had been so manifestly displayed, his skill was so well known, his judgment was so mature, and his fidelity so unquestioned, as to lead his friends to believe that a brilliant future awaited him. Drawn from the peaceful pursuits of life, by his love for the country and a desire to serve her welfare, he was rapidly making an honorable place for himself in the army—indeed had already secured that place—when the fortune of war and the decree of Heaven put an end forever to his career on earth. Isaac P. Rodman was born at South Kingstown on the 18th of August, 1822. His father was a manufacturer, and the boy was carefully reared at home, thoroughly instructed at school, and at a proper time was trained to the business of his father. He was soon distinguished for faithfulness, industry and integrity. The manly qualities of his character won for him the esteem and affection of his fellow citizens, and with great credit to himself, he filled various offices of trust to which his townsmen were always glad to elect him. On the 15th of June, 1847, he was married to Miss Sally, daughter of Hon. Lemuel H. Arnold, who, with a family of five children, survives him. At the breaking out of the rebellion, he was moved by an ardent patriotic feeling, which would not permit him to remain at home at his ease while so many of his fellow countrymen were hastening to the scene of duty and danger. He gave up his business, exercised his influence in raising troops, commenced by himself the study of military subjects, and upon the organization of the 2d Regiment of Rhode Island Volunteers, was commissioned Captain, June 1, 1861. The regiment was actively engaged in the battle of Bull Run, and there Captain Rodman won his first laurels in the field. He was especially distinguished for his coolness and valor and gained the approving notice of his superior officers, whose high respect he had previously secured by his unwearied faithfulness in the discharge of duty in the camp.

Soon after the organization of the 4th Rhode Island regiment, he was appointed Lieutenant Colonel, his commission dating October 19, 1861. Eleven days after, October 30th, he was promoted to the Colonelcy. Here his administrative and executive abilities were particularly marked, in the high degree of discipline and efficiency to which he soon brought his regiment. It became one of the best in the Army of the Potomac, and greatly assisted in gaining for Rhode Island the reputation which she holds among her sister States for the excellent character of her troops. When General Burnside was appointed to the command of the North Carolina expedition, he solicited and obtained the 4th Rhode Island for a portion of his army. The services which Colonel Rodman and his regiment rendered in the battles of Roanoke Island and Newbern have already been enumerated. The gallant charge which they made in the last named action gave Colonel Rodman a wide celebrity and attracted the attention of the War Department at Washington. He was accordingly promoted to Brigadier General, his commission dating April 28, 1862, a few days after the surrender of Fort Macon, in operations against which Colonel Rodman had been engaged.

Upon the reorganization of General Burnside's command, General Rodman was appointed to the command of a brigade. Returning home on sick leave soon afterwards, he spent a few weeks at his residence in South Kingstown. He rejoined the army on the 6th day of August, reporting to General Burnside at Fredericksburg. He was assigned to the command of the third (General Parke's late) division, and in that capacity entered upon the Maryland campaign. Here, as elsewhere, his courage and skill were abundantly proved. He led his division at South Mountain and again at Antietam with the same gallantry which he had displayed at Newbern. Shunning no danger, avoiding no duty, he was everywhere fearless and always faithful. He received his death wound in the final struggle that took place beyond the bridge of Antietam, near the close of the battle. He fell in the front with his face to the foe. He was borne from the field and carefully attended. Removed to the house of Mr. Rohrback, near Sharpsburg, close by the scene of the fight, nursed by his wife, tenderly treated by the best available medical skill, he lingered for twelve weary and painful days, and, on the morning of the 30th of September quietly breathed his last. He retained all his mental faculties to the latest moment. Knowing from the first, that all which friendship and affection could do was not sufficient to save his life, he was perfectly submissive and thoroughly trustful. Not a complaint or murmur escaped his lips, though he was at times suffering great pain from internal bleeding. But he endured all with the calmness and composure of a brave, true and Christian man. His Bible was his daily companion, and, after he fell, it was found beneath his uniform stained with his blood. He was particularly kind-hearted, of great nobility and manliness of character, of a pure Christian faith, and possessed to a degree not often witnessed among those who have been trained to middle age in the pursuit of a civil life, the capabilities and tastes of a good soldier. He brought the fidelity, which characterized him in business and domestic life, to the duties of the army, learned both how to obey and to command, and made himself by his own unwearied exertions a sagacious and skillful officer. His career is an additional illustration of the words of the poet:

> "The path of duty was the way to glory;
> He that walks it, only thirsting
> For the right, and learns to deaden
> Love of self, before his journey closes
> He shall find the stubborn thistle bursting
> Into glossy purples, which outredden
> All voluptuous garden roses.
> He, that ever following her commands,
> On with toil of heart and knees and hands,
> Through the long gorge to the far light has won
> His path upward and prevailed,
> Shall find the toppling crags of duty scaled
> Are close upon the shining table lands,
> To which our God Himself is moon and sun."*

---

* Soon after General Rodman's death, General Burnside testified to the estimation in which he held his late friend and companion in arms, by the following order addressed to the Corps:

"The Commanding General announces to the Third Division the death of their late commander, Brigadier General Rodman, caused by a wound received at the battle of Antietam.

One of the first to leave his home at his country's call, General Rodman, in his constant and unwearied service, now ended by his untimely death, has left a bright record of earnest patriotism undimmed by one thought of self.

Respected and esteemed in the various relations of his life, the army mourns his loss as a pure-hearted patriot and a brave, devoted soldier, and his division will miss a gallant leader who was always foremost at the post of danger."

CHAPTER IV.

AFTER ANTIETAM.

THE morning of the 18th of September found the two hostile armies still confronting each other. General McClellan had been reënforced during the night, in numbers sufficient to cover the losses of the preceding day. But the right wing had been so badly shaken, and, to a degree, demoralized, that it was not deemed advisable to attack. General Burnside expressed the opinion that our army ought to renew the battle, for the enemy had been worse shaken than we, and an assault upon his position promised every success. General Burnside visited General McClellan's headquarters to urge this course, declaring that "with five thousand fresh troops to pass in advance of his line, he would be willing to commence the attack."* But the commanding general of the army was not disposed to recommence the strife, and though General Morell's division was sent over to relieve General Burnside's more advanced troops, there were no orders to attack. General McClellan thought the responsibility too grave, and dared not take it. On the other hand, the enemy was in no humor for more fighting. The 18th was accordingly spent by both armies in quiet. The wounded were collected and cared for, the dead were buried, and new dispositions for further movements made. Possibly the battle might have been renewed on the 19th; but General Lee did not wait for any such contingency. During the night of the 18th–19th, he quietly moved his entire army, with the exception of some wounded men, all his serviceable artillery,

* Report of Committee on the Conduct of the War. Part I. p. 642.

wagons, ammunition and supplies across the Potomac, and took post on the opposite bank, near Shepherdstown. He retired at his ease, wholly unmolested. "He leaves us," says an army correspondent,* "the debris of his late camp, two disabled pieces of artillery, a few hundred of his stragglers, perhaps two thousand of his wounded and as many more of his unburied dead. Not a sound field piece, caisson, ambulance, or wagon; not a tent, box of stores, or a pound of ammunition. He takes with him the supplies gathered in Maryland and the rich spoils of Harper's Ferry." General Lee seems to have been satisfied with the result. At all events, he put a bold face upon it, and declared that History recorded "few examples of greater fortitude and endurance than" his "army had exhibited."

At daylight on the 19th, therefore, at which time it had been determined to renew the battle, our troops found that there was nobody to fight. The enemy had disappeared. Our cavalry started in pursuit, but found, on reaching the Potomac, that batteries of artillery were frowning upon the opposite bank and forbidding further progress. General Charles Griffin, with a detachment from his own brigade and that of General Barnes, was sent across at dark on the evening of the 19th, and captured several pieces of artillery. A subsequent reconnaissance on the 20th, was attended with severe loss, and the reconnoitering party was driven back by heavy forces under the command of General Hill. Our troops recrossed the river, and for the time all hostilities were mutually suspended.

It is not within the province of this volume to discuss the military questions which have arisen respecting the issue of the battle of Antietam. There can be no question, however, that the result, so far as General McClellan was concerned, was seriously to impair what little confidence the country reposed in him after the disasters of the Peninsula. Even many of his friends, who had been willing to excuse the want of suc-

---

* New York Tribune, of Sept. 22.

cess in front of Richmond on account of the peculiar circumstances of the case, could not look with complacency upon his refusal to renew the battle on the 18th. If, as he declared, he had defeated the enemy, it was certainly his duty to follow up his victory. But, if there were no victory on his part, it was simply an additional failure, when he had every instrumentality by which success could be gained. If he could not win at Antietam, the public did not believe that he could win anywhere. There is no necessity of expressing any opinion upon the subject. But the fact that, instead of gaining, General McClellan lost the public confidence after Antietam is as significant as it is indisputable.

Perhaps the enemy was no better satisfied than we. It was thought, on the other side of the Potomac, that General Lee had not achieved a very remarkable success. Indeed, if the abandonment of his chosen position after the battle be the indication of defeat, or, at least, an expression of conscious weakness, the enemy had not much occasion for self-congratulation. General Lee had fought a great battle, had fought it well. But he had not defeated his adversary. He had only held him at bay. He had also left in his hands thousands of his dead and wounded, and, availing himself of the darkness of the night, had hastened to put a broad river between himself and his opponent. Thus, at least, he had confessed his inability to withstand another resolute attack. Mr. Pollard's statement—whatever estimate may be put upon his volumes as records of historical facts—may well be taken as the expression of the average public sentiment at the South upon the subject: "Let it be freely confessed that the object of General Lee, in crossing the Potomac, was to hold and occupy Maryland; that his proclamation issued at Frederick, offering protection to the Marylanders, is incontrovertible evidence of the fact; that he was forced to return to Virginia, not by stress of any single battle, but by the force of many circumstances, some of which history should blush to record; that, in these results, the Maryland campaign was a failure."* Nor did the reception which the people of Maryland gave to General Lee and his troops afford much encouragement to the Southern hopes. The whole number of recruits to the rebel army did not exceed eight hundred men. The Southern historian thinks that something of all this was due to the fact that the army of General Lee marched only through the two counties that contained the "most violent Union population in Maryland." Something was also due to the fact that there was no possibility of a successful rising in Baltimore against the overwhelming forces of "Federal bayonets," or the guns of Fort McHenry. "It is true, that the South could not have expected a welcome in these counties, or a desperate mutiny for the Confederacy in Baltimore. But," he adds, with a grim sort of sarcasm, "it was expected that Southern sympathizers in other parts of the State, who so glibly ran the blockade on adventures of trade, might as readily work their way to the Confederate army as to the Confederate markets; and it was not expected that the few recruits who timidly advanced to our lines would have been so easily dismayed by the rags of our soldiers and by the prospects of a service that promised equal measures of hardship and glory."† On the whole, we may conclude that the campaign, which, in Southern eyes, bore upon the surface so brilliant and glorious an aspect, was barren in results, and had not so promising a character when closely examined. The "Southern Confederacy" was no nearer recognition after it than when the Army of the Potomac beleaguered Richmond. Suffice it now to say that the South had gained nothing by the campaign of its army in Maryland. On the contrary, the cause of the Union had added to its strength. It was reënenforced by the Emancipation Proclamation of Mr. Lincoln, issued soon after the battle, to take practical effect on the 1st of January, 1863. Thenceforward, the war for the Union was emphatically a war for Liberty, and recognition of

* Pollard's History of the Second Year of the War, p. 141. ‡ Pollard, p. 142.

Southern Confederacies—one or many—became forever impossible!

For the next few weeks both armies rested on opposite banks of the Potomac. General Lee posted his forces in front of Winchester, reaching from Martinsburg to the Shenandoah river, thus guarding the entrance of the valley. General McClellan arranged his lines reaching from the Williamsport ford on the right to Harper's Ferry on the left. Both armies received reënforcements, but neither general thought himself strong enough to initiate an aggressive movement. The Ninth Corps was posted in Pleasant Valley, and for some time enjoyed the rest which the quiet autumnal season gave. Nothing of moment to this corps occurred during the time except the departure of the Kanawha division, which was peremptorily ordered to West Virginia on the 7th of October, and started on the 8th.* General Cox had proved himself an able soldier in the scenes of the Maryland campaign, and had won the hearty recommendation both of Generals Burnside and McClellan for promotion. "His gallant services," says General McClellan, "in the battle of South Mountain and at the Antietam, contributed greatly towards our success in those hard fought engagements. I concur in the recommendation of General Burnside, and request that the promotion be made at once." These recommendations had the desired effect, and on the 8th of October General Cox was appointed Major General by the President. The number of promotions, however, exceeded that authorized by Congress, and this appointment with others was not confirmed. He had been appointed Brigadier General of Volunteers from civil life in the early days of the war, his commission dating May 7, 1861. He served faithfully and well in West Virginia, and in the summer of 1862 was in command of the District of the Kanawha. On the 15th of August he started with a division, consisting of the 11th, 12th,

*The first order for General Cox's movement is dated October 4th, but General McClellan delayed obedience.

Eng.d by J. C. Buttre.

J. D. Cox

MAJ. GEN. J. DOLSON COX.

23d, 28th, 30th, and 36th Ohio Regiments, two batteries of artillery and one troop of cavalry—organized in two brigades, Colonel E. P. Scammon and Colonel A. Moore commanding—to reënforce General Pope in Virginia. The troops started from Flat Top Mountain, marched to the head of navigation on the Kanawha, a distance of ninety miles in three and one-fourth days, and were thence transported by boat and rail to Washington. They reached Washington several days before the second battle of Bull Run, and went into the fortifications around the city. Colonel Scammon's brigade was sent out to Union Mills, where the Alexandria and Orange railroad crosses Bull Run, on the 26th of August and did excellent service there in checking the enemy's advance in that direction. Colonel Scammon conducted the hazardous enterprise with great skill. He held the bridge a long time against a superior force, retired at last in good order, eluded the efforts of the enemy to surround him and brought off his command with but little loss.

Upon the reörganization of the Army of the Potomac, General Cox's division was assigned to the Ninth Corps, and the extremely good service which it and its commander rendered has been previously recorded. It manfully bore its part in every position and attested its gallantry by the losses which it suffered. General Cox, in his report of the battle of South Mountain, mentions with great commendation Lieutenant Colonel R. B. Hayes commanding the 23rd Ohio, who was severely wounded but refused to leave the field until compelled by loss of blood, Major E. M. Carey of the 12th Ohio, who was shot through the thigh after greatly distinguishing himself in the action, and Lieutenant Croome who was killed while personally serving a gun of his battery. He mentions in his report of the battle of Antietam the death of Lieutenant Colonel A. H. Coleman commanding the 11th Ohio, and of Lieutenant Colonel Clark commanding the 36th Ohio. They were both excellent officers and "were killed while heroically leading their men under a terrible fire of shell, canister and musketry." General Cox throughout the war always did his duty with effectiveness and promptitude. He was placed in command of the District of Western Virginia, and served in that quarter for a considerable time. In the winter of 1863–'64 he was in command of the twenty-third corps, and rendered the Ninth Corps great assistance in its campaign in East Tennessee. He afterwards distinguished himself in General Sherman's movement against Atlanta, in the pursuit of Hood after the occupation of Atlanta by our troops, in the battle of Franklin under General Schofield on the 30th of November, 1864, in the battle of Nashville under General Thomas on the 15th and 16th of December, and in the closing movements of General Sherman's great campaign through Georgia and the Carolinas. His command in the army of the Ohio under General Schofield was transferred from Tennessee after the battle of Nashville and was moved to North Carolina, arriving at Goldsboro' on the 21st of March, 1865. His advancement came tardily, but it came at last, and he was promoted to the rank of Major General—his commission dating December 7, 1864—for the gallant service which he had performed at the battles of Franklin and Nashville. At the close of the war he resigned his commission, and was elected Governor of Ohio on the 14th of October, 1865. In civil as in military life he has shown himself to be a prompt, efficient and gallant gentleman, wearing his honors modestly and gracefully, and giving promise of greater distinction in the future. His connection with the Ninth Corps was very creditable to himself, and General Burnside parted from him with feelings of real regret. General Cox's staff while in command of the corps was composed of the following named gentlemen: Captain G. M. Bascom, Assistant Adjutant General; First Lieutenant James W. Conine, First Lieutenant Samuel L. Christie, (both of the 1st Kentucky regiment,) Aides de Camp; Major W. W. Holmes, Medical Director; Captaiu E. B. Fitch, Quartermaster; Captain R. B. Treat, Commissary of Subsistence.

Upon the departure of General Cox, Brigadier General Orlando B. Willcox was assigned to the command of the corps.

Soon afterwards, Brigadier General W. W. Burns was assigned to the command of General Willcox's division and Brigadier General G. W. Getty to the command of that of the late General Rodman.

The chief event of interest at this time was a raid, which the rebel cavalry under General J. E. B. Stuart made, entirely around General McClellan's army. The enemy's party started from camp at midnight on the 9th of October, crossed the Potomac between Williamsport and Hancock at dawn on the 10th, marched rapidly up the Cumberland valley—passing the rear of General Cox's command but an hour behind—and arrived in the outskirts of Chambersburg, Penn., about nightfall. General Stuart immediately occupied the town and remained there through the night, carefully respecting the rights of private property, with a few exceptions, and treating the inhabitants with kindness. We had no military force at Chambersburg. Two hundred and seventy-five sick and wounded men were found in hospital and paroled. A large quantity of arms, ammunition and clothing belonging to the army was destroyed. The extensive machine shops and depot buildings of the railroad company were consumed. The next morning the enemy's cavalry left Chambersburg, entered Maryland at Emmetsburg, crossed the Monocacy at a point twelve or fifteen miles above Frederick, thence marched through Liberty, New Market and Hyattstown, and during the forenoon of the 12th escaped across the Potomac. This raid accomplished nothing beyond plundering the country of horses, forage, aud such light articles as could readily be carried and destroying the public stores at Chambersburg. But it was a daring feat, and it was accomplished with but insignificant loss to the enemy. The expedition was a source of considerable mortification to General McClellan and of some alarm to the people of the North, who perceived how easily an adventurous leader with a small band of partizans could penetrate an undefended territory, and, by rapid marching and skillful manœuvering, elude pursuit and make good his escape. General McClellan complained, that he was deficient in cavalry and said that he must be better supplied with horses for remounts, and that too "within the shortest possible time." Otherwise, he declared, he would "be constantly exposed to rebel cavalry raids." Mr. Lincoln read the despatch and, with his accustomed shrewdness, directed General Halleck to suggest "that if the enemy had more occupation south of the river, his cavalry would not be so likely to make raids north of it."

The truth was, that the President and the country were becoming impatient on account of the continued inactivity of General McClellan and his army. As early as the 6th of October, the President directed General McClellan to "cross and give battle to the enemy, or drive him South." But General McClellan, instead of obeying this distinct command, still made excuses, found occasions for delays, objected to the different orders sent from Washington, endeavored to argue the cases presented, complained of want of supplies, and spent a large part of his time in correspondence with the heads of the different departments of the army in Washington. Horses, shoes, clothing and other needful things, in ample quantities, seem to have been sent from the Quartermaster's stores in Washington, but, by some miscarriage, could not readily reach the camps of the soldiers.* It began to be suspected that General McClellan did not wish to cross the Potomac, that he intended to go into winter quarters along the line of the Upper Potomac, and wait for the following Spring before he inaugurated another campaign in Virginia. It was supposed that the march of the army was to be delayed, under various pretexts, until the season had become so far advanced as to make any movement impracticable. Whether the latter supposition had any foundation in fact, cannot now be known. That the former opinion

---

* It was said at the time, that cars filled with supplies were allowed to remain unloaded at Hagerstown and other points. General Meigs's Letter to General McClellan, October 22, 1862, in Report of Committee on the Conduct of the War, I., 539. It is fair to add that General Ingalls denied the truth of the statement.

rested on good grounds, there can be but little doubt. General officers, who were friends and admirers of General McClellan, virtually admitted as much to the writer of these pages, in a familiar conversation with him in the latter part of the following December, at General Burnside's headquarters at Falmouth. General McClellan did not wish to march against the enemy in the neighborhood of Winchester. The authorities at Washington determined that he should move, and nearly the entire month of October was occupied in the discussion of this simple proposition. The President was particularly anxious that the army should move, and on the 13th wrote a long letter to General McClellan on the subject, which has been several times published. This letter was of so important a character and bearing upon subsequent operations, and exhibited so clearly the President's characteristics, as to make it desirable to reprint it here, though at the risk of repeating what may be already familiar to the reader:

"EXECUTIVE MANSION,
Washington, October 13, 1862.

"MAJOR GENERAL McCLELLAN:

"MY DEAR SIR,—You remember my speaking to you of what I called your over-cautiousness. Are you not over-cautious when you assume that you cannot do what the enemy is constantly doing? Should you not claim to be at least his equal in prowess and act upon the claim?

"As I understand, you telegraph General Halleck that you cannot subsist your army at Winchester, unless the railroad from Harper's Ferry to that point be put in working order. But the enemy does now subsist his army at Winchester, at a distance nearly twice as great from railroad transportation as you would have to do without the railroad last named. He now wagons from Culpepper Court House, which is just about twice as far as you would have to do from Harper's Ferry. He is certainly not more than half as well provided with wagons as you are. I certainly should be pleased for you to have the advantage of the railroad from Harper's Ferry to Winchester, but it wastes all the remainder of autumn to give it to you; and in fact, ignores the question of time, which cannot and must not be ignored.

"Again, one of the standard maxims of war, as you know, is 'to operate upon the enemy's communications as much as possible, without exposing your own.' You seem to act as if this applies *against* you, but cannot apply in your *favor*. Change positions with the enemy, and think you not he would break your communications with Richmond within the next twenty-four hours? You dread his going into Pennsylvania. But if he does so in full force, he gives up his communications to you absolutely, and you have nothing to do but to follow and ruin him; if he does so with less than full force, fall upon and beat what is left behind all the easier.

"Exclusive of the water-line, you are now nearer Richmond than the enemy is, by the route that you *can* and he *must* take. Why can you not reach there before him, unless you admit that he is more than your equal on a march? His route is the arc of a circle, while yours is the chord. The roads are as good on yours as on his.

"You know I desired, but did not order you to cross the Potomac below instead of above the Shenandoah and Blue Ridge. My idea was that this would at once menace the enemy's communications, which I would seize if he would permit. If he should move northward, I would follow him closely, holding his communications. If he should prevent our seizing his communications, and move towards Richmond, I would press closely to him, fight him if a favorable opportunity should present, and at least try to beat him to Richmond on the inside track. I say 'try;' if we never try, we shall never succeed. If he make a stand at Winchester, moving neither north or south, I would fight him there, on the idea that if we cannot beat him when he bears the wastage of coming to us, we never can when we bear the wastage of going to him. This proposition is a simple truth, and is too important to be lost sight of for a moment. In coming to us, he tenders us an advantage which we should not waive. We should not so operate as to merely drive him away. As we must beat him somewhere, or fail finally, we can do it, if at all, easier near to us than far away. If we cannot beat the enemy where he now is, we never can, he again being within the intrenchments of Richmond.

"Recurring to the idea of going to Richmond on the inside track, the facility of supplying from the side away from the enemy is remarkable—as it were by the different spokes of a wheel extending from the hub towards the rim—and this whether you move directly by the chord, or on the inside arc, hugging the Blue Ridge more closely. The chord line, as you see, carries you by Aldie, Haymarket and Fredericksburg; and you see how turnpikes, railroads, and finally the Potomac by Aquia Creek, meet you at all points from Washington. The same, only the lines lengthened a little, if you press closer to the Blue Ridge part of the way. The gaps through the Blue Ridge, I understand to be about the following distances from Harper's Ferry, to wit: Vestal's, five miles; Gregory's, thirteen; Snicker's, eighteen; Ashby's, twenty-eight; Manassas, thirty-eight; Chester's forty-five; and Thornton's, fifty-three. I should think it preferable to take the route nearest the enemy, disabling him from making an important move without your knowledge, and compelling him to keep his forces together, for dread of you. The gaps would enable you to attack if you should wish. For a great part of the way, you would be practically between the enemy and both Washington and Richmond, enabling us to spare you the greatest number of troops from here. When at length running for Richmond ahead of him enables him to move this way, if he does so, turn and attack him in rear. But I think he should be engaged long before such point is reached. It is all easy, if our troops march as well as the enemy, and it is unmanly to say they cannot do it. This letter is in no sense an order.

"Yours truly, A. LINCOLN."

It was evident, by the latter part of October, that the movement could not be delayed longer upon any pretext. But the weather had now become cold and stormy. The rains made the roads heavy, and the tops of the mountains began to whiten, as the early snows settled down upon them. General Halleck became more and more impatient, and somewhat sharp in his language. At last, on the 26th of October, the army commenced crossing the Potomac upon a ponton bridge, at Berlin, the divisions of Generals Burns and Sturgis of the Ninth Corps, being in advance, with General Pleasonton's cavalry. The weather was very bad, and the troops suffered much. Having spent the fine weather in camp, the army moved in a storm. Two detached divisions, respectively under the command of General Stoneman and General Whipple, were now added to the command of General Burnside, and these, with the two divisions of the Ninth Corps already across, formed the vanguard of the army. The command, with the exception of General Stoneman's division, marched to Lovettsville and on the night of the 26th there encamped. On the 27th General Getty's division crossed. The cavalry advanced to Purcellsville. General Stoneman's division crossed at Edwards' Ferry on the 29th and occupied Leesburg. The other portions of the army crossed at different times between the 26th of October and the 2d of November, at Berlin and other places below. The movement, thus commenced, was continued with commendable promptness—both with caution and celerity. The Ninth Corps, having the advance with General Pleasonton's cavalry, came occasionally into collision with the enemy's skirmishers. But in general the march was made with but little serious interruption. The gaps of the mountains were successively occupied, and the army wound its way along upon the eastern side of the Blue Ridge.

On the 2d of November the Ninth Corps advanced to Bloomfield, Union and Philomont. On the 4th it was at Upperville. On the 5th it was beyond the Manassas Railroad, between Piedmont and Salem, with one brigade guarding

Manassas Gap. On the 6th the corps had moved up to and occupied Waterloo and its neighborhood on the Rappahannock. The army was closed up on the two following days, and on the evening of the 9th the entire command was in position as follows: "The first, second and fifth corps, reserve artillery and general headquarters were at Warrenton; the Ninth Corps on the line of the Rappahannock, in the vicinity of Waterloo; the sixth corps at New Baltimore; the eleventh corps at New Baltimore, Gainesville and Thoroughfare Gap; Sickles's division of the third corps on the Orange and Alexandria Railroad from Manassas Junction to Warrenton Junction; Pleasonton across the Rappahannock at Annissville, Jefferson, &c., with his pickets at Hazel river facing Longstreet, six miles from Culpepper Court House; Bayard near Rappahannock station."* The enemy had not yet emerged from the Shenandoah valley with his entire force. General Longstreet "was immediately in our front near Culpepper," with the advance of the rebel army. But the remainder of the enemy's command had not yet come up. General Jackson with—as supposed—Generals A. P. and D. H. Hill, was near Chester's and Thornton's Gaps, and the most of their force was west of the Blue Ridge. A heavy snow storm set in on the morning of the 7th, and continued for two days, changing to rain. The situation was excessively uncomfortable, and the roads were in very bad condition. But the entire command was well closed up. And as no apprehensions were entertained of any immediate trouble with the enemy, the army was in good spirits, "perfectly in hand" and in "excellent condition to fight a great battle."

Late on the night of the 7th, a special messenger from the War Department at Washington arrived at General McClellan's Headquarters, bearing the following order:

"WASHINGTON, Nov. 5, 1862.

"By direction of the President of the United States, it is ordered that Major General McClellan be relieved from the

---

*McClellan's Report, p. 237.

command of the Army of the Potomac, and that Major General Burnside take the command of that army.

"By order of the Secretary of War,
E. D. TOWNSEND, *Ass't. Adj't. Gen.*

On the 9th of November General Burnside assumed the command of the Army of the Potomac, and issued the following order:

"HEADQUARTERS, ARMY OF THE POTOMAC,
"WARRENTON, VA., Nov. 9, 1862.

"General Orders, No. 1.

"In accordance with General Orders, No. 182, issued by the President of the United States, I hereby assume command of the Army of the Potomac.

"Patriotism and the exercise of my every energy, in the direction of this army, aided by the full and hearty coöperation of its officers and men, will, I hope, under the blessing of God, ensure its success.

"Having been a sharer of the privations and a witness of the bravery of the old army of the Potomac in the Maryland campaign, and fully identified in their feelings of respect and esteem for General McClellan, entertained through a long and most friendly association with him, I feel that it is not as a stranger that I assume this command.

"To the Ninth Corps, so long and intimately associated with me, I need say nothing; our histories are identical.

"With diffidence for myself, but with a proud confidence in the unswerving loyalty and determination of the gallant army now entrusted to my care, I accept its control with the steadfast assurance that the just cause must prevail.

"A. E. BURNSIDE,
"*Major General Commanding.*"

General Burnside's assignment to the command of the Army of the Potomac separated him for a time from the intimate, personal control of the Ninth Corps which he had heretofore exercised. The confidence and esteem which had existed between the men and officers of the corps and himself continued unabated. But they were now obliged to look to another commander, to be immediately present with them in the scenes of danger and duty which were now before them. Major General Parke followed his friend and became Chief of Staff of the Army of the Potomac. Brigadier General Orlando B. Willcox, who had been assigned to the command of the Ninth Corps upon the retirement of General Cox, was still continued in command. The organization of the corps at this time was as follows: First Division under the command of Brigadier General W. W. Burns, consisting of two brigades, respectively under the command of Colonels Thomas Welsh and B. C. Christ; Second Division under the command of Brigadier General Samuel D. Sturgis, consisting of two brigades respectively under the command of Brigadier Generals James Nagle and Edward Ferrero; Third Division under the command of Brigadier General G. W. Getty, consisting of two brigades respectively under the command of Colonels R. C. Hawkins and Edward Harland. The artillery was distributed as follows: First Division, Dickinson's Battery E, 4th New York artillery, and Durell's Battery A, 104th Pennsylvania artillery; Second Division, Benjamin's Battery E, 2d United States artillery, Cook's 8th Massachusetts battery; Third Division, Whitney's howitzer battery, 9th New York, Edwards's two sections each of batteries L and M, 3d United States, and Muhlenburg's battery A, 5th United States Artillery. General Willcox had already seen much and painful service and it may not be inappropriate to insert here a brief account in detail of his career up to this point.

Orlando Bolivar Willcox was born in Detroit, Mich., April 16, 1823. Securing an appointment to the Military Academy at West Point, he graduated from that institution, the eighth in his class, June, 1847. He was promoted to Second Lieutenant July 1, 1847, was soon after assigned to Light Battery

G, 4th United States Artillery, joined his company in Mexico, and served with faithfulness and efficiency in that country, on the Western Plains, in Texas and in Florida. He was also stationed at different times at Forts Washington, Ontario, Mifflin and Independence. He was promoted to a First Lieutenancy in 1850. But his tastes afterwards led him towards civil life, and on the 10th of September, 1857 he resigned his commission in the army, was immediately admitted to the bar at Detroit, and commenced the practice of the profession of law in his native city. He was gradually winning his way to an honorable place in his new profession, when the rebellion broke out. Like other army officers who had retired to civil life, he heard the summons to arms—as though it was personally addressed to himself. He accepted the command of the 1st Regiment of Michigan Volunteers, and was mustered into the service of the United States as Colonel on the 1st of May, 1861. When the decision was made to march into Virginia, the 1st Michigan was selected to form a portion of the force. Colonel Willcox led his regiment into Alexandria on the night of the 24th of May, and captured a company of rebel cavalry that was quartered there under command of Captain Ball. He was appointed Military Governor of the city upon its permanent occupation by our troops. In the advance on Manassas, Colonel Willcox was assigned to the command of the Second Brigade in Colonel Heintzelman's Division, and, marching on Fairfax Station, July 17th, took eleven prisoners and one stand of colors.

In the battle of Bull Run on the 21st of July, Colonel Willcox's brigade was engaged about noon and fought very bravely, until its commander was severely wounded and taken prisoner, when its position was turned, and the army was driven back to Centreville. Colonel Willcox tasted the bitterness of Southern imprisonment, at Richmond, Charleston, Columbia and Salisbury, at one time being held as one of the hostages for some captured privateersmen whom we held in our hands. For a period of twelve months and twenty-six days he

Engd by A.H. Ritchie.

O. B. Willcox
Brig. Genl. Vols.

was a prisoner in the hands of the enemy. In August, 1862, he was released, to the great joy of his friends, and was immediately appointed Brigadier General of Volunteers, his commission dating from the day of the battle of Bull Run, July 21, 1861.

On the 8th of September he joined the Ninth Corps at Leesboro', Md., and was assigned to the command of the division lately under the command of the lamented General Stevens. From that time forward until the end of the war, General Willcox was connected with the Ninth Corps, serving sometimes in command of the Corps, sometimes in command of a division, and proving himself, as the reader will have occasion to see in the course of this narrative, a gallant soldier and an honorable gentleman. He had long been an intimate friend of General Burnside, and the two companions in arms shared together many a scene of peril and of glory.

CHAPTER V.

TOWARDS FREDERICKSBURG.

WHAT to do with the large army now entrusted to his guidance was now the anxious question which General Burnside discussed with himself. He accepted the command with the greatest reluctance. With as genuine a modesty as that which characterized Washington himself, when he was appointed Commander-in-Chief of the armies in our Revolution, he shrank from the responsibility and the task. He confessed that he was not competent for the command. Washington, with all his consciousness of the possession of great gifts, did not hesitate to write to his wife and his intimate friends, that he considered the duty as "a trust too great for" his "capacity;" and also to declare in his place in the Congress that appointed him: "I beg it may be remembered by every gentleman in the room, that I this day declare, with the utmost sincerity, I do not think myself equal to the command I am honored with." But, in writing to his wife, he said, "I shall rely confidently on that Providence which has heretofore preserved and been bountiful to me." General Burnside had as sincere a humility and as profound a trust. He has never rated himself at as high an estimate as his friends are accustomed to place upon him. He has cherished no particle of that overweening self-confidence which considers itself equal to every duty and every occasion, and which boastfully promises large results ere yet the enterprise has fairly commenced. It might have been an undue self-distrust that led him to say that he did not consider himself competent to command the Army of the Potomac, but the remark was made with entire sincerity.

General Burnside's feelings at this time may be clearly understood by the language which he used in a letter that he wrote to one of his friends, under date of November 21, 1862. "You," he wrote, "who know how much I feel any responsibility placed upon me, can readily imagine how much of my time is occupied with this enormous command. You will remember that when I was with you in the field with a comparatively small command, I felt that I could do nothing of myself, and I then felt, more than ever in my life, the need of an entire reliance upon an all-wise Creator. But now the responsibility is so great that at times I tremble at the thought of assuming that I am able to exercise so large a command. Yet, when I think that I have made no such assumption; that I have shunned the responsibility, and only accepted it when I was ordered to do it, and when it would have been disloyal and unfriendly to our government not to do it, then I take courage, and I approach our Heavenly Father with freedom and trustfulness, confident that if I can act honestly and industriously, constantly asking His protection and assistance, all will be well, no matter how dark everything now seems to me." In the spirit of such a noble self-distrust and of such a complete faith in Divine Providence did General Burnside take command of the Army of the Potomac.

It was a vast responsibility. All the forces that were guarding the Upper Potomac, and those that were in the defences around Washington, were then subject to the orders of the general commanding this army. Not only was General Burnside to fight the foe immediately before him, but he was also to guard the approaches to the Capital by flank and rear. In round numbers, there were, on the 10th of November, two hundred and twenty-five thousand men, fit for duty, distributed around the points which have been named. Of these, one hundred and twenty-seven thousand five hundred and seventy-four officers and men were in the immediate front facing the enemy.

The command of this immediate army was a position and duty of no small magnitude. It was a force which must be effectively used upon the foes of the country. It must not be allowed to remain inactive. Though the season was now far advanced, and the frequent storms that had prevailed seemed to indicate that winter had set in, it was yet hoped that a decisive blow might be struck. Early in the autumn a levy of three hundred thousand men, for nine months' service, had been made, and it would be ruinous to the finances and faith of the country to leave this immense force unemployed. The country, the President and the General-in-Chief had been impatient of the slow policy which General McClellan had seen fit to adopt, and it was deemed best that the Army of the Potomac should take the aggressive. General Burnside believed that there was ample time yet to carry on a campaign against Richmond. The military strength of the Union seemed to lie in the Army of the Potomac. He who could lead that army to a victory, which would break the military power of the rebellion residing in General Lee's "Army of Northern Virginia," would be hailed as the deliverer of the Republic. Such a victory would be a great public benefit, as well as a prize brilliant enough to satisfy any man's ambition. But it could not be won by any hand that derived its strength from personal ambition. Whatever was to be done must be done with a spirit of humble, loyal, faithful duty.

Having received the order assigning him to the command of the Army of the Potomac, General Burnside's next step was to devise some plan for future operations. A movemeut upon Gordonsville, or even upon Culpepper, appeared hardly feasible, as it was liable to the risk of fighting an uncertain battle at a distance from the base. It is most probable that General McClellan had been contemplating a movement in a different direction, as on the 6th of November, before he had been relieved of command, he had given orders for the removal of his ponton train from Berlin to Washington, with a view to its further use at a subsequent and early day.* General Haupt, the superintendent of transportation, did not report encouragingly respecting the condition of the railroad from Alexandria for forwarding supplies. The President, in his letter of October 13th, had very strongly expressed his opinion respecting the proper route of the army towards Richmond. This letter was placed in General Burnside's hands at the same time with the order assigning him to the command. The suggestions thus made were not indeed to be considered as orders, but rather as indications of the President's plan of action. Of course, they had all the weight which Mr. Lincoln's sagacity and position could give to them. Some of them already had been followed. The army had moved down the east side of Blue Ridge, quite near to the enemy, "disabling him from making any important move without" the knowledge of the general commanding our army, and "compelling him to keep his forces together for dread of" us. But Mr. Lincoln had suggested another operation, viz.: moving upon the chord of a circle, while the enemy was moving upon the arc. He had

* General McClellan, in his report, endeavors to make the impression, without directly asserting it, that he was about to fight a great battle with the enemy at the time of his removal from the command. An examination of his language will show that he does not distinctly state that it was his real intention to fight. He hoped that he could either "separate the enemy's army and beat it in detail," or else force him to "concentrate as far back as Gordonsville, and thus place the Army of the Potomac in position either to adopt the Fredericksburg line of advance upon Richmond or to be removed to the Peninsula." "Had I remained in command," he says again, "I should have made the attempt to divide the enemy." Afterwards he declares that he followed the retreating enemy to a position where he was "confident of decisive victory, when in the midst of the movement, while" the "advance guard was actually in contact with the enemy," he was removed from command. His plan to divide the enemy was to march in between Culpepper Court House and Little Washington. Its success was problematical. He certainly had the Fredericksburg route in mind, and was preparing for it by ordering his ponton bridge to Washington, there to be put upon wheels and be in readiness to march at once. This train was certainly not intended for an early advance towards Gordonsville. What he says about his advance guard was entirely irrelevant, inasmuch as it had been "in contact with the enemy" from the day it had crossed the Potomac. At the time he was relieved, there were no indications of an impending engagement.

23

also expressly mentioned Fredericksburg as one of the places or points through which this chord passed, and within easy and uninterrupted communication with Washington and other parts of the country, by way of the railroad to Aquia Creek and the Potomac river.

With these suggestions in mind, General Burnside prepared his plan of operations. Accompanying the order assigning him to the command was an order from General Halleck, directing him to report what he "purposed doing with" his troops. On the 9th of November General Burnside prepared his plan, and on the 10th sent it to Washington by Major E. M. Neill, who, on the 11th, delivered it to General G. W. Cullum, General Halleck's Chief of Staff. That plan can best be stated in General Burnside's own words. It was as follows:

"In accordance with the order of the General in Chief, of the 5th inst., I have the honor to make the following report of the movement proposed for this army:

"To concentrate all the forces near this place, and impress upon the enemy a belief that we are to attack Culpepper or Gordonsville, and at the same time accumulate a four or five days' supply for the men and animals. Then make a rapid move of the whole force to Fredericksburg, with a view to a movement upon Richmond from that point. The following are my reasons for deciding upon this plan:

"If we move upon Culpepper and Gordonsville, with a fight there, or a general engagement, even with results in our favor, the enemy will have many lines of retreat for his defeated army, and will in all likelihood be able to reach Richmond with enough of his force to render it necessary to fight another battle at that place, and should he leave even one corps, with cavalry, on our right flank, it would render the pursuit very precarious, owing to the great lack of supplies in this country, and the liability to an interruption of our communications with Washington. Should the enemy retreat in the direction of Richmond upon our approach to Culpepper and Gordonsville, we would simply follow a retreating army well supplied with provisions, at least at depots in his rear, whilst this army would have to rely upon a long line of communications for its supplies, and as in the other case, a small portion of the enemy's force on our flank might tend to interrupt our communications. It may be well to add here, while on the subject of interrupted communications, that the enemy's sources for gaining information are far superior to our own. The General in Chief will readily understand the reason—the difference is more than usual in their favor at present, from the fact that nearly all the negroes are being run South, and kept under strict guard. Should the enemy retreat before us in the direction of Staunton and Lynchburg, the same difficulty would follow, with the certainty that he would also have a small portion of his force on our left flank. In moving by way of Fredericksburg, there is no point up to the time when we should reach that place at which we will not be nearer to Washington than the enemy, and we will all the time be on the shortest road to Richmond, the taking of which, I think, should be the great object of the campaign, as the fall of that place would tend more to cripple the rebel cause than almost any other military event except the absolute breaking up of their army. The presence of a large army on the Fredericksburg line would render it almost impossible for the enemy to make a successful move upon Washington, by any road upon this side of the Potomac. I take it that there are forces enough at Washington, and on the line of the Potomac connected with the fortifications about Washington, to repulse any movement of the enemy on the Capital by way of the Upper Potomac. It is hardly probable that he would attempt any serious invasion of Pennsylvania at this season of the year, and even should he make a lodgement in that State of any force that he can spare, the destruction of that force would be the result very soon after winter sets in. The destruction of property by him would be small in comparison with the other expenses of the war. Could the army before Richmond be beaten and the rebel capital taken, the loss of half a dozen of our towns and cities in the interior of Pennsylvania could well be afforded. A movement of the enemy upon Baltimore I consider altogether improbable, as an attack upon that place would render the destruction of the city certain.

"In connection with this movement in the direction of Fredericksburg, I would suggest that at least thirty canal boats and barges be at once loaded with commissary stores and forage and be towed to the neighborhood of Aquia Creek, from which place they can be brought into Belle Plain after the arrival of our force in that vicinity. These should be followed at once by enough stores and forage to subsist the army for forty days. A great portion of these, I think, could be towed up the Rappahannock under convoy of light draft gun boats, but that is a matter for after consideration. It will be also necessary to start at once, from Washington or Alexandria, by way of Dumfries, a quantity of beef cattle, and all the wagon trains that can be spared filled with small rations, such as bread, salt, coffee, sugar, soap and candles. This train should be preceded by ponton trains enough to span the Rappahannock with two tracks. But a small escort of cavalry for this train would be necessary, as we would be all the time between the enemy and the train. I will, however, if notified of its departure by telegraph, see that it is protected by my cavalry. During these movements, it would be well for General Sigel to remain with his force at Centreville and its neighborhood, holding Manassas Junction, Thoroughfare Gap, Aldie and Leesburg with forces sufficient to protect them against any light attack, any one of which can fall back on the main body if attacked by too large a force. The main portion of his cavalry can be kept in Loudon county, where there is an abundance of subsistence and forage. Below Fredericksburg, between the Rappahannock and the Potomac, there must be quite an amount of forage, which could be used by our broken-down animals after we reach Fredericksburg. We will need some fresh horses and mules on our arrival, which can be driven direct from Washington on this side the Potomac, or direct from

Baltimore to Smith's Point, opposite Aquia Creek, from which place they can be brought over in ferry boats, several of which it would be advisable to send us. An abundance of horses can also be brought by light draft vessels from New York and Philadelphia to a point near Belle Plain, where they can be thrown overboard and swim ashore. I cannot impress too strongly upon the General-in-Chief the necessity of furnishing by all these means an abundant supply of horses, mules and beef cattle. These should be sent to Fredericksburg, even at the risk of arriving after we have left. After reaching Fredericksburg, our wagon trains can be organized and filled with at least twelve days' provisions, when a rapid movement can be made upon Richmond direct, by way of such roads as are open to us; and as soon as the army arrives in front of the place, an attack should be made at once, and with a strong hope of success. The details of the movement from Fredericksburg I will give you hereafter.

"A great reason for feeling that the Fredericksburg route is the best is that if we are detained by the elements it would be much better for us to be on that line.

"I hope the General in Chief will impress upon the Secretary of War the necessity of sanctioning the changes which I now propose to make in this army:

"First, to divide it into three grand divisions, right, left and centre, under command of the three ranking Generals present.

"Second, to do away with the very massive and elaborate Adjutant General's office at these headquarters, and require the different commanders of the grand divisions and corps to correspond directly with Washington in reference to all such matters as resignations, leaves of absence, discharges, recruiting service, &c., &c., about which they necessarily know more than I do. I should have to be governed by their suggestions, and the attention to these matters in detail would surround me with a large number of staff officials and embarrass me with a responsibility which I cannot assume.

"Third, to make Brigadier General Seth Williams an inspector of the different staff departments of the command, by which means I shall ascertain if these duties are properly performed by the persons to whom they are delegated.

"To keep my own Adjutant General, Lieutenant Colonel Lewis Richmond at my Headquarters, and to use as far as possible my own staff officers, with promotions necessary to their positions. I shall make as few changes as possible, but I am very anxious to keep my staff as small as possible and to throw the labor and detail upon the officers immediately in command of the troops. A telegraph from you approving of my plans will put us to work at once."

General Burnside's plan was, in brief, to demonstrate towards Culpepper, and then to make a rapid march to Falmouth, to cross the Rappahannock upon pontons at that place, to seize Fredericksburg and the heights beyond, and to establish a temporary base of supplies at Aquia Creek. The movement beyond Fredericksburg was to be a matter for subsequent consideration. But it was in General Burnside's mind to push immediately on towards Richmond upon the roads leading through Spottsylvania Court House, Bowling Green and the villages beyond; have supplies in waiting at York river, then cross the peninsula rapidly to the James river, and with that for a base, march direct upon the city of his destination.

General Burnside did not fix upon his plan of operations without consultation with other officers. He was aware of the value which attached to the advice of those who had made the art of war a study, and he was ready to listen to any suggestions which his brethren in arms might make. He was not tenacious of his own opinion, except as it could be supported by reasons which he deemed more powerful than those adduced by others. General Sigel suggested to General Burnside a plan, which contemplated a march towards the James River, striking it above Richmond, near Louisa Court House. But this proposition was rejected on account of the difficulty of moving the army through hostile territory to so great a distance from the base of supplies in an uncertain season of the year. General

Burnside adhered to his own plan, as in all respects the most feasible of any that occurred or were proposed to him.

Immediately upon the reception of General Burnside's plan, General Halleck made arrangements for an early interview at Warrenton. The consultation took place on the 12th and continued through a considerable part of the night and the following day. Generals Meigs and Haupt accompanied General Halleck and occasionally participated in the council. It was a very important interview and had a decided effect upon the issue of the campaign. The two officers were very earnest in the support of their respective opinions and the points presented in General Burnside's paper were fully examined and discussed. General Halleck urged the expediency of continuing the march of the army, retaining its present base, which would carry it towards Culpepper, assuming that that was the line suggested by the President. General Burnside was strenuous in his advocacy of the plan which he had already submitted, contending that that was in accordance with Mr. Lincoln's letter. After a long discussion, it was agreed that General Halleck would not take the responsibility of ordering the movement, but would consult the President in relation to the matter. If that functionary approved the new plan, General Halleck would telegraph from Washington to that effect, immediately upon his return. General Burnside also represented to General Halleck that, if the movement on Fredericksburg was made, telegraphic communication with Washington would necessarily be broken, and that General Halleck would be relied upon to provide for carrying out such parts of the plan as required action at Washington. He was assured that due attention would be paid to the subject by General Halleck, and that the General in Chief himself would at once "order by telegraph the ponton trains spoken of" in the plan, and "would, upon his return to Washington see that they were promptly forwarded."* Thus matters stood at the conclusion

*Burnside's Report.

of the interview, and on the afternoon of the 13th General Halleck returned to Washington. On the morning of the 14th, he telegraphed to General Burnside: "The President has just assented to your plan. He thinks it will succeed if you move rapidly, otherwise not." General Burnside immediately issued his orders for the movement of the army.

A conflict of statement now appears between Generals Burnside and Halleck, which it is necessary to examine. General Halleck, in his annual report for 1862–'63, declares that "General Burnside did not fully concur in the President's views, but finally consented to so modify his plan as to cross his army by the fords of the upper Rappahannock, and then move down and seize the heights south of Fredericksburg, while a small force was to be sent north of the river to enable General Haupt to re-open the railroad and to rebuild the bridges, the materials for which were nearly ready in Alexandria. I however refused," adds General Halleck, "to give any official approval of this deviation from the President's instructions. On my return to Washington on the 13th, I submitted to the President this proposed change in the plan of campaign, and on its receiving his assent, rather than approval, I telegraphed authority to General Burnside to adopt it. I here refer, not to General Burnside's written plan to go to Falmouth, but to that of crossing the Rappahannock above its junction with the Rapidan."* He again declares that General Burnside's "plan of marching his whole army from Warrenton to Falmouth," "was never approved, nor was he ever authorized to adopt it." Again he says, that General Burnside "could not possibly have expected supplies and pontons to be landed at points then occupied in force by the enemy"—meaning, it is presumed, Aquia Creek and Fredericksburg. Here are three distinct assertions, viz.: that General Burnside was deviating from Mr. Lincoln's instructions; that the written plan was not approved, but that some other verbal plan was assented to; and that certain points,

*General Halleck's Report, in Report of Secretary of War, 1863-'64, p 17.

at which General Burnside expected supplies, were occupied in force by the enemy. These statements are contained in a document dated November 15, 1863. All these assertions are both in substance and in form incorrect.

Mr. Lincoln had given suggestions, not instructions. His words in closing his letter to General McClellan are: "This letter is in no sense an order." General Burnside did not deviate from the President's wishes, if these are to be understood by his words. He refers particularly to Aquia Creek and Fredericksburg, as points through which supplies were to be forwarded, as the army moved upon a "chord line." The lines would be "lengthened a little, if you press closer to the Blue Ridge part of the way." The President, in another paragraph of his letter, says that he "would press closely" to the enemy, "fight him, if a favorable opportunity should present, and, at least try to beat him to Richmond on the inside track" It cannot be denied that General Burnside's plan was completely in accordance with the spirit of the President's letter, and even with the language of that document when rationally interpreted. General Halleck, therefore, in accusing General Burnside of deviating from the President's instructions, is accusing wrongfully.

The second statement, that the President assented to some other plan than that which was written is disproved by General Halleck's own testimony given before the Committee on the Conduct of the War, on the 22d of December, 1862. The following questions by Mr. Gooch and answers by General Halleck are conclusive upon this point: "Q. 'When you were there [at Warrenton] was the time considered that it would take to move the army from where it was to Falmouth, opposite Fredericksburg?' A. 'No, sir; for it was not determined at that time that the movement should be made.' Q. 'Was it not determined it should be made provided the President assented to it?' A. 'Yes, sir; and he was immediately to commence his preparations as though it had been assented to until telegraphed to the contrary, but not to make any movement.'

Q. 'Was or was not the time requisite for the movement of the army from where it was to Falmouth considered at that time?' A. 'It may have been spoken of in conversation. We had a long conversation of three or four hours, and it may have been alluded to; nothing definite was decided upon in relation to the time it would take. Indeed, I remarked when I left him that he was of opinion that he would cross a portion of his forces at the fords above the junction of the rivers. That was the opinion that he expressed before I left.' Q. 'And the residue at Falmouth?' A. 'Yes, sir.'"* Here the chief thought, both in Mr. Gooch's and General Halleck's minds, was the movement to Falmouth. Only casually did the idea of crossing at the upper fords occur, and that too in relation to the crossing of a portion of the army. It is evident that the written plan of General Burnside was the only plan which General Halleck, on the 22d of December, believed to have received the President's assent. His idea of another verbal plan, as spoken of in the following November, was without question an after thought. Corroborative evidence on this point is given in the testimony of General Meigs on the same day. He says: "From what little I heard of the discussion between General Halleck and General Burnside—I only heard a part of it—I expected that a portion of General Burnside's army would cross above Fredericksburg, and I think he used the expression, that within twenty-four or forty-eight hours, I do not remember which, after he got permission to move, his cavalry would be in Fredericksburg, the main body of his army, however, not crossing above but crossing at Falmouth." General Haupt's testimony before the same committee has not one word favoring the declaration of General Halleck—that a "small force was to be sent north of the river to enable General Haupt to reöpen the railroad and re-build the bridges" while the army was to cross by the upper fords. All of General Haupt's testimony shows that he had in mind the necessity of making provision for the

*Report of the Committee on the Conduct of the War, Part I., pp. 675.

transportation of the supplies of a large army from Aquia Creek to Fredericksburg and beyond. He declares, moreover, that "on Friday, November 14, General Halleck informed him that the change of base was approved by the President."*

General Halleck's third assertion is that the points in question were held in force by the enemy. There were but a few pickets at Aquia Creek, and those ran away as soon as some of our troops—a small part of the engineer brigade—landed there. At Fredericksburg there was not a large force. Captain Dahlgren had made a dash into that place with a few cavalrymen not long before the army moved, and General Sumner testified, that he thought he "could have taken Fredericksburg and the heights on the other side of it any time within three days after" his arrival, if the pontons had been at Falmouth, for he did "not think there was much force of the enemy there up to that time." A remark of General Halleck's, in the same report, respecting an expectation of General Burnside, that "gunboats were to cover the crossing" of his troops at Falmouth has no foundation whatever. Thus General Halleck stands open to the grave charge of attempting, in an official document, to mislead the public mind.

General Burnside, having received the President's assent to his plan, and trusting that General Halleck would be as good as his word in forwarding pontons and supplies, proceeded to put his designs in execution. In accordance with the President's suggestion, he determined to move rapidly. He had organized his army into three grand divisions, of two corps each, the right under General Sumner, the centre under General Hooker, and the left under General Franklin. General Sumner's command started at daylight on the 15th of November, and the remainder of the army on the 16th. The Ninth Corps made demonstrations towards the Rappahannock, and the cavalry guarded the fords as the army passed. General Sumner's advance reached Falmouth on the 17th, and was

*Report of Committee on Conduct of the War, Part 1., p. 683.

opened upon by a battery of artillery posted upon the opposite side of the river. One of our own batteries was brought up and soon silenced the enemy, who fled, leaving four guns unprotected. General Sumner wished to cross, but as his orders were simply to occupy Falmouth without crossing, and as the fords in the neighborhood were impracticable, he halted his troops until the remainder of the army should come up. General Franklin concentrated his command at and near Stafford Court House. General Hooker was upon the road for three days, reached Hartwood on the 19th, and remained there over the 20th. While he was at Hartwood he addressed a letter to General Burnside suggesting that he could cross his grand division at one of the fords in the vicinity, and march on Sexton's Junction. He requested permission to do so, alleging that he could live on the country through which he passed. General Burnside declined allowing this march to be made, for the reason that the army was not sufficiently supplied for such a detached movement, and also because he was unwilling that a body of men, not over twenty-five thousand in number, should march out upon an isolated expedition into an enemy's country and in the face of a superior hostile force. Such a movement, though partaking of the characteristic daring of General Hooker, was not sufficiently prudent to ensure its success.

General Burnside left Warrenton on the 16th, and on the 19th arrived at Falmouth. To his great surprise, no ponton train was there, and there was no intelligence of any. The movement had been made with great celerity as the President had suggested. But beyond Falmouth there was no possibility of an advance. A wide and deep river lay between the army and the coveted heights beyond Fredericksburg. There were no means of crossing. Below Falmouth not a wheeled vehicle could cross without boats. Above, the fords were impracticable without pontons except for a few cavalrymen in line, or infantry jumping from rock to rock. Moreover, rain began to fall, the river commenced rising, supplies were short, and the roads were in bad condition. The enemy's cavalry had followed the army occasionally skirmishing with our rear guard. The movement had been developed, but it had failed. It had depended for success upon the prompt arrival at Falmouth of the ponton train. Without that nothing could be done. The fords were examined and pronounced to be impassable. Yet General Burnside hoped to "cross over by the United States Ford some cavalry and infantry with some light pieces of artillery." No enemy had yet appeared on the opposite bank in any great force, and the expectation of moving across the Rappahannock was not yet wholly dissipated. But, if General Burnside moved now, he must march his entire army, for General Lee was also moving. Precious time was passing. General Lee and the rebel government were somewhat puzzled to understand the reason of the sudden disappearance of our army from Warranton, and its as sudden reäppearance at Falmouth was still more inexplicable. But whatever was the motive, it was General Lee's duty to meet this force as speedily as possible and check its advance. Accordingly he hurried across the country and occupied the heights of Fredericksburg. The golden opportunity had passed. The unguarded avenue to Richmond was barred. The gates were closed. When General Burnside woke on the morning of the 22d, and looked across the river, he saw the enemy's cannon frowning on his position and the enemy's bayonets gleaming in the early light.

CHAPTER VI.

THE PONTONS.

THAT General Burnside's subsequent failure at Fredericksburg was due to the non-arrival of the ponton train at Falmouth, in season to cross the army before General Lee appeared, was acknowledged at the time by the grand division Commanders and has since become painfully apparent. The responsibility of that failure must therefore rest, to a certain extent at least, on the person or persons to whom the moving of the train had been committed. Whatever might have been General Halleck's intention, he certainly gave General Burnside the impression that he would do all that he could to expedite the business of sending forward the pontons and supplies. General Meigs, while at Warrenton, wrote an order for General Woodbury, the engineer officer in charge, to call upon the quartermaster at Washington for transportation for all his pontons and bridge material to Aquia Creek. This order General Halleck signed as General in Chief. Besides this order, General Halleck gave assurance to General Burnside to believe, that he would give his personal attention to the matter immediately upon his return to Washington. General Woodbury on the 12th ordered Captain Spaulding, in charge of the pontons at Berlin, to take up his bridges and transport them to Washington. This order had been anticipated by General McClellan's order of the 6th to his engineer officer Captain Duane. On the 12th this order was received, and Captain Spaulding was directed to move bridge material from Berlin to Washington, and to fit out a complete bridge train " on wheels as speedily as possible, with the necessary transportation, and be prepared to march at a moment's notice." Captain Spaulding immediately attended to the execution of this order by transporting his train by canal to Washington, arriving there himself on the 13th, and reporting to General Woodbury at midnight. General Woodbury requested him to call at nine o'clock the next morning. When Captain Spaulding called as appointed, he was desired to wait until General Woodbury had seen General Halleck. About an hour after, General Woodbury returned from his interview with General Halleck, and directed Captain Spaulding to put his ponton material in depot at the brigade shops near the Anacosti river as fast as it arrived from Berlin, and to go into camp with his men. Captain Spaulding supposed that the change of commanders had produced a change in the plan of operations, and that the ponton train would not be needed. The pontons commenced arriving at Washington on the 14th, and had all arrived soon after noon on the 15th. The bridges were placed in depot and the men in camp. On the morning of the 15th, General Woodbury, after another interview with General Halleck, repeated the order to put the train in depot as fast as it arrived. Captain Spaulding casually heard of a despatch from Lieutenant Comstock, General Burnside's chief engineer, to General Woodbury, inquiring as to the whereabouts of the pontons. In the course of the same day, Captain Spaulding was directed to make up "two trains of twenty-four boats each in rafts to go by water, a train of twenty boats with transportation for forty to go by land, to draw the necessary number of additional horses and harness required for the land train, to prepare it as soon as possible and march his detachment with it to Fredericksburg."*

Both these directions were carried out during the afternoon. The two trains that were to go by water were made up, towed below the bridge over the Anacosti, and made fast to the steamer Hero, that was to tow them to Belle Plain. The steamer was

*Captain Spaulding's memorandum.

delayed by fog, and did not start as soon as was expected. When fairly on her voyage she ran aground on some shoal place in the river, and after considerable delay, arrived at Belle Plain on the 18th. No wagons were sent with the boats and bridges,* as no intimation was given to Captain Spaulding that the pontons were needed for immediate use. General Woodbury himself had received no such intimation. General Halleck had evidently treated the matter as not of pressing importance. Had anything been said by any person of the immediate need, the wagons would have been sent with the raft, horses could have been procured of the Quartermaster at Belle Plain, and the pontons could easily have arrived at Falmouth by the night of the 18th.

The land train was equally unfortunate. Captain Spaulding drew his horses, two hundred or more, and had them in camp on the 16th. The harness was furnished in boxes, and had to be put together and fitted to the horses. Many of the animals had apparently never been in harness before, and it was difficult to find leaders that could be guided by one rein, in the ordinary manner of horses in the army trains. Besides this labor, drivers were to be procured, rations and forage drawn, and the boats loaded on the wagons. It was not till the afternoon of the 19th, that Captain Spaulding fairly got off upon the road. He passed through Alexandria that night, and encamped outside the city. Rain commenced falling before the train left Washington, and continued, with little intermission, for the next three days. The roads became very heavy and constantly grew worse. In many places, the wagons could only be moved

---

*It was General Meigs's opinion that "the best way to get pontons and ponton trains from Washington would be to pack the flooring, ropes, anchors, &c., of the bridges in the ponton boats and tow them down the river by steamer, while the wagons, on which they were ordinarily transported when moving by land, with their horses and harness, should march under guard from Alexandria to Aquia Creek, there to take up the ponton trains and transport them to Falmouth by the common road. By this means the wagons would go light and would get through more rapidly and with less wear and tear to the horses." But even this arrangement was not made.

by the greatest exertions, the men lifting them out of the mire. But slow progress was made, and Captain Spaulding, finding that it was useless to think of proceeding in this way, sent back an officer to Alexandria on the 22d, with a request to the Quartermaster at that post to send a steamer to the mouth of the Occoquan, to take the bridge and rafts to Belle Plain. The steamer was sent down on the 23d. On the afternoon of the 22d, Captain Spaulding marched to the Occoquan, built a bridge two hundred and fifty feet in length, crossed and encamped on the other side. Early the next morning the bridge was dismantled, made up in rafts, all the bridge material loaded on the rafts, and the animals sent forward by land. The wagons were also taken apart and loaded upon the rafts. Descending the river, the rafts grounded upon the flats near the mouth, and could not be floated till the rise of the tide at four o'clock on the morning of the 24th. Captain Spaulding took his rafts out to the steamer in waiting, and making fast to her the train was towed to Belle Plain, arriving at the wharf there just before dark. Quartermasters' teams were there procured for him, and by midnight the wagons had been put together and the boats and material loaded. At four o'clock A. M., on the 25th, the train started and arrived near the general headquarters about three o'clock in the afternoon. Captain Spaulding's animals had gone by land, and on the 24th had reached Falmouth in safety.*

By this extraordinary series of misfortunes, such delays in the transportation of the pontons occurred as made any attempt abortive to cross the army before the enemy appeared in force. But of these mischances General Burnside knew nothing. He had supposed that the officials at Washington were as desirous as himself of forwarding the army towards its destination. He thought that they were as fully impressed as himself with the necessity of expedition. General Halleck had transmitted the President's suggestions for a rapid movement; but he had ne-

*Captain Spaulding's Memorandum.

glected to carry out the promises made to General Burnside, to send on the pontons without delay. Even if he had believed that General Burnside was to take his army down the south bank of the Rappahannock, he must also have known that the army needed supplies, and that the supplies could not reach beyond Falmouth without the means of crossing the river. In any view of the case, the pontons were sorely needed at Falmouth. General Halleck must certainly have known the fact of that necessity. Yet he neglected to furnish the very material which he was expected, and which—according to General Burnside's conviction—he had promised to provide.

General Woodbury's account of the affair places the conduct of the General in Chief in no more favorable light. In the interviews which he had with General Halleck, he was not informed "that the success of any important movement depended, in the slightest degree, upon a ponton train to leave Washington by land." General Burnside, supposing of course, that General Halleck would inform General Woodbury of the necessity of despatch, did not think it requisite to hasten the preparations of an officer who was known to be faithful and energetic in the discharge of his duty. He did, however, through Lieutenant Comstock, inform General Woodbury on the 14th, that he desired "to have one more complete train mounted and horses as soon as possible, and with the other, sent with a company, at least, and Captain Spaulding in command, by land to Fredericksburg." General Woodbury declares that this was the only order that he had received in relation to transportation by land. It seems, that soon after the reception of this order, he saw General Halleck and found him averse to sending more than one train by land. That train, as General Woodbury telegraphs, could "be got ready to start Sunday or Monday morning." But on Monday, the 17th, it was found that Captain Spaulding had more work to do than was supposed, and General Woodbury telegraphed that the train would probably start the next morning. On the next day, the story was the same, and Captain Spaulding could not start till the afternoon of the 19th. In the meantime, the pontons that were to go by water had been despatched.

At the outset of the expedition, moreover, General Woodbury had requested General Halleck to delay the army for a few days. "General Halleck's order to me, of the 13th," says General Woodbury, "made it apparent that the army was preparing to march to Fredericksburg. As to the time when the movement would be made, I never received any information. Fearing, however, that the movement would be precipitate, I went to General Halleck's office and urged him to delay the movement some five days, in order that the necessary preparations might be made to insure its success. To this he replied, that he would do nothing to delay for an instant the advance of the army upon Richmond. I rejoined that my suggestion was not intended to cause delay, but rather to prevent it. Had the emergency been made known to me in any manner," he adds, "I could have disregarded the forms of service —seized teams, teamsters and wagonmasters for instant service wherever I could find them. Then, with good roads and good weather, they might possibly have been in time. But I had no warrant for such a course, which, after all, could only have been carried out by the authority of the General-in-Chief."* That General Halleck understood the exigency and the absolute need of celerity in sending off and transporting the pontons, is simply to claim for him the possession of ordinary intelligence and powers of observation. But with this knowledge, he neglected to inform the officer in charge of the operations that any emergency existed, and when he ascertained that it was almost impossible, without some special order, to get the ponton train off in time, he neglected to use the means which he held in his own hands for its despatch. When appealed to by General Woodbury to delay the movement of the army—which he could do by a single word—until the ponton train was ready, he utterly refused. It certainly was unfortunate that wagons

* Report of Committee on the Conduct of the War, I., 665.

were not sent with the train which went by water. That was a lamentable oversight on the part of General Woodbury. But the omission was doubtless caused by the ignorance of General Woodbury that any special need for haste existed, and by his supposition that the wagons would go by land, and would reach headquarters in ample season for the operations that were contemplated. General Halleck could have enlightened his subordinate, but did not choose so to do. From a careful review of all the facts, no other conclusion can be reached than that the failure of the pontons, and consequently the failure of General Burnside's plan of advance, must be laid to the negligence of the General in Chief in discharging the trust reposed in him.

General Hooker is disposed to divide the responsibility between the General in Chief and the Quartermaster General. He said, in his testimony before the Committee on the Conduct of the War,* that he "heard General Meigs or General Halleck assure General Burnside that they (the pontons) would be here (at Falmouth) in three days." In answer to the question, "As the matter was left at the time of the conversation, did you understand that the responsibility of having the pontons and supplies here rested upon General Burnside, or upon General Halleck and General Meigs?" General Hooker replied, "I think it necessarily rested upon General Halleck and General Meigs, because it was beyond the control of General Burnside, who was not where he could control it." General Sumner was positive, that if he had had the pontons within three days of his arrival at Falmouth, he could have occupied the heights in rear of Fredericksburg without material opposition. General Franklin wished "to impress as firmly upon the committee as it" was impressed upon his own "mind, the fact that the whole disaster had resulted from the delay in the arrival of the ponton bridges. Whoever is responsible for that delay is responsible for all the disasters which have followed."†

* Part I., 671. † Report of Committee, I., 662.

Perhaps it would have been better, if General Burnside had sent an aide or some trustworthy staff officer to Washington, especially upon the errand of despatching the pontons. It certainly would have been better, if he had held his army at Warrenton until he had received positive assurances, that the pontons had started and were well on the way under sufficient guard. But he trusted in General Halleck's promises and in General Woodbury's despatches. Between the two the movement failed, and General Burnside paid dearly for his misplaced confidence.

On the 22d of November, while awaiting the arrival of the pontons, General Burnside addressed the following letter to General Cullum:

"By reference to my plan of operations, submittted by order of the General in Chief, it will be found that one of the necessary parts of that plan was to have started from Washington at once ponton trains sufficient to span the Rappahannock at Fredericksburg twice, and I was assured that at least one train would leave as soon as the General-in-Chief and General Meigs returned, and I proposed that, if an escort was required and I was informed of the departure of the train by telegraph, I would furnish it from my cavalry. Receiving no information of its departure, I ordered Lieutenant Comstock to telegraph in reference to it.

"It is very clear that my object was to make the move to Fredericksburg very rapidly, and to throw a heavy force across the river before the enemy could concentrate a force to oppose the crossing, and I supposed the ponton train would arrive at this place nearly simultaneously with the head of the column. Had that been the case, the whole of General Sumner's column, of thirty-three thousand strong, would have crossed into Fredericksburg at once over a ponton bridge in front of a city filled with families of rebel officers and sympathizers with the rebel cause, and garrisoned by a small squadron of cavalry and a battery of artillery, which General Sumner silenced within an hour after his arrival. Had the ponton bridge arrived, even on the 19th or 20th, the army would have crossed with trifling opposition, but now the opposite side of the river is occupied by a large rebel force under General Longstreet, with batteries ready to be placed in position to operate against the working parties building the bridge and the troops in crossing.

"The ponton train has not yet arrived, and the river is too high for the troops to cross at any of the fords.

"You can readily see that much delay may occur in the general movement, and I deem it my duty to lay these facts before you, and to say that I cannot make the promise of probable success with the faith that I did, when I supposed that all the parts of the plan would be carried out.

"Another very material part of the proposition, which I understood to be approved as a whole, was that all the surplus wagons that were in Washington were to be loaded with bread and small commissary stores, and sent to this place at once, which would probably have supplied our army with from five to ten days' provisions. These trains could have moved with perfect safety, as they would have been protected by the movements of this army.

"I do not recall these facts in any captious spirit, but simply to impress upon the General in Chief, that he cannot expect me to do as much as if all the parts of the plan had been carried out. In fact, a force can be arrayed against us at this place that would very materially retard us.

"The work of the Quartermaster and Commissary Departments at Aquia Creek and Belle Plain has been most completely accomplished, and I am not prepared to say that every effort has not been made to carry out the other parts of the plan, but I must in honesty and candor say, that I cannot feel that the move indicated in my plan of operations will be successful, after two very important parts of the plan have not been carried out,—no matter for what reason.

"The President said that the movement, in order to be sucful, must be made quickly, and I thought the same."

General Halleck replied on the 23d, by telegraph:

"WASHINGTON, 12.20 P. M., Nov. 23d, 1862.

"MAJOR GENERAL BURNSIDE:

"You are aware that I telegraphed from your quarters in Warrenton to General Woodbury to send the ponton trains to Aquia Creek. Immediately on my return I saw him myself to urge them forward. He left for Aquia Creek with his brigade to report to you. He is there, under your command. If there has been any unnecessary delay, call him to an account. There has been no delay at these Headquarters in ordering him as you requested.

"H. W. HALLECK, General-in-Chief."

In the above correspondence, it is taken for granted by both that the main body of the army is at Falmouth.* General Halleck expresses no surprise that such is the fact. He has no word of censure for a movement which he afterwards characterized as made without authority. So far as appears in subsequent correspondence, General Halleck did not discover that General Burnside had moved the main body of his army in a different direction from what was intended and agreed upon at Warrenton, until after six weeks had passed, a great battle had been lost, and the General in Chief was suffering therefor in the public estimation.

---

* In regard to this subject the question would naturally arise: suppose, that General Burnside had taken the main body of his army across the upper Rappahannock and brought it down to Fredericksburg, how would it have been supplied? One hundred thousand men with animals would have to be fed, yet General Halleck would have put them in a position, between which and their depot of supplies a deep river would flow with no means of crossing.

CHAPTER VII.

AT FALMOUTH.

THE question with General Burnside now was: "Shall I put my army into winter quarters, or shall I, with the means at my disposal, press the enemy, as the country expects, the President and General in Chief advise, and my own sense of duty enjoins upon me to do?" The decision to which he came was this: "I did not take command of this army simply to idle away another winter, but to do what I could to end the rebellion. The strength of this treasonable movement lies in the rebel army upon the other side of the Rappahannock. I must at least try to break it. If I fail, it will not be for the want of a vigorous effort. If I succeed, the only reward I ask is the consciousness of having performed my duty." He was now convinced that the Army of the Potomac and the army of Northern Virginia must again enter into conflict. The indolence of winter quarters was as distasteful to him as to the public. He determined to fight, not for the sake of winning glory if victorious, but because he felt that his duty to the cause and to the country demanded it. He immediately set about his preparations. In the course of the next three weeks, he had made himself and his command ready to deliver battle.

Where and how? It was clear that General Lee had no intention of assuming the offensive. He had been badly shattered by the unsuccessful invasion of Maryland and the battle of Antietam. He wished to recuperate his forces by giving them a winter's rest along the Rappahannock, and, for convenience of subsistence and supplies, on the line of the railroad between Fredericksburg and Richmond. He therefore brought down his army from the upper waters and the mountains to the heights behind Fredericksburg, and occupied the country in the rear and below, reaching as far as Bowling Green in one direction and Port Royal in the other. The hills behind Fredericksburg were immediately selected as sites for defensive lines and were soon covered with earthworks, large and small redoubts. Rude works were also thrown up opposite the fords. The south bank of the river was picketed for a distance of fifteen and twenty miles. Guinney's station became the chief depot of supplies, and General Lee established his headquarters at Alsop's, about five miles distant from the river. The rebel army was preparing for a desperate resistance against any attempt to dislodge it from its position, or seize the road to Richmond.

General Lee had well chosen his position for defence. The country in the rear of the Rappahannock was admirably calculated for that kind of warfare, in which the enemy was most proficient. Like the banks of most American rivers, the land on either side rose in successive natural terraces, cut here and there by little streams making their way to the main channel. On the first of these, immediately upon the bank, but sufficiently high above the river level to escape the inundations of the spring freshets, lies the chief part of the city of Fredericksburg, regularly laid out, with the streets crossing each other at right angles. The plain which it occupies is about a mile and a half in length by a half mile in width. Two bridges once spanned the river, one belonging to the Richmond, Fredericksburg and Potomac Railroad Company, the other the continuation of the county road. The railroad bridge was a half mile below the public bridge. Both had been destroyed in the course of the war. The railroad, after crossing the river and passing through the town, follows down the bank for a distance of about three miles, and then turns southward towards Richmond. From the lower part of the town, a road runs out towards Port Royal. About two miles below Deep Run, another road strikes off from this to the right, crosses the railroad and the Massaponax Creek, and thence makes connection with a road leading to Richmond. It has thus received the name of the "old Richmond road." In the neighborhood of a point about two miles from the river, where this road crosses the railroad, and near the edge of the hills, is Captain Hamilton's estate, and the place is known as Hamilton's crossing. The county road, after crossing the river, is continued through the town under the name of Hanover Street, becomes a plank road, which climbs the hills, and, turning to the West, extends through Chancellorsville to Orange Court House.

Half a mile beyond the town, after ascending the gentle acclivity, a road diverges to the left turning southward and gradually reaching up the slope to the second terrace. A gentleman's house and grounds, comprising a very handsome estate, stand above this road near the northern extremity of the first fortified line of hills. This is "Marye's." These grounds are supported, where they come down to the road before spoken of, by a heavy bank-wall of stone. On the side of the road opposite the same and towards the town, is a similar wall in length nearly half a mile. This road, after leaving the plank road, winds along the edge of the second terrace with a gradual ascent, then crossing a small stream called Hazel Run, climbs the third terrace and extends into the country beyond, in a southerly or southwesterly direction. It is called the telegraph road. The lawn in front of the Marye mansion was crossed by a line of rifle pits, and in the southerly portion of the grounds was thrown up a small redoubt. Other rifle pits and small earth works were raised on the northerly and westerly side of the plank road.

Southeasterly from the telegraph road nearly parallel with the river and about two miles distant from it rises the second terrace. This is cut by Deep Run, which, after reaching the plain, makes a long curve towards the town and flows into the Rappahannock a mile below Hazel Run. One mile and a half below Deep Run, the Massaponax cuts the terrace, makes a long curve in the opposite direction—thus producing between the two streams a large and nearly level ellipse—and flows into the Rappahannock four miles below. The plain which is formed by the first terrace is about six miles in length from the upper part of the town to the Massaponax and varies in breadth from one to two miles. It slopes nearly up to the edge of the second terrace with almost the gentle incline of the glacis of a fortress, except that it is broken here and there by low ridges, shallow ravines and garden fences. The part of the plain above Fredericksburg is cut by a canal, which runs from the dam at Falmouth to a point within the upper portion of the town. A few houses are scattered over the plain. The second terrace was crowned with earth works and rifle pits, which were armed with field artillery and a few heavy guns. The natural position was very strong and could be defended by a resolute force against double its number. Beyond the second terrace rose a third of a character similar to the other but of much smaller dimensions. The third crest was fortified to some extent but by no means so strongly as the second. Upon the two lines of defence there were twelve or fifteen large and small works, lunettes and redoubts. These were of hasty construction but of sufficient strength to give great confidence to troops stationed behind them. In the rear of the first line of works, from the old Richmond road to the telegraph road, the enemy had cut another road, beginning near Hamilton's crossing, connecting his right with his left and affording easy communication between the two wings.

Above Fredericksburg the range of hills which General Lee had fortified subsides as it approaches the river, and four or five miles further up the country becomes less broken. But beyond that is an extensive tract of forest land—the Wilderness. Into this country a way is opened by means of two fords, Banks', about five miles, and United States ford, about ten miles distant from Fredericksburg. A mile above the latter ford the Rapidan empties into the Rappahannock. A mile beyond this debouche is Richards' ford crossing the Rappahannock, and four miles above, crossing the Rapidan, is Ely's ford. The road from Richards' to Ely's ford may be taken as the base of a triangle, the two sides of which are formed by the two rivers. These fords were strongly guarded by the enemy. Twelve miles above Richards', and twenty-four miles from Fredericksburg is Kelly's ford across the Rappahannock, and four miles above Ely's across the Rapidan at Germania mills is still another good ford. But these two latter points were considered by General Burnside as too far from Falmouth to make a successful demonstration against the enemy's line in that direction. Moreover, none of these fords were at that time practicable for crossing a large force without pontons.

Below Fredericksburg the Rappahannock gradually widens and the country on the right bank is comparatively open. But the river deepens as it widens, and is indeed navigable for steamers and other vessels of light draught within a mile or two of Fredericksburg. A crossing at any point below Falmouth must be made by means of pontons. Just above Falmouth, a dam is built across the river at the head of tide-water, and immediately below the dam the deep water commences. Eighteen miles below Fredericksburg are two towns, Port Royal on the right and Port Conway on the left bank of the river. A few miles above Port Royal the river makes a decided bend to the north and east, then turning south again, forms a peninsula bearing the name of Skinker's Neck. The gunboats of the Potomac flotilla could easily reach that point. Thence to Bowling Green, fifteen miles distant, is a good road. If a successful crossing could be made in the neighborhood of Port Royal, the rear of the rebel line would be threatened and the works at Fredericksburg would be almost valueless. Here then was an important point. General Burnside turned his attention to it and gave it a careful examination. Compared with the other points which were considered, it seemed as though Skinker's Neck or Port Royal would he a better point for turning the enemy's position than any point above. General Burnside thought that a crossing at Skinker's Neck might be made, and accordingly decided so to dispose his forces as to seize Port Royal, if possible, with the purpose of turning the enemy's right without hazarding his own communications. General Franklin, who had been stationed at Stafford Court House, was ordered to move his command down the river within convenient distance of Port Conway. A portion of the Potomac flotilla under command of Lieutenant Edward P. McCrea proceeded up the Rappahannock and took a position in the river between Liberty Hill and Port Royal. On the 1st of December, our lines extended from King George Court House to Stafford Court House, thence with guards upon the road to Alexandria. General Sigel with one corps was at Fairfax Court House and vicinity. General Slocum was in command at Harper's Ferry; General Morell commanded the defences of the Upper Potomac.

Upon this side of the Rappahannock the topographical features of the country differ but little from those upon the south bank. Opposite the plain upon which lies the city of Fredericksburg is another plain, very similar to the first though somewhat more limited in extent. From the river bank extends the first terrace, crescent-shaped and sloping gently upwards to the crest of the second plateau. This plateau commences at Falmouth a short distance from the bank, and sweeps around in an elliptical curve, broken about the centre by the railroad that runs up from Aquia Creek, and striking the river bank again nearly opposite the mouth of Deep Run, two and a half or three miles below Falmouth. Upon the two extremities of the curved line were established batteries—that at Falmouth known as Pettit's, that below as Tyler's. About midway between them upon the lower terrace, somewhat nearer to Falmouth than to Tyler's and not far from the river, stood the Lacy House, an old mansion surrounded by all the appurtenances of a wealthy Virginia planter. At a point about two thirds of the distance below Falmouth upon the edge of the upper plateau stood the Phillips House, a beautiful and costly mansion elaborately decorated and richly furnished. It was distant from the river about three quarters of a mile. It was occupied for the permanent headquarters of General Sumner, and became the headquarters of General Burnside on the day of the battle. It commanded an entirely unobstructed view of the town of Fredericksburg and all its environs, and it dominated the first and second terraces upon the opposite side of the river. This point was also the central signal station of the army during its encampment in the vicinity.

In times of peace the prospect from the Phillips mansion must have been remarkably charming and delightful. The green slopes, the fields of yellow grain, the distant hills, the rich forests and the widening river must have presented a landscape of rare beauty. The two houses were doubtless the abodes of generous hospitality. The rooms were filled with smiling faces and graceful forms and the roofs rang with merry laughter. But all this was now changed. The smiling landscape had become a waste, desolated by the ravages of war. The turf was trampled by the careless feet of man and beast, the lawns and hillsides were broken by rifle pits and redoubts, the forests were fast losing their pride and glory, the fields were bare. The mansions, occupied only in part or wholly abandoned by their owners, were converted into officers' quarters, in which the refinements of life were hardly expected to have a prominent place. The cruel hand of war was reaping an abundant harvest of devastation, destruction and death.

Beyond the second terrace the land stretched back to Aquia Creek in an undulating plain broken by occasional hills, some of which were heavily wooded, and produced an agreeable diversity in the landscape. This plain was divided into two nearly equal parts by Potomac Creek, which, flowing through a deep ravine, emptied into the Potomac at Belle Plain. This creek was spanned by a bridge, that for strength, rapidity in its construction, and its adaptability to the uses for which it was built was a miracle of engineering. The first bridge built by the Government during the war was constructed in May, 1862, while General McDowell occupied Fredericksburg. It was composed chiefly of round logs, and the legs of the trestles were braced with round poles. It was in four stories, three of trestle and one of crib-work. Its total height from the bed of the stream to the rail was nearly eighty feet. Its length was about four hundred feet. It bore daily from ten to twenty trains loaded with supplies, and successfully withstood several freshets. It contained more than two million feet of lumber and was constructed in nine days by the soldiers under the superintendence of General Herman Haupt, chief of railroad construction and transportation. This bridge was destroyed or dismantled upon the evacuation of this section by General Burnside in August, 1862. It was again built substantially in the same manner, and after the same plan, in six days after General Haupt for the second time commenced work upon it, on the 18th of November.

The month of November had passed in cold and storm. December at its first coming had brought no more genial weather. Ice began to appear in the Potomac, in Aquia Creek and in the Rappahannock. Affairs began to look doubtful for any movement for several months to come. The gunboats in the Rappahannock were even in danger of being caught and frozen up. Still General Burnside continued his preparations, carefully keeping his secret, and looking forward hopefully to the future. As December went on, the weather moderated. The ice disappeared. More genial suns shone down upon the hostile camps. An Indian Summer took the place of Winter, and it seemed as though October had returned. With the advent of a milder temperature fogs began to prevail. They crept up the river in the afternoon and retired most reluctantly before the morning's sun. This circumstance was both favorable and unfavorable. For while it concealed our movements from the enemy, it also threatened to become the occasion of considerable confusion among our own troops when they should be brought into action. Through all, General Burnside ventured to hope for success in the conflict which he was determined to hazard. Earnest himself in the discharge of his duty and trustful of his subordinates even to a fault, he believed that all around him were devoted with equal earnestness to the cause which claimed their fidelity, and relied upon their zealous coöperation in the contemplated strife.

To replace the command of General Franklin at Stafford Court House and vicinity, General Sigel was ordered down from Fairfax Court House. To occupy General Sigel's vacated position, General Slocum was ordered from Harper's Ferry, of which General Morell took charge. Finally all was ready. But meanwhile, General Lee had concentrated all his available forces around his position in the rear of Fredericksburg. He seems to have suspected that General Burnside intended crossing at Port Royal, and accordingly sent General Jackson to that point with a large force, to act as circumstances might determine—either as an army of observation or to dispute the passage of the river. Indeed, a large, perhaps the larger portion of the enemy's forces was stationed at the threatened point. The plan of crossing at Port Royal was abandoned, while yet feints were kept up in that direction. Then General Burnside decided to adopt the bold plan of throwing his bridges across the river, a part immediately in front of Fredericksburg itself, and the remainder at a point two miles below, between Deep Run and Massaponax Creek. It was supposed that the main body of the enemy was in the vicinity of Port Royal, and that a rapid crossing immediately in front of our position, and a swift advance upon the heights would be a successful surprise. There was another circumstance which doubtless had its weight. The town made an admirable *tete de pont.* It had a rebel population. It was rebel property. General Lee's batteries on the hills could not prevent the crossing of our troops without destroying the lives and property of the friends of his cause. He would naturally hesitate before committing such an act. But, on the other hand, the town would lie at our mercy. If the houses of Fredericksburg should become shelter for the enemy's infantry, which could alone oppose our passage of the river, our artillery was at hand to demolish them. The town, once occupied, afforded shelter to our own forces. For General Lee would still be restrained from destroying it by his reluctance to injure his friends. Moreover, it was hoped that our columns, after crossing, would move through the town and charge the enemy's position. General Burnside did not expect to meet with much difficulty or opposition in crossing the river. That was thought to be a comparatively easy task. The chief labor was to be performed after the passage of the river had been effected. There was one difficulty, however, which may not have been duly appreciated. It is possible that it had in it an element of great weakness for our troops. It consisted in the occupation of an abandoned town by a hostile army. The unoccupied houses and stores, many of which belonged to persons of considerable wealth, would offer opportunities for plunder too tempting to be missed. Here was an influence of demoralization which was not to be disregarded. The numerous camp followers that hung upon the skirts of the army, in several instances the soldiers themselves, would be exposed to a temptation which would make a proper measure of discipline exceedingly difficult. This may be thought a minor consideration. But upon matters of less moment have the most important movements sometimes hinged.

Beyond the town lay the slope up which the army was to march in order to reach the enemy's lines. Above the slope frowned the enemy's batteries. The main task was to carry those heights, bristling with bayonets and dark with cannon. It was a perilous undertaking. For the first time in its history, the Army of the Potomac was to "move on the enemy's works" for a determined assault. It had shown itself unequalled for defensive warfare. Could it successfully take the aggressive? The answer to that momentous question was soon to be given in fire and blood!

CHAPTER VIII.

THE BATTLE OF FREDERICKSBURG.

WHAT assurance of success had General Burnside in carrying his plans into successful execution? By the consolidated morning reports of the Army of the Potomac, it appears that, on the 10th of December, there was in front of the enemy an effective force of one hundred and eleven thousand eight hundred and thirty-four officers and men of all arms. The artillery consisted of three hundred and twelve guns of different calibre, mostly field pieces. Of the three grand divisions,* the left, General Franklin's, was the largest, consisting of forty-six thousand eight hundred and ninety-two officers and men and one hundred and sixteen pieces of artillery, and was composed of the first corps, General J. J. Reynolds, and the sixth corps, General W. H. Smith. General Reynolds's division officers were Generals Meade, Gibbon and Doubleday; General Smith's were Generals Newton, Brooks and Howe. The centre grand division, General Hooker's, numbered thirty-nine thousand, nine hundred and eighty-four officers and men and one hundred pieces of artillery, and was composed of the third corps, General Stoneman, and the fifth corps, General Butterfield. General Stoneman's division commanders were Generals Sickles, Birney and Whipple; General Butterfield's were Generals Sykes, Humphreys and Charles Griffin. The right grand division, General Sumner's, numbered twenty-two thousand seven hundred and thirty-six officers and men and

*For the sake of convenience of reference the organization of the army is stated in detail, notwithstanding some of the particulars have already been given.

sixty pieces of artillery, and consisted of the Ninth Corps, General Willcox, and the second corps, General Couch. General Willcox's division commanders were Generals Getty, Sturgis and Burns; General Couch's were Generals French, Hancock and Howard. The brigade of engineers, numbering fifteen hundred and five officers and men, was under the command of General D. P. Woodbury, to whom was assigned the duty of laying the bridges for the crossing. The signal corps, under the command of Captain Samuel T. Cushing, numbered one hundred and fifty officers and men. General Patrick's Provost Guard numbered about two hundred officers and men. General Ingalls' Quartermaster's Department numbered one hundred and fifty officers and men, and the headquarters escort about two hundred officers and men. A certain portion of the whole army was occupied in guarding the railroad and performing picket and outpost duty. The cavalry was held in reserve. There was, probably, in round numbers, an available force of one hundred thousand officers and men, who were either actively engaged or held in support, and thus, in a measure, exposed to the fire of the enemy at some time during the day of the battle of Fredericksburg.

The time for action came. On the 10th of December, the army was concentrated along the river front, within short marching distance from the bank, but concealed as much as possible from the enemy by the undulations of the land. During the night the artillery was posted along the edge of the plateau, from Falmouth to a point opposite the mouth of the Massaponax. Orders were issued to the engineers under General Woodbury to be ready for work at three o'clock on the morning of the 11th, and a sufficient force of infantry and artillery was detailed to cover the crossings and protect the working parties. Three points were selected for throwing the bridges:—the first at a short distance above the place where the county bridge had stood; the second opposite the lower end of the town, and the third about a mile below Fredericksburg nearly opposite the mouth of Deep Run and not far from the estate of a planter named Bernard. At the first of these points two, at the second one, and at the third three bridges were to be laid. Upon these six bridges the army was to cross the Rappahannock, occupy the town and move rapidly to the assault. The left, by a vigorous and decisive attack, was to pierce the enemy's line near Captain Hamilton's crossing, seize the road in the rear and compel the evacuation of the works upon the crest. Then the right and centre, in support of the left attack, were to force the enemy from the heights in front and pursue along the telegraph or the plank road, according to the direction of the enemy's retreat. The success of the plan of attack was to depend upon the celerity and vigor with which the troops were pushed to its execution.

The morning of the 11th dawned raw, cold and foggy. The engineers—among whom were volunteers from the 8th Connecticut regiment of the Ninth Corps—were promptly at work upon the bridges. But little opposition was made to the operations of General Franklin's working parties below the town, and after considerable labor, his three bridges were laid, secured and strengthened. At eleven o'clock in the forenoon he reported to General Burnside that he was ready to cross his grand division. But operations immediately opposite the town had not proceeded so satisfactorily as General Burnside had hoped, and General Franklin was ordered to hold his bridges, but not to cross the main body of his troops till the upper bridges were completed. The latter work was destined to meet with considerable opposition. As the day came on the design of crossing was revealed to the enemy's forces in the town. About two thirds of the work of laying the bridges had been accomplished, when the sharpshooters of General Barksdale's Mississippi brigade posted in the houses and streets directed a destructive fire upon the working parties. Then our artillery opened along the whole line opposite the town. Amid the deafening roar of cannon, the shrieking and bursting of shells, the crash of falling timbers, as solid shot pierced the walls, our men attempted to finish the bridges. Soon the exploding shells set several houses on fire, and a portion of the city broke out into flames. But the persistent sharpshooters of the enemy obstinately held their position, and poured in a withering fire. Our engineers were brave, but they were unable to work, exposed as they were to the deliberate aim of riflemen that rarely missed their mark. General Woodbury reported to General Burnside that the bridges could not be built. "They must be built," replied the chief. "Try again." Once again our men engaged in the useless endeavor. Once again they were obliged to desist. Once again General Woodbury reported his inability to complete his task. Our artillery could not dislodge those Mississippian riflemen from their position in the town.

At noon the fog lifted, and the enemy's fire became, if possible, more deadly. General Burnside had been at the Lacy house through most of the morning, anxious and impatient to put his troops across the river. Upon receiving the last report of General Woodbury, he immediately went down to the riverside himself. He at once saw the difficulty. He also saw the remedy. Consulting with his chief of artillery, General Hunt and other officers, he decided to call for volunteers to cross the river in boats, drive out its defenders and hold the town till the bridges should be built. Soldiers from three regiments—the 7th Michigan, the 19th and 20th Massachusetts—sprang forward at the call. Men of the 50th New York were ready to take the place of oarsmen. With the flag of the Union floating in the van, the brave fellows turned the prows of their boats towards the enemy and pushed off from the shore. A few minutes' strong pulling through the storm of death, and the opposite shore was reached. A party from the 89th New York, of General Getty's division, crossed at a point where the middle bridge was thrown, and our troops soon had the enemy in flank and rear. They rushed eagerly up the bank, along the streets, through the rifle pits, into the houses, and in half an hour's time the city of Fredericksburg was in our possession. The remnants of the Mississippi brigade, with the exception of a few that managed to escape, fell into our hands as prisoners of war. The engineers immediately proceeded in their work and the bridges were laid.

It was now four o'clock in the afternoon. The precious day had been almost wasted. Nothing more could be done than to cross a portion of the troops to hold the bridge heads. General Devens's brigade of General Smith's corps—the 2d Rhode Island regiment in advance—crossed by the lower bridges, and brushing away the enemy's skirmishers, held the position. Colonel Hawkins's brigade—the 46th New York in advance—and General Howard's division crossed by the upper bridges and occupied the town. By this time the night had settled down, and our troops, after establishing their picket lines well out towards the enemy, bivouacked in the streets and gardens of Fredericksburg. No soldiers were allowed to enter the houses, and the provost guard was vigilant. Still, some cases of plunder occurred, but they were so few as to speak well for the discipline of the army.

The 12th was occupied in crossing the remainder of the troops, with the exception of General Hooker's grand division, which was held in reserve on the hither side of the river. The residue of General Franklin's grand division, consisting of the balance of General Smith's corps, the whole of General Reynolds's corps, and General Bayard's brigade of cavalry, began the crossing at daylight, and completed it at one o'clock in the afternoon. The troops were put in position—two divisions of Smith's corps in line of battle and one in reserve near the old Richmond road, Reynolds's corps nearly at right angles with Smith's, *en potence*, as it were, his right resting on Smith's left and his left on the river. These dispositions were made in the face of a spiteful but almost harmless fire from the enemy's skirmishers and artillery. The road was bordered by an earthen parapet and ditch, but the ground was generally level. In front of General Reynolds's right was a considerable tract of forest land, traversed by the railroad, and bordered nearer the hills by the old Richmond road. General Sumner, on his part, sent across the river the remaining part of the right grand division, the balance of General Couch's and General Willcox's corps. General Couch held the town, and General Willcox connected with General Franklin's right. These movements were made under an occasional fire from the enemy's batteries on the heights, but without any material loss. General Hooker moved General Butterfield's corps and General Whipple's division of General Stoneman's corps to the support of General Sumner's movement, and the remainder of General Stoneman's corps to the support of General Franklin. Another day was thus consumed. General Burnside visited and inspected his lines and conferred with his grand division and some of his corps commanders during the night of the 12th, and returned at a late hour to his headquarters on the Falmouth side of the river. General Lee made his dispositions for defence. He brought General Jackson up from Port Royal, and massed his troops somewhat heavily upon the right of his line.

At an early hour on the 13th, written orders were issued to the several grand division commanders, in accordance with the plan of battle adopted by General Burnside and after full verbal instructions. General Franklin's order was despatched at fifty-five minutes past five o'clock. It was carried to him by General Hardie, who remained at General Franklin's headquarters during the day. The principal part of the order was as follows: "The general commanding directs that you keep your whole command in position for a rapid movement down the old Richmond road, and you will send out a division at least, to pass below Smithfield to seize, if possible, the heights near Captain Hamilton's, on this side of the Massaponax, taking care to keep it well supported and its line of retreat open. He has ordered another column of a division or more to be moved from General Sumner's command up the plank road to its intersection with the telegraph road, where they will divide with a view to seizing the heights on both those roads. Holding those two heights, with the heights near Captain Hamilton's, will, he hopes, compel the enemy to evacuate the whole ridge between these points. Two of General Hooker's divisions are in your rear at the bridges, and will remain there as supports." General Sumner's order was sent at six o'clock, and was as follows: "The general commanding directs that you extend the left of your command to Deep River, connecting with General Franklin, extending your right as far as your judgment may dictate. He also directs that you push a column of a division or more along the plank and telegraph roads, with a view to seizing the heights in the rear of the town. The latter movement should be well covered by skirmishers, and supported so as to keep its line of retreat open. The column for a movement up the telegraph and plank roads will be got in readiness to move, but will not move till the general commanding communicates with you." General Hooker, at seven o'clock, was simply ordered to "place General Butterfield's corps and General Whipple's division in position to cross at a moment's notice at the three upper bridges, in support of the other troops over the river, and the two remaining divisions of General Stoneman's corps in readiness to cross at the lower bridges, in support of General Franklin." General Burnside was to meet both Generals Sumner and Hooker at the Phillips house at an early hour, and accordingly deferred completing his orders until he could deliver them at a personal interview. In General Sumner's case, the reservation was made in regard to moving the troops, in order that such movement should be withheld until General Franklin's attack should have been sufficiently developed to promise a complete success. The artillery, under the direction of General Hunt, was distributed among the different corps, and the batteries moved in connection with their respective commands. The watchword of the day, given in order to prevent collision among our own forces in the fog, was "Scott." Each general of grand division received a copy of the orders given to the others.

General Franklin established his headquarters near the Bernard house, or Mansfield, as it is sometimes called; General Sumner's headquarters were at the Lacy house; General

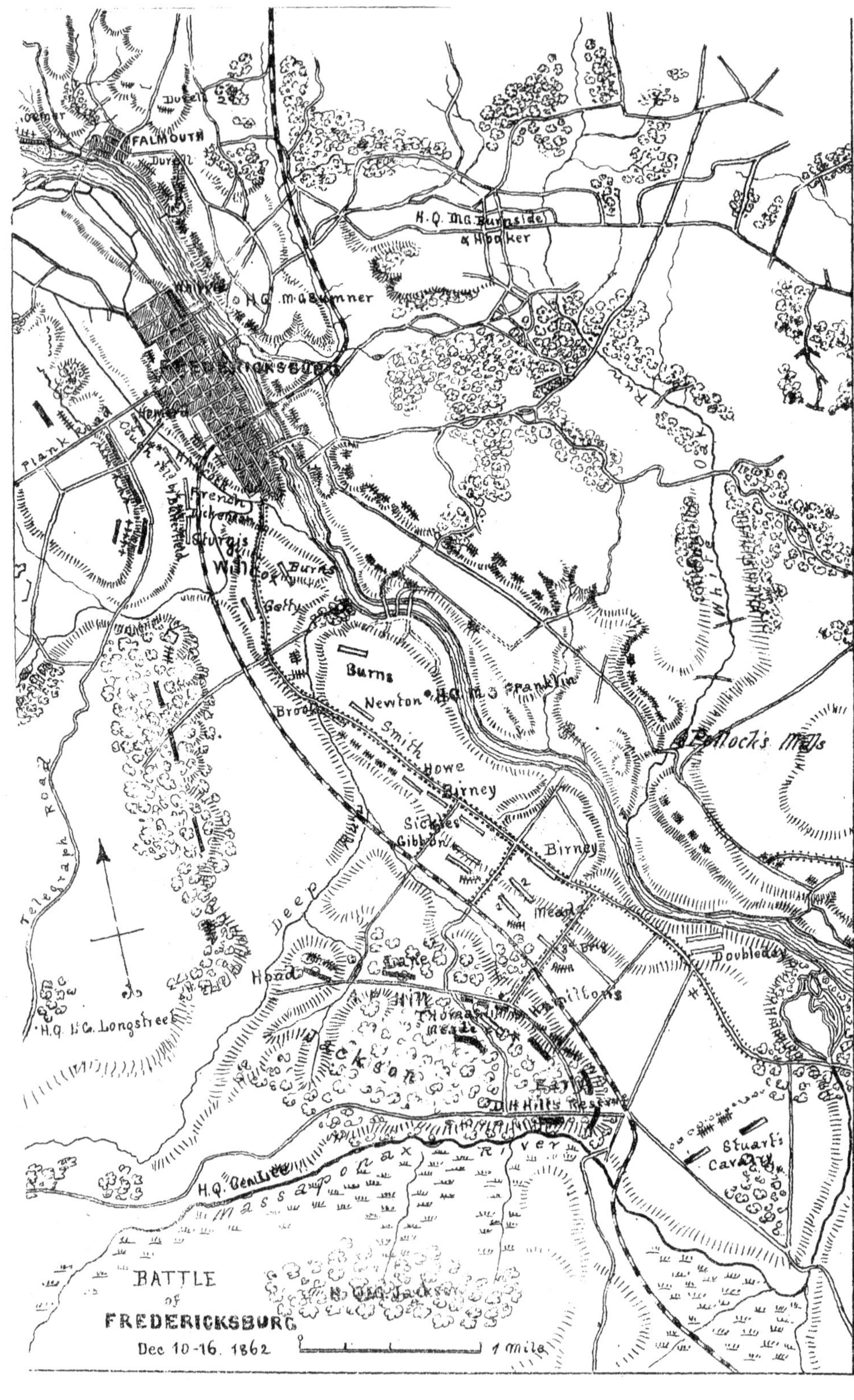
FALMOUTH
H.Q. Mc. Burnside & Hooker
H.Q. Mc. Sumner
FREDERICKSBURG
Plank Road
French
Sturgis
Burns
Getty
Burns
Newton
Smith
Howe
Birney
Sickles
Gibbon
Birney
Meade
Doubleday
Pollock's Mills
Telegraph Road
Deep Run
Hood
A. P. Hill
Jackson
D. H. Hill's Reserve
H.Q. Lt. G. Longstreet
Stuart's Cavalry
Massaponax River
H.Q. Gen. Lee
BATTLE
of
FREDERICKSBURG
Dec 10-16. 1862
1 mile

Hooker and Burnside's headquarters were at the Phillips House. The troops were put in readiness, and all parties anxiously awaited the lifting of the fog. The instructions seemed to be ample and sufficiently clear. General Franklin's task was to seize the heights near Captain Hamilton's at once, preparatory to a movement by the entire left wing along the old Richmond road. As soon as that was in process of accomplishment, General Sumner was to move up the telegraph and plank roads and seize the heights on the enemy's left, advancing his whole command against the enemy's lines. General Hooker was promptly to support the other two attacks with a view to pursuit, if they were succcessful, and to gathering in the fruits of victory. The main battle was to be on our left, and the attack was to be delivered "at once." General Franklin was esteemed a brave, skilful, cool and determined officer. He had the largest portion of the army. His bridges were guarded, his flanks and rear were perfectly secure, both by the infantry and the heavy artillery posted on the heights on the hither side. But General Franklin's temperament, as is perfectly well known, is somewhat sluggish. He did not seem to comprehend General Burnside's plan of battle. He even has since appeared to doubt if General Burnside had any definite plan at all. He professed to think that the main attack was to be upon the enemy's left, and that his own movement, to be made immediately and with a view to piercing the enemy's lines, was an armed reconnaissance. He had been averse to the movement from the first, as also had been some of his inferior officers, and neither he nor they were especially zealous to contribute to its success. All of them were good and brave soldiers. None in the army were more so. General Reynolds was particularly gallant and determined, and would have carried out the wishes of the commanding general had he been properly supported. No one of the corps commanders indeed would disobey a superior officer, even when it conflicted with his own judgment. But though obedience was rendered, it was evident that there was in it a lack of enthusiasm. Obedience is sometimes given in such a half-hearted way as to render it almost nugatory. When the will is wanting, it is easy to find obstructions in the way. Under such circumstances, the simplest order becomes difficult of execution. General Franklin ordered General Reynolds to send out " a division at least," to seize the heights. General Reynolds sent one division under General George G. Meade.

At nine o'clock, General Meade moved out on the old Richmond road. General Doubleday supported him with a division. But on advancing, General Doubleday was obliged to move to the left to protect the left flank of the army against a demonstration made by General Stuart with cavalry and artillery. General Gibbon's division took General Doubleday's vacated position. General Meade's skirmishers were soon engaged with those of the enemy, and the division became exposed to an artillery fire in front. General Meade's advance was very slow. He was obliged to clear away the enemy's artillery in front and flank, and to make frequent halts for the purpose of closing up his own columns, and to allow the division following to come within near supporting distance. At eleven o'clock, he had only gained half a mile, though suffering no loss of great importance. General Reynolds soon after developed his whole line, posting General Doubleday on the left, General Meade in the centre, and General Gibbon on the right—General Meade being in advance and General Gibbon in the rear, his left overlapping General Meade's right. General Franklin supposed that he was greatly outnumbered, and feared an attack from the enemy's forces on his extreme left. Instead of boldly attacking, as General Burnside had intended, he was thus far standing on the defensive. General Meade's advance seems to have been made simply to give room for further disposition of the troops. General Franklin appeared to be more disposed to hold his position than to take the aggressive. He ordered General Stoneman to cross one division, General Birney's, to support his left and occupy the gap which would remain after General Meade's advance. General Sickles's division crossed the river soon after noon and took position in General Reynolds's line. The troops upon the left were thus formed from left to right: Doubleday, two brigades of Birney, with Meade in front; Sickles, with Gibbon in front; the remainder of Birney's division, Howe, Newton and Brooks.

The enemy's line was formed with General Longstreet's corps upon the left, occupying the works on the Marye estate, the stone wall along the telegraph road, and the heights beyond; General Jackson's corps occupied the right opposite General Franklin; General A. P. Hill held the first line in front of and near Hamilton's crossing; General Taliaferro, commanding Jackson's old division, held the second line in General Hill's rear; General D. H. Hill held the third line behind the crest. On the slope of the hill commanding the crossing, Colonel Lindsay Walker had posted his artillery, consisting of Pegram's, McIntosh's, and sections of Crenshaw's, Latham's and Johnson's batteries. On the left of this line, near the avenue leading from the Bernard estate, was Davidson's artillery, twenty-one guns, and on the right of that position were twelve guns under Captain Brockenborough. General Jackson's left joined General Longstreet's right, which was under the command of General Hood, and constituted the centre of the enemy's line. It will thus be perceived that General Meade had no ordinary work to perform. With five thousand men, he was sent by General Franklin to perform a task which required four or five times that number.

By twelve o'clock, most of the dispositions on our side were made, and General Meade began to advance with earnestness and vigor. His division consisted of three brigades, of which the third was on the left, the first on the right, closely followed by the second. General Gibbon's division was ordered to hold itself ready as a support. The troops went forward with great spirit and resolution. In handsome style they charged up the road, regardless of a hot fire from the enemy, crossed the railroad, ascended the heights beyond, broke through the enemy's first line, penetrated very nearly to the enemy's second line under General Taliaferro, and gained a position near Captain Hamilton's house, capturing and sending back three hundred prisoners and more. Nothing could be better than this gallant charge. It was made in the midst of a destructive fire of musketry in front, and a severe enfilading fire of artillery, and for a time carried everything before it. Finding an interval in the enemy's line between the brigades of Archer and Lane, General Meade took advantage of it, and wedged his advance in, turning the flanks of both brigades and throwing them into confusion. He next struck Gregg's brigade and broke it to pieces, with the loss of its commanding officer. General A. P. Hill's line was thus pierced, and General Meade's next duty was to break the line of General Taliaferro. But this was not so easy. For an hour and a half had the gallant little division pushed forward in its successful career. But it was now bearing the brunt of a contest with the entire corps of General Jackson, which had been ordered to meet the audacious attack, and it could not maintain itself without continued support. General Doubleday was not actively engaged on the left, except to prevent Stuart's advance. There was no strong attack from the enemy in that quarter. Two corps were resting quietly near the river and down towards the bridges, engaged very diligently in "keeping the line of retreat open."

General Meade most urgently desired support. General Reynolds ordered General Gibbon in, and that officer hastened to the aid of the imperilled division. Ward's brigade of General Birney's division was also ordered forward. But it was too late. All the enemy's right wing—except the command of General Stuart, which General Doubleday was holding in check—was now concentrated upon two small divisions of our army, and, after an unavailing struggle of another hour, General Meade was forced back. General Gibbon was slightly wounded, and the two divisions were badly cut up. General Newton's division of General Smith's corps, and General Sickles's division of General Stoneman's were sent forward to aid the engaging forces in extricating themselves from the position.

General Meade had come within a hair's breadth of achieving a great success. His attack had been so vigorous as to be almost a surprise. His troops had come upon the enemy, in some cases, before he had time to take the muskets from the stacks. General Meade was very decidedly of the opinion, that "if large reënforcements had been thrown in immediately after" his "attack, we could have held that plateau, and, if we had done that, the result of the operations there would have been very different from what they were."* General Meade undoubtedly felt as though a victory could have been gained, had he received the support to which he was entitled. He thought that one or two divisions at the bridge heads would have been sufficient to hold them securely and keep open the line of retreat. Out of the five divisions in his rear, he had a right to suppose that a larger force than a single brigade would have been sent to his assistance. Even for that small reënforcement, he was obliged to send no less than three separate times—putting the last appeal into the form of a peremptory order. When the brigade from General Birney's division came, the most it could do, though bravely advancing, was to help in giving to the exhausted forces that had made so gallant an advance, an opportunity for retiring in comparative safety. The remainder of our troops upon that wing were not actively in contact with the enemy beyond a little skirmishing and some artillery fire.

General Burnside at thirty minutes past one o'clock sent a written order to General Franklin† to advance with all his available force and carry the heights in his front, which General Meade had previously won and lost. Orders to the same effect had already been given, but had not been zealously obeyed. General Franklin did not think fit to regard this last order of General Burnside with any better feeling. Indeed, he seems to have been disposed to treat it somewhat contemptuously. "I look upon the order," he says,‡ "as the attempt

* Gen. Meade's testimony before the Committee on the Conduct of the War, I., 692.

† Order received at 2.25 P. M. ‡ New York Tribune of March 24th, 1866.

of a man frantic with desperation at the failure due to his inefficient orders of the morning, to retreive his reputation by the last resource of all weak generals, an attack along the whole line. Knowing as I did, that darkness would overtake us before we could reach the enemy, I did not make the attack ordered, and I explained to General Burnside that night my reasons for not making it." The question naturally arises in the mind of a candid observer, whether General Franklin could not now have reached the enemy sooner, if he had vigorously advanced in the first place at an earlier hour in the day. "It would have required two hours or more," he says, "for either of General Smith's divisions to have reached the enemy's works on the summit of the ridge, on account of the natural and artificial obstacles in the way." But it would appear as though it would not have taken so long a time, had the proper dispositions been previously made. The reason for the failure in making those dispositions has not yet been satisfactorily shown.

The favorable opportunity for making any decided impression upon the enemy's lines had been allowed to pass. The languid nature of the operations upon our left—always with the glorious exception of General Meade's attack—had permitted the moment of victory to glide away from our hands. General Jackson had now massed his forces in front of General Franklin's position. Instead of waiting for an attack, he threatened to deliver one and also detached a force to hold the divisions of Generals Howe and Brooks in check. Growing more bold as he perceived the hesitation of our forces, he actually made a spirited assault upon General Franklin's batteries in front, but was speedily repulsed with the loss of prisoners. The short winter's day was drawing to a close, and nothing further could be done on either side. At half-past four o'clock, General Franklin reported that it was "too late to advance either to the left or front," and so far as the left grand division was concerned, the battle of Fredericksburg was over. During the day, it had suffered the loss of three hundred and seventy-three killed, two thousand, six hundred and ninety-seven wounded, and six hundred and fifty-three missing—of whom three hundred and fifty-three killed, two thousand three hundred and sixty-eight wounded and five hundred and eighty-eight missing belonged to the first corps, General Reynolds. The sixth corps, General Smith, had not been permitted to participate to any extent in the engagement during the entire day. Resting on its arms, it had been obliged to witness the advance and retreat of the two divisions of Generals Meade and Gibbon without being allowed to go to their aid.

The centre of our line was formed by the Ninth Corps. On the morning of the 13th General Willcox was directed to hold his corps in readiness to support the attacks to be made upon the left and right. He connected his own right with General Couch's line, and his left with General Franklin's, holding the ground between Hazel and Deep Runs, below the town. General Sturgis's division was posted on the right, General Getty's in the centre, and General Burns's on the left. The corps remained quietly in position until noon, when General Sturgis's division was sent to the right to support General Couch. Dickinson's battery was posted in a good position to cover the advance. General Ferrero's brigade went gallantly forward, and succeeded in checking the enemy, who had repulsed General Couch's left, and was following up his advantage. General Ferrero's men met the foe with their accustomed spirit and quickly drove him back to the cover of his rifle pits. Captain Dickinson, who had served his battery with great efficiency, was killed, and his battery suffered considerable loss in men and horses. Major Sidney Willard, of the 35th Massachusetts regiment, an accomplished officer, also fell during this movement. Ferrero's brigade, suffering severely from the enemy's fire, was reënforced by General Nagle's brigade, and soon afterwards by the 51st New York under Colonel Potter. "All these troops," says General Willcox in his report of the battle, "behaved well, and marched under a heavy fire across the broken plain, pressed up to the field at the foot of the enemy's sloping crest, and maintained every inch of their ground with great obstinacy, until after night fall. But the position could not be carried." Lieutenant Colonel Welcome B. Sayles and Major Jacob Babbitt of the 7th Rhode Island fell during this movement, the former killed and the latter mortally wounded. The 7th Rhode Island, Colonel Bliss, belonged to General Nagle's brigade, the 11th New Hampshire, Colonel Harriman, belonged to the brigade of General Ferrero. Both were new regiments, and both received at Fredericksburg their initiation of blood. They stood at their posts with the steadiness of veterans, they advanced with the enthusiasm of genuine soldiers, they won the encomium of all who witnessed their valor on this their first day of battle.

During the afternoon, General Whipple sent over to the line of the Ninth Corps Colonel Carroll's brigade, consisting of the 84th and 110th Pennsylvania and the 163d New York, to assist General Sturgis's operations. A brigade of General Griffin's division from the fifth corps also lent a timely aid. Captain Phillips's battery from General Hooker's command did good service, and Captain Buckley's Rhode Island battery—D, 1st Rhode Island light artillery—belonging to the Ninth Corps, made itself conspicuous for its gallantry and well delivered fire. But all efforts to dislodge the enemy were in vain, and about half-past seven o'clock in the evening General Willcox withdrew General Sturgis from the advanced position, which he held close under the enemy's works, and from which he was relieved by the division of General Griffin.

At three o'clock in the afternoon General Burns's division crossed Deep Run in support of General Franklin's command. By this movement it was thrown out of the action altogether and could do little more than look as a spectator upon movements in which it could not participate. General Franklin did not choose to employ it, and by such a movement he could only neutralize, or at least impede the operations of the centre of the army. But for General Getty's division a more active duty was required. It was held—up to a late hour in the afternoon—

as a reserve and a guard to the left of the town. At four o'clock, General Willcox determined to send it into the fight, with the hope that it might create a diversion in favor of our troops that had been hotly engaged through the greater part of the day, and possibly find a weak place in the enemy's line. The Division, forming in two lines under the fire of the enemy, marched bravely forward, advancing over the plain, crossing the railroad, a dry canal trench and some marshy ground, and with considerable exertion gained a position on the left of General Couch's line, within less than a hundred feet of the enemy's strongest position. Here a severe fire of musketry was added to the artillery, whose shot and shell had already thinned the ranks of the Division and the first line composed of Colonel Hawkins's brigade, was forced back under a storm of fire in front and flank. The second line, Colonel Harland's brigade, advanced in the midst of a storm of shell and shrapnel, to within a short distance from the railroad, and established pickets. The night had now settled down, and nothing further could be done. But in the short time of Colonel Harland's advance, the brigade had met with a severe loss in the death of Lieutenant Colonel J. B. Curtis of the 4th Rhode Island, who fell, while bravely cheering on his men. Lieutenant Colonel Curtis was a most intrepid officer and had already shown abundant signs of great promise. He had distinguished himself at Antietam and was valiantly discharging his duty when he fell. His loss was severely felt in the regiment to which he belonged and throughout the entire brigade.

On the right of our line, the battle was indeed sanguinary. The stone wall that lined the telegraph road was like the wall of a fortification. The ground sloped away from it with such an inclination as to enable the enemy's artillery and musketry to make it a field of carnage. But to the work of storming this position, the troops advanced with a determination that deserved success. The enemy's reports of the battle acknowledged that the "Yankees" fought that day with a bravery that had never before been witnessed to an equal degree. General Sumner's

Grand Division showed the highest soldierly qualities. General Couch's corps which bore the brunt of the bloody engagement, behaved in a most handsome and gallant manner. The troops moved out of the city and up the plank and telegraph roads. General French's division was in advance, followed promptly by the division of General Hancock. Both divisions marched bravely up to the enemy's works and undertook to carry them by assault. But the stone wall proved too strong for the valor of our troops. Never did a hotter fire greet an advancing party. The plain in front of the enemy was a sheet of flame. Our men replied with spirit. Our artillery was taken up to within one hundred and fifty yards of the enemy and was faithfully served. Some breaches were made in the wall. But it was all to little purpose. No troops in the world could stand in the midst of such destructive fire. Our line wavered, stopped, recoiled, fell back. It was again formed and again it advanced, only to meet with the same terrible resistance. It was now three hours past noon. The morning had passed away with only the result of General Franklin's partial success—lost because not followed up. General Sumner, who was on this side of the river at the Lacy House, longed to cross and lead his troops in person. To have died on that field of battle would have satisfied the brave old soldier's ambition. General Burnside was not willing to consent to such needless exposure. But the time had come to support General Couch, who was persistently carrying on the unequal conflict. General Hooker, crossing the river, ordered General Butterfield to advance his corps. General Couch's command was formed in front of the enemy, with General Howard's division on the right, General Hancock's in the centre and General French's on the left. Of General Butterfield's corps, General Griffin's division relieved General Howard's; General Humphrey's relieved General Hancock's; General Sykes's relieved General French's, and held the position, throwing pickets out in advance as the day declined. General Whipple's division crossed the river early and remained through the day occupying the city and guarding the bridges. The fresh troops of the fifth corps, under the personal direction of General Hooker, attempted the assault with equal bravery to their predecessors on the same field, but with no better success. The sun was sinking in the west. The day was closing, and, as the twilight fell, a few scattered shot proclaimed that the battle was drawing to a close. The Ninth Corps continued for some time after dark to engage the enemy. But on the right of the line the deadly struggle ceased, as the shadows deepened on river, town and plain. All became silent except the groans of the wounded and dying, and the sharp report of the picket firing as the extreme outposts came in contact with each other. General Burnside returned to his tent, disappointed by the result, but firmly resolved to renew the battle on the subsequent day.

When the Commanding General left headquarters on the morning of the 14th, he had made every preparation to recommence the action by storming the heights. He knew in such an emergency the Ninth Corps would not fail him, and he accordingly selected the troops whom he had before led to victory, to make the attack. He had decided even to direct the assault in person. A column of eighteen regiments was formed, and every thing was ready for the movement, when the three Grand Division Commanders earnestly appealed to him to abandon the attempt. He could not refuse to listen to their persuasions and arguments. General Sumner was a most brave and experienced soldier. General Hooker was unsurpassed for daring. General Franklin was cool and steady. After mature deliberation and a careful revision of the whole matter, General Burnside suffered himself to be convinced that the attack was not feasible. The orders were countermanded, and the day passed without incident. There was considerable spiteful skirmishing at different points along the lines. But General Lee kept his troops under cover of his intrenchments, and General Burnside had concluded to remain quietly in his lines. The severely wounded were cared for and transported across the river. The slightly wounded found relief in the regimental hospitals. The 15th passed in the same manner. A portion of the dead were buried. The night came on cold and stormy, and, concealed from the enemy by the darkness, General Burnside silently withdrew his army without loss across the Rappahannock. The bridges were taken up, and on the 16th the weary soldiers found rest in their former camps. The casualties in this battle were severe, but not disproportionate to the number of men exposed to fire. The subsequent operations of the Army of the Potomac were accompanied by greater losses, especially at Chancellorsville, and in General Grant's campaign of 1864. During the movements of the four days which General Burnside's army passed in Fredericksburg, one thousand three hundred and thirty-nine officers and men were reported killed, nine thousand and sixty wounded, and one thousand five hundred and thirty missing and prisoners. Of the wounded but one thousand six hundred and thirty were treated in general hospital, and of those reported missing, a large number were stragglers and skulkers who rejoined the army soon after the battle.* The loss of the enemy was reported at five thousand three hundred and nine killed, wounded and missing. It was smaller than our own, as he fought mostly behind his works or in the shelter of the woods.

It is not altogether useless now to discuss the causes of this unfortunate disaster. That the battle was well planned, there can be no question. That the plan was either misunderstood, or but feebly carried out by those officers to whom its execution on the left wing was entrusted, is equally without question. General Burnside is a man of quick perceptions and of great activity of mind. It is possible that he may have supposed that his subordinate officers comprehended the movements which he designed as well as he did himself, and so he

*Dr. Letterman, Medical Director of the army, declares that "while the battle was in progress and after it was over, nearly one thousand men (no one of whom had a wound of any consequence, and many were uninjured) jumped in the cars and climbed on the top, at the depot near Fredericksburg and went to Aquia Creek, where they knew no hospitals were established." Medical Recollections, p. 88.

may have neglected to explain their character and scope as fully as their importance demanded. It is characteristic of such minds to project themselves, as it were, upon the minds of others, and to take many things for granted which require an elaborate unfolding. General Burnside supposed that he had made it perfectly clear to General Franklin, both in conversation and by his orders, that the heights near Captain Hamilton's were to be occupied, "if possible," and that that was to be done "at once"—early in the morning—by "a well supported" attack, and moreover, that the whole command upon the left was to kept "in readiness to move at once, as soon as the fog" should lift. Had General Franklin possessed the quickness of appreciation for which his chief had generously given him the credit, and had he strongly resolved upon a successful obedience to the command which he had received, the result would have been more creditable to our arms. General Franklin must have known that a most important movement was expected of him. Else why had a hundred thousand men been sent across the river, and a very large portion of them placed under his command? The heights near Captain Hamilton's were the key to the enemy's position. Had they been occupied successfully, the rebel army would have been cut in twain and handsomely routed. The road to Richmond would have been opened, for, at that time, no intrenchments and defensive works existed. General Meade had the coveted point in his possession, but lost it because he was not supported, while fifty thousand men were standing idle within two miles of him in his rear. It was an additional illustration to those in which the war of the rebellion was fruitful, of the loss of great advantages through a want of coöperation or a miscomprehension of the importance of the occasion on the part of subordinate officers.

General Meade was very confident at the time that victory would have rested with our arms had his attack upon General Lee's right wing been properly supported. Not only did he express this opinion before the Committee on the Conduct of the War, but also before the public. An address which he delivered, on the occasion of the presentation of a sword by a number of the officers and men of his division, a few months after the battle, was reported and printed in the public journals of the time. In the course of that address, General Meade said: "I speak of Fredericksburg, where the Pennsylvania Reserve corps crossed and led the advance, unaided and alone, up the heights, and held their position for half an hour while the others crossed. Had they been followed and supported by other troops, their courage that day would have won a victory."

Corroborative evidence of this fact is to be found in a declaration, first made in Daniels's, and repeated in Cooke's Life of Stonewall Jackson—one of those instances of unconscious testimony which are so valuable in determining questionable points. It was at the time of General Meade's withdrawal from his attack, when he was pressed back by Jackson's entire corps, that Jackson had determined to assault in turn. "Those who saw him at that hour," says the narrative, "will never forget the expression of intense but suppressed excitement which his face displayed. The genius of battle seemed to have gained possession of the great leader, ordinarily so calm; and his countenance glowed as from the glare of a great conflagration." Such excitement does not occur, in persons of such military ability as Jackson undoubtedly was, except upon great emergencies—in times when great perils have been escaped, or when great enterprises are upon the eve of successful consummation, or when all the resources of the nature are required to command and change unfavorable circumstances and give a new character to unfortunate events. That this was a time of exceeding danger to the enemy's army, which demanded the exercise of every military resource to avert disaster, no one can doubt who has followed in thought the charge of General Meade, and has judged what the result would probably have been if General Franklin had followed up and supported the gallant advance of the Pennsylvania Reserves !*

General Franklin had one of the finest opportunities ever offered to a man for gaining a world-wide distinction—and he neglected to improve it. He was unequal to the occasion. A glittering prize was within his grasp, and he refused to reach forth and take it. Was he wilfully blind, or was he unable to perceive its value? However it may have been, it was a loss which could not be remedied. Such an opportunity comes but seldom in a life-time. It did not come again to General Franklin, and, since that day, he has quietly settled into obscurity. A subsequent failure in Louisiana, springing from causes similar to that at Fredericksburg, extinguished his hopes of military renown, and, having been dropped to his regimental rank in the regular army, as Colonel of the 12th infantry, he resigned his commission soon after the close of the war, and retired into private life.

General Burnside, however, wished to spare his subordinate commanders, and was unwilling to adopt the cheap expedient of throwing upon them the blame of the defeat. His language concerning them has always been particularly generous. But for the honor of our military service, the country would have been glad to witness and record a heartier coöperation of many

---

* The following conversation, which is authentically reported as having taken place between Generals Meade and Lee, at the headquarters of the latter, shortly after his surrender, may throw some light upon the subjects discussed in the text:

GENERAL MEADE. At Fredericksburg, General Lee, I pierced your line, and if I had been supported, as I expected to be, I should have defeated you.

GENERAL LEE. Yes, General; that is true.

MEADE. After I was driven back to the banks of the river, why did you not follow up your success? You then had the Army of the Potomac at an advantage at which you never held it before nor since.

LEE. I knew that at the time, and issued order after order to attack you; but I could not succeed in getting my orders obeyed.

MEADE. Indeed! How was that? We always thought that the discipline of your army was almost perfect.

LEE. (*Bitterly.*) Far from it, General. That disposition which my officers had to think and act for themselves, prevented me from reaping the benefits of almost all my successes, and thwarted almost all my plans of campaign.

of the officers of the Army of the Potomac with their commanding general.

General Lee did not receive a great amount of commendation for his conduct of the battle of Fredericksburg. It was thought by the people of his section of the country that he might have done more with the means which he possessed for the injury of General Burnside's army. It certainly exhibited no surpassing skill to keep one's troops in a defensive position, and to be content with simply resisting an attack from sheltered and almost impregnable works. Why did he not come out from his defences on the second day, and make an assault upon our forces in the open field? If the victory had been as decisive as some had thought it, he had every facility for disabling the Army of the Potomac to such a degree as virtually to destroy it as an organized force. If this army had suffered such a disastrous defeat as was represented, why was it allowed to remain unmolested for two days? With a river in its rear, it could have made but slight resistance to a vigorous assault, delivered by an army already flushed with a great success, gained at little cost. Or, if General Lee did not wish to take the risk of such an attempt, he could at least have opened his batteries upon the force which lay beneath his guns, incapable of further exertion. It is hinted, by Southern writers, that some sinister influence was at work at the enemy's headquarters, which prevented the gathering of the spoils which were within the grasp of the rebel army. By what secret force the hand of General Lee was restrained, it is now impossible to say. Whether there was any such force or not is a matter of question. The fact doubtless was that General Lee, a man of slow mind, had formed no plan of defence which could be made available for attack. He was in doubt respecting General Burnside's intentions for a subsequent movement, and he hesitated to take the initiative, preferring to await the development of events. It is possible, also, that General Lee's resources of ammunition and other supplies did not warrant him in a renewal of hostilities. Both his generalship and his material were equally lacking. Moreover, it may have been the case—and this is doubtless the true reason for General Lee's inaction—that the Army of the Potomac had not suffered so serious a disaster as the exaggerated reports of the battle at first led the country to believe. General Burnside would not have been sorry to have met General Lee outside his intrenchments. President Lincoln's address to the army, which was published a few days after the battle, contained a truthful declaration when it stated, that " the attempt was not an error nor the failure other than an accident." The Army of the Potomac, though it had been somewhat rudely shaken, was still in effective condition. There was no general demoralization or despondency, and it was soon ready to prove, on other and more successful fields, that it possessed those qualities of persistence, courage and self-reliance which would, in " the fullness of time," ensure for it a complete and permanent triumph!

NOTE TO CHAPTER VIII.

The result of the battle of Fredericksburg gloomily affected the loyal people of the country. General Burnside had personally so strong a hold upon the public regard, as to induce many persons to feel that he had been led to fight against his better judgment, and that the authorities at Washington were responsible, not only for the battle itself, but also for the failure. In order to do away with such an impression, which was impairing the public confidence in the wisdom of those who were conducting military affairs at Washington, General Burnside, of his own generous motion and from the magnanimity of his nature, wrote to General Halleck the letter which is given below. It was published throughout the country, and had the desired effect, of relieving our military authorities from the distrust which had begun to form. It also had another effect which was entirely unexpected on the part of the writer. It called forth the highest commendations both in public and private, and General Burnside, instead of losing by the want of success at Fredericksburg, rather gained in public estimation, having by his generosity increased the respect of all whose respect was worth securing for his fine qualities as a man and a soldier:

"HEADQUARTERS ARMY OF THE POTOMAC,
Falmouth, Dec. 17th, 1862.

"To MAJOR GENERAL HALLECK, General in Chief of the armies of the United States, Washington:

"GENERAL: I have the honor to offer the following reasons for moving the Army of the Potomac across the Rappahannock sooner than was anticipated by the President, Secretary of War and yourself, and for crossing at a point different from the one indicated to you at our last meeting at the President's.

"During my preparations for crossing at the place I had first selected, I discovered that the enemy had thrown a large portion of his force down the river and elsewhere, thus weakening his defences in front, and also thought I discovered that he did not anticipate the crossing of our whole force at Fredericksburg. And I hoped by rapidly throwing the whole command over at that place to separate, by a vigorous attack, the forces of the enemy on the river below from the forces behind and on the crest in the rear of the town, in which case we could fight him with great advantage in our favor.

To do this we had to gain a height on the extreme right of the crest, which height commanded a new road lately made by the enemy for the purpose of more rapid communication along his lines, which point gained, his positions along the crest would have been scarcely tenable, and he would have been driven from them easily by an attack on his front in connection with a movement in the rear of the crest.

How near we came of accomplishing our object future reports will show. But for the fog and unexpected and unavoidable delay in building the bridges, which gave the enemy twenty-four hours more to concentrate his forces in his strong positions, we would almost certainly have succeeded, in which case the battle would have been, in my opinion, far more decisive than if we had crossed at the places first selected. As it was, we came very near success.

"Failing to accomplish the main object, we remained in order of battle two days, long enough to decide that the enemy would not come out of his stronghold to fight us with his infantry, after which we recrossed to this side of the river unmolested and without the loss of men or property.

"As the day broke, our long lines of troops were seen marching to their different positions as if going on parade. Not the least demoralization or disorganization existed.

"To the brave officers and soldiers who accomplished the feat of thus recrossing the river in the face of the enemy, I owe everything. For the failure in the attack I am responsible, as the extreme gallantry, courage and endurance shown by them was never exceeded, and would have carried the points had it been possible.

"To the families and friends of the dead I can only offer my heartfelt sympathies, but for the wounded I can offer my earnest prayers for their comfort and final recovery.

"The fact that I decided to move from Warrenton on to this line, rather against the opinion of the President, Secretary of War and yourself, and that you left the whole movement in my hands without giving me orders, makes me responsible.

"I will visit you very soon and give you more definite information, and finally I will send you my detailed report, in which a special acknowledgment will be made of the services of the different grand divisions, corps and my general and personal staff, of the departments of the Army of the Potomac, to whom I am much indebted for their hearty support and co-operation.

"I will add here that the movement was made earlier than you expected and after the President, Secretary of War and yourself requested me not to be in haste, for the reason that we were supplied much sooner by the different staff departments than was anticipated when I last saw you.

"Our killed amount to one thousand one hundred and fifty-two, our wounded to about nine thousand, and our prisoners seven hundred, which last have been paroled and exchanged for about the same number taken by us. The wounded were all removed to this side of the river, and are being well cared for, and the dead were all buried under a flag of truce. The surgeons report a much larger proportion of slight wounds than usual, one thousand six hundred and thirty only being treated in hospitals.

"I am glad to represent the army at the present time in good condition.

"Thanking the Government for that entire support and confidence which I have always received from them, I remain, General,

"Very respectfully,

"Your obedient servant,

"A. E. Burnside,

"*Major General Commanding Army of Potomac.*"

CHAPTER IX.

AFTER FREDERICKSBURG.

AFTER the battle of Fredericksburg, General Burnside still believed that the enemy's position could be carried, or, at all events, successfully turned. The weather continued favorable, and the idea of going into winter quarters was unwelcome to an active mind. He immediately made preparations for another movement. A plan proposed by General Averill for making an extensive cavalry raid around the enemy's lines, destroying his communications and exciting alarm in the rebel capital was approved with some modifications. The army was to assist in the execution of the plan by a demonstration across the river, by which it was to withdraw the attention of the enemy from General Averill's movements sufficiently to give good promise of success to the operations in his rear. General Averill's plan contemplated a movement across the Rappahannock at Kelly's Ford, and the Rapidan at Raccoon Ford. Thence, according to order, the troops were to make a detour around the enemy's position, with detached parties to cut the telegraph wires between Gordonsville and Culpepper Court House on one side and those between Louisa Court House and Hanover Junction upon the other side. The main body was to "pass down near Louisa Court House to Cartersville or Goochland Court House, cross the James river, destroy one or more locks on the canal which runs along the left bank of the James river, destroy the bridges across the Appomattox river and Flat Creek, destroy whatever bridges might be found on the Petersburg and Lynchburg railroad, and the bridges across the Nottoway river and Stony Creek on the Petersburg and Weldon railroad."*

General Averill hoped to make a junction with General Peck at Suffolk, who was to be instructed to send out strong reconnoitering parties to the Blackwater river. Two signal officers were to accompany General Averill, two were to be sent to General Peck. A code of rocket signals had been prepared, by which communications could be interchanged over a distance of twenty miles. A picked force was organized, consisting of five hundred volunteer and five hundred regular cavalry, of the best men and most trustworthy officers, with four pieces of light horse artillery and an engineer party furnished with "proper tools and all the materials for destroying the bridges and blowing up the stone structures." The party was to go without baggage, or wagons, or pack animals, or anything to encumber the expedition. A division of infantry and an extra brigade with a battery and a few hundred additional cavalry were placed at General Averill's disposal to go as far as Morrisville, to be distributed along the upper fords of the Rappahannock. The enemy's cavalry were at the time attempting a raid upon our own lines near Fairfax Court House, and it was hoped that this extra force might cut off and capture the raiding party or disconcert its plans. In the meanwhile, General Burnside was to engage the enemy's attention by making a feint of attack upon his lines in front or flank. The officers and men in the cavalry force were eager to go upon this expedition, and burned for the opportunity of giving some eclat to their branch of the service.

On the 26th of December, General Burnside ordered preparations for a movement to be made, intending to cross the river at a point called Hayfield, some six or seven miles below Fredericksburg, and seize the railroad in the enemy's rear. On the 30th the cavalry started, and on the next day the head of the column had arrived near Kelly's Ford, intending to cross and en-

---

*Order to General Averill.

ter upon the real work of the expedition. Every thing was promising a great success. The infantry had well performed its work and the additional cavalry had had a successful skirmish with the enemy at Warrenton. The army was ready to coöperate.

A very serious and unexpected interruption took place, which changed the entire aspect of affairs. On the afternoon of the 30th, a despatch was received at headquarters from the President, in the following words: "I have good reason for saying that you must not make a general movement without letting me know of it." General Burnside was surprised by such a communication. What could it mean? It was supposed that the President had some information which rendered any movement impracticable, and accordingly orders were sent to General Averill to halt his column and await further directions. On the night of the 31st, General Burnside went to Washington, and on the following day had several long interviews with the President, Mr. Stanton and General Halleck, in which were discussed the various military questions which the battle of Fredericksburg had raised. To his great astonishment, he ascertained that two officers of his army, having solicited leave of absence for a few days, ostensibly on private business, had visited the President, and, by exaggerated statements of the condition of the army, of the magnitude of the preparations, and the feeling of the officers and men towards General Burnside, had induced him to believe that a movement was going on which would result in a second battle, more disastrous than the first had been. The President was alarmed, and under the influence of the erroneous information which had been given him, was induced to send the despatch above referred to. General Burnside returned to his camp early in the morning of January 2d, 1863. He found that the enemy's raid had been frustrated and had come to nought, mainly by the judicious management of General Stahl, commanding at Fairfax Court House. But he also found that the plan of his own movement had, by some means, become known to the enemy. Nothing remained but to recall General Averill and to give up the thought of active operations for the time. The troops were reëstablished in camp. Thus the third attempt of General Burnside to use his army against the enemy was brought to failure by the intrigue of his subordinate officers. That the President did not dismiss those officers on the spot, was due more to his humanity of heart than to their desert!

The incidents above related gave rise to the tender of his resignation on the part of General Burnside, and to some correspondence between him and the President and General Halleck. On the 5th, General Burnside wrote to Mr. Lincoln: "Since my return to the army, I have become more than ever convinced that the general officers of this command are almost unanimously opposed to another crossing of the river; but I am still of the opinion that the crossing should be attempted, and I have accordingly issued orders to the engineers and artillery to prepare for it. There is much hazard in it, as there always is in the majority of military movements, and I cannot begin the movement without giving you notice of it, particularly as I know so little of the effect that it may have upon other movements of distant armies.

"The influence of your telegraph the other day is still upon me, and has impressed me with the idea that there are many parts of the problem which influence you that are not known to me.

"In order to relieve you from all embarrassment in my case, I inclose with this my resignation of my commission as Major General of Volunteers, which you can have accepted if my movement is not in accordance with the views of yourself and your military advisers.

"I have taken the liberty to write to you personally upon this subject, because it was necessary, as I learn from General Halleck, for you to approve of my general plan, written at Warrenton, before I could commence the movement, and I think it is quite as necessary that you should know of the important movement I am now about to make; particularly as it will have to be made in opposition to the views of nearly all my general officers, and after the receipt of a despatch from you informing me of the opinion of some of them who have visited you.

"In conversation with you on New Year's morning, I was led to express some opinions which I afterwards felt it my duty to place on paper, and to express them verbally to the gentlemen of whom we were speaking, which I did in your presence after handing you the letter.

"I beg leave to say that my resignation is not sent in any spirit of insubordination, but, as I before said, simply to relieve you from any embarrassment in changing commanders, where lack of confidence may have rendered it necessary."

On the same day, General Burnside wrote to General Halleck: "I have decided to move the army across the river again, and have accordingly given the directions to the engineers and artillery to make the necessary preparations to effect the crossing.

"Since I last saw you, it has become more apparent that the movement must be made almost entirely upon my own responsibility, so far as this army is concerned, and I do not ask you to assume any responsibility in reference to the mode or place of crossing, but it seems to me that, in making so hazardous a movement, I should receive some general directions from you as to the advisability of crossing at some point, as you are necessarily well informed of the effect at this time upon other parts of the army of a success or a repulse. You will readily see that the responsibility of crossing without the knowledge of this effect, and against the opinion of nearly all the general officers, involves a greater responsibility than an officer situated as I am ought to incur.

"In view of the President's telegraph to me the other day, and with its influence still upon me, I have written to him on this subject, and enclosed to him my resignation, directed to the Adjutant General, to be accepted in case it is not deemed advisable for me to cross the river. I send this resignation, because I have no other plan of campaign for this winter, and I am not disposed to go into winter quarters.

"It may be well to add, that recent information goes to show that the enemy's force has not been diminished in our front to any great extent."

The replies of the officials thus addressed sufficiently indicate the wishes of the military authorities at this time. On the 7th, General Halleck wrote to General Burnside: "Your communication of the 5th was delivered to me by your Aide-de-Camp at twelve o'clock, meridian, to-day.

"In all my communications and interviews with you since you took command of the Army of the Potomac, I have advised a forward movement across the Rappahannock. At our interview at Warrenton, I urged that you should cross by the fords above Fredericksburg, rather than to fall down to that place; and when I left you at Warrenton, it was understood that at least a considerable part of your army would cross by the fords, and I so represented to the President. It was this modification of the plan proposed by you that I telegraphed you had received his approval.* When the attempt at Fredericksburg was abandoned, I advised you to renew the attempt at some other point, either in whole or in part, to turn the enemy's works or to threaten their wings or communications; in other words, to keep the enemy occupied till a favorable opportunity offered to strike a decisive blow. I particularly advised you to use your cavalry and light artillery upon his communications, and attempt to cut off his supplies and engage him at an advantage. In all our interviews, I have urged that our first object was, not Richmond, but the defeat or scattering of Lee's army, which threatened Washington and the line of the Upper Potomac. I now recur to these things simply to remind you of the general views which I have expressed, and which I still hold. The circumstances of the case, however, have somewhat changed since the early part of November.

* This is the first intimation of General Halleck's idea of a plan other than that which has already been given.

The chances of an extended line of operations are now, on account of the advanced season, much less than then. But the chances are still in our favor to meet and defeat the enemy on the Rappahannock, if we can effect a crossing in a position where we can meet the enemy on favorable or even equal terms. I therefore still advise a movement against him.

"The character of that movement, however, must depend upon circumstances which may change any day and almost any hour. If the enemy should concentrate his forces at the place you have selected for a crossing, make it a feint, and try another place. Again, the circumstances at the time may be such as to render an attempt to cross the entire army not advisable. In that case, theory suggests that, while the enemy concentrates at that point, advantages can be gained by crossing smaller forces at other points, to cut off his lines, destroy his communications, and capture his rear-guards, outposts, &c. The great object is to occupy the enemy, to prevent his making large detachments or distant raids, and to injure him all you can with the least injury to yourself. If this can be best accomplished by feints of a general crossing and detached real crossings, take that course; if by an actual general crossing with feints on other points, adopt that course. There seems to me to be many reasons why a crossing at some point should be attempted. It will not do to keep your large army inactive. As you yourself admit, it devolves on you to decide upon the time, place and character of the crossing which you may attempt. I can only advise that an attempt be made, and as early as possible."

On this, the President made the following endorsement:

"JANUARY 8, 1863.

"I understand General Halleck has sent you a letter, of which this is a copy. I approve this letter. I deplore the want of concurrence with you in opinion by your general officers, but I do not see the remedy. Be cautious, and do not understand that the government or country is driving you. I do not yet see how I could profit by changing the command of the Army of the Potomac, and if I did, I should not wish to do it by accepting the resignation of your commission.

"A. LINCOLN."

Fortified by these opinions, and deeming it best, with General Halleck, that both the army and the enemy should be occupied, General Burnside was encouraged to believe that something might yet be accomplished which would redound to the honor of the country and effect its deliverance from the burdens which the rebellion had brought. He did not yet, by any means, despair of success. With the hopeful temperament which enabled him to bear the burden of repeated failure with equanimity, he was still resolute. In the long-continued good weather, he saw reason for encouragement, and he determined to make at least one more effort to accomplish a favorable result. His new plan was, to cross his army either above or below Fredericksburg, and thus turn the position, draw General Lee into the open field, and then fight him at better advantage. He decided to cross at the upper fords, and turn General Lee's left flank. Careful reconnaissances were made, for many miles up and down the river, by experienced officers, and it was finally determined to make the passage at Banks's ford and United States ford. Demonstrations were made at a point below Fredericksburg, and a portion of the enemy's forces were drawn down towards Port Royal. General Lee, suspecting some movement, also sent a force up to the United States ford, leaving Banks's ford comparatively unguarded. General Burnside resolved to throw his entire army across the river at the latter point, and with this view the ponton trains were sent up to the neighborhood of the ford, and engineer parties were set busily at work to prepare the roads. He succeeded in deceiving the enemy by his movements, and with an advantage of nearly forty-eight hours' start, he moved his command to the neighborhood of the upper fords.

The army marched out of its encampments on the morning

of the 20th of January. For the first day all went well. The men were in good spirits, the sun shone bright, and all hoped for success. Towards evening, the omens were not so favorable. Heavy clouds began to gather, and at sunset the sky was overcast. The army bivouacked near Banks's Ford with the preparations for crossing nearly completed. But after nightfall a most furious storm burst upon the scene. The wind roared through the forests, along the plains, over the hills. The rain fell in torrents. The roads were soon reduced to a mass of mud and mire. The artillery, the wagons, horses and mules and men were stopped as effectually as though a hundred armies blocked the way. Winter, which with extreme forbearance had held off until that moment, now came on with relentless rigor.

It was utterly impossible to fight the elements, and General Burnside on the morning of the 22d, finding further efforts useless, ordered the army to return to its former position. The march back to Falmouth was made with extreme difficulty. The troops, on their arrival, went into winter quarters, and all idea of moving again until the spring opened, was abandoned. General Burnside, for the purpose of freeing the Administration from embarrassment, again tendered his resignation to the President, who again refused to accept it, preferring to relieve him in Virginia, and to retain his services for use in other quarters. General Burnside was accordingly relieved of the command on the 25th of January. General Hooker was appointed in his place. General Franklin was relieved by order of the Secretary of War. General Sumner, who was General Hooker's senior in rank, was relieved at hisown request. General Burnside immediately proceeded to Providence, where he was received by his fellow-citizens with every demonstration of welcome and esteem.

It was not strange that General Burnside should have failed in command of the Army of the Potomac. Any officer who should have immediately succeeded General McClellan would have met with the same fate. That army was divided by jealousies and partizanship. Army correspondents spoke of these strifes and bickerings as "notorious and scandalous." No man could have secured a cordial coöperation from his subordinate officers. Thus the efficiency of the command was seriously impaired by its internal dissensions. The feeling in favor of General McClellan in some quarters was so strong as to manifest itself on several occasions, not only in expressions of dissatisfaction with his successor, but also in assemblages which are described as "almost seditious in their character." In other quarters there were equally strong expressions of disapproval of General McClellan. These however did not take the form of support to General Burnside, but of laudations of this, that or the other general officer, who was supposed to be the best fitted to command the Army of the Potomac. The feeling even proceeded so far as to affect questions of comparatively minor importance. On the march from Fredericksburg and in camp at Falmouth if any delay occurred or supplies were short, or the railroad was not put in order as soon as was expected, the hardships were contrasted with the plenty enjoyed in Maryland and the blame laid at General Burnside's door. The partizans in the army had their friends and partizans at home. General McClellan allowed himself to be identified with a political movement, which culminated in a public declaration, a year or two later, that the war was a failure. The disloyal press of the country, in its greed for everything that would make against the Administration and the conduct of the war, seized upon the existence of this feeling in the army as an occasion for using expressions, which had for their object the diminution of confidence in the commander of the Army of the Potomac. Every quarrel was nursed, every difference of opinion was exaggerated, every conflict of feeling was fostered.

It required all General Grant's military genius and the strength of his silent, persistent, inflexible will, to control the discordant elements, and not until he exercised a personal supervision over the command was the Army of the Potomac able to perform its proper work. General Hooker, at Chancellorsville suffered a most disastrous failure. General Meade came very near it at Gettysburg. General Burnside did as much and as well as any man could have done with the materials which he then had in hand. Coming from the warm friendships and the cordial coöperation of his officers in North Carolina, the cold atmosphere that prevailed in the Army of the Potomac chilled him. He was unaccustomed to such want of enthusiasm and zeal. But he was resolved to do his duty, however difficult that might be. He failed to achieve success, because those who should have helped him refused to give the needful aid.

So keenly did General Burnside feel this lack of friendship and coöperation, and so strongly was he impressed with the thought of the injury which it was inflicting upon the country and the cause, that he was induced at one time to resort to extreme measures. He even contemplated the necessity of dismissing from the service several officers high in rank, and relieving others from duty with the Army of the Potomac. An order to that effect was prepared, signed and issued in due form, but as it required the approval of the President before it could be executed, General Burnside submitted it in person to Mr. Lincoln. The interview was held at Washington a day or two after the failure of the last movement. The President referred the matter to the Secretary of War, the General in Chief and other military advisers. They decided against the execution of the order, and the President accordingly withheld his approval. At the same time, it was very positively decided that General Burnside should not be permitted to resign. He was relieved from command, and he spoke from his heart when he said to the President at the end of the interview: "Neither you nor General Hooker will be a happier man than myself if he shall gain a victory on the Rappahannock." After General Burnside left the Army of the Potomac, the order known as "Order No. 8," found its way into the newspapers and became the occasion of considerable comment.

Other causes operated to produce in the army itself some

discontent. A long delay occurred in the payment of the troops. Many regiments had not been paid for six months, some for eight months or more. Again the disloyal press raised its clamor. The Administration was sending the army to destruction while officials at Washington were plundering the public treasury. Such was in substance the cry which began to be heard about the camps. Many of the soldiers were even credulous enough to believe it, and the feeling which it engendered had a bad effect upon the morale of the army. Even mutinous demonstrations were made and the commanding general was obliged to use force to secure obedience and quiet. The camp of a certain battery was at one time surrounded by a force of infantry and artillery in hostile array before the men would consent to come to terms. But there were other instances of discontent among the more intelligent and obedient soldiers, who could not regard the situation with feelings of entire equanimity. They heard of their families at home as being in great destitution, or becoming objects of public charity. They had no pay. They saw no immediate prospect of having any. They could not enter into battle with the enthusiasm which men would have who felt that a grateful country was ever ready to assist them, and that the government for which they were fighting was discharging to them and theirs its just obligations.

Another fruitful cause of failure was the training which the Army of the Potomac had had in the method of fighting with the spade rather than with the musket. The system which the campaign on the Peninsula had established grew almost into a disease. The army could not go forward with that *élan* which is a necessary requisite for victory. Compare the fighting under Sheridan in the valley of the Shenandoah with that under McClellan on the Peninsula! The two systems are put in admirable contrast, and the former bears away the palm. The difference was not in the men of the two armies, for they were the same in both. It arose from the training to which they had been subjected under the two commanders. In subsequent days, under a different system of warfare, the Army of the Potomac showed that it was not excelled by any army in the world. It was always brave and steady, but in its earlier days, it had not that celerity of movement, that quick mobility, which is indispensable for effective operations and decisive triumphs. The officers and soldiers, thus accustomed to fight behind defensive works, would look upon themselves as being led to slaughter when directed to charge upon the enemy's fortifications. In consequence, the advance would naturally lack vigor, and if extraordinary activity was required, there would arise a feeling that the army was ill used. It is true, that too much impetuosity is oftentimes as dangerous as too little. The Army of the Potomac never erred in the former particular. The proper combination of enthusiasm with steadiness is the requisite for genuine success in every enterprise—most of all in war. The Army of the Potomac—through no fault indeed of the men who composed it, for it was made up of the finest material—had been trained more to prudence than to boldness. The result of its early education was to be noticed in the long and severe campaigns to which it was subjected. In judging of General Burnside's course and its issue in this period, the above considerations are to be taken into the account.

On the 26th of January, General Burnside took leave of the Army of the Potomac in the following order:

"By direction of the President of the United States, the Commanding General this day transfers the command of this Army to Major General Joseph Hooker.

"The short time that he has directed your movements has not been fruitful of victory or any considerable advancement of our lines, but it has again demonstrated an amount of courage, patience and endurance that under more favorable circumstances would have accomplished great results;—continue to exercise these virtues, be true in your devotion to your country and the principles you have sworn to maintain, give to the brave and skilful General who has so long been identified with your organization, and who is now to command you, your full and cordial support and coöperation, and you will deserve success.

"In taking an affectionate leave of the entire Army, from which he separates with so much regret, he may be pardoned if he bids an especial farewell to his long tried associates of the Ninth Corps.

"His prayers are that God may be with you, and grant you continual success until the rebellion is crushed."

A few days before the last movement of the army was made, a change had been effected in the organization of the Ninth Corps. General John Sedgwick had been ordered to report to General Sumner, and, after a temporary assignment to the command of the second corps, had been ordered to relieve General Willcox in the command of the Ninth. General Willcox resumed command of the first division, relieving General Burns. General Sedgwick was well and favorably known throughout the army. He had acquired great renown in the Peninsula campaign and at the battle of Antietam, where he was twice severely wounded. He was born in Connecticut, and graduated at the Military Academy at West Point in the class of 1837, the twenty-fourth in a class of fifty. He was commissioned Second Lieutenant in the 2d Artillery, July 1, 1837, and First Lieutenant, April 19, 1839. He achieved an enviable fame in the Mexican war, winning a brevet Captaincy, August 20, 1847, for gallant and meritorious conduct in the battles of Contreras and Churubusco. He was brevetted Major, September 13, of the same year, for gallant and meritorious conduct in the battle of Chapultepec. On the 26th of January, 1849, he was made a full Captain of Artillery. Upon the organization of the 1st United States Cavalry, he was appointed Major, dating March 8, 1855, and served as such in Kansas during 1858, 1859, and 1860. When the rebellion broke out, he was in command of Fort Wise.

On the 16th of March, 1861, he was commissioned Lieutenant Colonel of the 2d United States Cavalry, and on the

25th of April, he was promoted to Colonel of the 4th United States Cavalry. On the 31st of August, he was commissioned Brigadier General of Volunteers. Serving on the Peninsula, he won by his valor a brevet as Brigadier General in the regular army, dating May 31, 1862, and in the following March, was nominated and confirmed as Major General of Volunteers, to rank from July 4, 1862. He was particularly noted for his skill and courage at Yorktown, Fair Oaks, Savage Station, Glendale and Antietam. He was one of the very best officers in the army, distinguished for his bravery, modesty, kindness of heart and manly integrity. His officers and men were very strongly attached to him, and he never disappointed their trust and affection. Had he remained as General of the Ninth Corps, he would doubtless have endeared himself as strongly to the soldiers of his new command, as to those who had previously been under his direction. But his stay with it was very brief. He only remained long enough for the Corps to claim his record as a part of its own honorable history. He was transferred to the command of the sixth corps on the 5th of February, 1863, and Major General William F. Smith was assigned to the position which he had vacated.

General Smith was a native of Vermont, and a graduate of the Military Academy at West Point in 1845. He was the fourth in rank in a class of forty-one. He was appointed a brevet Second Lieutenant in the corps of Topographical Engineers, July 1, 1845. He was acting Assistant Professor of Mathematics at West Point, from November 6, 1846, to August 21, 1848. He was promoted to Second Lieutenant, July 14, 1849. In common with other members of the corps, he served on the plains and among the mountains of the far West. The Pacific Railroad Survey found in him one of its efficient engineers and explorers. At the commencement of the war, he was a Captain, and at the time of his assignment to the Ninth Corps, he was on the eve of his promotion to be Major. He was commissioned Brigadier General of Volunteers, August 13th, 1861, and Major General, March 9, 1864, served with some distinction on the Peninsula, under General McClellan, and at the battle of Fredericksburg, where he was in command of the sixth corps. He afterwards, by direction of General Hooker, exchanged places with General Sedgwick, when the Ninth Corps was transferred to Newport News. He continued in command until March, 1863, when he was relieved by Major General John G. Parke.

General Parke was an old companion in arms of the corps to the command of which he was now assigned. He had won great distinction in North Carolina, as has already been set forth in these pages. A very dear and trusted friend to General Burnside, he became chief of staff to that officer both when the Ninth Corps, the left wing, and the entire army of the Potomac were placed in his charge. At different periods in the history of the Corps, General Parke was in command, and always acquitted himself in the best and most creditable manner. He is a man of singular excellence of character, and has ever inspired the confidence and esteem of those with whom he has been associated to a remarkable degree.

John G. Parke was born in Pennsylvania, in 1827, and graduated, second in his class of forty-three members, at the Military Academy at West Point, in 1849. He was appointed brevet Second Lieutenant, July 1, 1849, in the corps of Topographical Engineers. As a member of this corps he had performed, previous to the rebellion, distinguished services in different parts of the country, particularly in the west and south-west. He had acted as Secretary of the Light House Board and of the River and Harbor Improvement Board. He had also been active in the operations upon the plains of the West, in New Mexico, in the Boundary Commission, and the Surveys of the routes of the Pacific Railroad. In 1851, he prepared a map of New Mexico, which is declared to have been "a careful compilation of all the available and reliable information in relation to New Mexico which could be obtained at that date from trappers and hunters, as well as from actual survey. It was prepared by Lieutenant Parke, while in that country, by order of brevet Colonel John Munroe, United States Army, commanding Ninth Military Department."* During the same year he accompanied Captain Sitgreaves on an exploring expedition from Santa Fe to San Diego. In 1853, he assisted Lieutenant R. S. Williamson in a survey through the passes of the Sierra Nevada and Coast Range. The expedition occupied three months' time, and in the course of it, Lieutenant Parke conducted an independent expedition to Los Angelos, the San Gabriel and Santa Anna valleys.

In 1854, Lieutenant Parke made a successful reconnaissance for a railroad route between Punas Village and El Paso. He left San Diego on the 24th of January, with a party of twenty-three men and an escort of twenty-eight dragoons, under Lieutenant Stoneman, and made a careful examination of the country, from the Gila River to the Rio Grande, travelling by way of Tucson, San Xavier, Rio San Pedro, Chiricahui Mountains, and Fort Fillmore. The report of the expedition is published in the second volume of the Pacific Railroad Reports, and is a very valuable statement respecting the characteristics of the country through which the journey was made, and its facilities for the construction of the proposed road. Advanced to his next grade, July 1, 1856, Lieutenant Parke became, in 1857, the Astronomer of the Northwest Boundary Commission for establishing the line between the United States and British America. In all these positions, he was distinguished for the patient fidelity, modest, yet manly bearing and firmness in the discharge of duty which have characterized him in later years. In his early professional life, he laid the foundations of a solid, substantial reputation, which has never been weakened, but has continually strengthened in his subsequent career.

Lieutenant Parke's maps, contained in the eleventh volume of the Pacific Railroad reports, are models of accuracy and clearness of delineation. He had richly deserved his promotion to a captaincy in his corps, which he received on his arrival at Washington, his commission dating September 9, 1861.

* Reports of Explorations and Surveys of Pacific Railroad. Vol. xi,, p. 60.

Eng^d by A. H. Ritchie.

GEN. JOHN G. PARKE.

When General Burnside organized his expedition, he desired and secured the valuable aid and companionship of his old friend and school fellow. Captain Parke was commissioned Brigadier General of Volunteers on the 23d of November, 1861, and from that time his history was identified with that of the Ninth Corps through its entire term of service. For his services in North Carolina, he was brevetted Lieutenant Colonel in the regular army and promoted to Major General of Volunteers, his commission dating July 18, 1862.* General Parke's pure, noble and unselfish disposition had made him profoundly beloved by all the officers and men of the Ninth Corps, and his assignment to the command was hailed with sentiments of undisguised approbation and joy.

On the 10th of February, 1863, the Corps was separated from the Army of the Potomac, and was sent down to Newport News, where it remained inactive for the next six weeks. General Getty's division was transferred to Suffolk, where the enemy was making a demonstration against our works and even for a time threatened a siege. The two remaining divisions were respectively under the command of General Willcox and General Sturgis. General Getty's division did not again join the corps as a complete command. The regiments composing it were dispersed among the different armies in that quarter, after the retirement of General Longstreet, and only two of them—the 4th Rhode Island and the 9th New Hampshire—returned to the Corps, when, in the following year, it again formed an integral part of the Army of the Potomac.†

The two divisions that were left at Newport News were destined to more active service on distant fields. The West

*General Parke's promotion, with that of Generals Reno and Foster, was at first dated April 26, 1862, but, by the influence of General McClellan and the western generals, other corps commanders were allowed to out-rank General Burnside's officers and the commissions of the latter were re-dated as above.

†The detached regiments never forgot their alliance with the Ninth Corps, and, when transferred to other commands, their tents were still inscribed with the initials "9th A. C.," by which they were proud to be known.

and the Southwest were to be the scenes of their valor and endurance. They were to assist in opening the Mississippi to the unobstructed trade of the country, and in freeing a long-suffering people from the thraldom of a tyrannical government. The record which the Corps had written for itself in North Carolina, Maryland and Virginia, was to be illustrated by new and even brighter deeds. Under the able direction of General Parke, it had other fields to conquer and other laurels to win. The work which it had already performed was but the promise of more important labors, which had for their end faithfully to discharge its entire duty to the Republic. How thoroughly and well the work was done, it remains for the subsequent pages of this narrative to record!

NOTE TO THE ARMY OF THE POTOMAC.

Mr. William Swinton, a former correspondent of the New York Times, has recently published a volume entitled "Campaigns of the Army of the Potomac." Whatever worth the book may have as a record of the career of other generals, it has very little in reference to that of General Burnside. Every man has a right to form and express an opinion as to the merits or demerits of every public officer, so far as his official conduct is concerned. But in making up the estimate, there must be a strict accordance with facts. Mr. Swinton scarcely speaks of General Burnside and the Ninth Corps without a contemptuous sneer, and applies derogatory epithets to every military movement in which they were engaged. At South Mountain, "the key point of the whole position was overlooked" by General Reno. At Antietam, "Burnside's tentatives were frivolous in their character," and "five hours passed before the work that should have been done in the morning was accomplished." For the determination of the first point, the military judgment of General Reno can safely be put over against that of Mr. Swinton. For the decision of the second, it is but necessary to refer to the reports of Generals Burnside and Cox, and of other officers who were present in the action at the bridge.

That which Mr. Swinton calls a task of "comparative ease" was judged to be one of great difficulty by those who were most interested in performing the work. Three hours, not five, were occupied in carrying the position, and in those three hours the Ninth Corps lost some of its best officers and men. Every reader of military history knows that a narrow bridge is not an easy position to carry in the face of a resolute enemy, even though the numbers arrayed for the assault be greatly superior to the number of the defenders. Only a few can make the direct attack at any time. Those who were engaged in the strife did not consider their "tentatives" frivolous. There were no better troops in the Army of the Potomac, than the men of the Kanawha division and those of the Ninth Corps, who attempted and finally carried the bridge. The losses in killed and wounded sustained by the Corps as compared with the rest of the army will show whether or not every thing was done that could be done at the "Burnside Bridge" and on the heights and plateau beyond. The second corps was more roughly handled by the enemy than any other, and lost a little more than twenty-five per cent. of its number; the first corps lost a little less than sixteen per cent.; the twelfth corps lost a little more than sixteen per cent.; the Ninth Corps lost a little less than sixteen per cent. Of the two corps that were not actively engaged for any length of time, the fifth lost less than one, the sixth a little more than three per cent. The fight on the right of our line was especially severe as every one knows. Yet there is no great disparity between the losses on the two wings, and if the number of casualties affords any ground of judgment, it must be allowed that "frivolous tentatives" are equal to a combat which was "very murderous to each side"—or else that there were no frivolous tentatives at all, but downright fighting. Nor is it to be supposed that General Lee, able officer as he was, and the object of Mr. Swinton's admiration, would have left the bridge upon his right so poorly defended as to make General Burnside's task "one of comparative ease."

It is in "the Campaign on the Rappahannock" that Mr. Swinton falls into the grossest errors of statement. Without stopping to comment upon his reasoning from the unfounded premise of General McClellan's "manœuvering to fight a great battle," it is only necessary to examine the spirit and declarations of the author in his attempt to disparage General Burnside and his services. His statement of General Burnside's plan at the outset shows that he had no adequate knowledge of the subject upon which he was writing. "In point of fact," he says, (note to page 233,) "General Burnside had not matured any definite plan of action, for the reason, that he hoped to be able to postpone operations till the spring. He did not favor operating against Richmond by the overland route, but had his mind turned towards a repetition of McClellan's movement to the Peninsula; and, in determining to march to Fredericksburg, he cherished the hope of being able to winter there upon an easy base of supplies, and in the spring embarking his army for the James River." Every single assertion in the above extract is precisely the reverse of the truth. General Burnside had his plan matured, did intend to operate against Richmond by the overland route, did not have his mind turned to a repetition of McClellan's experiment, did not cherish the hope of going into winter quarters, was greatly averse to spending the winter in inaction, and had no notion of embarking his army for the James. It could not be possible for an author to put more misstatements into a single sentence than Mr. Swinton has done.

General Burnside's plan has been stated in the text, to push forward rapidly beyond Fredericksburg, keeping to the eastward, changing his base of supplies successively from Aquia Creek to Port Royal, to White House and some point on the James River below Richmond. His plan was substantially the same as that followed by General Grant in the campaign of 1864, except that he intended keeping nearer to Chesapeake Bay, unless a favorable opportunity occurred of thrusting in his army, well supplied and ready for battle, between General Lee and Richmond. He had the advantage of being considerably in advance of General Lee, and of marching on a shorter line, and through a defenceless territory. That this was General Burnside's plan at the time, I know through my correspondence with him, and frequent and familiar conversations at Falmouth and elsewhere, during the Winter of 1862–'63.

Mr. Swinton is equally unfortunate in his conception or interpretation of the plan of attack at the battle of Fredericksburg, and accuses General Burnside of an afterthought in his declaration that the main attack was to be made by the left wing of our army. That certainly was the plan of battle if General Burnside is to be believed; and those who know him best will not judge lightly of his veracity. General Franklin was to attack with one division, but he was to keep it well supported and have his entire command in readiness for a rapid movement along the old Richmond road. General Sumner was to form his division for attack but was to await directions. The subject has been fully stated in the text, and when Mr. Swinton tries to make it appear that General "Franklin was directed to make a partial operation of the nature of a reconnaissance" he is doing himself and his theme injustice. Nor is he more happy in his apparent attempt to disparage the fighting of our soldiers, when he tries to produce the impression, that but a small force was in the front of General Sumner's command. Two brigades he allows as the entire force, used by General Longstreet, to repel the attacks made by our right wing upon "the stone wall and rifle trenches at the foot of Marye's heights"—the chief scene of fighting in that quarter. In a note on the 250th page, he quotes with evident satisfaction an extract from General McLaw's report of the battle, which states that seventeen hundred men were all that were necessary "to repulse the numerous assaults made by the Union columns." Yet on the 253d page, he quotes another note to the purport, that General Longstreet's loss in fighting General Sumner's attack was "three thousand four hundred and fifteen"—or about twice as many as his subordinate found necessary to repulse the Union assaults. It is curious to notice how easily a man falls into error, when once he is predetermined to make the event of which he speaks wear the worst possible appearance. With such premises, of what value is the reasoning deduced from them?

Surely it may be said of Mr. Swinton somewhat as Sheridan said in his reply to Dundas, that he is indebted to his prejudices for his arguments and "to his imagination for his facts."

The animus of the book, to which I have thus called the reader's attention, so far as General Burnside is concerned, is one of contempt or malevolence—sometimes expressed directly, sometimes by innuendo. The cause of the author's spitefulness dates back to the time when he was a correspondent of the New York Times. In the issue of that paper of January 16, 1863, he characterized General Burnside's letter of December 17th to General Halleck as one "in which there is nothing his but the signature, and to which his good nature, not his conscience, consented." Mr. Swinton being questioned as to his authority for such an extraordinary declaration, gave, after some delay and with great reluctance, the name of General Sedgwick. But General Sedgwick, on being confronted with the correspondent at General Burnside's headquarters, declared the statement utterly unfounded. A friend of Mr. Swinton requested that the matter might be overlooked, and General Burnside was content, after such an exposure, to let the crestfallen writer go with an admonition to refrain from such unworthy practices in the future. Since that time, Mr. Swinton's animosity against General Burnside has been so strikingly marked through the public press, and now through his "Critical History," as to give but little value to his opinions.

THE DELIVERANCE

OF

EAST TENNESSEE.

THE DELIVERANCE

OF

EAST TENNESSEE.

CHAPTER I.

THE DEPARTMENT OF THE OHIO.

AFTER an interval of rest for a few weeks in Providence, General Burnside was appointed to the command of the Department of the Ohio, which comprised the States of Ohio, Indiana, Illinois, Michigan and Eastern Kentucky, with the prospective addition of East Tennessee. Headquarters were at Cincinnati. General Burnside was assigned on the 16th of March, 1863, reached Cincinnati on the 23d, and on the 25th, assumed command,* relieving Major General Horatio G. Wright. Affairs were not in a particularly flourishing condition in that quarter. Rebel raids were devastating portions of the State of Kentucky, and causing considerable alarm and anxiety

*To the officers of the commissioned staff of the corps, there were several additions at the time that General Burnside was appointed to the command of the Department of the Ohio. Among these are especially to be mentioned Mr. Daniel R. Larned, appointed March 13th, 1863, Assistant Adjutant General, with the rank of Captain, and Mr. W. Harrison French, who was appointed Commissary of Subsistence, with the rank of Captain, February 19th, 1863. Captain Larned had been General Burnside's private secretary from the beginning of the North Carolina expedition, and continued to act in that capacity until the end of the war, when he retired with the brevet of Lieutenant Colonel. Captain French had been assistant secretary.

among the inhabitants. Considerable disaffection, amounting in some cases to actual disloyalty, existed in certain parts of Ohio, Indiana and Illinois. Large numbers of rebel prisoners were confined in camps and barracks on Johnson's Island, and in the immediate neighborhood of the city of Chicago, and it was known that rebel sympathizers, outside the prison walls, were ready to afford aid and comfort to the prisoners. The Governors of the States were disposed to yield all needed assistance to the military authorities, but, as martial law had not been proclaimed in the Department, except in Kentucky, freedom of speech and of the press was exercised to an extent but a little removed from license. Such extreme liberty, in case of a civil war, becomes absolutely dangerous and injurious to the welfare of the country. The management of affairs required the utmost tact and ability on the part of the officer commanding the Department.

General Burnside, immediately upon his appointment, saw the necessity of a larger military force than was then in the Department, for the purpose of restoring the peace of Kentucky, of impressing the disaffected among the people of Ohio, Indiana and Illinois with a wholesome sense of the presence of military authority, and of accomplishing the deliverance of East Tennessee. He requested and obtained permission for the transfer of the two divisions of the Ninth Corps, then in camp at Newport News, under Generals Willcox and Sturgis, to his new command. Upon the departure of the corps, General Sturgis was relieved of his command, and General Robert B. Potter assigned to the position.* This reënforcement was rendered especially necessary at that time, as the rebel General Pegram, with a force of three thousand men, was devastating central Kentucky almost without opposition, had plundered much from the residents along his line of march, had captured and occupied several towns, had penetrated as far as Danville, and was even threatening Louisville with capture, and Indiana

* Colonel Potter, of the 51st New York, was promoted to Brigadier General on the 13th of March, 1863.

with invasion. General Burnside, upon his arrival at the scene of operations, immediately took measures to check the advance of the bold partisan. The two divisions of the Ninth Corps were hurried westward, and the small number of troops then scattered through Central Kentucky were hastily concentrated at Lebanon and Hickman's Bridge, under command of Generals Gillmore and Boyle. General Burnside proceeded to Louisville and ordered a simultaneous attack to be made on Pegram at Danville, on the 28th. The order was quickly obeyed, the enemy retreating southward as our force advanced. On the 30th, General Gillmore, with his cavalry, overtook the enemy at Somerset, and, after a smart engagement of five hours' duration, completely routed him, and drove him in confusion across the Cumberland river, with a loss of five hundred killed, wounded and prisoners. Our troops also recaptured a large portion of the plunder that had been seized.

Early in April, the two divisions of the Ninth Corps began to arrive in the Department. Their presence gave assurance of security to the harassed people of Kentucky. But it is simply declaring a matter of familiar knowledge to state, that the New England troops in the Ninth Corps, when they first entered Kentucky, were not cordially received. A strong prejudice against "the Yankees"—particularly the Massachusetts Yankees—existed among the people. Some of the regiments were even treated with open insult or half-concealed dislike. Kentucky did not want these abolitionists among her communities, said the people. But no long time was required to dispossess the inhabitants of their unjust and unworthy prejudices. In cases where the regiments of the corps were engaged as garrisons in the towns, the troops, by their thorough discipline, the intelligence and gentlemanly demeanor of their officers, and their general good conduct, fairly conquered the popular feeling and turned its direction. They won their way into the respect and even affection of those who were at first disposed to regard them with complete aversion. One noteworthy instance is given in the case of the 21st Massachusetts. It was sent down to Mount Sterling, on the 5th of April, to hold the place and, with other troops, to secure the neighborhood against the occurrence of rebel raids, to which that section was peculiarly open. The regiment was very coldly received. It remained at this post for three months, and during that brief period, coldness was changed to cordiality, contempt to unwonted esteem, aversion to hospitality and kindness. When the regiment was to be ordered away, the inhabitants of the town actually petitioned the commanding general to allow the troops to remain for their protection. Two loyal cavalry regiments raised in the vicinity had been stationed near the town, and were still to hold the position. But the citizens were even more ready to trust themselves to the care of the Yankees than to the keeping of their own neighbors. The same result ensued wherever the Eastern troops were stationed, and Kentucky thus learned to respect New England.

With the force which was now at his disposal, General Burnside could more effectually provide for the protection of the people entrusted to his care. His line of defence was necessarily long, and had its weak points. But his officers were vigilant and his men were trustworthy. His line extended from the mouth of the Big Sandy river to that of the Cumberland, running through Louisa Court House, Irvine, Somerset, Franklin and Hopkinsville. The State of Kentucky was at the time divided into three military districts. The Western was under the command of Brigadier General J. T. Boyle, with headquarters at Louisville: the Central under Brigadier General Q. A. Gillmore, with headquarters at Lexington; the Eastern under Brigadier General Julius White, with headquarters at Louisa. Immediately upon the arrival of the troops of the Ninth Corps, they were ordered to the front. General Gillmore, who had applied for leave of absence after his defeat of Pegram, was relieved by General Willcox, and did not return to the Department. The troops were posted at London, Somerset, Liberty, Glasgow, Louisa, and near Tompkinsville. Fortifications were thrown up along the lines of railroads leading to the extreme front in Western Kentucky and Tennessee, then held by Major General Rosecrans, the protection of whose lines was a part of General Burnside's duty. Every precaution was taken to prevent the incursions of the enemy's cavalry and guerillas. Our force was not large, and occasionally predatory bands would be able to evade the guards. But their success was short-lived, and gave but little encouragement for a multiplication of such practices. Still, for the purposes of his Department, General Burnside felt that his present number of troops was inadequate. Congress had already authorized the organization of a force of twenty thousand men in Kentucky, and to this duty the commanding general gave his immediate attention.

The civil affairs of the Department also began to assume prominence. Domestic enemies were busy in attempting to thwart the plans of the government, to prevent enlistments of troops, and to give aid and comfort to the public enemy. The character of the general in command of the Department became an object for the shafts of slander and malice. For the latter, General Burnside did not care. But he could not and would not endure the former. He judged that the exigencies of the service demanded some special attention, and called for an act of unusal stringency. Accordingly, on the 13th of April, he issued a general order, which became, among the people of that section, a topic of earnest and, in some cases, acrimonious discussion. This document is known as "General Order No. 38," and its importance claims for it a place in these pages. It was dated at Cincinnati, on the 13th of April, and was as follows:

"The commanding general publishes for the information of all concerned, that hereafter all persons found within our lines who commit acts for the benefit of the enemies of our country, will be tried as spies or traitors, and, if convicted, will suffer death. This order includes the following classes of persons:

"Carriers of secret mails.

"Writers of letters sent by secret mails.

"Secret recruiting officers within the lines.

"Persons who have entered into an agreement to pass our lines for the purpose of joining the enemy.

"Persons found concealed within our lines belonging to the service of the enemy, and in fact all persons found improperly within our lines, who could give private information to the enemy.

"All persons within our lines who harbor, protect, conceal, feed, clothe, or in any way aid the enemies of our country.

"The habit of declaring sympathies for the enemy will not be allowed in this Department. Persons committing such offences will be at once arrested, with a view to being tried as above stated, or sent beyond our lines into the lines of their friends.

"It must be distinctly understood, that treason, expressed or implied, will not be tolerated in this Department.

"All officers and soldiers are strictly charged with the execution of this order."

The effect of this order upon the affairs of the Department was marked and decisive. In Kentucky, it was especially beneficial. The emissaries of the rebel government had heretofore practised their schemes with comparative impunity. But now they felt upon them the pressure of a strong hand. The civil authorities of the State were encouraged in their endeavors to preserve the allegiance of the citizens unimpaired. The disloyal elements were suppressed, and a condition of tranquillity not previously experienced was the result. In the States north of the Ohio, a feeling of stronger opposition prevailed in some quarters. Many persons were of the opinion that their rights of free speech were violated, and they gave vent to their grievances through the public press, and on the rostrum. But General Burnside steadily pursued his course, and it was not long before an occasion was presented which gave all parties to understand that the authority of the government was supreme.

Another important order, issued about this time, had reference to the vexed question of slavery. The citizens of Kentucky had experienced some trouble in relation to the escape of their slaves, who had not been included in the Proclamation of Emancipation. They had not been tenacious in their observance of the rights of slaves from other States who had been made free. It was found necessary to remind all such persons, that the laws of Kentucky and of the United States were still in force and must be obeyed. An order, issued April 28th, contained the following provisions:

"I. In accordance with the spirit of the Proclamation of the President of the United States, dated January 1, 1863, it is ordered, that all persons, belonging to or following the Army in this Department, are forbidden to interfere with or impede the operation of any civil process in the State of Kentucky, having in view the recovery of slaves of citizens of the State, and they are likewise forbidden to aid or abet in their escape from their homes, or to employ such persons against the consent of their owners, except in cases where military necessity requires their impressment, which impressment must be made in accordance with regulations governing such cases.

"II. All slaves made free by the war measures of the President of the United States, by Congress or by capture during the war, are entitled to their freedom, and no one in this Department has a right to interfere with that freedom. Any sale of such persons in this Department is void. The rights of citizens must be respected by the army, and the war measures of the Government must be sustained."

This order had, likewise, a tranquillizing effect, and resulted in great good to all concerned. The soldiers learned that military authority was not always the sovereign power. The citizens of Kentucky understood, that, if they claimed the protection of the law, they were not to make the law an instrument of oppression. Demanding their pound of flesh, they yet could take no drop of blood with it. The slaves were not to be mocked with delusive hopes of freedom, and those already emancipated were assured of the amplest protection and security.

Foremost among the opponents of the government in the State of Ohio was Mr. Clement L. Vallandigham, recently a member of Congress and a politician of some note belonging to the Democratic party. On more than one occasion, he had seen fit to declaim with great vehemence against the Government, and boldly defied its power. He delivered an address at Mount Vernon, Knox County, on or about the 1st of May, in which he was more than usually violent. The President, the army, General Burnside and the orders of the Department received a large share of his vituperations. His language was such as to induce General Burnside to adopt measures for his trial and punishment. Orders were accordingly issued, on the 4th of May, to Captain Charles G. Hutton, Aide de Camp, to proceed to Dayton, Mr. Vallandigham's place of residence, arrest the offender, and bring him to Cincinnati for trial. Captain Hutton went immediately to Dayton with a sufficient force to prevent resistance, and, on the night of the 4th, succeeded in taking Mr. Vallandigham without any disturbance, and returned to Cincinnati with his prisoner. On the 5th a charge was preferred, in which it was specified, that Mr. Vallandigham had declared the war to be "wicked, cruel and unnecessary," "for the purpose of crushing out liberty and erecting a despotism," "for the freedom of the blacks and the enslavement of the whites;" had stated that "if the Administration had so wished, the war could have been honorably terminated months ago;" had characterized General Orders No. 38 as a "base usurpation of arbitrary authority;" had invited his hearers "to resist the same by saying, 'the sooner the people inform the minions of usurped power, that they will not submit to such restrictions upon their liberties, the better;'" and had affirmed that he "was at all times and upon all occasions, resolved to do what he could to defeat the attempts now being made to build up a monarchy upon the ruins of our free government." These words were considered as tending to "aid, comfort and encourage those in arms against the Government," and to "induce in his hearers a distrust of their own government, sympathy for those in arms against it, and a disposition to resist the laws of the land"—as Mr. Vallandigham "well knew." The exact words of the charge upon which the prisoner was tried were as follows: "Publicly expressing, in violation of General Orders, No. 38, from Headquarters Department of the Ohio, sympathy for those in arms against the Government of the United States, and declaring disloyal sentiments and opinions, with the object and purpose of weakening the power of the Government in its efforts to suppress an unlawful rebellion."

A Military Commission was immediately convened for trial. Brigadier General Robert B. Potter was assigned as President and the following gentlemen constituted the court: Colonel John F. De Courcy, 16th Ohio infantry; Lieutenant Colonel E. R. Goodrich, Commissary of Subsistence; Major J. M. Brown, 10th Kentucky Cavalry; Major J. L. Van Buren, Aide de Camp; Major A. H. Fitch, 115th Ohio infantry; Captain P. M. Lydig, Aide de Camp. Captain J. M. Cutts, 11th United States infantry, was appointed Judge Advocate. The trial at once proceeded. It continued through the 5th and 6th days of May. Witnesses were examined on both sides. Mr. Vallandigham protested against the jurisdiction of the Commission, declaring that, as a citizen of the United States not in either the land or naval forces of the United States, nor in the militia in the actual service of the United States, he was not triable for any such cause as the charge alleged. He also declared that he was subject to arrest only by due process of law, and demanded to be tried, if tried at all, by a civil court according to the ordinary methods adopted in the State of Ohio. The case was submitted without argument. The Commission examined the prisoner's protest, refused to admit its validity, found Mr. Vallandigham guilty of the charge, and the chief portion of the specification, and sentenced him "to be placed in close confinement in some fortress of the United States to be designated by the commanding officer of this Department, there to be left during the continuance of the war." General Burnside, on the 16th of May, reviewed the proceedings, approved and confirmed them, and ordered the prisoner to be confined in Fort Warren, Boston Harbor.

In the meantime, Mr. Vallandigham, through Hon. George E. Pugh, made application to the Circuit Court of the United States for the Southern District of Ohio, for the allowance of a writ of habeas corpus. The Court met and received the application on the 9th of May. The case was argued on the 11th, before Hon. Humphrey H. Leavitt, Judge of the Court, an old, experienced and able lawyer, who had held the office which he adorned for nearly thirty years. General Burnside submitted a brief statement of his case, basing the authority of his action upon the fact of the existence of a civil war, and the necessity in times of public peril, for "the operation of some power that moves more quickly than the civil," and affirming that his duty to the government required him to "stop license and intemperate discussion which tends to weaken the authority of the government and the army." He deprecated the violence of the public addresses to which the people in their assemblies were accustomed to listen. He fixed upon the public orators the responsibility of attempting to undermine the authority of the government by passionate and inconsiderate appeals. "They must not use license," he says with emphasis, "and plead that they are exercising liberty. In this Department, it cannot be done. I shall use all the power I have to break down such license, and I am sure I will be sustained in this course by all honest men. At all events, I will have the consciousness, before God, of having done my duty to my country; and when I am swerved from the performance of that duty by any pressure, public or private, or by any prejudice, I will no longer be a man or a patriot."* Mr. Pugh ap-

* It is a curious fact, when viewed in the light of recent events, that, at the time General Burnside prepared this paper, Mr. Andrew Johnson, now President of the United States, was in Cincinnati, and heard this statement read by General Burnside before it was submitted to the Court. He not only approved the language and spirit of the paper, but he also condemned Mr. Vallandigham's course, without mercy. The only objection that he expressed in regard to General Burnside's action was that it was too lenient.

peared for the petitioner, and made an able argument in his behalf, based upon the allegation of his being a citizen and not under the authority of martial law, and therefore not liable to be tried and condemned for "offences alike unknown to the articles of war and to the ordinary laws of the land." If Mr. Vallandigham was to be tried, it must be before a jury of his peers, and not by courts or commissions composed of military officers.

The District Attorney, Flamen Ball, Esq., assisted by Hon. Aaron F. Perry, appeared for General Burnside. Mr. Perry replied to Mr. Pugh, and based his reasoning, as an advocate for the legitimacy of Mr. Vallandigham's trial, upon "the obligations, duties and responsibilities of General Burnside as a Major General in command of an army of the United States in the field of military operations, for the purposes of war and in the presence of the enemy." Under the laws of war, arrests of a certain kind, by military officers, are certainly justifiable. The arrest of Mr. Vallandigham was a legal and justifiable act. In a state of civil war, all persons take sides. Those who favor the government are the supporters of the means required for carrying on the war. Those who oppose the government and embarrass its operations, intended to save the nation from utter destruction, are enemies to the country, for they aid the public enemy. Mr. Vallandigham came within this category, and consequently his arrest was imperative. Being lawfully held by the authority of the United States, there was no occasion for the exercise of the power contained in the writ of habeas corpus. Individual rights may, in such cases, be sometimes abridged. But the public safety requires such abridgement, and, according to the laws of war, when the country itself is in peril, "everything may be done which the necessities of war require."

The District Attorney followed on the same side, giving a very clear and compact statement of the legislation of Congress respecting the writ of habeas corpus from the beginning. He argued that, under such legislation, Mr. Vallandigham was excluded from the privilege which it conferred, and that General Burnside not only had the right to make the arrest, but that he would also be obliged, in case the writ should issue, to make return that he was acting under the authority of the President of the United States, who, in a state of civil war, was the judge of the necessity which required an extraordinary exercise of power.

Mr. Pugh replied to the arguments of the counsel appearing for General Burnside, quoting authorities both foreign and domestic, to make good the points which he had before argued, and to show that "a military officer has no right to arrest and detain a person not subject to the Rules and Articles of War, for an offence against the laws of the United States, except in aid of the judicial authority, and subject to its control; and if the party is arrested by the military, it is the duty of the officer to deliver him over immediately to the civil authority, to be dealt with according to law."

Judge Leavitt, after a most patient hearing of the case, gave his decision, refusing the writ. Besides considering the necessity of the case and the exigency which demanded the action of General Burnside, the Court referred to a decision which had already been given by the Circuit Judge, Mr. Justice Swayne, in a similar case. Judge Swayne "distinctly held that this Court would not grant the writ of habeas corpus, when it appeared that the detention or imprisonment was under military authority." "It is clearly not a time," says Judge Leavitt, "when any one connected with the judicial department of the government should allow himself, except from the most stringent obligations of duty, to embarrass or thwart the Executive in his efforts to deliver the country from the dangers which press so heavily upon it." It was not necessary that martial law should have been in force to justify General Burnside in making the arrest. "The power vested by virtue of the authority conferred by the appointment of the President," under which General Burnside became the commander of the Department of the Ohio. Occupying such a position, General

Burnside made the arrest. "It was virtually the act of the executive department under the power vested in the President by the Constitution; and I am unable to perceive," adds the judge, "on what principle a judicial tribunal can be invoked to annul or reverse it." The judge also took occasion to animadvert, with some severity, upon what he called "the pestilential leaven of disloyalty in the community," and concluded his able and patriotic opinion by the gratifying words: "For these reasons I am constrained to refuse the writ."

General Burnside made all necessary provisions for removing his prisoner secretly and swiftly from Cincinnati to Boston, and only awaited the order of the President confirming the sentence of the Military Commission. But the President deemed it best to commute the sentence of the commission, and on the 19th of May, General Canby, in behalf of Mr. Lincoln, despatched to General Burnside the following order: "The President directs that, without delay, you send C. L. Vallandigham, under secure guard, to the headquarters of General Rosecrans, to be put by him beyond our military lines, and that, in case of his return within our lines, he be arrested and kept in close custody for the term specified in his sentence." Under this order, Mr. Vallandigham was transferred into the hands of General Rosecrans, and was by him delivered, on the 25th, into the custody of the rebel authorities. General Bragg transferred him to Richmond. But the enemy's government evidently considered him an unwelcome guest. No great amount of cordiality was expended upon him, and he was finally sent, or betook himself out of the country. He found an asylum in Canada, and remained there in comparative retirement through the following autumn and winter, when, in the waning days of the rebellion, he returned home and was permitted to remain unmolested.

The arrest and trial of Mr. Vallandigham naturally excited the public mind. Threats of rescue were freely made at Dayton, Cincinnati and other places. Dayton and its neighborhood were immediately placed under martial law. The disloyal people of that section soon ascertained that resistance to the authority of the government was useless, and the loyal people of the State rejoiced to feel that their security was assured. Mr. Vallandigham's friends in Cincinnati endeavored to make arrangements, under cover of a complimentary serenade, for an attempt to rescue the prisoner. But General Burnside had taken the precaution to lodge him at headquarters, in a room immediately above his own, to place him under the most strict and vigilant guard, and to give his friends to understand that he would not be delivered alive into their hands. The ferment in the city subsided, and Mr. Vallandigham's partizans relinquished their unwise and ineffectual schemes. They were subsequently determined to bring his name more prominently before the country, and accordingly procured his nomination, as the candidate of the democratic party, for Governor of Ohio. The people of that State indignantly rejected him, and he was ignominiously defeated, in a spirited canvass, by a majority of over one hundred thousand votes. The vote of the soldiers was very decided, as a very bitter feeling existed in the army against this enemy in the rear. He was thus bereft of the last consolation of politicians —the sympathy of the members of his own party. He has since been more signally rebuked by the miscarriage of all his schemes to embarrass the government, has even been compelled to withdraw from a convention of his friends, and is now buried so deeply beneath the obloquy which his countrymen have heaped upon him, that no one cares to exhume his dishonored name. Deprived of honor, both North and South, he has met the doom which such a character must always be exposed to, and his career and end furnish a profitable lesson to all who may contemplate a similar course.

The arrest, trial and conviction of Mr. Vallandigham have given rise to much discussion throughout the country, and the policy and justice of General Burnside in the premises have been commended or condemned, according to the differing opinions of his critics. On the one hand it has been argued, that, as martial law had not been proclaimed in Ohio, whatever offences might have been committed by civilians should have been brought under the examination of the civil authorities, and the civil courts; that the principles of freedom of speech and of the press were too precious, and too firmly established by the struggles and sacrifices which they had cost, to become the object of a military commission, which, in such case, would be mere despotism; and that the loyal cause was too strong and too just to be placed permanently in danger by the frenzied utterances of a demoralized press, or the insane appeals of inflamed public orators. On the other hand, it was replied, that if civilians committed offences against public order, which were detrimental to the success of our armies in the field, by attempting to create a public sentiment hostile to the prosecution of the war, by the discouragement of enlistments, and by actual hindrance of military operations, such civilians were giving aid and comfort to the public enemy, and were justly answerable to the swift process of military tribunals; that when freedom of speech and the press degenerated into licentiousness, it was an abuse of the principle which could not be too speedily corrected, a nuisance in a loyal community which could not be too soon abated, a crime even in a season of civil war, which could not be too promptly and severely punished; and that no cause was so strong as not to be liable to be undermined and defeated by that meanest kind of craft which is the characteristic of traitors in disguise. General Burnside thought that the time had arrived when the military necessity required that the lines should be strictly drawn between those who were faithful to the national cause and those who were disposed to betray it. He determined to affix the stigma of treason upon the disloyal opponents of the government. He acted not as a politician. He had no personal feelings to gratify. He had no ill will against his prisoner, or the friends or partizans of the culprit. But he conceived that it was his duty, as commander of a Department in which an offence against good taste, good order, good morals and good government had been committed, to take cognizance of it, and to provide against its recurrence. He judged it to be his duty, as a loyal servant of the government, to see that the Republic should receive no injury from the action of its internal enemies, or from his own negligence. Especially he believed that it was necessary for him, as a sincere patriot, to strip off the speciousness of the disguise with which such men as those whom he proscribed cloaked their nefarious designs, and to hold them up, in all their ugliness and deformity, to the scorn of his countrymen and of mankind, as TRAITORS. The brand of treason—basest of all crimes—was to be forever fixed upon these offenders. When this was once done, and the practice of speaking and acting against the government was made infamous in public estimation, the hour of danger to the Republic would have passed.

Certainly if success is allowed to justify a measure of the kind which General Burnside adopted, he has been amply rewarded. The change of affairs and character in the Department of the Ohio was decidedly marked for the better. The treason that on his arrival was ripening into notoriety—expressing itself both in private and public, in the drinking of sentiments and toasts to the success of the rebel cause, in the loud proclamation of sympathy with the rebels, on the street corners, in the shops, in the hotels, in social intercourse, in public assemblies, in the columns of the press—suddenly felt that a master hand was laid upon it. The fate of Mr. Vallandigham was a significant and serious warning not to be overlooked or despised. There was a healthier public sentiment at once, loyal men breathed more freely, treason sank back abashed and was remanded into silence, and the authority of the Government was established more firmly than ever throughout the entire North West.

A few public journals, however, were indisposed to let the subject drop, and discussed the matter in the most acrimonious terms. Foremost among these were the Cincinnati Enquirer, the Chicago Times, and the New York World—all of which had long pursued a course which was aiding the cause of the rebels. The editor of the first, after being warned, proposed to General Burnside to submit his articles to inspection before they were printed. But General Burnside declined this, with the understanding on both sides, that for the future the tone of the paper was to be loyal. The second was suppressed and a military guard placed in possession of the office. The circulation of the third within the limits of the Department was prohibited. These acts of justice were performed in the latter part of May, but early in June the President disapproved them, and the papers in question were once more allowed to distil their venom. But a salutary warning had been given, and a more moderate tone was perceptible in their criticisms. The stigma of treason could not be removed. The line had been drawn. The President, the Cabinet, the public sentiment of the country pronounced its approval of General Burnside's course.

While General Burnside was thus engaged in securing his rear, he was by no means negligent in pushing forward his preparations for a movement in front. The enemy was somewhat disposed to alarm, and if possible, break through our attenuated lines. The Blue Grass Region of Kentucky was too fertile a country and too tempting in its abundance of supplies to be left in complete security from disturbance by the rebel forces. Predatory bands issued from the fastnesses of East Tennessee and South Western Virginia, and crossing the mountains, sought to harass and plunder the neighboring section. The lines of communication, upon which General Rosecrans relied for his means of offensive warfare, ran through General Burnside's department, and it became an object of some importance, on the part of the enemy to disturb them, and on the part of our own forces to prevent such disturbance. At different times during the months of April and May, the rebel partizans, Morgan, Wheeler, Pegram, and Clute, attempted to ravage central Kentucky, and to interfere with the lines of General Rosecrans. The affairs were not of much consequence in themselves, being scarcely more than skirmishes. But they served to keep our troops constantly on the alert, and subjected them to considerable annoyance, without permitting the accomplishment of any great result. In all cases, the roving bands of the enemy were met, checked and driven back, and their incursions rendered ineffectual. The people of Kentucky were made secure and General Rosecrans's communications were not interrupted for a day.

On the 27th of April, the War Department issued an order, directing "that the troops in Kentucky not belonging to the Ninth Army Corps, be organized into the twenty-third army corps, to be commanded by Major General G. L. Hartsuff." Measures were immediately taken to carry this order into effect, and on the 22d of May, General Burnside had completed the organization of the force, and the twenty-third army corps—composed of troops from Kentucky, Ohio, Illinois, Indiana and Michigan—came into existence as a constituent part of the Army of the Ohio. With the two corps, it was hoped that the contemplated movement upon East Tennessee might be made. General Burnside had repeatedly asked that General Getty's division should be sent out to him to fill up the Ninth Corps to its complement, but the request had been as repeatedly evaded or refused. With the two divisions, therefore, under General Willcox and the twenty-third corps under General Hartsuff, hastily organized as the latter had been, the enterprise must be undertaken. General Burnside submitted to General Rosecrans a plan for a coöperative movement upon East Tennessee. With the advice of General Thomas it was accepted and preparations were accordingly made by the two commanders. The troops were properly concentrated for the movement, and on the 2d day of June, General Burnside left his headquarters at Cincinnati, and proceeded to Lexington to take the field. The time was ripe for the operation, and officers and men were eager for the service. The Ninth Corps, strengthened by a division under General Carter, was to march directly into East Tennessee by way of Monticello. General Hartsuff was to follow in support. General Rosecrans was to advance upon Chattanooga.

CHAPTER II.

THE CAMPAIGN IN MISSISSIPPI.

THE Ninth Corps was not to have the honor of expelling the foe from the beautiful region which he had so long oppressed. On the very eve of marching, the destination was changed, and a more arduous duty was demanded. The deliverance of East Tennessee must be postponed. A more imperative necessity existed. A more important enterprise must first be brought to a successful conclusion. Just before leaving Cincinnati General Burnside had received a despatch from Washington inquiring if any troops could be spared from the Department of the Ohio to assist General Grant in the siege of Vicksburg. The despatch seemed ominous. Preparations were made for any exigency. Baggage of officers and men was cut down to the lowest amount, and nothing was wanting but the order to move. The order came, reaching General Burnside at Lexington on the 3d of June. General Grant must be reënforced with eight thousand men. It was like cutting off General Burnside's right arm. But it was obeyed on the instant. On the 4th, the Ninth Corps, with General Parke in command, was put *en route* for Vicksburg. The 12th Rhode Island, Colonel George H. Browne, did not accompany the Corps in its Mississippi campaign. This regiment was raised for nine months' service, and joined the Corps a short time previous to the battle of Fredericksburg, where Colonel Browne distinguished himself for his gallantry and the regiment suffered severely. It went west with the Corps, but as the expiration of its term of service was at hand, it was retained in Kentucky for a time and was at Cincinnati for a few days during the Morgan raid. By its services at Somerset, Jamestown and other parts of Kentucky, it won for itself a good reputation for all soldierly qualities. General Burnside desired to accompany his forces, but General Halleck would not consent to his departure, deeming his presence in the Department of the first importance. Accordingly, General Burnside remained behind, parting with his companions in arms with unaffected regret. He had the satisfaction of receiving, on the 7th, from Secretary Stanton the following despatch: "You will accept the thanks of the President and Vice President, for your alacrity and promptness in sending forward reënforcements to General Grant."

The Corps left Crab Orchard and vicinity, where it had been concentrated for the march upon East Tennessee, on the 4th of June, and bivouacked that night at Camp Dick Robinson. On the 5th, the march was resumed for Nicolasville, where the troops took cars for Covington. They proceeded thence by rail on the 5th towards Cairo. All along the route, they were welcomed by the people with every manifestation of interest and cordiality. Flags were waved, cheers filled the air, good wishes were uttered on every side. The Ninth Corps had come to be known and regarded throughout the Department, with the warmest sentiments of respect and admiration. On the 9th, the Corps arrived at Cairo, and left in steamers on the 10th for Memphis. It reached Memphis on the 11th, left there on the 12th, and on the 14th General Parke reported with his entire command to General Grant. On the 15th the troops were all disembarked at Sherman's Landing nearly opposite Vicksburg, and on the following day they were ordered to move down the river to a point opposite Warrenton. A portion of the Corps had started upon the march, when the order was countermanded, and a new point designated as the object of the movement. On the 17th, the men were again embarked, transported up the Yazoo River, and landed at Haines's Bluff. The Corps went into camp about two miles from the landing.

General Grant had been persistently carrying on the siege of

Vicksburg since the 22d of May. With that remarkable tenacity of purpose, and skill in the management of armies, which has made him the first soldier of the war for the Union, the Commander of our forces in that quarter had been more and more closely investing the enemy's stronghold. General Pemberton, who was in command of the post, had been doing all that was possible to avert the impending disaster. There was no help for him except what might arise from a movement upon General Grant's rear, by forces detached from the other armies of the enemy. General Jos. E. Johnston had been assigned to the work of raising the siege of Vicksburg, by an attempt upon our lines from the interior of Mississippi. To check any such attempt and to prevent any movement designed by the enemy for the relief of the beleaguered garrison, the Ninth Corps, with other troops, was posted at Haines's Bluff. The duty was more of observation than of direct contact with the enemy. It was General Johnston's part to take the aggressive. But this he declined and our forces had a fortnight of comparative quiet. The only incident which broke the monotony of camp life was a reconnaissance made on the 25th by the 6th New Hampshire and 7th Rhode Island, under command of Colonel S. Z. Griffin. The enemy was found quietly but vigilantly on the watch, and the troops returned to camp. The time was occupied in throwing up defensive works, to render General Grant's rear perfectly secure. Two intrenched lines were formed. The first extended along Oak Ridge, guarding the roads across the Big Black river. The second in rear of the first, extending from Haines's and Snyder's Bluffs, through Milldale and along the high ground east of Vicksburg, commanding all the approaches from the North and East.

General Johnston was thus foiled, and the enemy was doomed. On the 4th of July, General Pemberton surrendered his post with its garrison of thirty-seven thousand officers and men, arms and munitions of war sufficient for an army of sixty thousand, cannon, locomotives, cars, steamboats, cotton and other public property. By a happy coincidence, the Army of the

Potomac, under General Meade, who had superseded General Hooker in command, achieved on the same day a signal victory over General Lee at Gettysburg, and thus the victorious cannon peals of East and West proclaimed the declining fortunes of the rebellion.

Immediately upon hearing the intelligence of Pemberton's surrender, General Johnston fell back from his advanced position upon the Big Black, and retired towards Jackson. General Sherman, with the Ninth Corps to which was assigned General Smith's division of the sixteenth, his own corps and other forces, under command of Generals Steele and Ord, started in pursuit of the retreating enemy on the afternoon of the day of the surrender. The first division of the Ninth Corps was then under command of Brigadier General Thomas Welsh,* the second under that of General Potter. The command left camp towards nightfall on the 4th, and moved out towards the Big Black river, intending to cross at Jones's Ford and Birdsong's Ferry. On reaching the river, the enemy was found in force on the opposite bank, disposed to hinder the progress of the march. The configuration of the land and the heavy timber which covered it enabled him with a small force to check our advance, until the evening of the 5th, when an examination of the ford disclosed the fact that bridges would be necessary to cross the troops. A lodgement was effected on the opposite bank, and by constant exertions a bridge was constructed at Birdsong's by the men of Colonel Bowman's brigade† of the first division. During the afternoon and night of the 7th, the corps, with its supply trains and baggage, was safely got across. The ferry boat, which had been disabled by the enemy and sunk, was found, raised, put in order and used for transporting the division of General Smith. Colonel Griffin's

*Colonel Welsh of the 48th Pennsylvania had been promoted to the rank of Brigadier General on the 13th of March. General Welsh had relieved General Willcox who had been assigned to command the District of Indiana.

†The brigade consisted of the 36th Massachusetts, 45th Pennsylvania, 17th and 27th Michigan.

brigade and Captain Roemer's battery of the second division crossed at Messenger's Ferry.

On the evening of the 7th, the entire command moved out from Birdsong's, and at ten o'clock bivouacked at Robertson's, in the close vicinity of Jefferson Davis's plantation near Bolton. Other parts of the army were posted upon the plantation itself and Mr. Davis's house and library were thoroughly examined. The Corps marched out on the main road towards Jackson in the afternoon of the 8th, but, on coming in contact with General Steele's command, was obliged to make a detour upon a side road, along which the march was continued till ten o'clock, when the Corps bivouacked near Hall's Cross Roads. On this day's march Griffin's brigade and Roemer's Battery brought up the rear and guarded the trains. On the 9th, the Corps moved about twelve miles, cutting a road through the timber and across the plantations for a portion of the way, and encountering the enemy's cavalry about dark. A slight skirmish took place, in which the artillery of both sides was brought up and put into the action. The proximity of the enemy rendered great vigilance necessary.

On the 10th, the enemy retiring before our advance, our forces were early on the road, and pushing on across the country, through large plantations, came out at night, on the Livingston road, five miles north of Jackson. The next morning, General Sherman moved his army up to the suburbs of Jackson and found the enemy strongly entrenched. In front of the Ninth Corps was the ridge of land upon which is situated the State Lunatic Asylum—a natural position of considerable strength, and then well defended by lines of earthworks. The enemy fell back into his entrenchments, as the Corps moved forward upon him. General Welsh, commanding the first division, formed his command into line of battle, in the afternoon of the 10th, and prepared for an attack. The first brigade, Colonel Bowman, was placed upon the right; the third brigade, Colonel Leasure, upon the left; the 45th Pennsylvania regiment, Colonel Curtin, and the 79th New York, Colonel

Morrison, were thrown forward as skirmishers. The division advanced; our skirmishers soon came in contact with the enemy's videttes near the Mississippi Central Railroad. A general engagement seemed impending. But the enemy declined fighting in the open field, and, night coming on, General Welsh, after advancing to the neighborhood of the enemy's works, established his line securely and went into bivouac. The 2d Michigan, Colonel Humphrey, relieved the 79th New York, and the 46th New York and 50th Pennsylvania guarded the Canton road. The Second Division was moved up, leaving Griffin's brigade to guard the cross roads, and the entire Corps occupied a line at right angles with the Canton road, and extending from near Pearl river to the Livingston road, crossing the Mississippi Central Railroad.

The enemy's defences consisted of a line of works which, combined with the natural strength of his position, enabled him to make a decided resistance to any attempt which we might make to dislodge him. Opposite the right of our line were two forts, one an earthwork, the other constructed of cotton bales, and both well armed. In front of our centre was a six gun fort, the artillery of which was well manned and numerously supported. Opposite our left was an earthwork, armed with field artillery. All the works were connected with lines of rifle pits, and a large number of troops could be seen behind them. General Johnston seemed disposed to hold his position, and a very determined attack would be required to drive him out. The weather was excessively hot, and the troops were considerably worn. General Sherman decided to feel the enemy and to make an attempt upon his position.

On the 11th, our lines were advanced, the first division of the Ninth Corps moving out of bivouac at daybreak. Our line of skirmishers came almost immediately into conflict with the enemy's outposts, and a sharp engagement took place. The enemy's skirmishers were quickly driven in, their reserves pushed back upon their supports, and the advanced forces of the enemy were fairly compelled to seek the shelter of the fortifications. As our troops continued to advance, the enemy opened with his artillery, showing a formidable front. General Welsh halted his division, established his line, sheltering his men from the enemy's battery, and taking up a good position upon a ridge immediately facing the enemy's defences. The 2d Michigan on the left skirmished up to the immediate vicinity of the opposing lines, but not being supported, fell back to the main line, bringing in its wounded. On the right, the 45th Pennsylvania advanced to within five hundred yards of the enemy's works, and retained its position. The rest of our line advanced to the close proximity of the opposing lines. But the enemy was found too strongly posted, and General Sherman, judging the sacrifice of life too great a price to pay for an assault, proceeded to establish his lines, and awaited the arrival of heavier artillery and supplies of ammunition.

For the next few days, the two armies lay watching each other. The men got what shelter they could from the burning rays of the sun in the forests that bordered their position. But neither party was in the finest condition for fighting. A spiteful fire was kept up between the pickets. The 7th Rhode Island lost fifteen men killed and wounded in a single day, and two officers were captured. Early on the morning of the 13th, the enemy made a sudden and vigorous sortie from his works, hoping to break our lines and disturb our investing operations. Colonel Griffin was, at the time, in command at the trenches, and quickly made his dispositions to meet the foe. The enemy was received with so destructive a fire as to induce him quickly to retrace his steps. A speedy and disastrous repulse was the only result of his reckless attempt. The city was closely invested, and dispositions were made to cut off the retreat of the enemy. The supply trains came up, and General Sherman, on the 16th, ordered a reconnaissance for the purpose of developing the enemy's position and his force. General Potter's division, which had relieved General Welsh in the advanced lines, made a gallant movement, which discovered the enemy still strongly posted and in force behind his intrenchments. His formidable batteries made free use of shrapnel, canister and shell upon our troops, causing some casualties, among which was the severely wounding of Lieutenant Colonel Brenholts, of the 50th Pennsylvania, a gallant and worthy officer. General Smith's division at the same time advanced in fine style, but was met by a hot fire, which caused severe loss. The troops were finally withdrawn, after ascertaining the enemy's force, and preparations were made for a general assault, to take place on the following morning.

On the night of the 16th, General Ferrero was in command in the trenches. At nine o'clock in the evening, a report was brought in that artillery and infantry could be distinctly heard moving in an easterly direction through the town. General Ferrero investigated the matter, found that the information was correct, and that the enemy was actually in motion. The intelligence was communicated to his superior officers, but the darkness prevented any movement. At two o'clock in the morning of the 17th, General Ferrero's brigade occupied the skirmish line, and at daylight, the skirmishers were advanced to ascertain the true condition of affairs. No opposing force was found, a white flag was waving from the earthworks, and it soon became clear that the enemy had evacuated the city. General Ferrero at once brought up his command, at six o'clock entered Jackson—the 35th Massachusetts in advance—placed guards over the public property, and sent out parties of men to pick up the stragglers from the ranks of the retreating rebels. One cannon, a 32-pounder, was found in the works, about a thousand stands of arms, and a large quantity of ammunition were secured, and one officer and one hundred and thirty-seven men were captured. But General Johnston had made good his escape, and placed the Pearl river between himself and the pursuit. The city of Jackson was left to our mercy. The railroad depot and a few buildings, containing the enemy's property, were destroyed. The town itself and the public property of the State of Mississippi were guarded and preserved from harm.

On the 17th, General Welsh moved out his division upon the Canton road, with the hope of intercepting the enemy's cavalry, which were supposed to be making for the Pearl river in that direction. No enemy appeared, and on the 18th, the men were engaged in disabling and destroying the Mississippi Central Railroad. During that day and the following, the work of destruction was carried on, and by the evening of the 19th, fifteen miles of the track were rendered unfit for service, the ties were burnt, and the rails bent in the fire. On the morning of the 20th, the Corps commenced its return, and on the evening of the 23d, after a very harassing and exhausting march, the troops reached their old position at Milldale and Oak Ridge.

The Corps remained at this point for two weeks, waiting for transportation, which was procured, after various delays, in the early part of August. The boats on which the troops finally embarked were crowded to their utmost capacity; the voyage to Cairo occupied an unusual time, the men suffered terribly from disease engendered by their exposure to the enfeebling climate, and many died on the passage and were buried on the river bank. Such was the deficiency of transports, that the Corps, in different detachments, was upon the river for two weeks. On the 15th, the last of the troops reached Cairo, in a most lamentable plight. They were received with every kindness and attention, and after a short stay, proceeded to Cincinnati, where they arrived on the 20th. They were soon afterwards transferred to Kentucky, and allowed a week or two of rest and recuperation. General Grant heartily thanked the Corps in general orders, dated July 31st. "In returning the Ninth Corps to its former command," said he, "it is with pleasure that the general commanding acknowledges its valuable services in the campaign just closed. Arriving at Vicksburg opportunely, taking a position to hold at bay Johnston's army, then threatening the forces investing the city, it was ready and eager to assume the offensive at any moment. After the fall of Vicksburg, it formed a part of the army which drove Johnson from his position near the Big Black river into his intrenchments at Jackson, and, after a siege of eight days, compelled him to fly in disorder from the Mississippi Valley. The endurance, valor and general good conduct of the Ninth Corps are admired by all; and its valuable coöperation in achieving the final triumph of the campaign is gratefully acknowledged by the Army of the Tennessee.

"Major General Parke will cause the different regiments and batteries of his command to inscribe upon their banners and guidons, 'Vicksburg' and 'Jackson.'"

This campaign in Mississippi was especially severe in its effects upon the officers and men of the Ninth Corps. The excessive heat, the malaria that settled like a pall of death around the camps upon the Yazoo river, the scarcity of water and its bad quality, the forced marches and the crowded condition of the transports told fearfully upon the troops. All the accounts of the movement agree in their statements respecting the amount of disease and mortality which accompanied it. The hardships which all were obliged to endure were excessive. Water, which the horses refused to drink, the men were obliged to use in making their coffee. Fevers, congestive chills, diarrhœa, and other diseases attacked the troops. Many sank down upon the road side, and died from sun-stroke and sheer exhaustion. The sickness that prevailed on board the transports upon the return voyage was terrible and almost universal. Nearly every night, as the boats lay up on account of low water and the consequent danger of the navigation, the twinkling light of the lanterns on shore betokened the movements of the burial parties, as they consigned the remains of some unfortunate comrade to the earth.

When the troops reached Cairo, the men were scarcely able to march through the streets. They dropped in the ranks, and even at the market house, where the good citizens had provided an abundant and comfortable meal for the worn-out soldiers, they fell beside the tables, and were carried away to the hospitals. More than half the command were rendered unfit for duty. There were not able men enough belonging to the batteries to water and groom the horses. In such circumstances, instances of brave, even of heroic endurance were not rare, and the soldiers deserved the commendations which their officers freely bestowed. The diseases which the campaign engendered continued to afflict their subjects long after the close of the operations. Many of the officers and men are suffering to this day from the effects of their unwonted exposure. Some valuable lives were sacrificed. Lieutenant Eli Wentworth, of the 6th New Hampshire, died at Milldale on the Yazoo, on the 18th of August. Assistant Surgeon William H. Paine, of the 20th Michigan, died on board the transport in the Mississippi river, August 5th, exhausted by his severe and trying duties.

Brigadier General Thomas Welsh, the commander of the first division, contracted disease from which he never recovered. On the return of the Corps, he was so reduced by sickness as to be unablé to reach his home in Columbia, Pennsylvania. He was carried to Cincinnati, where he died on the 14th of August. He was a very brave and efficient officer, and by his skill and courage won the high encomiums of his superior officers. He joined the service as Colonel of the 45th Pennsylvania regiment, and went through the campaigns at Port Royal, in Virginia, under General Pope, in Maryland and in Virginia a second time, with great credit, gradually winning his promotion by his gallant and meritorious conduct. Assigned by General Parke to the command of the first division, he added to his already honorable reputation as a soldier, and gave promise of future distinction. Though not wholly in accord with the spirit of the times in respect to the subject of slavery, and not agreeing with the Administration in its policy of Emancipation, he was yet too good a soldier to make his opinions a pretext for any want of zeal in the service. He was always prompt in his obedience and always faithful and vigorous in his discharge of the duties of his position. Honest, straightforward and fearless, he made himself felt in the command, and his death was considered a loss to the service which could not easily be supplied. His name is to be added to the list of the departed brave whom the Ninth Corps has contributed to the preservation of the Republic.

CHAPTER III.

JOHN MORGAN'S RAID.

WHEN General Lee moved from his encampments on the Rappahannock after the battle of Chancellorsville, he had evidently given all the troops in the "Confederacy" to understand that it was a signal for commencing an offensive campaign along the entire line. The government of Jefferson Davis was tired of being kept on the defensive, and the invasion of Pennsylvania was determined upon. In West Virginia and Kentucky, the rebel force felt the impulse and exhibited signs of unusual activity. One raiding party reached as far as Maysville, but was there met by Colonel De Courcy, with four regiments of cavalry, and was broken to pieces and driven off in complete rout.

General Willcox, who was in command in Central Kentucky, had proposed a counter raid into East Tennessee, under Colonel W. P. Sanders, a very brave and skilful cavalry officer. The plan was approved, and the necessary preparations were made. General Willcox was, however, transferred to the command of the district of Indiana, on the 10th of June, in order to quiet some trouble which the disaffected and disloyal people in that quarter were disposed to foment. General Willcox very discreetly and very effectually performed his delicate duty, and was retained in that command. General Hartsuff, succeeding him in Kentucky, completed the preparations for the raid and Colonel Sanders was soon upon the road. The expedition was very successful. Colonel Sanders struck the Virginia and Tennessee Railroad at Loudon, moved up the road, destroying portions of it on the way, threatened Knoxville, burnt the important bridge across the Holston river at Strawberry Plains, captured ten pieces of artillery, a great number of small arms, and four hundred prisoners, and destroyed a large quantity of the enemy's stores. He returned to our lines on the 26th, having gained great credit by his gallant and daring feat. Other movements of troops took place, under Generals Julius White and S. P. Carter, in the direction of Monticello, to distract the attention of the enemy and to support Colonel Sanders's operations.

But the enemy himself was not inclined to accept the situation quietly. He prepared for a raid, whose magnitude was to eclipse all former efforts of that description, and to cause considerable alarm throughout the Department. The plan of the enemy was to break through our lines in Western or Central Kentucky, cross the Ohio, plunder the southern tier of counties of Indiana and Ohio, and either escape into West Virginia, or make a bold march through Pennsylvania, and join General Lee's invading army. It was a design of considerable daring, and, had it been successfully executed, would have caused great trouble to our military authorities East and West. The time was happily chosen. The Ninth Corps was absent. The new levies had hardly become thoroughly accomplished in the duties of the soldier. Colonel Sanders's raid had taken away a considerable portion of our cavalry, that were scarcely fit for arduous service upon their return. General Carter's troops who had been stationed on the Cumberland had been engaged in assisting Colonel Sanders. General Halleck had unwittingly done much to cause a feeling of false security to prevail among the people of the Department South of the Ohio, by repeatedly telegraphing during the month of June, that Kentucky was safe, and that the time was ripe for a movement into East Tennessee. General Burnside might possibly have been disposed to feel, under the influence of such despatches, that his lines were more secure than they really were. Even as late as the 6th of July, the General in Chief stated that there was "no need of keeping large forces in Kentucky." Had General Burnside listened too attentively to the suggestions of his superior, instead of acting upon his own more accurate information, Morgan would doubtless have had an unimpeded ride through Indiana and Ohio, and would have got safely off with his booty. As it was, the raid came to a disastrous and ignominious end.

On the 2d day of July, General John H. Morgan, an intrepid and active partizan, with General Basil Duke as second, crossed the Cumberland river at Burkesville and its neighborhood, with a force of four or five thousand men,* well organized, mounted, equipped and armed for a long expedition. Immediately upon receiving intelligence of the movement at head-quarters, General Burnside took measures to check the advance of the bold raider, and if possible to cut off his retreat. In the confusion of the moment, our officers and men were hardly prepared for such an incursion. They rallied to their work, however, as promptly as could naturally be expected, but in despite of their efforts, Morgan succeeded in eluding the troops sent to intercept him, and obtained a start of forty-eight hours in advance of his pursuers. Rainy weather came on, and the roads became difficult. On the 3d, in a skirmish with one or two companies of Colonel Wolford's cavalry, our men were worsted. On the 4th, Morgan met with different fortune, as he attempted to cross Green River Bridge at Tebb's Bend, near Columbia. The post was held by Colonel Orlando H. Moore, with five companies of the 25th Michigan infantry. Colonel Moore selected his ground for defence most judiciously, and awaited the attack. Morgan approached, at half-past three o'clock in the morning, and demanded the surrender of the force. Colonel Moore replied with spirit: "The Fourth of July is not a proper day for me to entertain such a proposition." Morgan at once attacked; but Colonel

* This is the estimate of our officers in Kentucky. The enemy's statement is that Morgan had "two thousand and twenty-eight effective men, with four pieces of artillery."

Moore showed that he had not spoken without good warrant. He and his men made a most gallant fight of three and a half hours, and, after an obstinate contest, succeeded in beating off the enemy. Morgan was actually forced to retire, with a loss of over fifty killed, among whom were a Colonel, two Majors, five Captains and six Lieutenants, and two hundred wounded. Our own loss, out of two hundred men, was six killed and twenty-three wounded. The fight was very spirited. "At times, the enemy occupied one side of the temporary breast-works of fallen timber, while the men of the 25th held the other. After the battle, the enemy, under a flag of truce, requested permission to bury his dead, which was granted. For this defence, the thanks of the Kentucky Legislature were tendered unanimously and by acclamation, to Colonel Moore and his comrades of the 25th."*

On the 5th Morgan attacked the garrison at Lebanon, and forced it to surrender, after a short but desperate fight. The town was plundered. Thence moving to Springfield, the rebel chief divided his force, one column threatening Louisville, another Columbia, and others moving off towards Lexington and Frankfort. But the pursuit had now become well organized and vigorous. Generals Hobson, Judah and Shackleford formed a junction with Colonel Wolford, and the combined forces formed a formidable array of mounted men, infantry and artillery. Morgan drew in his detached parties that had been ravaging the country, securing supplies and seizing horses, and, uniting his forces, made a bold push for the Ohio, by way of Bardstown. Our pursuit was difficult, as the country was scoured clean by the raiders, who secured fresh mounts at every point, while our men were compelled to do the best they could with their jaded animals. On the 7th the pursuing party reached Bardstown, and, pushing on to Shepherdsville, encamped near that town for the night. Morgan was now about twenty hours ahead in this exciting race. He crossed Rolling Fork,

* Report of Adjutant General of Michigan, 1863.

burnt the bridges behind him, reached the Ohio at Brandenburg at an early hour on the 8th, found and captured two steamers at the landing, put his troops on board, ferried them across during that day and night, and, having placed them all safely on the Indiana shore, burnt his transports. Our forces reached the bank just in season to witness the spectacle of the burning boats, and to hear the derisive shouts of triumph that the successful enemy raised from the opposite shore.

The lower range of counties in Indiana now seemed to lie at the disposal of the rebel chief, and those who sympathized with his cause had the opportunity of learning, that even his tender mercies were cruel. He burnt the town of Salem, destroyed the railroad bridge and track, and ravaged the neighboring region without regard to friend or foe. For a time he seemed to conduct the affair with great skill. He made the authorities at Indianapolis believe that he was threatening the Capital, while he kept our forces at Louisville on the *qui vive* by making feints of attempting a passage at Jeffersonville. But General Burnside was by no means idle. He disposed his available forces in Kentucky either for defence or pursuit, he ordered the river to be patrolled by the gunboats in his Department, arranged a system of fortifications and defence for Louisville, employed the militia of Indiana and Ohio in conjunction with Governors Morton and Tod, aroused the people, stationed his improvised forces in the most advantageous positions for checking the career of the adventurous raider, and urged on the forces already in pursuit. Morgan found that his plans for further progress in ravaging had met with a serious interference, and, when Generals Hobson, Judah and Shackleford had reached the opposite bank on the morning of the 10th, with their forces in pursuit, the rebel chief became seriously baffled, and sought only to escape in safety. He fled through the counties of Harrison, Jefferson, Scott, Ripley and Dearborn, harassed by the militia. He more than once attempted to find a crossing place into Kentucky, but was foiled at every point by the vigilance of our naval force. Without doing much damage, he reached the Ohio line at Harrison on the White Water river in Hamilton county, followed as closely as the condition of the roads would permit by our indefatigable cavalry.

The following dates will show his progress: On the 10th of July he was at Vernon, Ind.; on the 12th near Versailles; on the 13th one column near Aurora, and another at Harrison, and on the 14th he crossed the Miami river at Miamisville. At the latter place, our forces were but three or four hours behind him. Such dispositions were made at Hamilton and Cincinnati, as effectually to secure the safety of those two cities, and Morgan, passing to the eastward on the night of the 13th and during the 14th, endeavored to reach the Ohio by way of Batavia. Again prevented and closely pressed, Morgan's escape became simply a question of the comparative endurance of our men and his own. Day and night, through Sardinia, Winchester, Jackson, Jasper, Pikeston, Linesville and Chester, the pursuit continued without cessation. The loyal people of Ohio turned out to harass the invaders at every cross road and afforded every facility to our troops. Provisions, forage, horses were willingly furnished, or,—if any reluctance was occasionally manifested,—were pressed into the service. General Judah led a column along the river roads, Generals Hobson and Shackleford in the interior. A division of small gunboats kept the river itself on Morgan's right flank, and threw shell and shot among his columns, whenever opportunity offered. With some difficulty, the gunboats were warped over the shoals and forced up the rapids. The gallant officer in command, Lieutenant Commander Le Roy Fitch, clearly understood the exigency and faithfully met its requirements.

Eastward the flight and the pursuit continued through Southern Ohio until the 19th of July, when the enemy was brought to bay near Chester by our land forces. He had previously attempted to cross the river near Buffington Island, but had been handsomely repulsed and driven back into the country in confusion by Lieutenant Commander Fitch, leaving horses, carriages, boots, shoes, small arms and the like, strewn

who followed him with unabating persistence. For fifty-seven miles did this energetic officer pursue, until at three o'clock in the afternoon of the 20th, General Shackleford, with the aid of Colonel Wolford with the 45th Ohio infantry, had driven the foe to a high bluff near the river, from which escape was difficult. An unconditional surrender was demanded, and forty minutes were allowed for consultation. During the interval, Morgan, with six hundred men, managed to slip away unperceived, and the remainder of the enemy's force surrendered. The captures on that day amounted to over twelve hundred officers and men, with their arms and equipments. General Shackleford, exasperated by the treachery of Morgan, called for volunteers who would be willing to "stay in the saddle, without eating and drinking," until Morgan was captured. A thousand and more responded; but, as only five hundred horses were found serviceable, that number of men started, on the morning of the 21st, determined to run down the coveted game.

The chase had become decidedly animating and highly interesting. For three days and three nights longer were our troops in hot pursuit, until, on the morning of the 24th, Morgan was overtaken near Washington, in Guernsey county, but succeeded, by destroying bridges, in eluding our forces and causing them considerable delay. Still General Shackleford was persevering and vigorous, and pushed persistently on through Athens, Harrison county, Springfield and Salem, Jefferson county, capturing two hundred and thirty of the enemy by the way. Major W. B. Way, with the 9th Michigan cavalry, after a forced march of a day and night, succeeded, at eight o'clock on the morning of the 26th, in bringing Morgan to an engagement about a mile and a half from Salinesville. Fighting continued for an hour or more, and resulted in scattering the enemy in all directions. The enemy lost seventy-five killed and wounded, two hundred prisoners, and one hundred and fifty horses, with equipments and arms. Finally, General Shackleford had the extreme satisfaction, on the morning of the 27th, of overtaking Morgan and the remnant of his command, about four hundred in number, near New Lisbon, in Columbiana county, and compelled them to an immediate surrender. The rebel partizan, with characteristic craft, pretended to have surrendered himself to a militia officer who had paroled him. But as, in the course of the interview, he had expressed considerable contempt for the militia of Ohio which had endeavored to check his career, and deemed them of no consequence, General Shackleford rightly judged his story to be a fabrication. The prisoner, therefore, and the officers who accompanied him, were immediately carried to Cincinnati and delivered over to General Burnside. The capture of the guerilla chief was immediately reported to the authorities at Washington. General Halleck at once ordered that Morgan and his officers be placed in close confinement in the penitentiaries of the State of Ohio. The order was obeyed, and the captured men were accordingly distributed among the prisons and confined under the usual regulations. Morgan, however, and a few of his officers succeeded, at a subsequent period, in escaping, and, assisted by disloyal persons within our lines, finally rejoined his friends. But the signal failure of his raid had not added to his reputation among his fellow officers. He seems afterwards to have fallen into some disgrace, and did not again become in any way prominent.

The admirable conduct of Generals Hobson, Judah and Shackleford and the pursuing party was beyond all praise. The Governors of Indiana and Ohio were very efficient in their dispositions of the militia of the two States. The committees of safety in the different counties were exceedingly active, and rendered very efficient service. The loyal people of Ohio turned out, and, by felling trees across the roads, organizing in squads to harass the fugitives, and adopting such other measures as the emergency suggested, gave valuable assistance to the parties in pursuit. Occasionally, the militia showed signs of faltering and fear, but, in general, they were very prompt and effective.

General Scammon, whom we have already seen at South Mountain and Antietam, was now in command in West Virginia, and kept his command well posted to prevent the escape of Morgan. The naval forces did incalculable service. Lieutenant Commander Fitch, with the few boats which he had for a nucleus, organized an impromptu squadron, and, placing a gun or two and a few men on every boat that he could use, succeeded in guarding the river most thoroughly, and in thwarting every attempt of the enemy to cross into Kentucky or West Virginia. The battle of Buffington Island and Chester was doubtless the crisis of the pursuit, and in this affair, our land and naval forces were equally conspicuous and gained an equal glory. In fine, all the subordinate officers and men were zealous, energetic and faithful in the discharge of every duty. But the guiding mind of the pursuit was that of the commander of the Department. From the first rupture of his lines until the capture of Morgan, he was on the alert, active in disposing his forces, in furnishing fresh relays of horses and men, in pushing on the pursuit, in arranging his river guards, in corresponding with the authorities along the route of the guerilla chief, in communicating with the commanding officers of the neighboring Departments, in warning, encouraging and impelling all whom he could reach. Though suffering at the time from an illness which was peculiarly enervating, his energies seemed inexhaustible. So effectual were the measures which were adopted and executed, as to confine the track of the rebel raider to the belt of counties lying along the river bank, and at last to bring his expedition to a most disgraceful end. Very few of those who first crossed the Cumberland with high and hopeful hearts, succeeded in returning to the enemy's lines. Many of them were killed and disabled. Most of their plunder was recaptured. No expedition of the kind on either side during the war was so effectually and completely brought to nought. The capture of the rebel partizan and his men was an exploit for which General Burnside, his subordinate officers and his troops well deserved the thanks of their countrymen, for their vigilance, persistence and fidelity.

CHAPTER IV.

OVER THE MOUNTAINS.

FOR East Tennessee at last! The raid of General Morgan had somewhat disturbed the plans of General Burnside, but immediately upon its defeat and conclusion, the campaign against the enemy in Knoxville was commenced. General Burnside had hoped that, upon the fall of Vicksburg, the Ninth Corps would be ordered back to the Department of the Ohio. Such had been the repeated promise of the authorities at Washington. But, as has already been perceived, the promise could not well be fulfilled, while General Grant needed the services of the corps to operate against the forces of General Johnston. It is true that the movement upon Jackson resulted in little except to inflict great losses upon our troops in the diseases which were caused by the rapid marches of the campaign. But, as it was thought necessary to place the safety of Vicksburg beyond even the shadow of a doubt, our officers and men acquiesced in the operations with a steadfast loyalty, and endured the terrible hardships of the campaign with a heroic patience. Before the arrival of the Ninth Corps in Kentucky, the movement over the mountains had been arranged, and actually commenced. But even if this had not been the case, the troops were in no suitable condition to join the advancing columns. They required rest and recuperation. General Burnside must accomplish his great task without the aid, at first, of the tried and bronzed veterans who had proved their valor, devotion and patriotism on so many ensanguined fields. It was with the troops of the twenty-third corps, reënforced by some fresh levies made in Kentucky, East Tennessee itself, and the States North of the Ohio, that the advance was to be made. The troops of the Ninth, as fast as they arrived, were brought down towards the frontier and distributed at the proper points, that they might be sent forward as reënforcements when their presence was required.

From the commencement of the war, East Tennessee had been a prominent point in the calculations and plans of both the contending parties. Its occupation was a matter of prime importance. Lying in the valley of the Tennessee and Holston rivers, between the lofty and difficult range of the Cumberland mountains on the north and west, and the Blue Ridge, with its outlying spurs and ranges composed of the Stone, Bald, Smoky and Iron mountains on the south and east, it was easily defensible by the rebels, while it contained the great line of communication between their left and right flanks—the Virginia and Tennessee Railroad. While this road remained intact, there was an unbroken and continuous connection between the two grand armies of the enemy, under General Bragg in the West and General Lee in the East. In the rear of the railroad lay the comparatively prosperous communities of the interior of the Gulf States and the Carolinas, as yet unvisited by the devastations of the war.

East Tennessee was also the home of a most loyal community. All the best and leading men in the district were firm supporters of the Federal Government, and a large majority of the people were prompt to follow their guidance. But the peculiar position of the country, isolated as it was from the North, and held by the large armies of the rebel "Confederacy," placed these loyal men at the mercy of their inveterate foes. Some were driven off, and compelled as refugees to procure a precarious subsistence from their Northern allies. Some were imprisoned and maltreated in the most barbarous and cruel manner. Some were tortured, others murdered, and others hung by the rebel authorities and their cruel subordinates. The history of this unfortunate war contains no sadder chapters than those which narrate the atrocities that were inflicted upon the loyal people of East Tennessee. Whether the authorities at Richmond were responsible for these dreadful wrongs, or the officers in immediate command, acting under the influence of their brief authority, were disposed to allow their personal hatreds full exercise, the fact remains clear and indisputable. No people were so mercilessly treated as these. No region became the scene of so much horror. Yet, amidst all their calamities and wrongs, the East Tennesseeans preserved their loyalty unshaken, and looked eagerly forward to the time when the advancing armies of the Union should give them their deliverance, and their opportunity for revenge.

The succor of these unfortunate victims of rebel rage, no less than the rupture of the rebel lines, had long engaged the attention of the government. The occupation of East Tennessee by the Union armies would at once deliver the loyalists there, and would deal a staggering blow to the insurgent power. It would in effect become a bisection of the "Confederacy," and would be a necessary preliminary to the triumphant advance of the national flag through all parts of the South. Were East Tennessee regained and permanently held, the result of the war would be no longer doubtful. The success of the Union would be placed beyond a question. The work of opening this region devolved upon General Burnside and General Rosecrans. To the former was given the task of proceeding directly into East Tennessee; to the latter that of marching on to Chatanooga, demonstrating towards Atlanta. General Rosecrans, during the summer, had pushed his lines forward as far as Winchester and the banks of the Elk river, and there made further preparations for prosecuting his campaign. On the 16th of August, he advanced across the Cumberland mountains, reached the Tennessee river on the 20th, established his headquarters at Stevenson, Alabama, and prepared for a further advance. On the 9th of September, General Crittenden's corps of his army occupied Chatanooga, and pressed forward in pursuit of the retreating enemy.

Meanwhile, General Burnside had rapidly performed his portion of the work. On the 16th of August, the very day of the departure of General Rosecrans from Winchester, General Burnside started from Lexington. The route which he had chosen for his own march lay through Crab Orchard, Mount Vernon, London and Williamsburg, with other columns, under command of General Hartsuff, moving on his right flank by way of Tompkinsville, Albany and Somerset, and a column of cavalry under Colonel Foster upon the left, to march directly upon Knoxville by way of Jacksboro'. The design was to cross the mountains by unfrequented roads, and even by those hitherto deemed impassable by a large army, and therefore left undefended by the rebel forces. This would introduce an army into East Tennessee to the surprise of the commanding general there, force his surrender or the evacuation of the position, and give our own forces an undisturbed possession of the entire region. The design was admirably carried out. Sending a force, under Colonel De Courcy, to take position in front of Cumberland Gap and occupy the attention of the enemy, General Burnside crossed the Cumberland mountains at the more westerly gaps. It was a work of extreme difficulty and was performed with great rapidity, considering the obstacles which were overcome. Preparations had been made for forced marching and ready fighting. The troops were in light marching order. All unnecessary impediments were cast aside. Pack mules were procured for the transportation of supplies. A part of the army was mounted. Wagon trains were to follow on the more accessible roads, while the troops on foot and on horseback clambered the heights.

On the 21st of August, General Burnside left Crab Orchard, and then followed fourteen days of as hard marching as was done by any army in the course of the war. The soldiers climbed the rugged ways with indomitable persistence and courage. The horses and mules connected with the army were tasked to their utmost, and many of them gave out exhausted by the severities of the march. In several instances, the animals utterly failed to drag the artillery up the acclivities; and their places were filled by men, who, with hands upon the drag ropes and shoulders to the wheels, dragged or lifted guns, caissons and wagons from height to height. The road was in some places strewn with the fragments of the broken vehicles and harness. But the soldiers were in good heart and cheerful spirits. Their commander knew not what it was to yield, and together they surmounted every difficulty. Crossing the summit, they easily descended into the plain below, and stood at last the conquerors of East Tennessee without a battle. A little skirmishing upon the road was all that betokened the nearness of an enemy. The rebel General Buckner, surprised by the suddenness of the advance, bewildered by the strange appearance of a large army, as though it had dropped from the clouds into the midst of his lines, and exaggerating the forces as they approached by different roads, immediately evacuated the region, retreated and joined General Bragg, actually leaving the garrison at Cumberland Gap without orders or even information of his movement. A portion of the rear guard was encountered by our cavalry, under General Shackleford, near Loudon, but succeeded in escaping, after burning an important bridge at that point. General Burnside, after a march of two hundred and fifty miles in fourteen days, found himself completely master of the situation.

Perhaps it may be well to place this march across the Cumberland mountains more in detail before the mind of the reader. The army of General Burnside, at the time, was composed of about eighteen thousand men. These were divided into five columns. The first marched from Glasgow, by way of Tompkinsville, Ky., to Livingston and Jamestown, Tenn.; the second from Columbia, by way of Creelsboro' and Albany, Ky., to Jamestown, Tenn., there joining the first; the third from Somerset, Ky., to Chitwoods, Huntsville and Montgomery, Tenn., where it was joined by the first and second; the fourth, which the commanding general accompanied, from Mount Vernon, by way of London and Williamsburg, Ky., over the Jellico mountains to Chitwoods, Huntsville — demonstrating towards Big Creek Gap—and Montgomery, Tenn., where the four columns formed a junction and pushed rapidly forward to Kingston. The fifth column, composed of cavalry, marched from Williamsburg directly on Jacksboro', passing through Wheeler's Gap, and occupied Knoxville on the same day upon which the infantry reached Kingston. Headquarters were at Crab Orchard on the 21st of August; at Mount Vernon on the 22d; at London on the 24th; at Williamsburg on the 25th; at Chitwoods on the 26th, 27th and 28th, delayed by the non-arrival of the supporting columns from Glasgow and Columbia, and of the supply trains; at Montgomery on the 30th; at Kingston on the 1st of September; and at Knoxville on the 3d of September.

Placing out of view the hardships of the road, the march over the mountains was not without beauty and picturesqueness. One officer* declared it to be "the most beautiful march of the war." The scenery of Tennessee has many attractive points. The mountains are not too high, and, seen at a distance, their lines are harmonious and graceful. The valleys are green, fruitful and, in some instances, of enchanting loveliness. The route travelled by the army lay through portions of the State that presented alternate beauty and wildness, and, as the troops emerged from the fastnesses of the mountain range, the valley of East Tennessee lay at their feet in all the luxuriance and mellowness of the early autumn.

But there was other business in hand than the enjoyment of the pictures which Nature offered to the contemplative eye. General Burnside entered East Tennessee as the deliverer of a cruelly treated and long suffering people. He was received as such. The troops were everywhere greeted with joyful acclamations. They were overwhelmed with kindness, and a generous welcome was offered them on all sides. The old flag, concealed under carpets, between mattrasses, buried in the earth itself, was taken from its hiding place and floated to the

* Captain W. H. Harris.

breeze from every staff. "Bless the Lord! the Yankees have come!" "The old flag's come back to Tennessee!" were the shouts that gave expression to the people's abounding joy. Gray-haired men, with tears streaming down their cheeks, women who had lost their all, children whose tender age had not escaped the cruelty of the rebel rule, came forth to greet the General and his officers at every turn, and to express their gratitude for the redemption which he had brought.

Dr. William H. Church, of General Burnside's staff, in a communication published at the time, gives a very interesting account of the reception of the troops. "The East Tennessee troops," he writes, "of whom General Burnside had a considerable number, were kept constantly in the advance, and were received with expressions of the profoundest gratitude by the people. There were many thrilling scenes of the meeting of our East Tennessee soldiers with their families, from whom they had been so long separated. The East Tennesseeans were so glad to see our soldiers that they cooked every thing they had and gave it to them freely, not asking pay and apparently not thinking of it. Women stood by the roadside with pails of water and displayed Union flags. The wonder was where all the stars and stripes came from. Knoxville was radiant with flags. At a point on the road from Kingston to Knoxville, seventy women and girls stood by the roadside waving Union flags, and shouting: 'Hurrah for the Union.' Old ladies rushed out of their houses and wanted to see General Burnside and shake hands with him, and cried: 'Welcome, General Burnside, welcome to East Tennessee!'"* The people felt that it was the time of their deliverance. It was also a time for action. They begged for arms, that they might join our forces and drive from their land the oppressors whose tyranny had lasted already too long. General Buckner was only too willing to escape before the swelling tide of popular indignation should rise and overwhelm him with its surges.

* Rebellion Record, Vol. VII., pp. 407–8.

On the 1st of September, General Burnside entered Kingston unopposed, and on the same day Colonel Foster with his cavalry occupied Knoxville without resistance. General Burnside, scarcely waiting for the thanks of an emancipated people, left Kingston, and passing through Lenoir's on the 2d, entered Knoxville, the objective point of his march, on the 3d of September. A considerable amount of public property, an arsenal, machine shop, cars, locomotives, pikes, &c., fell into his hands. From that day the rebel rule in East Tennessee was ended, the great Western line of rebel communication was taken from the hands that had abused its facilities, and the power of the Union became supreme. The frantic and desperate attempts which the rebels subsequently made to regain their lost authority were all completely foiled. Their season of triumph had passed. Their doom was sealed.

It was no matter of surprise, therefore, that General Burnside and his troops who had thus successfully carried out this great enterprise, should be welcomed at Knoxville with a joy which baffles all attempt at description. Their progress had already been a complete ovation. But here the people seemed to surpass all former demonstrations. An hour like that compensated for all the toils and anxieties of the wearisome march. As the general sought his quarters at the close of the day, he had the satisfaction of feeling, that he rested in the midst of as loyal a people as could be found in the land, who looked upon him as their saviour from the terrible and grinding despotism of the insurgent government. East Tennessee was now free, and he who had restored her liberty was the almost idolized commander of the army of the Ohio. The joy of such a triumph might well repay for the disappointment and defeat at Fredericksburg!

In the meantime the garrison at Cumberland Gap under General Frazer had fallen into direful straits. On the morning of the 4th of September, General Shackleford was sent forward from Knoxville to assist in capturing the garrison and occupying the Gap, and on the 7th General Burnside left Knoxville, with infantry and artillery, to assume a personal direction of the enterprise. A forced march of sixty miles was made in two days, and on the 9th General Burnside put his forces in position, and demanded the surrender of the post. Colonel De Courcy and General Shackleford had previously made the same demand, and had been refused. But the army now opposing the rebel commander was not to be trifled with. General Frazer endeavored to secure mild terms. General Burnside insisted upon an unconditional surrender. The rebel officer finding resistance useless gave up the post on the evening of the day of General Burnside's arrival. The captures consisted of a large quantity of ammunition, two thousand stand of small arms, eleven pieces of artillery, with their carriages and caissons and twenty-five hundred prisoners.

A portion of the garrison was composed of troops who had been taken on Roanoke Island a year and a half before, and now found themselves again in the hands of their former captor. The loss in this entire movement was but one man killed who fell at Tazewell as our advance was approaching Cumberland Gap. Thus expeditiously and successfully was the great enterprise carried through. Never again were East Tennessee and its loyal inhabitants to pass beneath the rebel yoke.

CHAPTER V.

CONQUEST AND OCCUPATION.

GENERAL Burnside and his troops had successfully occupied the principal commanding points in the section of East Tennessee to which they had been directed. What was doing by the coöperative column that was moving on Chattanooga? While at Cumberland Gap, General Burnside received the most gratifying intelligence from General Rosecrans. Every thing had gone forward in the most satisfactory manner, and so promising was the situation, that it seemed as though the work of the army of the Ohio had been completed. General Crittenden sent a despatch to General Burnside in terms of exultation and victory. It was dated at Chattanooga on the 10th, and was written at two o'clock in the morning of that day. Said General Crittenden: "I am directed by the General commanding the department of the Cumberland to inform you, that I am in full possession of this place, having entered it yesterday at twelve M., without resistance. The enemy has retreated in the direction of Rome, Ga.; the last of his force, cavalry, having left a few hours before my arrival. At day light, I make a rapid pursuit with my corps, and hope that he will be intercepted by the centre and right, the latter of which was at Rome. The general commanding department requests that you move down your cavalry and occupy the country recently covered by Colonel Minty, who will report particulars to you and who has been ordered to cross the river."

From this despatch, General Burnside naturally concluded, that General Rosecrans was making a very satisfactory and indeed an uninterrupted progress. If the enemy had been driven as far as Rome, East Tennessee was safe. Scarcely more was needed, than to occupy the principal strategic points with sufficient garrisons. He felt that such a work as that could as well and as easily be done by any other officer, as by himself. The principal duty had been performed. Subsequent events proved that General Crittenden had written in too enthusiastic terms. The enemy had not retreated so far as he had thought nor had our advance penetrated so far into the enemy's lines. But General Burnside had nothing to guide him but the information which General Rosecrans had sent. He was also suffering, at the time, from a severe attack of the disease which had prostrated him during the summer, and he considered that he required some relief from his constant and harassing duties. He had done his work well and he needed rest. He therefore tendered his resignation on the 10th, and, on the following day, returned to Knoxville. On the 12th, telegraphic communication was established with Washington, and on the 13th, General Burnside received from President Lincoln a kind but decisive despatch declining to receive his resignation. It was in the following words: "A thousand thanks for the late successes you have given us. We cannot allow you to resign, until things shall be a little more settled in East Tennessee." General Burnside accordingly proceeded, without further delay, to effect a more complete settlement of affairs, in the district which he had wrested from the enemy. He had sent troops up the valley of the Holston, immediately after the occupation of Knoxville, for the purpose of dismantling the railroad or occupying it as far as the Virginia line, and of threatening the salt works near Abingdon in Virginia. He had also stationed cavalry at Kingston under Colonel Byrd, who was directed to communicate with the cavalry of General Rosecrans. General Halleck's orders on the subject were positive. On the 11th, he sent a despatch to General Burnside as follows: "I congratulate you on your success. Hold the gaps of the North Carolina mountains, the line of the Holston river or some point, if there be one, to prevent access from

Virginia, and connect with General Rosecrans, at least with your cavalry. General Rosecrans will occupy Dalton, or some point on the railroad to close all access from Atlanta, and also the mountain passes in the West. This being done, it will be determined whether the movable force shall advance into Georgia and Alabama or into the valley of Virginia and North Carolina."

In accordance with this order, General Burnside disposed his troops. He put his forces in motion to occupy the different points necessary to guard his line of defence, the Holston river, and to hold the gaps of the North Carolina mountains. But these points were threatened by General Samuel Jones with a force of ten thousand troops, who were vigilant and active. The enemy had no intention of leaving East Tennessee in our undisputed possession. Its conquest was a severe loss to him, and the ease with which it had been accomplished was a source of especial mortification. He was by no means willing to sit down quietly and submit to such a derangement of his lines. General Jones was therefore occupied with harassing our outposts and carefully watching our lines, to take advantage of any weakness or negligence on the part of our officers. It was necessary, both for the safety of our own posts, and for a thorough obedience to General Halleck's order, to expel General Jones from the Department. Colonel Foster's brigade of cavalry had already been pushed out to observe the enemy and hold him in check. Colonel Carter, with his brigade, was acting in support of Colonel Foster. General Shackleford had the direction of the entire cavalry force. General Hartsuff was ordered to send all his infantry except Colonel Gilbert's brigade, together with Colonel Wolford's cavalry, to reënforce the troops, that were already in the presence of the enemy. General White's division and all of General Hascall's except Gilbert's brigade, were accordingly sent forward. The troops moved on the 13th and 14th, and made good progress on their march towards the threatened points. Every disposition was thus made to guard a line of one hundred and seventy-six miles in length from the left of General Rosecrans, with whom General Burnside was in direct communication, nearly to the Virginia boundary. The reader can easily understand what unceasing vigilance and vigor were necessary to maintain this long line, and to preserve an uninterrupted connection with the coöperating army.

But General Rosecrans himself was now in greater danger than had been supposed, and needed reënforcement. The enemy under General Bragg had not been so completely discomfited as had been believed. The information sent by General Rosecrans was of somewhat too hopeful a character. It was too good to be altogether correct. The enemy, instead of retreating into the interior of Georgia, was standing at bay a short distance beyond Chattanooga on the line of Chickamauga creek.

It was known at Washington that General Lee had sent General Longstreet's corps to the West to reënforce General Bragg, who could thus prevent any further advance by General Rosecrans, and who, it was feared, might take the offensive. General Halleck, accordingly, telegraphed in all directions, soliciting aid for General Rosecrans. The following despatch, dated Washington, Sept. 13th, went forward to General Burnside: "It is important that all the available forces of your command be pushed forward into East Tenneesee. All your scattered forces should be concentrated there. So long as you hold Tennessee, Kentucky is perfectly safe. Move down your infantry as rapidly as possible towards Chattanooga, to connect with Rosecrans. Bragg may merely hold the passes of the mountains to cover Atlanta, and move his main army through Northern Alabama to reach the Tennessee river and turn Rosecrans' right and cut off his supplies. In this case Rosecrans will turn Chattanooga over to you and move to intercept Bragg."

On the reception of the above order, on the evening of the 16th, General Burnside immediately telegraphed for the Ninth Corps to move with all possible despatch from its camping grounds in Kentucky to the scene of action in East Tennessee. On the morning of the 17th, he started in person to overtake the troops whom he had sent up the valley in obedience to General Halleck's first order, and to see that they returned at once to Knoxville and moved down "towards Chattanooga," in obedience to the second order. Though he had full confidence in his subordinates, he yet considered that the emergency demanded his personal supervision. On the 14th, General Halleck, now in great alarm, forwarded the following despatch: "There are several reasons why you should reënforce Rosecrans with all possible despatch. It is believed that the enemy will concentrate to give him battle. You must be there to help him." General Burnside received this despatch at Morristown, late on the 17th, and on the 18th ordered all his troops in that quarter back to Knoxville and Loudon. On the 19th General Rosecrans was attacked with great fury near Chickamauga Creek, and, after a very severe engagement of two days, in which the losses on both sides were exceedingly heavy, was obliged to withdraw his army within the defences of Chattanooga. The field of battle was at least one hundred and twenty miles distant from General Burnside's headquarters, and nearly two hundred from his outposts in the upper valley, and the lateness of the hour at which the orders from General Halleck were received, rendered it impossible for General Burnside to reach the Chickamauga, or even Chattanooga in season to be of any service. The contradictory orders from Washington were somewhat embarrassing. To hold the line of the Holston, to occupy East Tennessee, to secure the gaps of the North Carolina mountains, and to reënforce General Rosecrans at the same time, was clearly beyond General Burnside's power. The Ninth Corps was moving, but no portion of it had yet made its appearance. Knoxville could not be left without defence, for that would be an abandonment of the campaign. Nevertheless, General Burnside made his dispositions to aid his brother officer, and put his troops in motion. All were moving down the valley, except a force of cavalry and infantry, confronting the enemy at Carter's Station on the Watauga.

General Burnside hastened up to Henderson's Station by rail on the 20th, there took horse, and without slacking rein rode to Carter's, thirty-six miles distant. On the evening of the 21st, he received peremptory orders from the President to join General Rosecrans without delay. But the enemy was in front in his entrenchments, commanding a bridge that spanned the river at that point. Should General Burnside attempt the destruction of the bridge, his intention of withdrawal would at once be revealed. To retreat with the bridge intact would subject him to no little annoyance from the enemy's pursuit. But the order was to go, and General Burnside had no disposition to remain longer than was absolutely necessary. The question with him was important, as its answer involved the safety of his command and the assurance of his obedience. Should he attack, or retire without an engagement? His best course was evidently to attack. Preparations were immediately made for that purpose, and the order was given to force the enemy's lines at daylight on the next morning. The 22d dawned. It was discovered that the enemy had fled during the night, hastened by Colonel Foster's cavalry, that was demonstrating towards his rear; and, as he fled, he had set fire to the bridge. Additional combustibles were applied to ensure its destruction, the troops were immediately put on the march, and by noon, the column was well on its way towards Knoxville. The General and his staff rode back to Henderson's Station during that day and night, met the advance of the Ninth Corps at Morristown the next morning, and, late in the evening of the 24th, arrived at Knoxville. The troops were immediately concentrated and put in readiness to march to any point where their presence was demanded. Every exertion had been made to assist General Rosecrans, but meanwhile the battle had been fought, and the emergency had passed.

Immediately after its arrival from Mississippi, the Ninth Corps had been put into camp in central Kentucky, to give

Eng^d by A.B. Ritchie.

GEN. ROBERT B. POTTER.

the officers and men the opportunity for recuperation, and to prepare them for the operations in East Tennessee. The beneficial effect of the fresh breezes of the early autumn upon the exhausted soldiers was at once perceptible. The men soon recovered their health, tone and spirits. But little service was required of them, and, for a week or two, they enjoyed the ease and comfort of their situation with great content. When the order came to move into East Tennessee, they heard it with eagerness and obeyed it with alacrity. The old enthusiasm reawakened, and they trudged along the roads over the mountains in the cheerfullest mood. Their numbers had been greatly reduced. Only six thousand were fit for duty. But their spirit was unbroken, and they were as ready as ever before to meet the enemy. General Willcox had been engaged during the greater part of the summer in administering the affairs of the Districts of Indiana and Michigan, and, during the movement into Tennessee, had busied himself in organizing a division of reënforcements.* On the 1st of October, he put his command on the march. He reported for duty at Cumberland Gap on the 5th of that month, and was immediately assigned to the command of the forces in the upper valley, with his headquarters at Greenville. General Parke was made chief of staff of the army of the Ohio, and General Robert B. Potter was assigned to the command of the corps.

General Potter had won a high place in the estimation of his brother officers and of the country, by his bravery, faithfulness and skill. He had entered the service in 1861, as Major of the 51st New York Volunteers, and these pages have borne an honorable record of his services in every position which he filled. Promoted by successive steps, he was appointed Brigadier General soon after the battle of Fredericksburg, his commission dating March 13, 1863. From the command of a brigade, he soon passed to that of a division, outranking his

* General Willcox's new division consisted of the 115th, 116th, 117th and 118th Indiana Volunteers, and 12th Michigan, 21st Ohio and 23d Indiana batteries. He had also two companies of the 3d Indiana cavalry.

former Colonel, Ferrero, on account of the failure of the latter to obtain the confirmation of his first appointment as Brigadier General.* Although the two officers had thus singularly enough changed their relative positions, they ever cherished the friendliest feelings towards each other, and General Ferrero obeyed as gracefully as he had formerly commanded. General Potter, in the absence of General Willcox, was the ranking division commander, and accordingly took command of the corps when General Parke was transferred to another post of duty. During the time of his command, he led the corps with great ability, and established his military reputation beyond a question. His subsequent course earned for him high commendations, and he bears the scars of honorable wounds received in the gallant and faithful discharge of his duty. He is a son of the late Right Reverend Alonzo Potter, Bishop of Pennsylvania, in the Protestant Episcopal Church, and a grandson of the late Reverend Doctor Eliphalet Nott, President of Union College. He was born in Boston, Mass., July 16, 1829, was educated at Union College, but left before graduation. At the outbreak of the war he was a lawyer in the city of New York, having been admitted to the bar, May, 1852.

After the battle of Chickamauga, some correspondence took place between Generals Burnside and Halleck, ending in directions to General Burnside to maintain his position. Headquarters were retained at Knoxville, in the neighborhood of which most of the Ninth Corps was posted. General White's division of the twenty-third corps was sent to Loudon. Colonel Wolford's cavalry reënforced Colonel Byrd, on the south side of the Holston, who was occupied in keeping open the communications with General Rosecrans. The important point of Bull's Gap was held by Colonel Carter's cavalry, with Colonel Hoskins's brigade of infantry in support at Morristown.

General Burnside, having this force well in hand and ready

* General Ferrero was reappointed, after the adjournment of Congress, upon the earnest recommendation of General Burnside and others, and was duly confirmed by the Senate, to date from May 6, 1863.

for offensive action, proposed to the General in Chief a choice of three distinct plans of operations. He desired to perform some active service which would, as he thought, be decisive of the fate of the rebel army confronting General Rosecrans, or which would, at least, relieve that general from his pent up position at Chattanooga. General Bragg, largely reënforced, had delivered battle at Chickamauga with such energy as showed that he was an enemy not to be despised, and, since that day of fighting, had sat down, with most provoking persistence, in front of General Rosecrans, and, threatening his right flank, seriously incommoded our troops at Chattanooga in the matter of supplies. General Burnside's proposition took the form of a communication, dated at Knoxville, September 30th, and was in clear and decisive terms, which the reader can easily comprehend.

"My force is now concentrated and in readiness to move in accordance with either of the following plans:—First plan: To abandon the railroad and East Tennessee, leaving the present force at Cumberland Gap, and to move down with the remainder of the force, say twenty thousand men, on the north side of the Tennessee river, through Kingston, Washington and Smith's Cross Roads, and effect a junction with Rosecrans.

"Second plan: To move down along the line of the railroad as an independent force, leaving a body of troops at Cumberland Gap, another body at Bull's Gap and Rogersville, to cover Cumberland Gap and watch the enemy in that part of the State, and small garrisons at Knoxville and Loudon; then to attack the right wing of the enemy about Cleveland with, say fifteen thousand men, acting in concert with Rosecrans and according to his advice.

"Third plan: To move on the south side of the Tennessee, through Athens, Columbus and Benton, past the right flank of the enemy, sending a body of cavalry along the railroad, or on its west side, to threaten the enemy's flank and cover the movement of the main body, which, consisting of seven thousand infantry and five thousand cavalry, will move rapidly down the line of the East Tennessee and Georgia Railroad to Dalton, destroying the enemy's communications, sending a cavalry force to Rome to destroy the machine works and powder mills at that place; the main body moving rapidly on the direct road to Atlanta, the rail road centre, and there entirely destroying the enemy's communications, breaking up the depots, &c.—thence moving to some point on the coast where cover can be obtained, as shall be agreed upon with you. It is proposed to take no trains, but to live upon the country and the supplies at the enemy's depots, destroying such as we do not use. If followed by the enemy, as we undoubtedly shall be, Rosecrans will be relieved and enabled to advance, and, from the celerity of our movement and the destruction of bridges, &c., in our rear, the chances of escaping material injury from pursuit are in our favor. Our chief loss would probably be in stragglers. I am in favor of the last plan.

"All the information that we can derive from deserters and citizens within the rebel lines, shows that the enemy suffered very heavy loss on the 19th and 20th, and considers it a drawn battle. If Rosecrans is in such position as to hold his own until he receives help from other quarters, I am satisfied that we can hold this country and do the enemy material injury by operating in the direction of the rebel salt works and Lynchburg, which we were doing with fair chances of success when the President's order arrived. A heavy force of the enemy, infantry, cavalry and artillery, is pressing our forces down the railroad, and is now occupying Jonesboro' and Greenville. We will try to stop them at Bull's Gap. Inasmuch as we are now ready to move, the earliest possible answer is desirable."

To the above despatch, General Halleck replied under date of October 2d: "The purport of all your instructions has been that you should hold some point near the upper end of the valley, and with all your available force move to the assistance of Rosecrans. Since the battles of Chickamauga and the wear of our force to paper, you have been repeatedly told that it would be dangerous to form a connection on the south side of the Tennessee river, and consequently that you ought to march on the north side. Rosecrans has now telegraphed to you, that it is not necessary to join him at Chattanooga, but only to move down to such a position that you can go to his assistance should he require it. You are in direct communication with Rosecrans and can learn his conditions and wants sooner than I can. Distant expeditions into Georgia are not now contemplated. The object is to hold East Tennessee, by forcing the enemy south of the mountains and closing the passes against his return."

There was apparently some working at cross purposes in relation to affairs in East Tennessee. General Halleck, with a good theoretical knowledge of the art of war, had had but a very limited experience of the actual movements of large armies in the field. The only march that he made during the entire war was from Pittsburg landing to Corinth, to occupy a position which the enemy evacuated without loss. He fought no battle, and his conduct of an army was distinguished by no important incident. Confined to such a narrow practical knowledge of operations in the field of actual warfare, it was no matter of surprise, that he did not understand the precise character of the situation in East Tennessee. His orders were contradictory and his plans confused. They required General Burnside to divide his forces into two weak divisions, place them nearly two hundred miles apart, and do impossibilities with both. At one time East Tennessee was to be held, at another it was to be given up, and all the troops crowded within the narrow limits of the post at Chattanooga, where supplies were already short, and animals and men nearly at the point of starvation. At one time General Burnside's men were to be scattered, and before they had reached their points of destination, they were to be concentrated, without losing their hold upon the territory which they had freed from the enemy. Again, the loyal people of East Tennessee were to be left to their fate, and the country, with the enemy's line of communication, to be once more ccupied by the rebel forces. In the midst of these harassing circumstances, and these conflicting despatches and dispositions, General Burnside not only had to check the enemy in his threatening demonstrations from Virginia and Northern Georgia, but he had also to quiet the alarm, caused among the people by an apprehension of the return of the despotism, which had so long oppressed them. If General Burnside should now leave them, to whom could they turn for safety? If, by any inconsiderate action or order of the General in Chief, the valley of the Holston should be abandoned and the enemy's troops again return, the people might well fear that the very worst consequences would ensue. A few thousand arms had indeed been distributed among the loyal Tennesseeans, but what could three or four hastily organized regiments accomplish against the veteran soldiers of the rebel army? A feeling of despondency began to prevail, as though the government of the United States was about to relinquish the territory after having once extended over it a beneficent rule. The President endeavored to rectify the mistakes of the General in Chief, but hardly succeeded in his well meant efforts. The defeat at Chickamauga emboldened the enemy, who was disposed at all times to profit by any error upon our part. General Burnside's position was most difficult. The President had the fullest confidence in him, and did the best he could to make the situation agreeable and the duty easy. The people looked up to him as their deliverer and depended upon him with a grateful trust. He had the fullest faith, that East Tennessee could be held against the enemy's most determined attacks, and he was resolved to retain his conquest and make it productive of good results.

The plan which General Burnside proposed to General Halleck had been well considered. The third proposition in his despatch of September 30th, may not have been practicable then, and with the small force which he contemplated employing upon such perilous service. But the careful reader, studying the successful and grand campaign of General Sherman, a year or more subsequent to that time, can perceive that the germ of such a movement was contained in the less conspicuous plan of General Burnside. General Sherman proved that the "Southern Confederacy" was a hollow shell. Whether the Autumn of 1863 or that of 1864 was the proper time to break it, is of course a matter of question. The latter time had indeed a condition which the former did not possess:—the fact, namely, that General Grant was then General in Chief. It had a further condition—that General Grant is a thorough and accomplished soldier, and confides in the good judgment and skill of his subordinates.

General Rosecrans was disposed to favor the first of the plans submitted to General Halleck and desired that it might be adopted. But the state of affairs at Chattanooga rendered it impracticable. By some disarrangement of forces, the Quartermaster's department had been unable fully to supply the army which General Rosecrans already had under his command. The depots of provisions and supplies at Chattanooga, and along the line through Bridgeport and Stevenson, were very poorly provided, and great difficulties of transportation existed. Already the horses and other animals required for the artillery, cavalry and wagon trains were dying in large numbers for want of forage, and the army itself was on half-rations.* The addition of General Burnside's forces to those already occupying the half-starved camps around Chattanooga would have increased the complications of the case, and would have compelled the men of both armies to endure great sufferings.

There was another circumstance to be considered when speaking of such concentration. It would have been the complete loss of East Tennessee. The entire valley of the Holston would have been laid open to the inroads of the rebel troops from Virginia, the people would have been subjected to a renewal of the cruelties from which they had been happily freed, the position at Chattanooga itself would have been pres-

* General Halleck's Report for 1863.

sed in front and on both flanks to an evacuation, and the Summer's operations would have been frustrated. While General Burnside held Knoxville and the upper valley, keeping free the roads through Cumberland and Big Creek Gaps, ample lines of retreat lay open in case of disaster. But, with with both armies at Chattanooga, short of supplies and confronted and flanked by a superior force of the enemy, defeat was almost certain. The reüniting of the enemy's broken line of communication would enable him to send large bodies of his troops from Virginia and give him every advantage. Only one line of retreat lay open for our forces towards Nashville, and the enemy, crossing the Cumberland Mountains, could fall upon the rear of our troops and drive them in inglorious rout to the line of the Cumberland river. Kentucky would again lie at the mercy of the rebels, and the entire North West would have been threatened. The occupation of Knoxville and the upper valley was necessary for the prevention of such calamities. While our forces were thus disposed, the further reënforcement of General Bragg from Virginia was difficult; while, on the other hand, General Rosecrans was comparatively safe from attack. What would have been the consequences, if this great avenue of communication had been given up to the enemy, it is very easy to perceive. Happily for the Federal government, General Burnside understood precisely what to do in the premises, and persisted in doing it. He securely held the railroad and the line through Cumberland Gap. He protected the left flank of General Rosecrans, and completely foiled the rebel plans in that quarter.

The month of October was not prolific of great events on either side. The rebel General Wheeler attempted a raid upon the communications of General Rosecrans, reached McMinnsville and burnt a few wagons and some stores. But the cavalry of General Rosecrans succeeded in intercepting and driving off the enemy. General Burnside's cavalry passing farther down the river, made our lines secure from subsequent interruption. On the left of the army of the Ohio, General

Jones again became active. A large force of the enemy from Virginia was threatening our communications with Cumberland Gap, and demonstrating upon the south side of the Holston and Watauga rivers. Since the concentration of our own troops at Knoxville, the enemy had assumed a decidedly hostile attitude, and it became necessary to clear our left flank from his encroachments.

The Ninth Corps, under General Potter, and a considerable body of cavalry, under General Shackleford, were sent up the valley during the first week of October, and, on the 8th, were joined by General Willcox's division, reënforced by Colonel Hoskins's brigade, at Bull's Gap. General Burnside himself left Knoxville on the 9th, and advanced from Bull's Gap on the 10th, with the entire command. The enemy was found strongly posted at Blue Springs, and disposed to receive battle. Colonel Foster's brigade of cavalry was sent around to the rear of the enemy's position, with directions to occupy the road upon which the enemy must retreat, at a point near Rheatown. The main attack was to be made at the time when Colonel Foster was supposed to be in proper position, and meanwhile the attention of the enemy was occupied by our skirmishers. A desultory engagement was thus kept up till about half-past three o'clock in the afternoon, when General Potter was ordered to move up the Ninth Corps, attack, and, if possible, break through the enemy's lines. At five o'clock, General Ferrero's division, which had been selected for the attack, moved gallantly forward against the enemy, and by a bold push pierced his first line, and heavily pressed back his troops upon the reserves. Night coming on put an end to the conflict, and our forces were disposed to resume the battle upon the following day.

The enemy, finding his rear threatened by Colonel Foster's movement, decided to withdraw during the night, leaving his dead upon the field and many of his wounded in our hands. Colonel Foster was delayed by the roughness of the roads and other causes, and did not succeed in reaching his assigned position in season to intercept the retreating foe. The dangerous point was safely passed. But for this untoward circumstance, the entire force of the enemy, with his materiel of war, must have fallen into General Burnside's hands. But our cavalry was early in the saddle, and General Shackleford with his troops, made a rapid and energetic pursuit, pushing the enemy across the Watauga and beyond the Virginia line, and driving him onward whenever he attempted to make a stand. General Shackleford continued on the trail for several days, burning six bridges, capturing and destroying three locomotives and thirty cars, and even proceeding so far as to threaten the salt works at Abingdon and Saltville. Our loss in this engagement was about one hundred killed and wounded. The enemy suffered more severely, and left in our hands one hundred and fifty prisoners.

On the 16th, a regiment of loyal North Carolina troops captured Warm Springs and occupied Paint Rock Gap. The remainder of General Burnside's troops were concentrated at Knoxville and Loudon, picketing down to the left of the Army of the Cumberland, pushing out scouts and outposts on the south side of the Tennessee, and clearing the country between the little Tennessee and Hiwassee rivers. General Burnside, besides these operations, was occupied during the greater part of the month in organizing his loyal East Tennessee regiments, and in preparing for the new movements inaugurated by the advent, upon this interesting scene, of the successful soldier whose name had already filled the country in connection with his grand triumph at Vicksburg.

CHAPTER VI.

THE SIEGE OF KNOXVILLE.

ON the 18th of October, Major General Ulysses S. Grant, by order of the President, assumed command of the "Military Division of the Mississippi," composed of the three Departments of the Ohio, the Cumberland and the Tennessee. The changes that had taken place upon the military chess board required more concentration of command, especially in the West. As many as four different armies were operating upon the soil of Tennessee, and to ensure their efficient co-ordinate action, a single head was required. General Grant's merit and distinguished service pointed him out as the most suitable for such command.

Operations in this quarter were now almost solely occupying public attention. The Army of the Potomac, after the battle of Gettysburg, had contented itself with quietly following General Lee's retreating forces to the line of the Rapidan, where the two armies, with an occasional episode of conflict, subsided into comparative quiet. General Hooker was despatched with two corps—the eleventh and twelfth to the aid of General Rosecrans on the one side. On the other, General Longstreet had been sent westward by General Lee with a large reënforcement, and had even joined General Bragg in season to take a prominent and active part in the battle of Chickamauga. General Grant was returning from the successful siege of Vicksburg. General Parke, with the Ninth Corps, had already reached Knoxville, and General Sherman, with the fifteenth corps, was marching across the country from Memphis. It seemed as though the chief struggle of the war was impending among the mountainous regions of northern Georgia and East Tennessee. The two great combatants appeared to feel the importance of the occasion, and each prepared to do his utmost. While the East lay comparatively quiescent, the West was to become the scene of the contest of giants.

General Grant, upon his advent, made a few changes in his Military Division. General Burnside was retained in his command at Knoxville. General Sherman was appointed to the command of the Department of the Tennessee, General Rosecrans was relieved and General Thomas was appointed in his place, to command the Department of the Cumberland. Under such able guidance, the country looked with confidence to a successful result of the autumnal operations. The well-grounded hopes of the public were not destined to disappointment. General Grant repaired in person to Chattanooga, and, bringing up General Hooker with his command, speedily relieved the force there by pressing back the enemy from the Tennessee river beyond the passes of the overhanging mountains. General Sherman restored the communications with the Mississippi river. General Burnside held the line of the Tennessee on General Grant's left flank, from Knoxville down to Washington, with his communications northward through Cumberland Gap well guarded. In this position, the further developments of the campaign were awaited with undiminished trust.

In General Burnside's immediate front, indications of the enemy's approach began to be perceived as early as the middle of October. General Bragg, having been forced back from his position before Chattanooga, extended his right flank beyond Cleveland, and finally decided to detach General Longstreet to attack General Burnside, and sever his communications with the rapidly concentrating army of General Grant. On the 20th of October, Colonel Wolford, during the pendency of some negotiations respecting prisoners, carried on under a flag

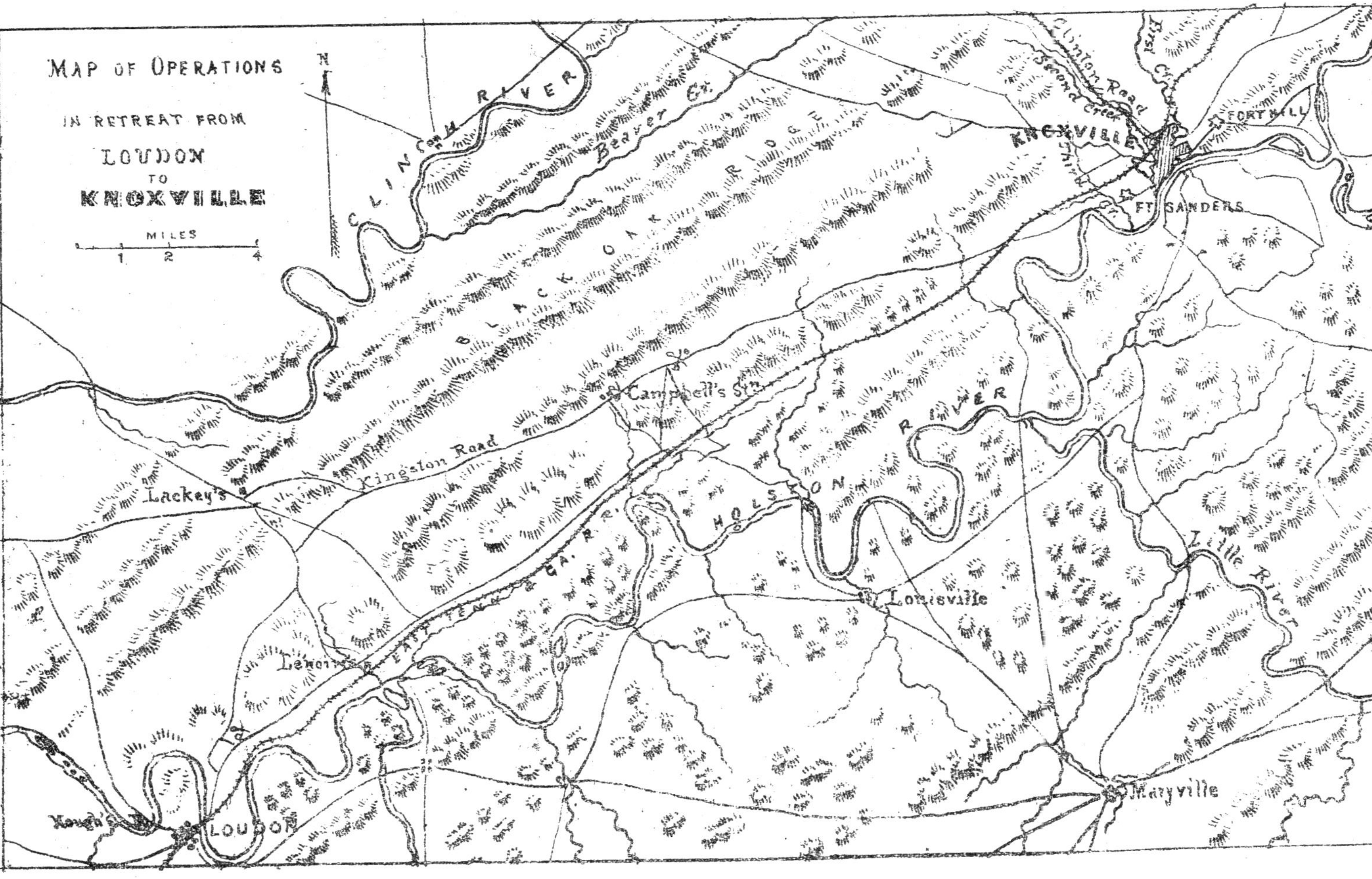
MAP OF OPERATIONS
IN RETREAT FROM
LOUDON
TO
KNOXVILLE
MILES
1 2 4
N
CLINCH RIVER
Beaver Cr.
BLACK OAK RIDGE
Clinton Road
Second Creek
First Cr.
KNOXVILLE
FORT HILL
FT. SANDERS
Campbell's Stn.
Kingston Road
Lackey's
HOLSTON RIVER
EAST TENN. & GA. R.R.
Lenoir's
Louisville
Little River
Maryville
LOUDON

of truce,* was attacked near Philadelphia by a large force of infantry, cavalry and artillery. After a severe fight of several hours, having inflicted a greater loss upon the enemy in killed and wounded than he had himself suffered, Colonel Wolford retreated to Loudon, leaving in the hands of the enemy six small howitzers, with thirty-eight wagons and between three hundred and four hundred prisoners. Our cavalry afterwards took the offensive, and drove the enemy back beyond Philadelphia, capturing from him a considerable number of prisoners. But it soon became evident that there was a force of the enemy in support of this movement which was really formidable in numbers and organization. Indeed, subsequent events proved that the affair at Philadelphia was the initiative of a desperate attempt to retake East Tennessee from our troops and drive them back into Kentucky. At the same time, some threatening demonstrations were made from Virginia, which were promptly met by General Willcox, in command at Greeneville.

The main attack, however, was to come from the forces now confronting us across the Tennessee river near Loudon. General Burnside had put General Sanders, a very brave and promising young officer, in command upon his right flank, where he and his forces performed many gallant and conspicuous services. He now withdrew his troops to the north bank of the Tennessee and occupied the heights above and opposite Loudon. Constant skirmishing occurred from day to day between the pickets of the hostile forces, with small losses upon either side. It was thought that the enemy's crossing might be prevented. But it was made manifest, before many days, that that portion of the rebel army which was operating in this direction was too strong for us successfully to oppose, except from a well fortified position. It was hoped by General Burnside, that a show of resistance might attract General Longstreet's forces sufficiently far away from General Bragg's main body to enable

* Captain Pell, of General Burnside's staff, was engaged in these negotiations, and was detained as prisoner by the enemy for a short time.

General Grant at Chatanooga to make a decisive attack upon his opponent. The situation was interesting enough to demand the personal presence of General Burnside, and on the 28th of October, headquarters were removed from Knoxville to the heights opposite Loudon, and the enemy's advance awaited. But the emergency for that time passed, and on the 31st General Burnside returned to Knoxville, preparing himself and his army for any further action which might become necessary.

Nothing of any great importance, however, took place until the 10th of November, when the attack came from another direction. A portion of the enemy's force, that had been threatening our left flank from Virginia, came down upon our garrison at Rogersville under Colonel Garrard, and succeeded in driving it out and back to Morristown, with a loss of about five hundred prisoners, four pieces of artillery, and thirty-six wagons. It was a severe demonstration upon our lines in that quarter, but beyond the single shock thus given, it was of little advantage to the enemy, as our posts were again immediately and fully secured. Our communications with Kentucky in that direction were undisturbed, and the balance of prisoners, besides those captured at Cumberland Gap, was still largely in our favor. The only two reverses which General Burnside's command suffered in its entire campaign in East Tennessee, were those at Philadelphia and Rogersville, and they were of comparatively little importance as affecting the result of the chief operations in the department.

An active campaign seemed about to open. Our troops near Loudon had prepared for winter quarters. They were somewhat rudely disturbed. General Grant became anxious in relation to the affairs of his military division, and was desirous of taking the offensive still more decidedly than he had already done, and of dealing a blow to the rebel army in his front, which should send it reeling back from its threatening position at Lookout Mountain. General Sherman was doing a good work on his right, engaged in clearing that flank of the combined armies. The presence of the enemy in large force below Loudon was thought to be troublesome. General Grant appeared at first to believe that it was desirable to evacuate the position at Knoxville and concentrate General Burnside's forces at Kingston in order that close communication might be made with our troops at Chattanooga. General Burnside was naturally unwilling to relinquish his hold upon the enemy's line of communication through Tennessee, and to abandon the people whom he had delivered to the renewed severities of the enemy's rule. He therefore preferred Knoxville to Kingston as the point of concentration. He also thought that General Grant would be materially aided by the withdrawal of General Longstreet from the main army of the enemy. If this detached force could be occupied in the neighborhood of Knoxville, General Grant would be able to inflict a very severe injury upon the enemy in his front. Knoxville moreover was partially fortified. General Burnside's chief engineer, Captain O. M. Poe, had inaugurated a system of defences at Knoxville as early as the 15th of September. Two earthworks had been erected near the town, and it was thought that these could be strengthened sufficiently to resist an attack and possibly to endure a siege. The communications with Cumberland Gap were secure, by which a retreat might be made in case of disaster. General Burnside laid these considerations before General Grant with the hope of his approval.

It happened that Mr. Chas. A. Dana, Assistant Secretary of War was visiting the West at the time to consult with the military authorities upon the character of the situation. He was then at General Grant's headquarters. In company with Colonel Wilson of General Grant's staff Mr. Dana visited Knoxville. The two gentlemen arrived on the 13th, and had an interview with General Burnside at which the questions involved in his operations were fully discussed. After hearing the reasons which General Burnside adduced to support his plans, they immediately telegraphed them in detail to General Grant. The information thus conveyed served to allay whatever anxiety existed in the mind of the commander of our armies in that quarter.

Meanwhile the enemy was making certain movements which confirmed the opinions that General Burnside had formed, and eventually proved them to be the best that could be followed in the existing circumstances. During the progress of the consultation at Knoxville, intelligence was received from the front which hastened the departure of Mr. Dana and Colonel Wilson. On Saturday morning, November 14th, General Longstreet with twenty thousand men threw his advance across the Tennessee river at Hough's Ferry, six miles below Loudon. By this manœuvre our position on the heights was turned. General Sanders had been previously relieved from the command at this point and was now operating with his cavalry on the south side of the Holston. Brigadier General Julius White with one division of the twenty-third corps was now holding the position, supported by General Potter with the Ninth Corps at Lenoir's. General White, upon learning the enemy's movement, sent the 23d Michigan infantry and a section of artillery to observe the enemy and if possible dispute his crossing. These troops were soon ordered back, and General White withdrew his command to Lenoir's. Intelligence of these movements broke up the council. General Burnside's guests immediately departed. The General himself went to the front, and on hearing the details which General White had to communicate decided to take charge of the movement of his troops in person. Entrusting General Parke with the command of Knoxville, he speedily arranged his plans for holding the enemy in check, until our troops could deliver battle successfully or securely withdraw. The first point was to harass the crossing at Hough's Ferry or, if that had been effected, to attack the advancing party. He ordered General White, supported by General Ferrero's division of the Ninth Corps, to assume the offensive. The odds were greatly against us. But General White, with the spirit of a true soldier, was ready and even eager for the combat. At four o'clock in the afternoon Colonel Chapin's brigade came in contact with the enemy's van-guard which had crossed the river. These troops were comparatively raw, but they charged upon Longstreet's veterans with the greatest gallantry, and supported by their comrades of the twenty-third corps they fairly forced the enemy's lines, and, pressing vigorously upon him, drove him for two miles back to the river. The night came on thick, rainy and very dark, and put an end to the engagement. The fight reflected great honor upon General White and his officers and men. The enemy had been checked in his advance. General Burnside contemplated another attack on the following morning, but the receipt of a despatch from General Grant was decisive in regard to the withdrawal of the troops. This despatch was received late at night. The officers of General Burnside's staff were gathered at his headquarters and the contents of the despatch naturally became a subject of conversation. "I shall withdraw my command to Knoxville," said General Burnside. "Why so?" said one of the young gentlemen, "you can easily beat the enemy as he is at present situated and drive him across the river. If we start we are lost. He will bring his entire force against us and we shall be defeated and ruined." "That may be true," replied the General; "but it will benefit General Grant if we can draw Longstreet away from his front more than it will injure us. If General Grant can destroy Bragg it is of no great consequence what becomes of ourselves. Order the troops to be ready to march in the morning."

At daylight the next morning, therefore, General Burnside retired his troops to Lenoir's,—Colonel Morrison's brigade of General Ferrero's division bringing up the rear—drawing off his artillery and trains in safety, with the exception of a single caisson, which became mired and had to be abandoned. The command was put in position at Lenoir's without molestation. Later in the afternoon, the enemy's skirmishers appeared in force, and were promptly scattered by a few well-directed shells from Captain Henshaw's battery of the twenty-third corps. During the night of the 15th, preparations were made for falling back to Campbell's station. The horses of the artillery had become so wearied and worn out, that the draft animals from the baggage train of General White's division were required to drag the guns, and a few wagons with their contents were destroyed.

Between ten o'clock and midnight, the enemy attacked our lines, but was quickly repulsed. Foiled in this, he attempted by a flank march, to anticipate our movements, and to seize the junction of the roads at Campbell's station. It was an admirable place for either attack or defence. Were the enemy able to occupy the coveted point, General Burnside's line of retreat would be cut and his army would be in extreme peril. He fully understood the importance of the movement, and prepared to meet and baffle the designs of the enemy. He knew that the possession of Campbell's station by General Longstreet would render the holding of Knoxville uncertain. But he also knew, that if the enemy could here be held in check, time would be gained for ensuring the safety of the army and the occupancy and fortification of the town.

The battle of Campbell's station was in reality the decisive battle of the campaign, and it was fought on both sides with great skill, courage and persistence. Its method, its progress and its result were all highly creditable to General Burnside and his officers and men. The disparity of forces was great. We had but six thousand; the enemy twice or three times that number. The preliminary movement was of course the occupation of the cross-roads. The main road to Knoxville runs nearly parallel with the Holston river and the railroad, in a north-easterly direction. From the west the approach is by the Kingston road striking the Knoxville road at an angle of about thirty degrees. From the North a narrow country road comes down from Clinton crossing the main road and continuing to the river. From the south-east another road comes up from the river. Campbell's station was thus the point of junction of roads leading from six different directions. Its importance can easily be understood. General Longstreet hoped to gain the desired point by throwing a body of troops along the Kingston road. General Burnside was on the alert. Just before daylight on the 16th, General Potter put the Ninth Corps in motion—Colonel Hartranft's division in advance, Colonel Humphrey's brigade in the rear. With rapid marching, Colonel Hartranft, always prompt and always reliable, succeeded in the early part of the forenoon, in reaching Campbell's station. He was but a quarter of an hour in advance of the foe. It was an exciting race and our troops won. Colonel Hartranft's command was immediately moved out on the Kingston road and deployed across it, with the left thrown forward to cover the Loudon road, along which our army and trains were moving.

It was just in time. Scarcely had the disposition been made, when the head of the rebel column appeared hastening up the Kingston road. A small body of cavalry that were with Colonel Hartranft, immediateiy attacked and forced the head of the column back. Our infantry also poured in such a sharp and destructive fire, as to check the enemy's advance and throw his leading regiment into some confusion. General Longstreet had not succeeded in his first movement, and though his flanking column made several attempts to break the lines of the covering brigade, and his pursuing column to press our rear guard under Colonel Humphreys, they met in both instances with nothing but repeated failure. Colonel Hartranft steadfastly held his ground until the remainder of the army and all the trains had safely passed the threatened point. Lieutenant Colonel Loring of General Burnside's staff was sent to select a position for the formation of the troops. The trains were directed upon the road to Knoxville. General Burnside rapidly arranged his line of battle upon the chosen position, a low range of hills about half a mile beyond the crosss-roads, slowly withdrawing his troops, regiment by regiment, from the advanced position near the village. The first line was found *en echelon*—General Ferrero's division on the right, General

White's in the centre, Colonel Hartranft's on the left. A small cavalry force was posted on the country roads on either flank, and the right of the infantry brigade on the right flank was partially refused. The heavy artillery was posted in the centre, the light batteries in the intervals between the infantry and cavalry, with proper support. In this position, General Burnside waited the enemy's onset.

The attack commenced about twelve o'clock, by a furious charge upon our right, where Colonel Christ's brigade had been posted. The rebels came on in columns of attack, hoping to crush in our right flank by the momentum of their assault. Our lines wavered a little. Colonel Christ rapidly changed front, and though his brigade was somewhat attenuated, it could not be broken. The desperate charges of the rebel host were most handsomely and successfully repulsed. Soon after this, a very formidable attack was made upon our left centre, held by General White's division. The enemy was received by the artillery, but moved steadily forward till within three hundred and fifty yards, when all our batteries in the centre and to the right and left of General White opened with canister and shell. The slaughter was terrible, and the enemy's first line was broken and forced to retire. Reforming once more, he returned to the attack, only to be repulsed again. Our troops were admirably handled and fought, and every attempt of the enemy to break our lines and force the position was effectually thwarted.

About two o'clock in the afternoon, our scouts reported that the enemy's forces were crossing the road and passing through some woods in their rear to attack our left. General Burnside had already decided to hold his first position until three o'clock, when he intended to retire to another defensive line in his rear. At fifteen minutes before three, he turned to Lieutenant Colonel Loring and asked the time. On being told, he said, "We will wait ten minutes longer, and then withdraw." Accordingly, at the designated hour, the troops were withdrawn as before to a second range of hills, and the second line was formed upon a position about a thousand yards in the rear of the first and commanding it. The withdrawal was accomplished by our officers and men with great deliberation and coolness, though made under a heavy continuous fire from the enemy's batteries. It was evident that General Longstreet, after failing to make an impression upon one flank, was intending to practise his favorite tactics by massing his troops upon the other, with the expectation of pushing back our left by a still heavier charge. Our centre was too strong to be forced. General Burnside formed his second line *en potence* on either flank—almost in the shape of a rectangle with three sides—massing his light artillery with Colonel Hartranft's brigade upon the left, where it was expected the enemy's attack was to be made. The cavalry scouts were well out as before, and the infantry was deployed across and upon either side of the road. On came the enemy, with a more resolute and determined bearing, if possible, than before; with frightful yells, they rushed down the opposite slope and up the acclivity, upon the crest of which our troops were posted. Our men poured in destructive volleys of musketry, and as the rebels, still undismayed, came within short range, the artillery opened with grape, canister and shell with fearful effect. No troops could withstand so withering a fire. The charging column staggered, recoiled, and finally broke and sought shelter from the storm of death. The enemy's artillery on the heights in his rear kept up a hot but ineffectual fire until sunset, when it ceased, and a sullen silence settled over the field. Our loss in this battle was twenty-six killed, sixty-six wounded, and fifty-seven missing. The enemy's loss was much greater, as he was more exposed. The manner in which our troops were handled, the movements executed, the withdrawal made from one point to another, and the final advantage secured, elicited the highest commendation from those who witnessed the progress of the engagement. "Never did troops manœuvre so beautifully and with such precision," says General Ferrero in his report of the action, "changing position several times while under a severe fire, brigades moving forward to relieve each other, others retiring, having exhausted their ammunition, changes of front, passing of defiles, were executed by men and officers so as to draw forth exclamations of the highest praise from all. In these movements, Colonel Christ particularly distinguished himself."

The conduct of the officers and men was beyond all praise, and the battle of Campbell's Station will always be proudly remembered by those of our troops who were fortunate enough to participate in its scenes. The soldiers of the Ninth Corps, with their comrades of the twenty-third, had met the flower of General Lee's army, and had inflicted upon it a most damaging blow. General Longtreet was surprised by the obstinacy with which he was met and fought, and was forced to feel that the reconquest of East Tennessee was not an easy task. General Burnside, having punished the enemy, mastered the field, and saved his trains, deliberately drew off to Knoxville during the night of the 16th, and prepared for the siege which General Longstreet would now be obliged to make. Captain Poe had already been sent from Campbell's Station, with instructions to select lines of defence around Knoxville, and to have everything in readiness to put the troops in position as they should arrive. Captain Poe was familiar with the ground, and was thus able to designate without delay the points to be occupied. General Burnside knew that he could trust his troops, and they knew that they could trust him. The Ninth Corps was always to be depended upon, and the valor of the twenty-third had sufficiently been proved at the battles of Lenoirs and Campbell's Station. General Longstreet had received a severe check, but was not disposed to relinquish his purpose of driving our troops from East Tennessee. General Burnside's retreat drew him still farther away from General Bragg. All General Burnside's plans were working admirably. If Knoxville were once reached and properly defended, there would be no cause to fear for the result.

When our troops were withdrawn from Loudon, the ponton bridge which they had used was conveyed to Knoxville and thrown across the Holston river. By this means, General Sanders's cavalry was enabled to cross to the south side and maintain an easy communication with our troops in the town. General Burnside anticipated some movement of the enemy upon the south side of the Holston, and General Parke reposed the utmost confidence in the valor and discretion of General Sanders. The anticipation was realized, the confidence was more than justified. On the night of the 13th, a large body of cavalry and mounted infantry, under Generals Forrest and Wheeler, crossed the little Tennessee river near Morgantown, and on the 14th, attacked our advance at Marysville. A portion of the 11th Kentucky cavalry fell into the enemy's hands. Our forces were drawn in and skirmishing continued, at different intervals, during the 15th, occasionally with very severe and sanguinary fighting, in which the 1st Kentucky and 45th Ohio mounted infantry suffered considerable loss. Our dead were stripped of clothing, rings, watches, and other articles of value, by the enemy. But General Sanders was too strongly posted to be attacked with any hope of success, and our lines were everywhere vigilantly guarded. After carefully observing our position, the rebel commander withdrew without a serious attack. In the course of the 16th, the enemy had entirely disappeared from the immediate front of Knoxville. Colonel Adams, with the 1st Kentucky cavalry and 45th Ohio, pursued the retreating foe for several miles, with occasional skirmishes. The battle at Campbell's Station relieved the garrison of Knoxville from the pressure of the hostile force.

General Sanders returned across the river with his command, and at once proceeded down the Loudon road to cover the retreat of our forces and hold the pursuing enemy in check. Colonel Pennebacker, with a brigade of mounted infantry, occupied the Clinton road. The enemy's cavalry could not reach General Longstreet in season to be of any service on the 16th, and our army retired unmolested. General Sanders stationed his outposts for a considerable distance down the road. On the 17th, the enemy vigorously attacked. General Sanders, drawing in his more exposed posts, concentrated his force, gallantly met the enemy's assault, and repulsed it after a brief but sharp engagement. During that night, he fell back to within a mile of the city defences, where the army was now getting into its proper position.

On the 18th, in the early morning, the enemy attacked with great fury. General McLaws commanded the assaulting force, and expected to push back our cavalry upon and into the town, and to enter in victory. But General Sanders was not a man who could be easily beaten. He fully appreciated the importance of the conflict in which he found himself engaged, and was resolute to prevent the execution of the enemy's plan. The fight that followed was of a most gallant description. For three hours, the engagement continued. The 112th Illinois, 45th Ohio, 3d Michigan, and 12th Kentucky mounted infantry regiments bore the brunt of the contest, and were especially conspicuous for their bravery. But the enemy's forces were too heavy for us, and they gradually forced back our left until under the cover of the guns of General Ferrero's position, they were finally checked. But General Sanders was not inclined to give up the contest, and it was necessary that the foe should be held back until our defences were made tenable. The battle was renewed later in the day, and became a sanguinary struggle. General Sanders himself was foremost in every scene of danger, performing wonderful deeds of valor. Most precious time was saved for our men who were at work in the trenches. The enemy's attack was completely repulsed, and he was fairly forced away from our lines. The prize had not fallen into his hands, and it is said that General McLaws was afterwards court martialed for his failure to drive our troops from Knoxville.

But the price of our victory was heavy. Among those who fell were Captain Clifton Lee, of the 112th Illinois, and Adjutant Charles W. Fearns, of the 45th Ohio, both promising young officers. But the chief and saddest loss was that of the brave commander of our troops. He fell in the midst of the hottest fighting, and at the very front, pierced by a minie bullet. He was tenderly conveyed into the town and received every attention. But no human skill could save him. On being told that his wound was mortal, he said: "Well, I am not afraid to die. I have made up my mind upon that subject. I have done my duty and have served my country as well as I could." The last consolations of religion were administered. General Burnside and some of the members of his staff stood by the bedside, and, amid the prayers and tears of his comrades and friends, the spirit of the fearless soldier took its heavenward flight.

General Sanders was but twenty-eight years of age, a native of Kentucky, and a graduate of West Point in the class of 1856. When the war broke out he was 1st Lieutenant of dragoons, and on the organization of the 6th Regiment of cavalry, United States army, he was promoted to Captain—his commission dating May 14th, 1861. He distinguished himself in the campaigns in Virginia and Maryland, and in 1863 was appointed Colonel of the 5th Kentucky cavalry. His raid into East Tennessee has already been mentioned. At the earnest request and solicitation of General Burnside, who had early perceived his merits, he was promoted to Brigadier General about three weeks before his death. He was immediately assigned to the command of a cavalry division, and in that position, by his daring, skill and generosity of disposition, gained the admiration and affection of his officers and men to a remarkable degree. His death cast a gloom over the entire command. It was felt that a most brilliant and promising name had been lost from the roll of the army. General Burnside felt his loss most keenly, and ordered that the earthwork, in front of which the engagement in which he fell had taken place should be named Fort Sanders in honor of his memory. He also placed on record his estimation of the fallen soldier's worth by the issue of a general order in which occur the following appreciative words: "A life rendered illustrious by a long record of gallantry and devotion to his country has closed while in the heroic and unflinching performance of duty. Distinguished always for his self-possession and daring in the field, and in his private life eminent for his genial and unselfish nature and the sterling qualities of his character, he has left, both as a man and a soldier, an untarnished name."

After this engagement, General Longstreet decided that he would be obliged to lay siege to the place, and to carry our works, if at all, by regular approaches. Accordingly he moved up the right bank of the river and posted his main body between the river and the Clinton road, investing about half the circuit of the town upon the northern, western and southwestern side. Communication with Cumberland Gap was cut on the night of the 16th of November by the enemy's cavalry, and by the night of the 18th, the enemy's forces were well up and the siege established. The southern part of the town was free from the presence of the foe. A bridge spanned the Holston, affording easy communication with the opposite heights which were diligently fortified. The country was open in that direction as far as Marysville. On the north side, our engineers, under the direction of Captain Poe and Lieutenant Colonel Babcock were not idle. Fortifications were thrown up around the town, and a continuous line of rifle pits was added. A *chevaux de frise* of pikes captured from the enemy at Knoxville was set up in front of the rifle pits. The skirmishers were kept out from five hundred to a thousand yards beyond the line of the rifle pits. The men were in good spirits, and supplies had been accumulated, which with economy would suffice for two or three weeks' consumption.

An excellent article in the Atlantic Monthly for July 1866, by Major Burrage of the 36th Massachusetts, gives a very correct and graphic description of Knoxville and its defences as they appeared at the time of the siege. "Knoxville is situated on the northern bank of the Holston river. For the most part the town is built on a table land which is nearly a mile square, and about one hundred and fifty feet above the river. On the the northeast, the town is bounded by a small creek. Beyond this creek is an elevation known as Temperance Hill. Still farther to the east is Mayberry's Hill. On the northwest this table land descends into a broad valley; on the southwest the town is bounded by a second creek. Beyond this is College Hill, and still farther to the southwest is a high ridge running nearly parallel with the road which enters Knoxville at this point. Benjamin's and Buckley's batteries occupied a bastion work on the ridge known as Fort Sanders. Roemer's battery was placed in position on College Hill. These batteries were supported by Fererro's division of the Ninth Corps, his line extending from the Holston river on the left to the point where the East Tennessee and Georgia railroad crosses the creek mentioned above as Second Creek. Hartranft connected with Ferrero's right, supporting Gittings' and the 15th Indiana Batteries. His lines extended as far as First Creek. The divisions of White and Hascall of the twenty-third corps occupied the ground between this point and the Holston river on the northeast side of the town, with their artillery in position on Temperance and Mayberry's Hills."* After the fortifications were completed, they were truly formidable. General Sherman examined them after the siege, and declared them to be "a wonderful production for the short time allowed in the selection of ground and construction of work. They seemed to be nearly impregnable."

After the withdrawal to Knoxville, General Burnside received a despatch from General Grant dated on the 14th of

* Roemer's battery on College Hill was supported by Colonel Morrison's brigade of the first division, Ninth Corps. The batteries in Fort Sanders were supported by the brigades of Colonels Humphreys and Christ of the same division. The artillery supported by White and Hascall was composed of Captain Simms's twenty-fourth Indiana battery, Captain Henshaw's battery and Captain Shield's Ohio battery and one section of Captain Thomas's "Wilder's" Indiana battery. Two sections of "Wilder's" battery and Captain Konkle's battery were posted on the heights south of the river, supported by Colonel Cameron's brigade of the third division, twenty-third Corps. One section of howitzers covered the bridge head and was manned by soldiers detailed principally from the regiments of loyal Tennesseeans. These batteries and troops were posted by Captain Poe as they arrived from Campbell's Station.—Captain Poe's Report.

November, having reference to the visit of Colonel Willson and Mr. Dana. General Grant's despatch was as follows: "Your despatch and Dana's just received. Being there, you can tell better how to resist Longstreet's attack than I can direct. With your showing, you had better give up Kingston at the last moment, and save the most productive part of your possessions. Every arrangement is now made to throw Sherman's force across the river, just at and below the mouth of Chickamauga Creek, as soon as it arrives. Thomas will attack on his left at the same time; and, together, it is expected to carry Missionary Ridge, and from there rush a force on to the railroad between Cleveland and Dalton. Hooker will at the same time attack, and, if he can, carry Lookout Mountain. The enemy now seems to be looking for an attack on his left flank. This favors us. To further confirm this, Sherman's advance division will march direct from Whiteside's to Trenton. The remainder of his force will pass over a new road just made from Whiteside's to Kelly's Ferry, thus being concealed from the enemy, and leave him to suppose the whole force is going up Lookout valley. Sherman's advance has only just reached Bridgeport. The rear will only reach there on the sixteenth. This will bring it to the nineteenth as the earliest day for making the combined movement as desired. Inform me if you think you can sustain yourself till that time. I can hardly conceive of the enemy breaking through at Kingston, and pushing for Kentucky. If they should, however, a new problem would be left for solution. Thomas has ordered a division of cavalry to the vicinity of Sparta. I will ascertain if they have started, and inform you."

On the 15th, having received full despatches from Knoxville, and also from General Halleck in regard to the danger of the abandonment of East Tennessee, General Grant sent the following despatch to General Burnside, which was received very nearly at the same time with the preceding:

"I do not know how to impress on you the necessity of holding on to East Tennessee in strong enough terms. Ac-

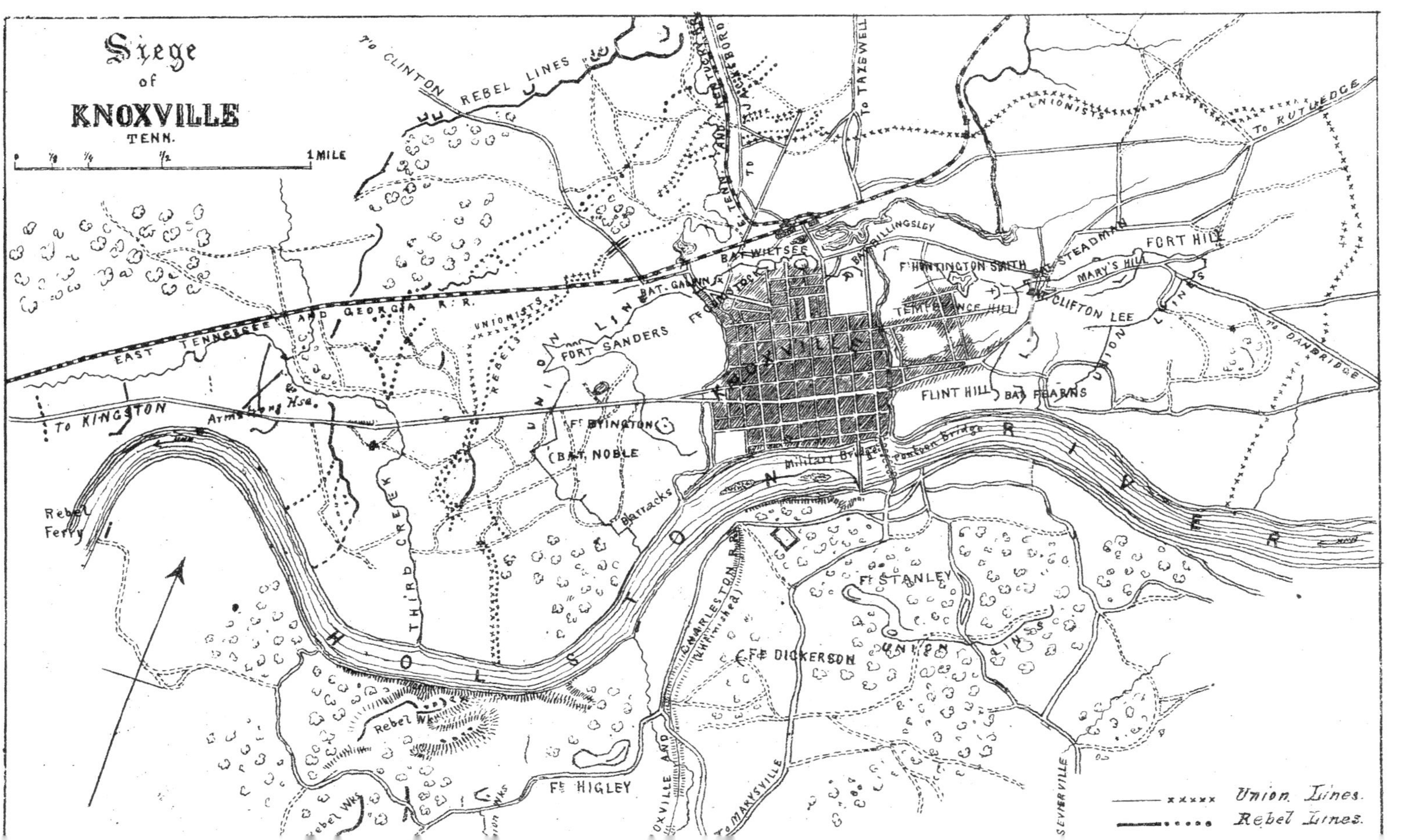

Siege of KNOXVILLE
TENN.
0 1/8 1/4 1/2 1 MILE
To CLINTON
REBEL LINES
To TAZEWELL
To RUTLEDGE
UNIONISTS
REBELS
EAST TENNESSEE AND GEORGIA R.R.
E. TENN. AND KENTUCKY R.R.
To JACKSBORO
To KINGSTON
Armstrong Hse.
Rebel Ferry
THIRD CREEK
UNION LINE
FORT SANDERS
Ft. BYINGTON
(BAT. NOBLE
Barracks
BAT. GALPIN
Ft. COMSTOCK
BAT. WILTSEE
BAT. BILLINGSLEY
Ft. HUNTINGTON SMITH
TEMPERANCE HILL
KNOXVILLE
FLINT HILL
BAT. FEARNS
BAT. STEADMAN
MARY'S HILL
FORT HILL
CLIFTON LEE
UNION LINES
To DANBRIDGE
Military Bridge
Pontoon Bridge
HOLSTON RIVER
Ft. STANLEY
Ft. DICKERSON
UNION LINES
CHARLESTON R.R. (Unfinished)
KNOXVILLE AND
To MARYSVILLE
SEVIERVILLE
Rebel Wks.
Ft. HIGLEY
Union Lines.
Rebel Lines.

cording to the despatches of Mr. Dana and Colonel Wilson, it would seem that you should, if pressed to do it, hold on to Knoxville and that portion of the valley you will necessarily possess holding to that point. Should Longstreet move his whole force across the Little Tennessee, an effort should be made to cut his pontons on that stream even if it sacrificed half the cavalry of the Ohio army.

"By holding on, and placing Longstreet between the Little Tennessee and Knoxville, he should not be allowed to escape with an army capable of doing anything this winter. I can hardly conceive the necessity of retreating from East Tennessee. If I did at all, it would be after losing most of the army, and then necessity would suggest the route.

"I will not attempt to lay out a line of retreat. Kingston, looking at the map, I thought of more importance than any one point in East Tennessee. But my attention being called more closely to it, I can see that it might be passed by, and Knoxville and the rich valley about it possessed, ignoring that place entirely. I should not think it advisable to concentrate a force near the Little Tennessee to resist the crossing, if it would be in danger of capture; but I would harass and embarrass progress in every way possible, reflecting on the fact that the army of the Ohio is not the only army to resist the onward progress of the enemy."

General Burnside thus encouraged to believe that his plans had received the approval of his chief, and that he would be relieved from the presence of the enemy, as soon as General Grant could detach a force from Chattanooga, was doubly determined to hold on at Knoxville. He accordingly issued an order, to the effect that there was to be no further retreat and that the town was to be held at all hazards and to the last man. The enemy however seemed to labor under the impression, that his task was not difficult of accomplishment. All that was required was to remain patiently before the town until the supplies in our camps were exhausted, and starvation should compel surrender. In one of the fights on the south side of the river, the enemy charged with the cry "Vicksburg and mule meat!" But that point was far away, as he afterwards learned to his cost.

The weary days of the siege passed slowly away. The monotony was broken only by occasional skirmishing and cannonading, a sortie of our men upon some part of the rebel lines which was thought weaker than the rest, or an attempted advance of the enemy's pickets and batteries. The loyal citizens of the town were engaged in zealous emulation with the troops in perfecting the defences. It became necessary to seize and destroy some buildings outside of our lines of fortification, which afforded shelter to the enemy's sharpshooters and were in the way of our artillery fire. The work was gallantly and thoroughly accomplished, on the night of the 20th, by a detachment of the 17th Michigan. On the night of the 23d, the enemy made an attack upon the right of our lines, and succeeded for a time in gaining considerable advantage. But at daylight on the 24th, Colonel Hartranft, with the 48th Pennsylvania and the 21st Massachusetts, made a counter assault, which was successful in driving the enemy from his advanced position and in reëstablishing our own lines of defence. On the 24th Colonel Mott, with a small cavalry force, had a smart engagement with General Wheeler, near Kingston, and inflicted upon him a serious defeat. On the same day Colonel Cameron was attacked, on the south side of the river, but gallantly repulsed the assault, with considerable damage to the attacking party. During this time, also, the enemy had been engaged in felling trees and adopting other means for strengthening his position. A force was detached to pass above the town, cut down trees upon the river bank, and make a raft to float down upon our pontons which connected the garrison with the troops on the opposite heights. The movement was discovered and seasonably foiled.

General Longstreet was watching every opportunity and adopting every expedient to reduce the place. General Burnside was holding on with the utmost tenacity, and though his communications were cut, his supplies were lessening, his forces were inferior, he himself was suffering somewhat from illness, and affairs generally were gloomy, yet he never once lost his hope. At last, it became evident that an assault must be made by the enemy, or the attempt to regain East Tennessee must be abandoned. General Bragg had become alive to the magnitude of the blunder which he had made. General Grant was making his power felt upon the enemy's weakened lines in those grand operations at Lookout Mountain and Missionary Ridge, which, on the 23d, 24th and 25th of November, inaugurated the final and successful campaign against Atlanta. General Longstreet could not endure the thought of leaving his enterprise unfinished, or retiring from it baffled by an inferior force. His position had now become perilous. Grant's success made it impossible for him to rejoin Bragg. General Sherman's junction with General Grant threatened his position in the rear too seriously to be neglected. The rebel General determined to risk an assault, hoping thus to secure the long desired position and an unmolested line of retreat to Virginia. General Burnside was ready for him, and the attack came.

The day appointed was the 29th of November. The place selected for the assault was Fort Sanders. It had been strengthened by General Burnside's accomplished Engineers, Lieutenant Colonel Babcock and Captain Poe, assisted by Lieutenant Benjamin, with every art known to their profession or available for their purpose. The ditch was widened, abattis were thickly laid in front and flank, trees were felled, and wires stretched from stump to stump. It was a desperate enterprise on the part of General Longstreet, and cost the lives of many brave men to no purpose, except to prove that the defences of Knoxville were impregnable. During the night of the 28th—29th, the first demonstration was made by an attack upon our skirmish line to the right of the Kingston road, which resulted in some slight advantage to the enemy. Sharp skirmishing continued nearly all night, with little result, except in annoying our troops and preventing their needed rest.

In the gray of the morning of the 29th, the assaulting column, composed of three picked brigades, appeared. The garrison of the fort was awake and ready. Reënforcements were held in readiness to throw upon any point which was too hardly pressed. It was the men of the brave Ninth Corps that held the defences—the 79th New York for immediate garrison, with four companies of the 17th Michigan in support, and the men of Benjamin's and Buckley's batteries for cannoniers. It was a glorious day in the calendar of these invincible troops. Onward came the storming party—five regiments in columns by divisions closed in mass. They struck and stumbled over the wires amidst the deadly fire of our men. This obstruction was soon passed. A number fell amidst the entanglement, but the weight of the column carried it through. They came steadily on, with a courage which extorted the admiration of their antagonists. They cut away the abattis, never faltering beneath the withering musketry fire, and the destructive projectiles of the artillery. They filled the ditch. Their way was marked by carnage and death. Would nothing stop those devoted men? A few mounted the parapet. But they could go no further. Hand to hand, the conflict raged with unabated fury. One rebel, with a flag, endeavored to approach the embrasure, when Sergeant Frank Judge, of Company D, 79th New York, "seized him by the collar and dragged him with his flag into the fort." Grenades were thrown into the ditch. Lieutenant Benjamin, with his own hands, threw several lighted shells over the parapet among the masses of the struggling enemy. "It stilled them down," the Lieutenant said.

But even this stubborn resistance was not enough to stop the advancing troops. Two guns in the bastion poured triple rounds of canister in their faces. A gun upon the flank swept the ditch. Still they continued to press forward, until convinced that the attempt was useless, the assaulting column retired. But, as another column came up in support, the attack was renewed. The enemy was desperate, but our men were equally resolute. A more savage contest than the first, if that were possible, took place. The former scenes were reënacted, with yells and shouts and most infernal tumult. The storming party again filled the ditch, and some, more daring than their companions, climbed the parapet and succeeded in placing three of the enemy's flags there. It was a short lived triumph. The flags were quickly torn away. The foe met with a terrible resistance. Muskets were clubbed—bayonets, sabres, and even axes were employed in the dreadful work. A more determined valor has not been displayed on either side during the war than this fight in the trenches and in front of Fort Sanders. Mortal men could endure it but a brief period. The second assault was no more fortunate than the first. The enemy's column faltered, hesitated, stopped, was hopelessly broken, and at last retired in great confusion. One company of the 20th Michigan from the right, and one company of the 29th Massachusetts from the left, advanced into the ditch and captured two hundred prisoners and two flags. General Longstreet had attempted too much. He had sent his chosen men to useless slaughter. He was told, in fire and blood, that Knoxville could not be taken. He drew off his forces from the scene of his defeat. General Burnside, with characteristic humanity, immediately after the fight, directed General Potter to send a flag of truce, offering the enemy the privilege of removing the wounded and dead from the scene of the conflict. The permission was courteously acknowledged, the slightly wounded and others wounded and captured in previous engagements were exchanged, the dead were taken away and buried, and, before night, Fort Sanders had resumed its wonted aspect. The enemy's loss in this assault was nearly or quite one thousand four hundred in killed, wounded and prisoners, of whom three hundred unhurt fell into our hands. Our loss in the fort was eight killed, five wounded, and about thirty captured.*

* No less than ninety-six dead bodies were found in the ditch and within three or four yards of it. One regiment that was totally annihilated, and whose flag fell into our hands, was ascertained to be the 17th Mississippi, which had opposed the crossing at Fredericksburg.

A simultaneous attack was made by one brigade of the enemy upon our forces under General Shackleford upon the south side of the river, which was attended with some slight advantage to the enemy at first, but was finally repulsed with severe loss.

This action and its results were particularly creditable to the troops engaged, to Lieutenant Benjamin, who was in immediate command of the artillery, and to General Ferrero, who commanded that portion of our defensive line. Lieutenant Benjamin had prepared and armed the earthwork with great care, and had taken every precaution against surprise. The fort stood at the angle of our line to the southwest of the town, about a mile out and north of the main Kingston road. It was armed with four 20-pound Parrotts, four light 12-pounders, and two 3-inch guns, and well fitted with traverses. A hill a short distance from the work to the south was armed with two guns from Captain Buckley's battery. The northwest bastion was the salient. The fort was open in the rear and flanked by rifle pits. The parapet was partially covered with brush, for purposes of concealment, and the embrasures were arranged in such a way as to enable our officers, by removing a few shovelfuls of earth, to train the guns upon the approaches to the northwest bastion, which became the enemy's point of attack. The enemy ran a parallel about three hundred yards distant from the bastion, about half enveloping it. He also posted batteries, varying from seven hundred to fifteen hundred yards' distance from the fort, upon its different fronts:—on the west, one battery of six 12-pounders and another of one 20-pound Parrott; on the north, one battery of two 20-pound Parrotts and two 3-inch guns, and two batteries of two guns each; across the Holston one battery of six guns.

The prisoners taken belonged to eleven different regiments, with an estimated strength of from two hundred to four hundred each. The officers reported that there were two brigades to watch and fire upon our lines, one brigade to assault, and two more to support the attack. Two brigades actually reached the ditch. Our own men in the fort had been carefully drilled for their part. Each man had his proper post, ate and slept at it, so as to be ready at the instant of alarm. At night, one man in four was always awake. On the reception of an alarm from the outer picket, every man on watch immediately awakened his three comrades, who silently and at once took their assigned positions at the parapet.* The result justified these extraordinary precautions, and was an honorable testimony to the fidelity of the officer in command.

The enemy's forces in this action consisted of "three brigades of McLaw's division; that of General Wolford, the 16th, 18th and 24th Georgia regiments and Cobb's and Phillips's Georgia Legions; that of General Humphrey, the 13th, 17th, 21st, 22d and 23d Mississippi regiments; and a brigade composed of Generals Anderson's and Bryant's brigades, embracing, among others, the Palmetto State Guard, the 15th South Carolina regiment, and the 51st, 53d and 59th Georgia regiments."† Our own troops were reënforced by five companies of the 29th Massachusetts, two companies of the 20th Michigan regiments, and a brigade of General Hascall's division of the twenty-third corps.

---

* Lieutenant Benjamin's Report.

† Pollard's History, "Third Year of the War," pp. 161, 162.

CHAPTER VII.

AFTER THE SIEGE.

THE attack on Fort Sanders was the last important event of the siege of Knoxville. General Grant, on the 28th, ordered General Sherman to march, with a force of twenty-five thousand men, to proceed with all possible despatch to the relief of General Burnside. General Sherman marched upon the south side of the Tennessee river, to take General Longstreet in the rear. General Thomas, on the 26th, directed General Elliot, with his cavalry division, to proceed from Alexandria to Knoxville to aid in the relief of that place. These welcome reënforcements were within two or three marches of Knoxville on the 4th of December. On the morning of the 5th, our pickets reported that the enemy had retired, and that the siege of Knoxville was raised. On the same day, General Sherman, with his own corps and that of General Granger and a part of General Howard's, arrived at Marysville and despatched an aide-de-camp with the following hearty message: "I am here, and can bring twenty-five thousand men into Knoxville to-morrow; but Longstreet having retreated, I feel disposed to stop, for a stern chase is a long one. But I will do all that is possible. Without you specify that you want troops, I will let mine rest to-morrow and ride in to see you. Send my aide, Captain Audenried, out with your letters to-night. We are all hearty but tired. Accept my congratulations at your successful defence and your patient endurance."

General Sherman arrived at Knoxville on the 6th, and had a personal conference with General Burnside in regard to the situation. General Burnside was of the opinion that General

Granger's command was sufficient for all necessary operations. On the 7th, General Burnside wrote to General Sherman, acknowledging in the most grateful terms, the great services of his brother officer in relieving the besieged forces at Knoxville. "I desire," he said, "to express to you and your command my most hearty thanks and gratitude for your promptness in coming to our relief during the siege of Knoxville, and I am satisfied that your approach served to raise the siege. The emergency having passed, I do not deem, for the present, any other portion of your command than the corps of General Granger necessary for operations in this section; and, inasmuch as General Grant has weakened the forces immediately with him in order to relieve us, thereby rendering portions of General Thomas's less secure, I think it advisable that all the troops now here, except those commanded by General Granger, should return at once to within supporting distance of the forces operating against General Bragg's army. In behalf of my command, I again desire to thank you and your command for the kindness you have done us."

General Longstreet slowly retreated up the north bank of the Holston like a lion at bay. General Sherman was too far in the rear. General Burnside had no men or animals available for rapid pursuit, with the exception of a few cavalry for observation. A portion of the troops, however, marched out as far as Rutledge, but the enemy was in too strong force to warrant an attack. The only force which could in an effective manner impede the retreating foe, was a small body of troops from the neighborhood of Tazewell and Cumberland Gap, under General Foster. This force, outnumbered as it doubtless was by two or three to one, could do little more than threaten the enemy's line of retreat. Still our troops were full of daring, and marched up boldly against the retiring foe. They attacked him at Blain's Cross Roads, at Bean's Station, and in the passes of the Clinch Mountains, and succeeded in inflicting upon him some injury. General Longstreet, however, did not leave East Tennessee entirely until the following spring, when he rejoined

General Lee in season to take part in the memorable campaign of 1864.

General Willcox, to whom had been entrusted the charge of the operations in the upper valley and its neighborhood during the siege, had done excellent service in holding Cumberland Gap and in preventing a junction between General Longstreet and the enemy's forces advancing from Virginia. Previous to the interruption of communication with Knoxville, orders had been transmitted to General Willcox that, in the event of such a contingency, he was to gather up his garrisons and trains and withdraw to Cumberland Gap. His command at that time consisted of the Indiana regiments and the batteries already mentioned, with a skeleton regiment of recruits from North Carolina, and two brigades of cavalry under Colonels Graham and Garrard. With these, General Willcox was holding the passes of the Bull Mountains, and scouting towards Greeneville and Newport. At Morristown, he had the 32d Kentucky infantry, the 11th Michigan battery and a battalion of mounted Tennesseeans. At Mossy creek was a battalion of Tennessee recruits under Colonel Patten. He had an immense wagon train to carry in safety with these troops to Cumberland Gap, a distance of fifty-two miles. He conducted the movement with great skill. On the morning of the 18th, he sent out his cavalry to demonstrate against the enemy at Kingsport, and under cover of this feigned movement, quietly withdrew his infantry and trains. The roads were crowded with refugees and their property, and the march was slow. During the night of the 18th, he collected all his troops and trains without accident of any kind at Bean's Station. On the afternoon of the 19th, he put his command on the march, with his cavalry well out in front, on his flanks and in his rear, reached Tazewell safely on that night, and Cumberland Gap in the evening of the 20th. One of his cavalry parties, scouting towards Jonesville, surprised and broke up the camp of the 64th Virginia regiment, scattered the troops and drove them two or three miles, capturing and destroying a large portion of their arms and camp equipage.

General Willcox remained at Cumberland Gap during the remainder of the month, employing his men in scouting, gathering subsistence and forage, and obtaining what information was accessible. At one time he communicated with Knoxville by means of a courier, who bravely and cunningly made his way through the enemy's lines. Major Behr, with a battalion of Illinois cavalry, made a dash upon the enemy at Jonesville and drove him across the Powell river with considerable loss. General Willcox also organized an expedition against Abingdon and the salt works in that neighborhood, but owing to various circumstances, the party did not get off. On the 30th, General John G. Foster arrived at the Gap, and on the 1st of December, the entire command, with the exception of a small garrison left at Cumberland Gap to hold the post, started towards Knoxville to coöperate with the other columns moving up from Chattanooga. On the next day, Colonel Graham's cavalry, with two regiments of infantry and Captain Patterson's 21st Ohio battery, had a smart engagement with the enemy's cavalry under General Martin, near Walker's ford, and succeeded in punishing them quite severely. Our loss was about fifty in killed and wounded. The enemy's loss was considerably greater, and our cavalry captured one hundred and fifty prisoners.

With the successful termination of the siege of Knoxville closed the active services of General Burnside in East Tennessee. Before General Longstreet's withdrawal, the command of the Department of Ohio was transferred by the Secretary of War to General Foster. But General Foster did not succeed in reaching Knoxville until nearly the middle of December. On the 11th of that month, General Burnside formally committed the Department into the hands of his successor. The general orders, both of General Burnside and of General Foster, are expressive of such sincere and appreciative friendship as to deserve a place in these annals. General Burnside's order was dated at Knoxville, December 11th, and was as follows: "In obedience to orders from the War Department, the Commanding General this day resigns to Major General John G. Foster the command of the Army of the Ohio.

"On severing the tie which has united him to this gallant army, he cannot express his deep personal feeling at parting from men brought near to him by their mutual experiences in the eventful scenes of the past campaign, and who have always, regardless of every privation and every danger, cheerfully and faithfully performed their duty. Associated with many of their number from the earliest days of the war, he takes leave of this army, not only as soldiers to whose heroism many a victorious battle field bears witness, but as well tried friends, who in the darkest hours have never failed him. With the sincerest regret he leaves the Department without the opportunity of personally bidding them farewell.

"To the citizen soldiers of East Tennessee, who proved their loyalty in the trenches of Knoxville, he tenders his warmest thanks.

"With the highest confidence in the patriotism and skill of the distinguished officer who succeeds him, with whom he has been long and intimately connected in the field, and who will be welcomed as their leader by those who served with him in the memorable campaign in North Carolina, and by all as one identified with some of the most brilliant events of the war, he transfers to him the command, assured that under his guidance the bright record of the Army of the Ohio will never grow dim."

General Foster gracefully responded: "In compliance with the orders of the War Department, Major General John G. Foster assumes the command of the Army of the Ohio.

"He accepts with pride a position which his predecessor has rendered illustrious.

"After a long period of unbroken friendship, strengthened by the intimate relations of active service with him in a campaign which is prominent in the history of the war, he can add to the general voice his tribute to the high worth and stainless name of the recent commander of the Army of the Ohio. The work he has so ably planned and vigorously conducted, it will be the aim of the commanding general to complete.

"For the future of this command he has no fears. The results of their past are around them, and confident with these high evidences of what he may expect from their courage and their patriotism, he assures them that to the fulfilment of their mission his utmost efforts shall not be wanting."

General Burnside left Knoxville on the 14th, and arrived at his home in Providence on the 23d. While on his way, he stopped at Cincinnati for a day or two, and in the course of a public address in that city, he modestly disclaimed the honors which were offered him, declaring that they "belonged to his under officers and the men in the ranks." Major Burrage gratefully acknowledges the kindness of these words, and declares that it will ever be the pride of these officers and men to say: "We fought with Burnside at Campbell's Station and in the trenches at Knoxville." The Congress of the United States passed, and on the 28th of January, 1864, the President approved a resolution providing "that the thanks of Congress be, and they hereby are, presented to Major General Ambrose E. Burnside and through him to the officers and men who have fought under his command, for their gallantry, good conduct, and soldierlike endurance."

The deliverance of East Tennessee and its subsequent preservation from the hands of the enemy, were considered of so great importance by the President as to receive from him, not only his personal thanks, but also an official public recognition. On the 7th of December, he issued a proclamation referring, in congratulatory terms, to the fact that the enemy had retreated from before Knoxville, "under circumstances rendering it probable that the Union forces cannot hereafter be dislodged from that important position," and recommending that "all loyal people do, on receipt of this information, assemble at their places of worship, and render special homage and gratitude to

Almighty God for this great advancement of the national cause." The intelligence was received in all sections with the liveliest gratification. It was generally understood that the blow given to the insurgent cause was especially severe and damaging in its effects. General Lee so regarded it, and at one time was seriously inclined to strengthen General Longstreet, and make a grand combined effort to wrest this region from our grasp. But the advent of General Grant upon the scene of operations at the East convinced him that all his strength would be required in that quarter, and the rebel forces reluctantly turned their steps away from East Tennessee.

General Longstreet, however, caused our troops considerable annoyance during the winter. He retreated beyond our line of communication with Cumberland Gap, but established himself in the neighborhood of Rogersville and Morristown. Thence he occasionally sent out detachments of his force, and attempted to embarrass our troops in the matter of supplies. At one time in January, 1864, a portion of his army approached Knoxville and gave rise to certain apprehensions that another siege was contemplated. "Well informed refugees" reported that large reënforcements had been sent from General Lee's army in Virginia, and that a great battle was imminent. The emergency, if it ever really existed, soon passed, without a decisive engagement. A few lively skirmishes relieved the tedium of winter quarters.

General Willcox rejoined the Ninth Corps on the 17th of January, and relieved General Potter. On the 21st, a very brisk engagement took place at Strawberry Plains. The purpose of the movement was the destruction of the bridge near that point across the Holston river. The Corps moved from Blain's Cross Roads on the 16th, and encamped near the bridge. On the 20th, the enemy made a dash upon our pickets, but was speedily repulsed. The bridge was destroyed on the night of the 20th, and the next morning our forces formed in line of battle. Colonel Morrison's brigade of the first division was in front, with Gittings's battery of artillery. Colonel E.

W. Pierce's brigade guarded the fords two miles below, Colonel Collins's brigade of the second division was held in reserve. The enemy appeared at eleven o'clock A. M., on the south bank of the river, and placing a battery of six guns in position, opened fire upon our lines. Our own artillery promptly responded, and an artillery duel ensued, continuing for four hours, after which the enemy retired. But little loss was suffered on either side. The bridge was destroyed, and on the next day the Corps marched to Knoxville, followed by the enemy's cavalry at a very respectful distance, which was increased on the advance of the 27th Michigan regiment. On the 26th, General Willcox was relieved by General Parke, who had returned to Knoxville from leave of absence. General Willcox took command of the second division, which was posted at Lyon's Mill, below Knoxville. This division accompanied General Schofield in his advance upon Morristown in the latter part of February.

The conclusion of the siege of Knoxville may fairly be taken as the termination of the active campaign of the Corps in East Tennessee. There was but little additional fighting, but there was much hard service in watching the enemy and preventing him from making inroads upon our lines. Supplies of clothing and food were somewhat scanty, and the troops in some instances suffered severely in consequence. Mention is made, in some reports from that quarter, of the almost utter destitution to which the men were reduced. Six spoonfuls of flour and the scattered corn that could be picked up from under the feet of the animals, were all that could be procured for a week's rations. "One table spoonful of coffee was issued once in from three to five days. The men were unable to subsist upon such allowance, and each morning there could have been seen parties of two and three in search of food. Some of the loyal Tennesseeans would meet them with smiles; and upon being asked for bread, they would reply in their peculiar vernacular, that 'they were plumb out,' and had not 'a dust of meal in the house.'

Many of the men were barefooted, and raw hide was issued to be made into moccasins."*

Such were the circumstances amid which the movement for the redemption of the loyal people of Tennessee was consummated. The soldiers of the Ninth Corps exhibited as heroic a spirit in the endurance of hardships as in the achievement of victories. As no foes could appall them, so no privations could subdue. With cheerful and even eager alacrity, they were willing to take up new duties and bear new pains in behalf of the country for which they fought and suffered. They proved to the enemy that they could not be conquered, and he was forced to be content with the loss of the important section which they had wrested from his grasp. The Ninth Corps was soon to return to the East and participate in movements of a more startling and conspicuous nature. But it may safely be recorded, that, of the important operations of 1863, the DELIVERANCE OF EAST TENNESSEE deserves to hold an equal rank with the victory which turned the tide of invasion from Pennsylvania, and is not far behind the magnificent triumph which gave the Mississippi once more to the Republic!

---

* Letter from an officer in the 29th Massachusetts, in "Massachusetts in the Rebellion," p. 330.

THE LAST YEAR

OF

THE REBELLION.

THE LAST YEAR

OF

THE REBELLION.

CHAPTER I.

REORGANIZATION.

THE necessity of a change in the chief direction of the armies of the United States had, for a considerable time, been apparent both to the officers and soldiers of the army, and to the people of the country. The brilliant and most important successes of General Grant in Mississippi, Tennessee and Georgia, which were due to his military genius and his admirable persistence, pointed him out as the man best fitted for command. But General Grant had but just been appointed to the regular army,* and the jealousies of rank were to be avoided, if possible. Congress composed whatever difficulty might thus arise, by passing a bill to revive the full grade of Lieutenant General, the brevet of which had already been conferred upon General Scott. The President approved the bill on the 29th of February, 1864. The act provided that the person to fill the position should "be selected from among those officers in the military service of the United States not below the grade of Major General, most distinguished for courage, skill and ability." "Being commissioned as Lieutenant General," he was to be "au-

*Major General, July 4, 1863.

thorized, under the direction and during the pleasure of the President, to command the armies of the United States." The President immediately appointed General Grant to fill the honorable post, and on the 2d of March the appointment was confirmed and the commission issued. General Grant was summoned to Washington, and on the 9th the President, in the presence of the Cabinet and several distinguished personages, formally gave into the hands of the successful officer the commission which he had so bravely won. The wishes of the country and of the army had become so unmistakable, that General Halleck went through the formality of requesting to be relieved. On the 12th, General Grant was assigned to the "command of the armies of the United States," and on the 17th, he assumed the command, in General Orders. Headquarters were to be in the field and with the Army of the Potomac. Order, vigor, a settled purpose and plan at once took the place of the feeble and unstable policy which had characterized the previous administration of military affairs.

The discussion of this and other similar questions in Congress and among the people had directed the public attention to the necessity of vigorous measures. It was determined to fill the depleted corps of the different armies to their maximum number. Great exertions were made during the winter of 1863–'64 to place the entire army upon a basis of enduring strength, and to give to it such efficiency as would make the approaching campaign the great and final campaign of the war. With an effective army and able officers, the nation indulged the hope of complete success. The victories of the past were full of promise for the future. If the army was put into the field at the proper time, with proper materiel and a sufficient number of men, the result would be a glorious triumph. General Sherman was to conduct operations in the West, and his great march was already projected in the mind of General Grant. The Army of the Potomac was to fight over its old ground for its long-desired object. General Grant was determined to crush the strength of the rebellion by the utter defeat thorized, under the direction and during the pleasure of the President, to command the armies of the United States." The President immediately appointed General Grant to fill the honorable post, and on the 2d of March the appointment was confirmed and the commission issued. General Grant was summoned to Washington, and on the 9th the President, in the presence of the Cabinet and several distinguished personages, formally gave into the hands of the successful officer the commission which he had so bravely won. The wishes of the country and of the army had become so unmistakable, that General Halleck went through the formality of requesting to be relieved. On the 12th, General Grant was assigned to the "command of the armies of the United States," and on the 17th, he assumed the command, in General Orders. Headquarters were to be in the field and with the Army of the Potomac. Order, vigor, a settled purpose and plan at once took the place of the feeble and unstable policy which had characterized the previous administration of military affairs.

The discussion of this and other similar questions in Congress and among the people had directed the public attention to the necessity of vigorous measures. It was determined to fill the depleted corps of the different armies to their maximum number. Great exertions were made during the winter of 1863–'64 to place the entire army upon a basis of enduring strength, and to give to it such efficiency as would make the approaching campaign the great and final campaign of the war. With an effective army and able officers, the nation indulged the hope of complete success. The victories of the past were full of promise for the future. If the army was put into the field at the proper time, with proper materiel and a sufficient number of men, the result would be a glorious triumph. General Sherman was to conduct operations in the West, and his great march was already projected in the mind of General Grant. The Army of the Potomac was to fight over its old ground for its long-desired object. General Grant was determined to crush the strength of the rebellion by the utter defeat colored soldiers to form a division. General Burnside had, for a considerable time, been in favor of the employment of colored troops, and was desirous of incorporating them with his command. The matter was laid before the War Department as early as the 26th of January, and, after some delay, received the approval of the Secretary.

General Burnside also submitted, on the same day, a plan of operations, which contemplated the occupation of North Carolina and the reduction of that entire State to the Federal authority. Wilmington, which had long been the great entrepot of supplies for the rebellious government, was to be taken, and the railroads in the interior of North Carolina were to be occupied and held. This movement would compel the evacuation of Virginia and place Richmond at our mercy, or it would at least draw off a sufficient number of men from General Lee's army to make it easy for the Army of the Potomac to fall on and defeat, capture or destroy its steadfast enemy. General Burnside thus hoped to be employed upon a coastwise expedition, and, with his old soldiers of 1861 and 1862, complete the course of his public service on the fields which had been the scene of his early triumphs. It certainly would have been a fitting close to the history of his brave command. But the Lieutenant General had other objects in view. He already had his eye fixed upon the route which General Burnside had once essayed to follow, and, knowing its difficulties, which were now greater than ever before, and also its advantages, was disposed to use all his available means to achieve success. A coastwise expedition was not yet to be attempted. But, doubtless with the design of concealing the real plan of the campaign both from friend and foe, General Grant somewhat encouraged the hope, that the Corps would eventually be employed in North Carolina, and it was only within a short time of the opening of the campaign that General Burnside himself was apprised of his destination.

On the 8th of March, the Secretary of War designated Annapolis, Maryland, as the "depot and rendezvous" for the Ninth Corps. The new regiments were to be sent to that point as soon as their recruitment and organization were complete. The old regiments of the Corps then in East Tennessee were also ordered thither. General Parke had already come East, and General Willcox superintended the removal of the troops. The Corps left Knoxville on the 17th–23d of March, marched to Nicholasville, Kentucky, thence moved by rail, and arrived at Annapolis in the early part of the following month. The old regiments were filled up by reënlistments and new levies, five cavalry and twelve infantry regiments and five batteries of artillery, besides the colored troops, were added to the veterans of the Corps, and by the 20th of April, the strength of the command was fully twenty-five thousand men.

On the 11th of April, General Burnside left his home in Providence for his last campaign, and repaired immediately to Annapolis. For the next two weeks, he was occupied in arranging, reorganizing, equipping and arming the command. The Corps was formed into four divisions. General Parke was made Chief of Staff. Brigadier General Thomas G. Stevenson, once Colonel of the 24th Massachusetts, was assigned to the command of the first division; General Potter to that of the second; General Willcox to that of the third; and General Ferrero to that of the fourth, composed entirely of the colored troops. The expectation of embarking was still kept alive, and many a curious eye scanned the southern horizon, eagerly watching the waters of Chesapeake Bay to discover, if possible, the transports which were to carry the troops to North Carolina. Many would scarcely believe their senses, even while the harbor of Annapolis exhibited nothing but its usual monotonous quiet, and insisted that the transports were concealed in some retired creeks and inlets below the town, to be sent up at the instant of embarkation.

On the 7th of April, General Burnside was ordered to have his command in readiness to move from Annapolis at the shortest notice after the 20th of that month. Every arrangement was accordingly made, and on the 23d, at early morning, the Ninth Corps broke camp and took up its line of march. The direction was not towards the harbor, but into the interior, and the column was soon on the road to Washington, whither General Burnside repaired by rail. General Willcox had direction of the march, and, on the night of the 24th, encamped his command on the Bladensburg road, about six miles distant from the Capital. In Washington, it began to be rumored that the Ninth Corps would pass through the city, and that a division of colored troops, five or six thousand strong, was incorporated in the column. The citizens were on the *qui vive*, the members of Congress and the President were eager to witness the movement. About nine o'clock in the morning of the 25th, the head of the column entered the city, and by eleven, the Corps was marching down New York Avenue. Halting a short distance from the corner of Fourteenth street, the column closed up, and prepared to pay a marching salute to the President, who, with General Burnside and a few friends, was awaiting the coming of the troops. The President and his party occupied a balcony over the entrance of Willard's Hotel.

The scene was one of great beauty, spirit and animation. The day was superbly clear. A cool wind breathed through the soft air of the early Spring. Rain had fallen during the previous night, and there was no dust to cause discomfort to the soldiers or the spectators. The troops marched and appeared exceedingly well. Their soiled and tattered flags, bearing inscriptions of battles in six States, east and west, were silent and affecting witnesses of their valor and their sacrifices. The firm and soldierly bearing of the veterans, the eager and expectant countenances of the men and officers of the new regiments, the gay trappings of the cavalry, the thorough equipment and fine condition of the artillery, were all subjects of warm commendation. Multitudes of spectators filled the streets and greeted the column with enthusiastic cheers. General Ferrero's division was the first body of colored troops of any magnitude that ever marched through Washington, and their fine appearance and demeanor, though they had been but a week or two in the service, elicited numerous expressions of the heartiest approval. Mr. Lincoln himself seemed greatly pleased, and acknowledged the cheers and plaudits of the colored soldiers with a dignified kindness and courtesy. As they saw the modest and true gentleman who, with head uncovered, witnessed their march, a spirit of wild enthusiasm ran through their ranks. They shouted, they cheered, they swung their caps in the exuberance of their joy. They were now freemen. They had a grand and glorious object to live for. They would now make a history for their race, and there, looking down upon them, was the man who had given them this magnificent opportunity, and who was opening before them a new path of ambition and hope! It was a spectacle which made many eyes grow moist and dim. Through the greater part of the day, the column, with its long wagon train, filled the streets of the city. And thus the Corps that had never lost a flag or a gun marched through Washington! Crossing Long Bridge, the troops went into camp in the vicinity of Alexandria.

Even then, many of the officers and men had not entirely given up the thought of moving to some point upon the southern coast. They still cherished the hope that transports would be put in readiness for them at Alexandria. But the duty to which the Corps was now assigned effectually dispelled any such idea. To guard the Alexandria and Orange Railroad, from the Rapidan to the Potomac, was the immediate work to which General Grant had appointed the command. General Willcox, who was still in charge, established his headquarters at Manassas, and distributed the different divisions of the Corps along the railroad. In the course of the next few days, General Burnside had made his personal preparations to take the field. On the 27th, he proceeded to Manassas, and thence to Warrenton Junction, and, through all the stirring scenes of the next four months, commanded the Corps in person. It was definitely settled by the 1st of May, that the Ninth Corps was to operate in Virginia, in immediate connection with the Army of the Potomac. Once more the soil of Virginia was to be ensanguined with the blood of brave men, and to tremble beneath the roar of artillery and the march of armies.

CHAPTER II.

THE WILDERNESS AND SPOTTSYLVANIA.

THE Battle Summer of 1864 was a season of sanguinary conflicts, unsurpassed and even unequalled by any that had yet been recorded in the annals of this bloody war. General Grant had said that the "Army of the Potomac had never fought out its battles." He seemed determined now to carry his command through to victory, cost what it would. In his own words, he was resolved "to fight it out on that line, even if took all summer." General Lee was equally resolute in his resistance. The contending armies were equally brave. They were both composed of Americans, with all the courage and determination of the race—the finest citizen soldiers in the world. Able officers on both sides directed the movements of the opposing forces. The question was one of endurance and resource. Who could give, who could withstand the hardest "hammering"? Who could bring the largest number of men into the field? Who could animate those men with the liveliest hope, or endue them with the most persistent fortitude? It was sufficiently manifest that the first aggressive movement of either party, which had lain quiescent so long upon the banks of the Rapidan, would inaugurate the life and death struggle of the rebellion.

General Grant took the initiative. On the 3d of May, the Army of the Potomac was put in motion from its camps upon the north bank of the Rapidan. General Grant's plan was to turn the enemy's position upon the south bank, by a rapid march in the direction of Spottsylvania Court House. He hoped to draw General Lee out of his fortified position and fight him on more favorable ground. A part of the army crossed the Rapidan at Germania ford; the remainder crossed the Rappahannock at United States ford; all moved with promptness. On the afternoon of the 4th, the Ninth Corps was ordered to follow with all despatch, and reënforce the Army of the Potomac. The bulk of the Corps was then at the crossing of the Rappahannock by the Alexandria Railroad, holding that road back to Bull Run. It was to move as soon as a crossing of the Rapidan had been secured by the army in front. General Burnside at once put his Corps in motion, and proceeded with all speed to the scene of operations. He marched through the 4th until after midnight, went into bivouac for a few hours and was again upon the road at an early hour on the 5th. The advance of the Corps crossed the Rapidan at Germania ford on the night of that day. A cloud of dust upon the right showed that other movements were going on. It proved to be the march of General Longstreet's corps, that was hastening on a parallel road to the aid of General Lee. The two antagonists were once more pitted against each other, and arrived almost simultaneously upon the field where their chiefs were contending.

On the 5th, General Lee struck the Army of the Potomac amid the entanglements of the Wilderness, and for two days a stubborn and bloody battle raged. Among the trees, in the under brush, along the forest paths, the armies grappled with each other, mostly in detached bodies of regiments and brigades. But little artillery was used, except in the roads, and the ground was unfavorable for the movements of cavalry. It was almost entirely an infantry fight, and was illustrated by many individual instances of heroic daring. Early on the morning of the 6th, General Burnside led his corps into the action near the Wilderness tavern. The command had marched a distance of thirty miles—a portion ten or fifteen more—crossing both the Rappahannock and Rapidan rivers. The colored division had marched from Manassas Junction, leaving there on the 4th, arriving at Catlett's at two o'clock on the morning of the 5th, crossed the Rappahannock in the afternoon of that day and bivouacked at dark upon the banks of Mountain Creek. On the 6th, the division marched to the Rapidan and crossed at Germania Ford, relieving the troops that were at that time guarding the crossing. General Grant in his report of the operations of the campaign, with characteristic justice declares that, "considering that a large proportion, probably two-thirds of General Burnside's command, was composed of new troops, unaccustomed to marches and carrying the accoutrements of a soldier, this was a remarkable march."*

The arrival of General Burnside's corps was most opportune. The Army of the Potomac had been considerably shaken and its lines were disordered. Both contending armies indeed had suffered severely. Yet the spirit of the combatants was unabated, and on the 6th the battle raged once more with almost equal fury. General Longstreet put his corps into the action against General Burnside's command. The Ninth again vindicated its superiority, and the attack of the enemy was broken. In this engagement, the first division under General Stevenson fought with General Hancock's corps and did admirable service in connection with that gallant body of men. The second and third divisions were moved out upon the "Parker's store road," between the positions held by the second and fifth corps. General Potter, with General Willcox in support, attempted to seize Parker's on the plank road. Colonel Griffin's brigade in advance gained considerable ground, and was steadily pushing the enemy back, when an order arrived from General Grant to move all the available forces to the left, with the view of attacking the enemy in that quarter, in order to relieve General Hancock who was then hard pressed. General Potter's division was accordingly sent to the point of attack, and slowly but surely made its way through the dense undergrowth to the assigned position. General Willcox held the ground already occupied. General Potter, upon coming in contact with the

*Report of Lieutenant General Grant, p. 6.

enemy, charged and carried a portion of the opposing lines. Three times did the brave men of the second division advance upon the enemy's intrenchments, and though they gained considerable advantage, they were not able to carry the position.

General Willcox, after holding the Parker's Store road for some time, was finally enabled, about two o'clock in the afternoon, to withdraw his division and to go to General Potter's assistance. Colonel Hartranft's brigade had already moved forward to General Potter's right, and, with its usual gallantry, had attacked the enemy and punished him severely. But Colonel Hartranft, having once broken through the enemy's lines, found himself confronted by so strong a force as to make further progress impracticable. He did however succeed in maintaining his position, close by the enemy's intrenchments, where he was bravely supported by the brigade of Colonel Christ. An attack by the two divisions, in connection with the second corps, was contemplated at six o'clock. The enemy, ascertaining the arrangement, opened fire upon our troops, necessitating an earlier assault. The troops advanced about half-past five o'clock, made a singularly gallant charge upon the enemy, drove him into his works and even broke a portion of his line. But the obstinate resistance which he made and the strong position which he held, prevented a complete success. The two divisions held their ground in front of the enemy, and, when the sun set upon the second day's engagement and the two armies rested on their respective lines, the advantage was clearly with our men. General Lee did not venture upon a third day of fighting. After a demonstration upon our right, which created some confusion in the sixth corps, and at one time threatened very serious consequences, the enemy withdrew from our immediate front, into his fortified lines of defence.

The fourth division, with the cavalry, arrived at Germania ford at an early hour on the morning of the 6th, and at first expected to enter into the conflict. General Ferrero was ordered to report to General Sedgwick and was by him directed at first to press the enemy. But on the arrival of Colonel Marshall's provisional brigade, composed of some heavy artillery regiments, that had been garrisoning the defences of Washington and were now assigned to the Ninth Corps, General Ferrero's division was ordered to guard the bridges, roads and trains then near the Rapidan. The white troops were at once put into the conflict. A speck of danger appeared in the evening, when the enemy attacked General Sedgwick, but it soon vanished, and through the night, the fourth division moved up the trains nearer to the rear of the army. General Ferrero and his men would have been glad of more active and prominent service. But General Grant felt disposed to employ his white soldiers in the more dangerous duties of the campaign, and the men of the colored division had no opportunity of displaying their courage until a later day.

The losses of the Corps in the desperate fighting of the 6th were somewhat severe. The two divisions lost nine hundred and eighty-five killed, wounded and missing, among whom were several officers of promise. Colonel Frank Graves, of the 8th Michigan infantry, belonging to General Willcox's division, was mortally wounded while leading his regiment bravely in the battle, and unfortunately fell into the hands of the enemy. He was a gallant officer, and had done good service in former campaigns. Colonel Charles E. Griswold, of the 56th Massachusetts regiment, was killed early in the action. He was shot and fell dead without a groan. Hs was one of the most accomplished of the numerous young officers of merit that the State of Massachusetts has contributed to the war. His regiment was a model of neatness, regularity and good discipline. He was an excellent specimen of the patriotic New England citizen soldier;—brave, intelligent and skilful, always faithful to his duty, and ready to meet every danger and death itself with a calm and courageous soul. Of the enemy's forces immediately engaged with the Ninth Corps, General Longstreet was quite severely wounded.

On the 7th, General Grant discovered that the enemy was

not disposed to renew the battle except from behind his works. He determined to turn the position by marching by General Lee's right flank. On the night of the 7th, the movement towards Spottsylvania Court House commenced. General Warren, with the fifth corps, had the advance. General Burnside, with the Ninth Corps, brought up the rear. The first division immediately followed the fifth corps. The other divisions, with Colonel Marshall's provisional brigade, followed the sixth corps towards Chancellorsville, not gaining the road until daybreak of the 8th, on account of its occupancy by the sixth corps and its trains. The Corps moved through Chancellorsville and went into bivouac on the road beyond. The artillery reserve belonging to the Corps was ordered to join the artillery reserve of the Army of the Potomac, with which it remained until the 16th. The fourth division and cavalry covered the trains. Some skirmishing ensued during the march, whenever the enemy approached too near our columns, and always to his disadvantage.

The 9th passed with a more exciting train of events than the two preceding days. A very gallant affair was conducted by General Willcox with his division. He had been directed to move his command to the crossing of the Ny river on the Fredericksburg and Spottsylvania road. General Willcox was early on the march, and about a mile from the river his advance came in contact with the enemy's pickets. He quickly drove them to and across the river, and seized the bridge. Colonel Christ's brigade, with Roemer's and Twitchell's batteries of artillery, was immediately thrown across and posted on a little eminence about a quarter of a mile beyond. Colonel Christ was attacked while here by a considerable force of dismounted cavalry and a brigade of General Longstreet's corps. Colonel Hartranft sent over two regiments of his brigade to reënforce Colonel Christ. The enemy made repeated assaults upon our position, but was effectually repulsed at all points. Finding fruitless further attempts to dispute our progress, he finally retired, leaving about fifty prisoners and several of his wounded in our hands. About noon, the first division came up, and the point was secured against any danger of loss. The third division—and especially Colonel Christ's brigade—won this position in a very creditable manner, but at a cost of one hundred and eighty-eight killed, wounded and missing. The second division was brought up in the course of the afternoon, but too late to take any part in the brisk engagement which Colonel Christ had so finely carried through. The fourth division was occupied in guarding the rear of the entire army. In the course of the day, the 2d Ohio cavalry was attacked, near Piney Branch Church, by a brigade of the enemy's cavalry, with two pieces of artillery. The 23d regiment United States colored troops was sent to the assistance of the cavalry, and, with conspicuous courage, attacked and forced back the enemy. The cavalry pursued, and soon relieved the trains from the presence of a troublesome foe. Preparations were made by General Burnside for a further movement, to be undertaken on the following day.

The 9th had passed with considerable fighting by the other portions of the army. The enemy had divined the purpose of General Grant, and was not inclined to allow him to carry it out without opposition. General Lee, having the shorter lines, moved his army from the field of battle in the Wilderness to the defensive points around Spottsylvania Court House, and immediately crowned them with fortifications. General Grant found his progress once more stopped, and after one or two attempts to force the position, halted his army and prepared for another bloody battle.

The fighting of the 8th and 9th, though not of so important character as on the preceding days in the Wilderness, was yet sufficiently serious to result in considerable loss. On the 8th, General Warren had a brisk engagement, in which were manifested the steadiness and courage of the fifth corps and its commander. On the 9th, the sixth corps met with an incalculable loss in the fall of its commander, the brave General Sedgwick. After the Ninth Corps had passed from his command to that of General Smith, General Sedgwick had been assigned to the command of the sixth corps. In all the operations of the Army of the Potomac, subsequent to that time, he performed a distinguished part. When General Hooker moved upon Chancellorsville, it was General Sedgwick's duty to storm the heights of Fredericksburg, in order to create a diversion in favor of his chief. The work was most gallantly done, and the enemy's positions on Marye's hill and beyond were carried by a vigorous charge. General Hooker's failure let loose the greater portion of General Lee's army upon the sixth corps. But General Sedgwick was successful in extricating his command from its perilous position, though with severe loss, and crossed to the north bank of the Rappahannock above Falmouth.

In all the movements of the Army of the Potomac, General Sedgwick's corps was always found in the right place. So clear was his merit, that he was offered the command of the army itself. But with characteristic modesty, he declined the proffered honor. He preferred the more humble position of a corps commander, and in that capacity was remarkably faithful and trustworthy. By his presence of mind and coolness he saved the right wing of the army in the enemy's night attack of the 6th, and contributed very materially to the successes which were afterwards gained. He was killed while standing near an embrasure in one of our hastily erected earthworks. A bullet from the rifle of a sharpshooter of the enemy pierced his brain, and he fell dead. He was, without question, one of the bravest men and one of the finest soldiers to be found in all our armies. Modest, manly, skilful and courageous, without boastfulness, pretension or show of any sort, he has written for himself a bright and honorable name upon the records of his country, and impressed an ineffaceable image of his genuine manhood upon the hearts of all who love virtue, fidelity and heroism.

On the 10th, the fighting was of a very sanguinary character, but still without decisive results. "The enemy was obstinate," as General Grant found occasion to say, and was resolute in disputing every inch of his ground. His lines extended around Spottsylvania Court House, between the Po and Ny rivers in a position well supported by breastworks and protected by forest and marshy land. Our own lines were well brought up, the Ninth Corps holding the extreme left, General Willcox's division resting on the Ny, at the point which Colonel Christ had won. In the course of the afternoon, a determined attack was made by the corps, in conjunction with the Army of the Potomac. It resulted in placing our lines in immediate proximity with those of the enemy. General Potter's division attained a point within a short distance of the Court House. The advance was made in a very creditable manner, in the face of a heavy and destructive fire. After holding the position for a short time, General Potter was ordered to retire for nearly a mile, to a point selected by Lieutenant Colonel Comstock, under the direction of General Grant. The withdrawal was made against the remonstrance of General Burnside, and the mistake was afterwards seen—unfortunately not till it was too late to rectify it except by hard fighting.

But the Ninth Corps suffered a severe loss in the death of General Stevenson, the commander of the first division. He was killed early in the day by one of the enemy's riflemen, while near his headquarters. Born in Boston, on the 3d of February, 1836, Thomas Greely Stevenson was especially fortunate in his family, his education and his social position. He was the son of Hon. J. Thomas Stevenson, well known as an able lawyer and a sagacious man of affairs. He was educated in the best schools in Boston, and at an early age he entered the counting room of one of the most active merchants of that city. There, by his faithfulness in duty, his promptness and his generosity of disposition, he secured the entire confidence and love of his principal and the high esteem of the business community, and a brilliant commercial career opened before him. But when his country called him, he could not neglect her summons. The parting words of his father to himself and his younger brother, when they left home for the field, well express the appreciation in which his domestic virtues were held: "Be as good soldiers as you have been sons. Your country can ask no more than that of you, and God will bless you."

In the spring of 1861, he was orderly sergeant of the New England Guards, and upon the organization of the fourth battalion of Massachusetts infantry he was chosen Captain of one of its companies. On the 25th of April, the battalion was sent to garrison Fort Independence in Boston harbor, and on the 4th of May, Captain Stevenson was promoted to the rank of Major. In this position he was distinguished for an excellent faculty for discipline and organization which was subsequently of great benefit to him. On the 1st of August he received authority to raise and organize a regiment of Infantry for a term of three years, and on the 7th of September, he went into camp at Readville with twenty men. On the 9th of December, he left the State of Massachusetts with the 24th regiment—one of the finest and best drilled, organized, equipped, and disciplined body of troops that Massachusetts had yet sent to the war. His regiment was assigned to General Foster's brigade in the North Carolina expedition, and he soon gained the respect and friendship of his superior officers.

The conduct of the 24th regiment and its commander in North Carolina has already been made a matter of record. When Colonel Stevenson was assigned to the command of a brigade in April, 1862, the choice was unanimously approved by his companions in arms. General Burnside regarded him as one of his best officers. "He has shown great courage and skill in action," once wrote the General, "and in organization and discipline he has no superior." General Foster was enthusiastic in his commendation. "He stands as high as any officer or soldier in the army of the United States," said he, "on the list of noble, loyal, and devoted men." On the 27th of December he was promoted to the rank of Brigadier General, and on the 14th of March, 1863, he was confirmed and commissioned to that grade. In February, 1863, he accompanied General Foster to South Carolina, where his brigade was attached to the tenth corps, and where he served with great fidelity and zeal throughout the year under Generals Foster, Hunter and Gillmore. In April, 1864, he reported to General Burnside at Annapolis and was assigned to the command of the first division.

General Stevenson was peculiarly known and respected in the army for his bravery and coolness in action, his skill in organization, and for his faithful care of the troops under his command. He exercised a personal supervision over the execution of his orders, and was not content till he had fully ascertained that every thing had been done as it should be. The report of the 44th Massachusetts regiment, which was in his brigade in North Carolina, bears especial testimony to this trait in his character.

The language of a friend, who furnished the material for the above sketch of General Stevenson's career, will hardly be considered too strong or too partial an estimate of his character. Certain it is, that his loss was felt by all his brother officers with profound sorrow. A personal friend, a meritorious soldier, a trustworthy and noble man had been taken from the midst of them, and they will agree to the summary which a not too indulgent pen has traced. "In his military career he was honored far beyond his years, but not beyond his acknowledged deserts. Many, who were older and of larger experience than himself sought his counsel and his aid. He was peculiarly fit for a leader. Quick in the perception of danger, cautious in preparing for it, he was as bold as the boldest in confronting it. He shrank instinctively from all unnecessary display. Modest almost to bashfulness he was nevertheless very determined in the support of opinions which he had deliberately formed. He felt the weight of the large responsibilities which constantly devolved upon him, but he never shrank from them. Conscientious in the discharge of each duty, he made for himself a record of honor in the military annals of his country. True manliness was his marked characteristic.

Generous, truthful, liberal in his judgments of others, forgetful of self, genial in his disposition and frank in his intercourse with every one, he made many friends. The easy familiarity, for which he was noted, never detracted from the respect which the true dignity of his character inspired.

"Upon the arrival of his remains at Boston public honors to his memory were promptly tendered by the authorities both of the city and of the State; but his family, acting upon what they knew would have been his own wish, decided that the last tributes should not be attended by any public display."

The command of the first division devolved upon Colonel Leasure of the 100th Pennsylvania, until the arrival of Major General Thomas L. Crittenden, who had been assigned to the position. This officer had previously been on terms of intimate intercourse with General Burnside, had served with General Rosecrans in East Tennessee, and his arrival in camp on the 11th was a source of much gratification. But little was done by either army on this day except some very lively skirmishing. The weary soldiers enjoyed a brief period of repose, to which a refreshing shower of rain gave additional zest. It had been a week of toil and blood. The ground had been well fought over, and as General Grant changed his base of operations, from the Rapidan to Fredericksburg, the roads in the rear of the army, to the Rappahannock and the Potomac at Belle Plain, presented a sorry spectacle. Fredericksburg was filled with wounded soldiers. Even the forest recesses of the Wilderness hid many a poor fellow, who had crept away to die. Many of the severely wounded were still lying upon the field under the rude shelter of hastily constructed booths of boughs and canvas. The medical department worked with all diligence and the efforts of the delegates of the Sanitary and Christian Commissions were beyond praise. A large army leaves in its track desolation and misery. Such battles as had been fought since the opening of the campaign seemed to drench the soil with blood and fill the air with groans of pain. Scenes of most piteous interest were exhibited on every hand.

On many hearts and homes the shadows of darkest bereavement had fallen, and the bright spring time sun was clouded with grief. Patriotism and duty required a heroic sacrifice.

The battles of the week culminated on the 12th, when the fighting was resumed with redoubled energy. General Hancock's corps, in the early dawn, made a particularly gallant attack upon a salient of the enemy's works, striking them upon his right centre, and completely surprised the foe in that quarter, capturing and sending to the rear General Johnson's division almost entire, with its commanding general. Twenty pieces of artillery also fell into our hands. Our whole line was closed up. The Ninth Corps dashed into the fight with the utmost enthusiasm and speedily joined General Hancock's troops in their daring adventure. For an hour or two it seemed as though our men would carry everything before them. But at nine o'clock, the enemy had become fully alive to the necessity of resistance, and made a counter attack against our lines. For three hours longer the fight continued with exhibitions of the most desperate valor and with terrible carnage. The rebel columns of attack dashed in vain against our lines, advancing with unflinching resolution, and retiring only when broken up by the withering and destructive fire which was brought to bear against them. At noon, the enemy gave up his attempts to force back our troops, but he had succeeded in preventing our further advance.

General Grant was not yet ready to stop the conflict. He determined, if possible, to turn and double up the enemy's right flank. It was a desperate enterprise. The enemy's right was resting on marshy and difficult ground. But after a temporary lull, to afford a little rest to the tired troops, the battle was renewed in the early afternoon. Our troops were massed upon our left, the Ninth Corps occupying a conspicuous position. Rain had commenced falling in the morning, and the field of battle became a mass of gory mud. Still the struggle was once more entered upon with unflagging courage. Again and again did our troops press forward to be met with a most stubborn resistance. The rebels fought with remarkable obstinacy, and our men were not inferior in pertinacity to the determined foe. Step by step the ground was disputed with resolute courage. The fight was deadly. The slain and disabled covered the ground. The frightful carnage was only closed by the darkness of the night, so desperate was rebel hate, so persistent was patriot valor.

During the entire day, the Ninth Corps was effectively engaged, and lost heavily. At the outset, it had promptly moved up to General Hancock's support, and through the forenoon had been most active in the fight. The Corps had been posted across the Fredericksburg turnpike, upon the extreme left of the army, with dense thickets in front. The opposing corps of the enemy, protected by rifle pits and timber breastworks, was under the command of General A. P. Hill. In this movement, Colonel Griffin's brigade of General Potter's division had the advance, and connecting with General Hancock's left, shared in the glory and danger of the attack. The brigade succeeded in carrying a portion of the enemy's works, including a battery of two guns. In the successful result of that attack, General Hancock's command became somewhat disturbed, and was in turn the object of assault. Colonel Griffin's position enabled him at this moment to be of effectual service, the enemy was handsomely met and Hancock was saved. So prominent had been the gallantry of the brigade commander upon this and former occasions, that General Burnside recommended him for instant promotion. The remainder of General Potter's division was equally forward, both in attack and defence. The fruits of the movement were the capture of two lines of detached rifle pits, a number of prisoners, and a part of the enemy's main line. The rupture of the connection with the second corps enabled the enemy to check our progress, but he could not retake his lost ground.

General Crittenden's division was formed on the left of General Potter, and courageously sustained its part of the conflict. By some means, its left had become refused, and when General

Willcox brought up his division still further to the left, the formation of the line was somewhat irregular. But the men fought exceedingly well, and though no great gain was made, no serious repulse was experienced. General Willcox's division was at first held in reserve, but soon after the battle opened, was moved up *en echelon* to the immediate front. Colonel Humphrey's brigade on the left immediately came in contact with the enemy's skirmishers, and quickly drove them in. Colonel Hartranft's brigade upon the right quickly made connection with the first division, and actively entered into the engagement. Captain Twitchell's battery was posted on the right front, and Captain Roemer's in rear of Colonel Humphrey, to protect the left flank. The provisional brigade and the dismounted cavalry held the trenches in front of the Court House.

In this position and with this formation, after the temporary lull at noon, the Corps renewed the battle. Repeated charges were made upon the opposing lines, but without forcing them. General Burnside succeeded, however, in carrying his own lines within a few yards of the enemy, and could not be dislodged. Counter charges were made, particularly upon the left of the Corps, where the enemy massed heavy columns of attack. General Willcox had anticipated such a movement, and notified General Burnside of the probability of its occurrence. Lieutenant Benjamin, chief of artillery, was accordingly directed to prepare for such emergency. Two additional batteries were brought up, posted and made ready for the expected assault. The attack came. It was vigorously delivered and stubbornly disputed. Roemer's battery did great execution. Wright's battery lost all its cannoniers, and was in danger of being captured, when the men of the 2d Michigan manned the guns and splendidly retrieved the fortunes of the hour. Our infantry regiments changed front, and bearing down upon the foe, scattered Colonel Barber's brigade of the enemy's column and captured its commanding officer, with nearly a hundred of his men. Further to the right, the division suffered severely, and for some time considerable confusion prevailed in this part of the field. The efforts of the officers were successful in restoring order, and the enemy's attempt was effectually checked. The Corps had advanced about a mile, had successfully charged the enemy's first line, had repulsed his attack, inflicting heavy loss upon him, and ended the day with entrenching immediately in front of his works. The losses had been very severe—over a thousand killed, wounded and missing in the third division alone. Again the day closed upon a bloody field, and the enemy was still unsubdued.*

Among our dead was Captain James Farrand, commanding the 2d Michigan infantry, a very brave and promising officer, whose name is mentioned in reports of the battle in terms of high and well merited praise. He was killed while serving the guns of Wright's battery, which the men of his regiment had saved from capture. The 36th Massachusetts lost a good and faithful officer in Captain S. Henry Bailey, of Company G. He was killed early in the morning, while gallantly cheering on his men. He was twenty-nine years of age, was born at Northborough, Mass., and was a man of great probity of character. Sickness had struck him down at Harper's Ferry and again at Vicksburg. But he continued in the army in the faithful discharge of duty till the last. He served at one time in East Tennessee on the staff of General Ferrero, and won, in all positions, the confidence of his superior officers. He has left the pleasant memory of a true manhood to his friends, and the record of an honorable service to his country.

---

* Colonel Hartranft, as well as Colonel Griffin, earned his promotion to the rank of Brigadier General, in this well contested battle.

CHAPTER III.

TO THE JAMES RIVER.

THE battles around Spottsylvania Court House had been very fierce and sanguinary. Great losses had been suffered on both sides. The enemy had been considerably crippled, and was evidently reluctant to come out into the open field and fight in a fairly contested engagement. Acting henceforward on the defensive, he saved himself from suffering as much injury as he inflicted. Keeping close behind his intrenched lines, he had every advantage which the natural strength of his positions, increased by his labor, could afford. The army of General Grant was thus compelled to assault every fortified point, and, whether the point was carried or not, to suffer enormous losses. Scarcely less than thirty thousand men must have been killed, wounded and captured during the eight days of fighting. The number of stragglers and skulkers, who always take advantage of such opportunities, must have been nearly if not quite five thousand, thus reducing the effective strength of the army by a very considerable degree. The Ninth Corps had suffered its proportionate loss. No less than five thousand five hundred men had been disabled in the battles of the 6th and 12th and the skirmishings that had intervened. Of the staff, Lieutenant Benjamin had been severely wounded in the neck, but with characteristic bravery remained on the field until the critical moment had passed, directing his batteries.

General Grant was by no means discouraged by the losses to which he had been subjected, and the unexpected obstinacy of the enemy in clinging to his intrenched positions. The depleted ranks were filled up by reënforcements, drawn from the defences of Washington and elsewhere. The position at Spottsylvania was too strong to be forced. But Spottsylvania was not the objective point of the campaign. The Lieutenant General determined upon a second movement by the left flank, with the hope of drawing General Lee into an engagement away from his intrenchments. Yet, previous to this, he wished to make another direct assault. For a week after the 12th, every day was occupied with more or less skirmishing and artillery firing along the lines, but no general action was in any case contemplated by either party, until the 18th, when a heavy attack was made upon the enemy's works. General Lee, on the 13th, contracted his lines somewhat, by retiring about a mile towards the Court House, but still held tenaciously to the roads. On the 14th, the Ninth Corps was moved from the extreme left to the left centre, the fifth corps taking its place. On the 16th, the first and second divisions made a strong demonstration, for the purpose of feeling the enemy and reconnoitering the position, but beyond inducing the development of a large force, the movement accomplished no important result. The action of the 18th at one time threatened to be of considerable magnitude. At least one-half of the army was in the action, and some advantage was gained over the enemy by forcing him back a little from his most advanced positions and occupying points which commanded portions of his line.

The first and second divisions of the Ninth Corps were engaged in this attack, and, handsomely supported by the batteries of the third division, succeeded in gaining a position which rendered a part of the enemy's works untenable. Beyond that, however, nothing of value could be attained. The troops moved gallantly forward in three columns of attack, but on their arrival at the abattis that protected the enemy's front, found that an attempt to surmount the obstructions and charge the works would be hopeless. The other corps met with no better success. The entire demonstration proved that no advantage could be secured, and at eleven o'clock in the forenoon, the assault was abandoned and the troops were recalled.

These various operations confirmed the opinion of General Grant as to the necessity of moving to the North Anna, if he hoped to make any progress towards the completion of the campaign. Orders were accordingly issued to that effect, and on the 21st, the movement commenced. The fifth and second corps took the advance, and after they had sufficiently uncovered the roads, the Ninth moved down towards the Po river, followed closely by the sixth. General Grant had intended to move General Hancock's corps on the night of the 19th, sending him with as much cavalry as could be spared as far towards Richmond, on the line of the Fredericksburg railroad, as could be attained, "fighting the enemy in whatever force he might find them." While General Hancock was thus moving, the other three corps were to keep close up to the enemy's works and attack, if Hancock were followed. It was a bold plan, and would have forced the enemy into the open field if it had been successful. But General Lee himself interfered with the movement by sending General Ewell's corps, on the afternoon of the 19th, to attack our extreme right flank. The enemy marched around to our rear, hoping to disarrange and break our lines. The point that was assailed was guarded by a division of heavy artillery, then for the first time under fire. These troops met the enemy and repulsed him in a very brilliant manner. As he attempted to recross the Ny, on his withdrawal, he was set upon and thrown into confusion, with a loss of four hundred prisoners and many killed and wounded. This movement was sufficient to disturb General Grant's plans for the time, and the project of sending General Hancock off by himself was abandoned. Not a single corps, but the entire army was to move, and finally got upon the road after various delays.

The directions for the Ninth Corps were to march down the north bank of the Po river to a point near Stannard's Mill, and cross there, unless opposed by the enemy. If the enemy was in force, the Corps was to proceed to Guinney's Bridge. The provisional brigade had now become incorporated with the first division and was afterwards known and designated as the third brigade of that division. The entire Corps was promptly put in motion in the afternoon of the 21st. Colonel Curtin was sent in advance with his brigade from General Potter's division to seize and occupy the crossing. He met the enemy's pickets about a mile from Stannard's, rapidly drove them over the river, and prepared to cross. General Potter hastened forward with the remainder of his division, and found the enemy in considerable force on the opposite side of the river. He made his dispositions to carry the position, but as it was feared that it might bring on more of an engagement than was then contemplated, General Potter was restrained, and Colonel Curtin simply held the hither bank until the remainder of the Corps had passed. General Willcox had been detained to aid General Wright, who had been attacked just before sunset. He now came up soon after dark and the Corps marched through the night, halting at sunrise on the 22d near General Grant's Headquarters in the neighborhood of Guinney's Station. A rest of two hours refreshed the troops, and they were moved a few miles further by way of Downer's Bridge to New Bethel Church, and to Thornbury, in the neighborhood of which they remained through the rest of the day, holding the crossing of the Ta river and the roads beyond. At five o'clock on the morning of the 23d the march was resumed for Jericho Bridge, in order to cross the North Anna. General Hancock had already made Milford Station, and was directed to proceed to the North Anna and effect a crossing at New Bridge. The Ninth Corps was to act as a support to the second. The crossing was to be made at daylight on the 24th. Should General Hancock be able to force his passage without assistance, General Burnside was to march his corps to Ox ford and cross the river at that point if possible.

It is hardly within the province of this narrative to discuss the merits of General Grant's plan for the movement upon Richmond. His intention was to "beat General Lee if possible north of Richmond," making the rebel army his objective point. He had in mind the possibility of crossing the James above the enemy's capital, and thus of cutting off its communications with the South. He had hoped that General Butler would occupy the south bank of the James even to the points in the immediate neighborhood of Richmond. Being disappointed in that respect, and meeting with a more strenuous opposition from the army of Northern Virginia than he had reckoned upon, General Grant's object now seemed to be to place his army between that of General Lee and Richmond, or, failing in that, to transfer it to the south of the James and unite with General Butler. The movement upon Ox ford, New Bridge and other points on the North Anna would effect the first of these objects, provided General Lee did not anticipate it. But since the battle of the 12th, the utmost vigilance was exercised in the enemy's camp and every movement of our forces was observed with the greatest watchfulness. General Grant's army was scarcely on the move before General Lee had also started with his command. Having the main roads in his possession, the enemy could move with greater facility over equal distances. The march of our columns had to be made with great caution, and every available plantation road and pathway was used to push forward the troops. The enemy was too quick for our army, and when General Grant reached the North Anna, he found that the passage was to be disputed.

The army struck the North Anna, on the afternoon of the 23d at three points—the fifth and sixth corps on the right, at Jericho bridge, the Ninth near Ox ford, and the second near the railroad bridge. General Warren crossed the river during the afternoon. The North Anna at the points where the army reached the river makes a decided bend to the south, and then immediately to the north-east, thus nearly forming two sides of a triangle. The enemy's lines of intrenchments commenced two or three miles in the rear, and at their point of junction near Ox ford, formed an obtuse angle. The position of the Ninth Corps on the north bank was opposite the enemy's salient. A crossing at Ox ford was therefore impracticable without a very serious loss. The corps was here divided. General Potter's division was sent to the assistance of General Hancock, General Crittenden's to the aid of General Warren, and General Willcox's retained in the rear of the ford.

General Willcox on the 24th succeeded in seizing and holding a small island in the river near the ford. General Crittenden on the same day threw his division across the river at Quarles's ford. The troops pressed forwards, forded the stream with great celerity, marched up the opposite bank, and at once engaged the enemy. General Ledlie's brigade had the lead, and behaved most creditably, advancing beyond the river for at least a mile and a half with brisk fighting and forcing the enemy into his intrenchments. The troops held their position close to the enemy's lines for some time, but were finally obliged to retire. Two divisions of General Hill's corps marched out, attacked and attempted to outflank General Ledlie. The brigade withdrew from its advanced position to a point nearer the river. During the day it lost one of its finest officers, Lieutenant Colonel C. L. Chandler of the 57th Massachusetts, who fell at his post in the brave performance of duty. In these movements Major J. St. C. Morton of the Engineer corps, on General Burnside's staff, distinguished himself by leading a portion of the brigade in a gallant attack upon the enemy's lines.

General Potter's division crossed the river on the 24th, at Chesterfield bridge and in conjunction with the second corps engaged the enemy. The right of the division rested on a bluff near the river, the left was well advanced connecting with General Mott's brigade of General Birney's division. The line was held and well intrenched. On the 25th but little was done at this extremity of our lines, but on the 26th the enemy was disposed to be troublesome. In the afternoon of that day a sharp affair took place in which General Potter's division won fresh laurels. It drove back the enemy's entire line in front, and came near gaining a decisive advantage. As it was, General Potter succeeded in advancing his line for some distance, and in securing a highly favorable position for his command. In this operation, however, he had the misfortune to lose one of the best officers of his division, Lieutenant Colonel Pearson, commanding the 6th New Hampshire. This excellent soldier had manifested his bravery on many a well fought field, and was considered by all who knew him as one of the most promising among the volunteer officers in the army. General Potter spoke of him in terms of high commendation, and to the officers and men of his own regiment he was greatly endeared. He had entered the service in the early days of the war, and won his way through the several grades of office, by faithful service and distinguished gallantry. His manly and honorable qualities of character attracted the respect of his brother officers, and his bright and genial disposition made him at all times a welcome and agreeable companion. He was killed while watching from an exposed situation the progress of the movement on the 26th, and his death caused, throughout the brigade to which he was attached, emotions of genuine sorrow and expressions of sympathy and regret.

During the operations of this campaign General Burnside had perceived the difficulty of moving and fighting two independent commands. To this point the Ninth Corps had been a separate organization from the Army of the Potomac, and in reality constituted a distinct army. It is easy to see that some embarrassment might ensue. It not unfrequently happened that the Ninth Corps was called upon to reënforce the different corps of the army of the Potomac in positions where they were hard pressed. A division was sent here, another there, reporting to the different corps commanders, and General Burnside, thus called upon, willingly denuded himself of his command, to serve his brother officers. But these orders could only come from General Grant, and valuable time might be lost in their transmission. It was necessary that the Ninth Corps should be incorporated with the Army of the Potomac. But here a difficulty at once became apparent. General Burnside was superior in rank to General Meade, as was also General Parke. If the two armies were consolidated, General Meade, according to military usage, could not well hold chief command of the Army of the Potomac. But General Burnside was not willing thus to affect the position of an officer for whose feelings, as a skillful commander, he had a considerate regard. He therefore, with General Parke, generously waived all considerations of rank, and at his suggestion, an order was accordingly issued by General Grant on the 25th, incorporating the Ninth Corps with the Army of the Potomac. By this action General Burnside voluntarily placed himself under the command of his inferior, General Meade, as two years previously he had done in the case of General Pope. It was an act of generosity of not common occurrence among military men, and deserves this special mention.

The operations at the North Anna had not been so successful as to justify General Grant in hoping for the defeat of the enemy at that point. General Lee was not more disposed than previously to come out and deliver or receive battle at any distance from his fortified lines. Within his defences he could rapidly reënforce any threatened point, by simply moving his troops across the intervening space between his lines. General Grant had the disadvantage of being compelled to reënforce any point in his lines, by crossing his troops over two bridges, and marching over a distance at least twice that of his opponent. Nothing could be accomplished under such circumstances, and accordingly General Grant again determined to turn the enemy's position. It was a question whether he should attempt the right or the left. After carefully weighing the matter, he decided to continue his former tactics, and, moving by the left flank, to make his base of supplies at White House, cross the Pamunkey and essay a nearer approach to Richmond across the Tolopotomoy Creek, by way of Cold Harbor and Bethesda Church. Orders were accordingly issued and during the night of the 26th, the army was withdrawn across the North Anna and put on the march for the passage of the Pamunkey at Hanover Town.

The two divisions of the Ninth Corps, that had been temporarily under the command of Generals Hancock and Warren, were united with General Willcox's division, and on the 27th the entire Corps was concentrated near Mount Carmel Church and awaited orders to move. On the afternoon of that day, the movement towards the crossing of the Pamunkey, at Hanover Town, began. The second division, which was in the advance, reached the river bank and crossed at ten o'clock on the evening of the 28th. The rear division, General Willcox's, crossed at one o'clock on the morning of the 29th. The Ninth Corps took position between the second and fifth and intrenched. On the 30th General Burnside moved the Corps across Tolopotomoy Creek, skirmishing with the enemy at every point, particularly in front of the second division, and forcing back all opposition. On the 31st the entire line was moved forward from one to three fourths of a mile, under a brisk fire, and after a smart engagement, involving considerable loss, several detached lines of skirmish pits were carried, and our troops pushed closely up to the enemy's main lines.

The 1st and 2d of June were passed in changing, establishing and strengthening our lines, and in making such disposition of troops as promised the most decisive results. Almost continual skirmishing took place while these movements were going forward, and the sharpshooters on both sides were busily employed. On the 1st, particularly, there was severe fighting by the cavalry and infantry at different points of the line. But no very general engagement ensued. Several gallant charges were made by different divisions on either side, and the result of the operations was our occupancy of the country extending from a point near the Chickahominy to Bethesda Church. In the course of these two days the Ninth Corps was moved from the centre to the right. By the night of the 2d it was posted on the extreme right of the line, the right partially refused, the left resting, near Bethesda Church, the main line running part of the way parallel to the Mechanicsville road, then across to a point not far from the Tolopotomoy. The movement was made in the face of considerable opposition by the enemy, and with some loss of prisoners in General Crittenden's division.

The object of these movements was for the purpose of forcing the passage of the Chickahominy and driving General Lee into the intrenchments around Richmond. With this end in view, a force of sixteen thousand men under General W. F. Smith had been brought round on the 29th of May from Bermuda Hundred to White House, and had been instructed to march to New Cold Harbor in order to seize that important point. By a mistake in the transmission of the order, the name of the place had been wrongly given, and General Smith had unfortunately directed his command towards Newcastle. This deflection of the line of march lost us a great advantage, and General Grant was obliged to be content with the occupation of old Cold Harbor—a position of much less consequence. This was the centre of General Grant's—or rather, since the union of the Ninth Corps with the Army of the Potomac, General Meade's—position, his left resting near the Despatch Station road, and his right near Bethesda Church. General Lee's line extended from a point a few miles east of Atlee's Station beyond Shady Grove, covering New Cold Harbor, and commanding the public roads, with the Chickahominy in the rear. In front numerous thickets and marshy places rendered the approach difficult. The line was well intrenched, in some places formidably so, and defied attack. The key to the position was opposite General Hancock's corps on the left and was a redoubt or earthwork occupying a crest called Watt's Hill, with a sunken road in front. The ground had already been fought over in the Peninsular campaign of General McClellan, the position of the two armies being reversed. Our entire line was at least eight miles in length. The ground was varied, wearing the same features as the region north of the Pamunkey, woodland, marsh, hills, and open plain, a capital country for defence by inferior forces.

About sunrise on the 3d the assault commenced. Artillery opened along the line. In front of General Hancock, the two divisions of Generals Barlow and Gibbon made a magnificent charge, which swept before them all opposing forces, and gave them for a few minutes the summit of the enemy's position. Had these two brave divisions been promptly supported the day would have been our own, and General Grant's plan would have been grandly successful. But the supports were from some cause delayed, the enemy rallied, poured in a murderous enfilading fire, and our men were forced to give way and finally to abandon the captured work with its guns. Two or three hundred prisoners and an advanced position near the enemy's line were the only fruits of this gallant assault, and for these we paid dearly. "In less than an hour Hancock's loss was above three thousand."* The sixth corps and General Smith's command made gallant attempts to carry the enemy's position, but succeeded only in dislodging him from his exterior defences. These were brilliant charges, splendid heroism and immense sacrifice. But the inability of General Barlow to hold his advanced position had really decided the contest on our left, and proved the strength and determination of the enemy.

On the right, the brunt of the battle fell upon the Ninth Corps. The fifth was formed in a long attenuated line, and could do little else but hold the ground on which its ranks stood. The Ninth, formed with its right refused, could not make the attack quite so early in the day as the corps upon the left. General Wilson's cavalry division was pushed out on the extreme right, the two divisions of Generals Willcox and Potter were formed for attack, and General Crittenden's division was held in reserve. Colonel Curtin's brigade of General Potter's division made a daring charge, drove in the enemy's

*Swinton ; Campaigns of Army of Potomac, p. 486.

skirmishers, carried some detached rifle pits, forced the enemy—consisting of portions of Longstreet's and Ewell's corps—back into the inner works, and established itself in close proximity to his intrenchments. General Griffin's brigade came up in support, and held the right flank of the corps. Our artillery was brought forward and did effective service, silencing the enemy's batteries and blowing up two of his caissons. General Willcox's division attacked at an early hour, and recaptured a line of rifle pits that had been lost on the previous night. General Hartranft's brigade won additional distinction by the manner in which it advanced upon the enemy, driving him, as Curtin had done, into his interior works. Artillery was brought to the front, as on the right, and the Ninth was fairly established face to face with the foe at the shortest possible distance, ready for a second spring upon the stronger line of works.

Orders were given for a simultaneous attack by the two advanced divisions, to be delivered at one o'clock. Intelligence of the movement was communicated to General Wilson, and the suggestion made to him to move his command around the enemy's left flank and attack him in the rear. The plan of attack seemed certainly feasible, and had fine promise of success. But, as the movement had so signally failed on the left of the army, General Meade thought it best to suspend further operations, and just as the skirmishers of the Ninth Corps were advancing against the enemy, General Burnside received orders to cease all offensive operations. The skirmish line was accordingly drawn in, and our entire position strengthened. During the afternoon, the enemy made a sortie and ventured upon an assault, but was quickly and vigorously repulsed. The men of the Ninth Corps had bravely fought, and were on the point of winning a decisive advantage. They had shared in the honors and dangers of the movement. They also shared in its disappointments. Their blood had been freely spilt. Their losses had been severe. More than a thousand men had fallen killed or wounded. But all this heroic self-sacrifice had been as yet unsuccessful. The enemy's works still barred the road to Richmond.*

The issue of the battle of Cold Harbor was not what was

* Mr. Swinton, in his history of the Campaigns of the Army of the Potomac, is copious and severe in his criticisms of the entire movement from the Rapidan. He lauds General Lee and his principal officers, and correspondingly disparages General Grant and some of his associates. He does not appear to entertain a very high opinion of General Meade's ability or skill, and, in his remarks upon the battle of Cold Harbor, on page 487, he insinuates a very grave charge against the entire army. "The action was decided," he says, "in an incredibly brief time in the morning's assault. But rapidly as the result was reached, it was decisive; for the consciousness of every man pronounced further assault hopeless. The troops went forward as far as the example of their officers could carry them; nor was it possible to urge them beyond; for there they knew lay only death, without even the chance of victory. The completeness with which this judgment had been reached by the whole army was strikingly illustrated by an incident that occurred during the forenoon. Some hours after the failure of the first assault, General Meade sent instructions to each corps commander to renew the attack without reference to the troops on his right or left. The order was issued through these officers to their subordinate commanders, and from them descended through the wonted channels; but no man stirred, and immobile lines pronounced a verdict, silent, yet emphatic, against further slaughter."

This statement seems altogether incredible. It has been thought that there was some basis of fact in it, especially as it regarded some of the corps commanders; but how much, it is impossible to say. If true, it shows that the Army of the Potomac was affected by universal cowardice, or was in a state of downright mutiny. That the commanding general should issue a distinct order, and that the soldiers of his army should utterly refuse to take the first step towards its obedience, is not to be believed for a moment. Indeed, if the judgment of General Meade and other officers was not at fault, Mr. Swinton's declarations are to be considered as requiring considerable qualification. So systematically and persistently had he, while correspondent of the New York Times, given inaccurate accounts of the movements and operations of the army, as to draw upon him the notice both of General Grant and his subordinate officers. He was finally dismissed from the lines of the army by a formal order from General Meade, dated on the 6th of July. He was recited as "having abused the privileges conferred upon" him "by forwarding for publication incorrect statements respecting the operations of the troops." He was warned not to return, and corps commanders were advised, that should he be found within the limits of the army, he was to be "sent under guard to the Provost Marshal General" at headquarters. It is possible that the mortification caused by this expulsion from the army is the secret source of his unfavorable criticism of Generals Grant and Meade. What bearing this fact may have upon the worth of his volume, as an authority for the declarations which it contains any one can judge. An untruthful correspondent can hardly make a trustworthy historian.

expected or desired by General Grant. But it effectually proved that we could not cross the Chickahominy at this point, without the greatest opposition and a vast sacrifice of life. General Grant was not yet disposed to retire, and for the next few days the army intrenched itself, buried the dead, cared for the wounded, and prepared to enter upon new and more promising movements. The enemy made one or two assaults, which were beaten back with severe loss to the attacking force. At midnight, on the 6th, a heavy charge was made on General Burnside's position, which was very gallantly repulsed by the men of the Ninth. Meanwhile our line had been shortened by the withdrawal of the fifth corps to the rear for a reserve, and the substitution of the Ninth in its place. General Meade was manœuvring to prepare for a change of base, and for throwing his army across to the south bank of the James. It was a delicate and hazardous movement, and was gradually accomplished by moving our lines steadily to the left, refusing our right flank, until the time for marching the entire army should arrive. Upon the fifth and Ninth Corps devolved the most difficult of these manœuvres—the two commands alternating in moving by the flank and rear.

Of course the movements could not be made without the knowledge of the enemy, who endeavored to thwart them and harass our troops. A hill near our lines, in the vicinity of the Tucker estate, which was needed for fortifying, became the scene of some sharp fighting, and was at different times in our own and the enemy's hands. General Potter had taken the position and posted his skirmishers. Upon these the enemy advanced, on the afternoon of the 6th, and drove them off, capturing a few prisoners. He established batteries and commenced an ineffective cannonade. Withdrawing in the night, he left the hill once more free for occupation by our troops. Our skirmishers again took possession, and a working party dug a long line of rifle pits. But on the 7th, a heavy force of the enemy appeared, and again drove in our men. During the following night, General Potter, unwilling to yield that part of our line, advanced and forced the enemy away from the position. The hill was again occupied, strongly fortified and held securely. A flag of truce was flying during a portion of the afternoon of the 7th, for the burial of the dead and the removal of the wounded. But the enemy in front of the Ninth Corps did not appear to notice it, and even fired upon those who were assumed to be under its protection.

The four following days passed without event, with the exception of the retirement of General Crittenden, who was relieved at his own request from the command of the first division. Brigadier General Ledlie was assigned to the command by seniority of rank. Events proved it to be an unfortunate substitution. The usual amount of picket and artillery firing was kept up, and the working parties on both sides were greatly annoyed. Beyond that, small damage was done. Within the lines, it became manifest to all the soldiers in the army that another flanking movement by the left was contemplated. General Grant decided to place the Army of the Potomac on the south side of the James—an object which, he declares in his report, he had "from the start." He had hoped to have beaten General Lee before he did this; but whether General Lee was beaten or not, the point to take Richmond was certainly from the south. Accordingly, the railroad from West Point was dismantled and supplies were diverted to City Point. The cavalry was sent off in various directions to cut the enemy's communications, and the army moved. On the night of the 12th it began its march, and the great campaign in Virginia north of the James river was ended.

In reviewing these grand movements, extending over more than five weeks of time, almost every hour of which witnessed a combat at some point, it is impossible not to admire the wonderful resolution and bravery displayed on both sides. General Grant, in one of his despatches, says that the enemy seemed "to have found his last ditch." But if General Lee exhibited great capacity for defence, he soon discovered that he had met with more than his match in the tenacity, the determination and skill with which General Grant pushed on his aggressive operations. General Lee was very greatly aided by the peculiar formation of the country; rivers crossing the lines of march almost at right angles; forests of vast extent, which afforded concealment for the movements of an army on its defence or retreating; marshes which could be used for the protection of positions selected for a stand; hills, each one of which could speedily be made to become a fort; and all these strengthened by all the appliances of engineering skill which had leisurely constructed defensive works in view of just this contingency, or had hastily thrown them up as the emergency demanded. But all his skill, his ability, his resources, the advantages of his chosen positions, the very favorable opportunities which the natural features of the country supplied, were of little avail except to postpone defeat for a season. In the end they were compelled to give way before the indomitable will, the resistless and steady advance, the undaunted spirit, the matchless persistence and energy of General Grant and his army.

It is true, that the advance was slow, and that every mile was marked with brave men's blood. But still the advance was made. Positions which could not be successfully assailed without vast expenditure of human life, were turned by those flank marches in the face of an enemy, which, under the lead of unskilful men, are sure to result disastrously, but which, when made by a man of genius, are as successful as great battles won. In all these operations, the Ninth Corps participated in a manner to reflect the highest honor upon all its officers and men, and especially so upon its hopeful General and his division commanders. No campaign during the progress of the war was at all so severe in its demands upon human endurance and human courage as those forty days of marching and fighting. To say that the Ninth Corps in every position did all that was required of it, and commensurately suffered, is to declare sufficient praise for the living and the dead. More than one-fourth of the number of those who had crossed the Rapidan had been killed or disabled from service. In the second and third divisions, the reports of Generals Potter and Willcox state the losses to have been four thousand five hundred and thirty-two killed, wounded and missing. The losses in the first division were proportionately great. The remainder of the Army of the Potomac suffered in an equal degree.

The question whether General Grant could have placed his command on the south side of the James, without the great sacrifices which he was thus compelled to make, has often been discussed. With the army of General Lee confronting him on the Rapidan, and ready to improve every advantage which a false step on our part would give, a movement of General Grant's army to Alexandria or Aquia Creek, and thence by water to the James River, would have been very hazardous to the Capital and its defenders themselves. It was necessary to cover Washington while attacking Richmond. But Richmond was not so much the objective point as was General Lee's army. General Grant hoped to defeat General Lee as soon as he could bring him to action in the open field. But the Army of Northern Virginia was on ground with which its generals were perfectly familiar, and was not so easily to be beaten as was supposed. It is possible that General Lee may also have thought that he was to win an easy victory. He accordingly attacked with confidence in the Wilderness. But the very significant fact is to be observed, that he did not attack afterwards. From that moment, he fought defensive battles, and did not venture upon aggressive movements. Not even while General Grant was making his hazardous flank marches did the enemy dare to make more than feeble demonstrations. When, therefore, General Grant reached the James, he had an army in front of him, which considered itself safe only behind its defensive works. This was the result of General Grant's continuous "hammering"—and it was a great result. Moreover, the railroads leading to Washington from the south were destroyed or rendered useless, and the Capital was thus safe from serious attack. The difference between General McClellan's and General Grant's positions on the Peninsula was this :

the former found an enemy always ready to give, the latter found an enemy ready only to receive, battle. In war, success is the chief test of power. General Grant's magnificent success is a complete justification of the wisdom of his plans.

What if the Ninth Corps had been sent to North Carolina, and the grand interior line of communication broken between Richmond and the extreme South? A movement against Wilmington, Goldsboro' or Raleigh certainly seemed promising, and when it was finally made, proved most effectual. What if General Burnside had been sent to City Point, and the movement against Petersburg entrusted to him? It is not the design of this work to discuss probabilities. But, judging from the opinion which General Burnside had long before formed respecting the importance of a movement upon Petersburg, it is certain that he would have bent all his energies to achieve a complete success. But there is another question. What if the Ninth Corps had not reënforced the Army of the Potomac at the battle of the Wilderness? The result of the first day's fighting there was anything but promising. What the result of the second day would have been without the presence of the Ninth Corps, of course it is impossible to say. But that the reënforcement was most opportune, that it strengthened the disordered lines of General Grant, that it aided materially in checking the enemy, and gave General Grant confidence in his ability to cope successfully with his resolute antagonist, there can be no question. Whatever disappointment may have been felt by General Burnside or any of his officers, in the relinquishment of a coastwise expedition, was entirely lost in the satisfaction of knowing that the Ninth Corps was affording the Lieutenant General a very great assistance in carrying his plans to a triumphant conclusion.

CHAPTER IV.

IN FRONT OF PETERSBURG.

THE movement to the south side of the James, and the transfer of the scene of action from the front of Richmond to the front of Petersburg, has been universally considered as a master piece of military skill. Petersburg was in reality the citadel of Richmond, and would carry with it in its fall the fate of the Rebel Capital. It is curious to observe the series of disappointments to which General Grant was subjected in his operations against this important point. In the first place, General Butler failed to make any impression upon the line of communication between Richmond and Petersburg. Again, while General Grant was holding all the enemy's available force around Richmond, he ordered General Butler to send out a force against Petersburg. General Gillmore was despatched, on the 10th of June, to attack the city from the east, and General Kautz, with a division of cavalry, to make a detour and attack from the south. The works were held only by the local militia and a few troops of Wise's Legion. General Kautz was brilliantly successful, actually entering the city. General Gillmore was ingloriously unsuccessful. He marched up to a point where he could see the spires of the city, observed the defences, turned about and retired to Bermuda Hundred. General Kautz, deprived of his coöperating force, was obliged to loosen his grasp upon the prize, and also retired. Once more, as a preliminary to the movement of the army to the south of Richmond, the eighteenth corps was directed particularly against Petersburg. General Smith's command was put on transports at the White House and arrived at Bermuda

Hundred at midnight on the 14th. General Grant, who was then at that point, immediately ordered him forward to Petersburg. General Lee was still watching the movements of General Meade's army, and the defences of Petersburg were almost without a garrison.

"General Smith," says General Grant in his report, "got off as directed, and confronted the enemy's pickets near Petersburg before daylight next morning, but for some reason that I have never been able to satisfactorily understand, did not get ready to assault his main lines until near sundown. Then, with a part of his command only, he made the assault, and carried the line northeast of Petersburg from the Appomattox river for a distance of over two and a half miles, capturing fifteen pieces of artillery and three hundred prisoners. This was about seven P. M. Between the line thus captured and Petersburg there were no other works, and there was no evidence that the enemy had reënforced Petersburg with a single brigade from any source. The night was clear, the moon shining brightly, and favorable to further operations. General Hancock, with two divisions of the second corps, reached General Smith just after dark, and offered the services of these troops as he (Smith) might wish, waiving rank to the named commander, who he naturally supposed knew best the position of affairs and what to do with the troops. But instead of taking these troops and pushing at once into Petersburg, he requested General Hancock to relieve a part of his line in the captured works, which was done before midnight." On the 16th, General Lee threw in reënforcements, and the golden moment passed. In this movement, a division of colored troops, under Brigadier General Hinks, seem to have won the brightest laurels. They first attacked and carried the enemy's outpost at Bailey's Farm, capturing one piece of artillery in the most gallant manner. On their arrival before Petersburg, they lay in front of the works for nearly five hours, waiting for the word of command. They then, in company with the white troops, and showing equal bravery, rushed and carried the enemy's line of works, with what glorious success has already been related.

While these operations had been going forward, General Sheridan had proceeded with his cavalry as far to the rear as Gordonsville, having considerable fighting, and destroying the railroads running north from Richmond. With Washington secure and the eighteenth corps well on its way towards Petersburg, General Grant directed General Meade to move his army across the James.

The movement commenced on the night of the 12th. It was skilfully performed. The withdrawal of the troops was made almost without the knowledge of the enemy. Certainly General Lee did not know until he heard the intelligence of General Smith's attack upon Petersburg, to what point the Army of the Potomac was moving. He supposed, up to the last moment, that General Grant intended attacking Richmond by way of the river roads. General Warren, with his corps assisted in producing this impression by halting on the road through White Oak Swamp, and making a feint upon Richmond from that direction. The march of the army was thus completely covered from the enemy's observation.

The Ninth Corps was withdrawn with great secrecy. Even the retirement of the pickets was wholly unknown to the enemy, who continued for at least an hour after the departure of the Corps to fire artillery upon one of our vacant earthworks. The Corps moved out to Tunstall's Station, where it arrived about daylight on the 13th. The roads were filled with the trains of the army, which by some mistake, had got in the way of the marching columns. Considerable delay ensued, which the men improved by taking a little rest along the roadside. As soon as the way was cleared, the Corps was again put in motion, and, marching by way of Baltimore cross roads and Olive Church, gained a point about three-fourths of a mile from Sloane's Crossing of the Chickahominy about nightfall. The sixth corps was then crossing the river by a ponton bridge and the Ninth went into bivouac for the night. At an early hour the next morning, the Ninth Corps crossed the Chickahominy and marched on the 14th by way of Varden's, Clopton's, and Tyler's Mills, reaching the James river that evening and taking position on the right of the sixth corps. This position was fortified and the Corps remained there during the 15th. On the evening of the 15th, it crossed the James on a ponton bridge above Fort Powhattan, and immediately pushed on to Petersburg to participate in the operations of Generals Smith and Hancock. The sixth corps had been immediately in advance of the Ninth, but was now diverted to assist in an ineffectual movement upon the enemy's communications between Richmond and Petersburg. The second corps had been carried across by transports and ferry boats at Wilcox's Landing, landed at Windmill Point, and was now in front of Petersburg. The fifth corps followed the Ninth, and was also put *en route* for Petersburg. In the march of the Ninth a body of engineers under Major Morton of the staff led the van, General Willcox's division headed the main column and General Potter's brought up the rear. The entire movement was made by the whole army without casualty or molestation from the enemy. At ten o'clock on the morning of the 16th, the advance division had arrived at our lines before Petersburg awaiting orders for an assault. An hour or two afterwards the remainder of the command had come up, and at one o'clock in the afternoon, the entire Corps was placed in position upon the extreme left of the line.

The original design of General Meade was to attack the enemy at four o'clock in the afternoon. But some delay occurred and the assault was not made till six o'clock. The attack was delivered by General Barlow's division of General Hancock's corps. General Griffin's brigade, reporting to General Barlow, participated in this movement. The attack was not, however, attended with important results. General Griffin succeeded in securing a few rifle pits, and amid heavy skirmishing, the night came down upon the combatants. General Grant, not satisfied with previous operations, determined to make another attempt to carry the place by assault. During the night of the 16th, orders were issued to attack at an early hour on the morning of the 17th, to make trial of the enemy's defences, and if possible to secure them for ourselves.

General Potter's division was selected from the Ninth Corps for the assaulting column. General Ledlie was to support the attack with the first division. To General Griffin's brigade was assigned the post of honor and of danger, and to General Griffin himself was given the duty of planning and executing the immediate attack. Colonel Curtin's brigade was to support. General Griffin arranged the movement with great daring and skill. Under cover of the night, he led his troops to a ravine within a hundred yards of the enemy's position, and there formed his column of attack—his own brigade in two lines, the 17th Vermont, 11th New Hampshire, and 32d Maine in front, and the 6th and 9th New Hampshire, 31st Maine and 2d Maryland in support. Colonel Curtin formed his brigade with the 45th and 48th Pennsylvania, and 36th Massachusetts in front supported by the 7th Rhode Island, 2d New York Rifles and 58th Massachusetts. The enemy occupied an estate at the head of the ravine, belonging to a Mr. Shind, with his headquarters in the house, and his artillery commanding the approaches. So near were the enemy's lines, that only in whispers could the necessary orders be communicated. General Griffin enjoined the strictest silence upon his men, and ordered them, when advancing, not to fire a shot but to depend upon the bayonet for clearing the works. Even the canteens were placed inside the haversacks to prevent their rattling. At the first blush of the morning the word "forward!" was passed quietly along the column. The men sprang to their feet, and noiselessly, rapidly, vigorously moved upon the enemy—Griffin to the right, Curtin to the left. They burst upon him with the fury of a tornado. They took him completely by surprise. They swept his lines for a mile, gathering up arms, flags, cannon and prisoners all along their victorious pathway. A stand of colors, four pieces of artillery with their caissons and horses, fifteen hundred stands of small arms, a quantity of ammunition and six hundred prisoners were the fruits of this splendid charge. A wide breach was made in the enemy's lines, and it seemed as though the defences of Petersburg were within our grasp.* But the energetic movement of General Griffin was not followed up. Colonel Curtin had most gallantly done his part, and General Potter was promptly on the ground to direct the assault. But where were the supports? General Ledlie was not at hand with his division. Fallen timber and other obstructions lay across the way, and the men, stumbling over them in the darkness, made but slow progress. When the junction was finally made, it was too late to do any more than to secure the advantage already gained. Had the supporting division been present at time, a very brilliant and decisive victory would undoubtedly have been the result. As it was, General Potter could only maintain his position, pushing up his pickets and skirmishers close to the new line upon which the enemy had retired.

Not long after noon, General Willcox was ordered to attack. A little delay occurred in the formation of the troops and the direction of the assault. This being remedied, the troops were put in position and moved forward to the charge. General Hartranft's brigade dashed on to the attack in a specially vigorous and gallant style, and its left succeeded in reaching the enemy's main line of rifle pits. By some mischance the line was so deflected as to expose it to a tremendous fire both of musketry and artillery, which inflicted great loss upon this brave brigade. Notwithstanding the most resolute attempts, General Hartranft was compelled to withdraw his suffering troops, as his line was melting away beneath the hot fire of the enemy. Colonel Christ was more fortunate. His brigade secured a lodgement about midway between his first position of attack and the enemy's line. From this point all the efforts of the enemy could not push our tenacious troops. They held

---

*MS. Narrative of the 6th New Hampshire.

on in the midst of a murderous fire which sadly thinned their ranks but could not break their spirit, and received high encomium for their obstinate valor. In the afternoon General Ledlie made an attack, in which a part of Colonel Christ's brigade participated. One hundred prisoners and a stand of colors were captured, and a number of rifle pits carried. The position was held until late at night, when the enemy pressed down upon General Ledlie and forced his retirement from the line which he had gained.*

During this day of battle, the fighting was mostly done by the Ninth Corps. General Crawford's division of the fifth corps rendered General Ledlie an efficient support upon the left, and General Barlow of the second corps had given valuable assistance to General Hartranft. But beyond that, comparatively little had been done by the remainder of the army. The Ninth Corps, almost unassisted, had carried and now held the most advanced position of our lines in front of Petersburg. It was a brave and bloody exploit. Out of eighteen hundred and ninety officers and men in General Hartranft's brigade but about eleven hundred were ready for duty at the close of the day. Losses in other parts of the Corps were proportionate. But a very decided advantage had been gained, the Ninth Corps had proved its high and admirable efficiency, and had gained a position which threatened to make untenable the enemy's entire front line. During the afternoon, so well had our men done their work, that the batteries of the Corps were able to throw a few shells into the city of Petersburg itself.

On the 18th the Corps was again called into action. It was again successful. The enemy had fallen back to a point near the Norfolk and Petersburg Railroad and it became necessary to force him still further back and into nearer proximity to the

*Mr. Swinton in his imaginative way says (page 510) that "the enemy after dark leaped the breastwords Burnside had captured and drove him out." The truth is, that only that part of the line which General Ledlie's troops had captured was lost. General Potter's and Colonel Christ's conquest was still retained.

city. General Meade ordered a general assault at four o'clock in the morning, but a large proportion of the fighting again fell upon the Ninth Corps. General Willcox's division was to-day in the van of the attack, supported by General Crawford's division of the fifth corps. General Hartranft had the advance supported by Colonel Raulston's (late Colonel Christ's) brigade. The object was to dispossess the enemy of a piece of woods and the railroad cut which he held in force. The assault was vigorously made and was successfully carried through. The enemy was steadily but surely pushed back to the railroad, and after considerable fighting, he was dislodged from a portion of the ravine through which the road passed. The cut here was fifteen or twenty feet deep, with steep sides, in which "steps and holes had to be made to enable the troops to climb up on the bank." Very gallantly and creditably did the third division accomplish its difficult task, holding against all assaults the ground which it had gained, and fortifying extemporaneously with the rails, sleepers and ties which the men tore up from the track. Further operations were suspended until the afternoon, when after new combinations, the entire army was put in position for attack or support. The second corps furnished three brigades for the attacking force. The Ninth Corps supported this assault. The movement failed.

The brave men of the second corps did all that brave men could, but the enemy's lines could not be forced at the close of a wearisome, sultry summer's day. The fifth corps on the left was no more fortunate. The enemy retired to a fortified position in front and around Cemetery hill and there he bade defiance to our attacks. General Willcox, supported by Colonel Curtin's brigade, was a little more fortunate. For he succeeded in following up his advantage in the morning so well as to press the enemy still further back from his immediate front. He extended his lines well across the railroad, and even established himself in a position within one hundred and twenty-five yards of the enemy's salient work. It was gallantly done, though with great loss. But a thousand uninjured men were left in the ranks to intrench themselves when the night came on. This position was strengthened and made secure. It was the salient of our own lines during the entire subsequent siege of Petersburg. General Parke had the direction of the Corps during this day's action, and it is not less commendable to his ability than to the bravery of the troops, that General Burnside could justly say in his report, that "no better fighting has been done during the war, than was done by the divisions of Generals Potter and Willcox during this attack." During that night, General Potter made connections with the second corps on the right and the fifth on the left, holding the advance as an intrenched skirmish line. During the next few days the line in the immediate rear of the railroad was strongly intrenched and strengthened with traverses, abatis and covered ways. Afterwards two or three field works were built and armed. The skirmish line itself was so firmly strengthened in the course of the next week or two, and so well manned as to make it in effect a part of the main line.

The losses in the Corps during the operations of the 16th, 17th and 18th, had been especially severe. General Willcox's second brigade changed its commander three times on the 18th. Colonel Raulston of the 24th New York dismounted cavalry had succeeded Colonel Christ who had been wounded on the previous day. Colonel Raulston was shot at his post and Lieutenant Colonel Traverse of the 46th New York, who succeeded him, shared the same fate. Colonel Curtin of General Potter's division was severely wounded. Lieutenant Colonel George C. Barnes of the 20th Michigan, a gallant officer, who had greatly distinguished himself in previous actions, was mortally wounded while bravely leading on his men. He died on the 20th, greatly lamented by his fellow officers and the men of his command. Major Levant C. Rhines and Captain George C. Knight of the 1st Michigan sharpshooters fell on the 17th leaving an honorable record of their former bravery.

Among the great number of private soldiers who fell on this ensanguined field, the story of one has been preserved who is a very good representative of a large class of those who made up the rank and file of our volunteer army. Edward M. Schneider was a soldier in the 57th Massachusetts. He was the son of Rev. Mr. Schneider, a well known American missionary at Aintab. When the regiment was formed, he was a student at Phillips Academy, Andover, Mass., and but little more than seventeen years of age. He was a youth of great ambition, adventurous spirit, and a tender and affectionate nature. His patriotic feeling was extremely ardent, and against the wishes of his friends, he resolved upon a soldier's life. He was wounded at the North Anna, and was sent to Port Royal to be transferred to a hospital at Washington. But refusing this, he returned to his regiment at Cold Harbor. Among the very first, in the attack of the 17th of June, he was shot through the body and fell mortally wounded. When told that there was no hope, he said to the Chaplain of the regiment: "It is God's will. I wish you to write to my father and tell him that I have tried to do my duty to my country and to my God. I have a good many friends, schoolmates and companions. They will want to know where I am and how I am getting on. You can let them know that I am gone, and that I die content. And, Chaplain, the boys of the regiment—I want you to tell them to stand by the dear old flag! And there is my brother in the navy—write to him and tell him to stand by the flag and cling to the cross of Christ."* He lingered in great pain until Sunday morning, June 19th, when he died. He was one of many thousands—perhaps the expression ought to be hundreds of thousands—to be found throughout our entire army during the war, brave, intelligent, enthusiastic youth, the sons of educated and Christian parents, who early learned the lesson that duty was more imperative than affection, and devotion to principle of greater worth than personal safety and bodily life! The record of their lives, their courage, their death, is an illustrious vindication of the true character of the volunteer army of the United States.

* Coffin's Four Years of Fighting, p. 366.

But the greatest loss that fell upon the Ninth Corps was the death of Major James St. Clair Morton, chief engineer upon the staff of General Burnside. He was of a gallant, daring temperament, and, on one or two occasions during the campaign had led in person charges of the troops upon the enemy's intrenched lines. Always in the van, he had narrowly escaped with his life in former battles. On the 17th of June, he headed the advance of General Hartranft's brigade, and was killed while the troops were retiring from the attack. Major Morton was born in Philadelphia, Pa., September 24, 1829, and was the son of Dr. S. G. Morton, a distinguished physician of that city. He was appointed to the United States Military Academy at West Point at the age of eighteen, and graduated in 1851, the second in a class of forty-two members. He was assigned to the Corps of Engineers as Second Lieutenant, July 1, 1851. He was promoted to Captain, August 6, 1861, and to Major, July 3, 1863. On the 29th of November, 1862, he was commissioned a Brigadier General of Volunteers, but preferring his own department of service, he was mustered out of this appointment, November 7, 1863, and was remitted to his former rank in the Corps of Engineers.

From August 18, 1851, to May, 1852, Lieutenant Morton was employed in his corps upon Fort Sumter, and from May, 1852 to September, 1855, upon Fort Delaware. In 1856, he published "An Essay on Instruction in Engineering," and in 1857, "An Essay on a New System of Fortifications." He was assistant Professor of Engineering at West Point from September, 1855 to June, 1857; assistant Engineer in construction of fortifications at the mouth of New York harbor from June, 1857 to March, 1858; Engineer of the third light-house district of the Atlantic coast from March, 1858 to July, 1859; and Engineer in charge of the Potomac Aqueduct from July, 1859 to July, 1860. From the latter duty he was relieved and appointed Engineer of the expedition for the exploration of the coasts of Chiriqui from August, 1860 to the subsequent November, when he returned to Washington. He became the Superintendent of the fortifications on the Tortugas in April, 1861, and continued in charge till March, 1862. While engaged in the last named work, Captain Morton was prostrated by severe illness, from which he did not recover until the spring of 1862. When he entered into active service in May of that year, he was assigned to the staff of General Buell as Chief Engineer of the Army of the Ohio. In this position, he superintended the erection of the fortifications about the city of Nashville, and afterwards organized a pioneer and bridge brigade, which was found to be of the greatest service. General Rosecrans (who succeeded General Buell) himself an engineer of no small distinction, expressed the warmest approval both of this organization and of Captain Morton's subsequent fortification of Murfreesboro' and Chattanooga. Speaking of this brigade, General Rosecrans, in his report of the battle of Murfreesboro', says: "The efficiency and *esprit de corps* suddenly developed in this command, its gallant behavior in action, and the eminent service it is continually rendering the army, entitle both officers and men to special public notice and thanks, while they reflect the highest credit on the distinguished ability and capacity of Captain Morton, who will do honor to his promotion to a Brigadier General." Promoted to Brigadier General of Volunteers, he was engaged in the battle of Chickamauga, where he was wounded.

In October, 1863, Major Morton was relieved of his appointment on the staff of General Rosecrans, and soon after the reorganization of the Ninth Corps, he was appointed its Chief Engineer, very greatly to the satisfaction of General Burnside. Always prompt, energetic and trustworthy, he was conspicuous in every operation of the arduous campaign. General Burnside was strongly attached to him, having learned to hold his abilities in the highest estimation, and to depend upon him as one of his best, most intelligent and most reliable advisers. The other officers of the corps looked upon him as a gallant and skilful soldier. His death was keenly felt by all who had known him as a brilliant officer and a generous and genial friend. General Parke wrote of his deceased comrade in terms of warm and hearty commendation :—From the date of his appointment to the corps, May 18th, to the day of his death, Major Morton "performed the arduous and dangerous duties of his position with an activity, zeal and ability which often called forth the praise of his commanding general. He was noted in the Corps for his personal gallantry, and in the attack at the North Anna he took a conspicuous part, narrowly escaping death. On the morning of the 17th of June, he received orders from General Burnside to place the troops making the assault in their proper position, and to direct at what point they should strike the enemy's works. When this had been accomplished, feeling deeply interested in the success of the movement, he went forward with General Hartranft. When the attack failed, he was retiring with the troops when he was struck in the breast by a rifle ball and mortally wounded. Captain Shadley immediately went to him, but I believe he expired without a word. In his death, this Corps and his country lost a valuable officer, and his memory will long be cherished among those who were fortunate enough to have known him."

Major Morton's contributions to military literature were especially valuable, and were the result of close study and a wide experience. He was a vigorous writer, an original thinker, and an accomplished scholar in the special department to which he had devoted his time and thought. Major Morton's body was sent to his afflicted family in Philadelphia, where appropriate honors were paid to his heroic memory.

CHAPTER V.

THE MINE.

THE experience of the army in front of Petersburg induced General Grant to believe that the place could only be reduced by the slow process of a siege. He therefore decided to place the army of the James on the north and the Army of the Potomac on the south side of the James river, and in this way invest both Petersburg and Richmond. Parallels were accordingly laid out, traverses and covered ways built, trenches opened, earthworks of various sizes thrown up and armed, and all the different operations of a siege fairly entered upon. On the line which the Ninth Corps occupied were two batteries of two guns, one of four, one of six, two of eight, and in the centre, one of fourteen guns. Besides these were three mortar batteries. General Grant fixed his headquarters at City Point. Our lines extended from across the Jerusalem plank road in front of Petersburg to Deep Bottom, crossing the Appomattox and the James by means of ponton bridges. A force was also held at White House, and the York and Pamunkey rivers were patrolled by gunboats.

The enemy made one or two attempts during the summer to make diversions in other quarters, at one time pushing a considerable force into Pennsylvania and Maryland, and even attacking Fort Stevens, on the north side of the city of Washington. One party reached the Philadelphia, Wilmington and Baltimore Railroad, cut the telegraph wire and destroyed a portion of a bridge. Another party burned Chambersburg. But all such movements were insufficient to make General Grant give up his hold. The aggressive forces were swept away from the Capital, and General Lee found, before the summer had passed, that he could, by no exertion of his, loosen the gripe which General Grant had fixed upon the army of Northern Virginia, the rebel capital, and the fortunes of the "Southern Confederacy." An investment had been established which would not be raised until its object had been fully accomplished—the suppression of the rebellion.

On the 18th of June, the colored division of the Ninth Corps reported to General Meade, and was at once ordered to its own proper organization. General Ferrero had been separated from his brother officers of the Corps since the crossing of the Rapidan, and was now glad to renew his relations and come once more under the orders of his chief. During the interval, the division had been occupied in guarding the trains of the army—a necessary work, indeed, but somewhat troublesome, and especially lacking in that excitement of conflict which is the glory of the soldier's life. On the 6th of May, the division had been separated from the Ninth Corps, and placed successively under the orders of Generals Sedgwick and Sheridan, until the 17th. Then General Ferrero came under the direct command of the Lieutenant General himself, until the incorporation of the Ninth Corps with the Army of the Potomac. On the 9th, General Ferrero's command was strengthened by three regiments of cavalry—the 5th New York, the 3d New Jersey, and the 2d Ohio. These troops remained with him until the 10th of June, when the cavalry force was placed under the command of General Sheridan. From the 9th of May until the 17th, the fourth division occupied the plank road looking toward the old Wilderness tavern, covering the extreme right of the army, extending from Todd's tavern to Banks's ford. On the 17th, the division moved to Salem Church, near the main road to Fredericksburg. Here, on the afternoon of the 19th, it was drawn into the defence of our rear line against the attack made by General Ewell. The colored troops stood up well against the enemy and captured several prisoners.

The remainder of the record of the fourth division, up to the time of rejoining the corps, is simply that of the movement of the trains. On the 21st of May, the command was covering Fredericksburg and the roads leading thence to Bowling Green. On the 22d, it marched towards Bowling Green, and on the 23d, it moved to Milford Station. From that date to the 27th, it protected the trains of the army in the rear of the position on the North Anna. On the 27th, the division moved to Newtown; on the 28th, to Dunkirk, crossing the Mattapony; on the 29th, to the Pamunkey, near Hanovertown. On the 1st of June, the troops crossed the Pamunkey, and from the 2d to the 6th, covered the right of the army. From the 6th to the 12th, they covered the approaches from New Castle ferry, Hanovertown, Hawes's Shop and Bethesda Church. From the 12th to the 18th, they moved by easy stages by way of Tunstall's, New Kent Court House, Cole's ferry, and the ponton bridge across the James, to the lines of the army near Petersburg. The dismounted cavalry were left to guard the trains, and the fourth division prepared to participate in the more active work of soldiers. Through the remainder of the month of June and the most of July, the troops were occupied in the second line of trenches, and in active movements towards the left under Generals Hancock and Warren. While they were engaged in the trenches, they were also drilled in the movements necessary for an attack and occupation of the enemy's works. A strong feeling of pride and *esprit de corps* sprung up within the hearts of the blacks, and they began to think that they too might soon have the opportunity of winning some glory for their race and their country.

The presence of the colored soldiers, both in the eighteenth and the Ninth Corps, seemed to have the effect of rendering the enemy more spiteful than ever. Before the fourth division came, the closeness of the lines on the front of the corps rendered constant watchfulness imperative, and no day passed without some skirmishing between the opposing pickets. When the colored soldiers appeared, this practice seemed to increase. While, in front of the fifth corps, upon the left of our line, there was little or no picket firing, and the outposts of both armies were even disposed to be friendly, on the front of the Ninth, the firing was incessant, and in many cases fatal. General Potter in his report mentions that, when his division occupied the front lines, his losses averaged "some fourteen or fifteen officers and men killed and wounded per diem." The sharpshooters on either side were vigilant, and an exposure of any part of the person was the signal for an exchange of shots. The men, worn by hard marching, hard fighting and hard digging, took every precaution to shield themselves and sought cover at every opportunity. They made fire proofs of logs and earth, and, with tortuous covered ways and traverses, endeavored to secure themselves from the effects of the enemy's fire. The artillery and mortars on both sides were kept almost constantly at work.

Opposite the salient which the Ninth Corps occupied, the enemy had constructed a strong redoubt, situated a few hundred yards below the crest of "Cemetery Hill." In the rear of the redoubt, a ridge ran back nearly at right angles with the enemy's line, to the hill. This appeared to be a dominating position, and would, if carried, seriously threaten, if not entirely break up the enemy's lines. Was it possible to devise some bold plan, which promised success in an enterprise directed against this important point? An officer in General Potter's division, who had looked over the whole ground with a professional eye, thought that the enemy's redoubt might be destroyed. That officer was Lieutenant Colonel Henry Pleasants, of the 48th Pennsylvania—a regiment which was composed chiefly of miners from Schuylkill county. The soldiers, around their camp fires, had talked over the subject, and, at last, became so interested in the matter as to believe in the feasibility of running a mine under the intervening space between the line of the Ninth Corps and the enemy, with the design of exploding it immediately beneath the fort opposite. The distance to be mined was a little over five hundred feet. Lieutenant Colonel Pleasants was himself an experienced and skilful mining engineer, and, upon hearing the suggestion, consulted General Potter upon the subject. General Potter, on the 24th of June, laid the matter before General Burnside, who, after further consultation, directed that the work be commenced, and informed General Meade accordingly. The commanding general, however, was not favorably disposed towards such a plan. He did not consider the "location of the mine a proper one," as the point to be assaulted was commanded on both flanks by the enemy. Major J. C. Duane, Chief Engineer, also expressed an opinion not only unfavorable to the success of any such operation as General Burnside contemplated, but also somewhat derisive of its practicability. Yet with this opinion in mind, General Meade gave his official sanction to the continuance of the work, and expressed the hope that it "might at some time result in forming an important part in the operations" of the army. Having thus secured the reluctant authority of the commanding general, Lieutenant Colonel Pleasants proceeded with his task. He commenced work at twelve o'clock meridian, on the 25th of June.

At headquarters, the design of an assault was still entertained. General Grant could hardly endure the long delays of the necessary siege, and watched his opportunity for a *coup de main*. Meanwhile, Lieutenant Colonel Pleasants and men wrought with such earnestness and perseverance that, by the 23d day of July, a main gallery of five hundred and ten and eight-tenths feet in length was constructed, with two lateral galleries at the further end, one of thirty-seven, the other of thirty-eight feet in length. The fact was reported to the headquarters of the Army of the Potomac. Agreeably to General Burnside's plan, four magazines were to be placed in each of these lateral galleries, to be established at intervals equidistant from each other, two upon each side of the gallery, and to be charged with about half or three-fifths of a ton of powder each. The magazines were to be connected by troughs of powder with each other and with the main gallery, five or six fuses and two wires were to be run out to the mouth of the mine, there to be fired—the fuses in the ordinary way, the wires to be charged by a galvanic battery. It was supposed by General Burnside that these preparations would insure the explosion of the mine at the appointed moment, and he accordingly made his requisitions upon the proper officers for the needful supplies. After some delay, the powder for furnishing the magazines—about eight thousand pounds—was forwarded, and the ten days following the 18th were occupied in strengthening the mine and charging the magazines. The powder was put into the magazines on the 27th of July, three lines of fuses were laid for a distance of ninety-eight feet, and the mine was tamped during the night of the 27th and through the day on the 28th—the work ending at six o'clock in the afternoon.

Lieutenant Colonel Pleasants's account of the construction of his mine, as given in his report, is very interesting. It seems that no general officers encouraged the work but Generals Burnside and Potter. He was obliged to carry out the earth in cracker boxes, and to cut down bushes to cover it from the sight of the enemy. He could not obtain a theodolite without sending to Washington, although there was a very good one at the headquarters of the Army. The excavation was ventilated by means of a tube made of lumber picked up about the camps or taken from a rebel bridge and a saw mill, some five or six miles distant. The ground through which the mine was dug was in some places very wet and difficult to work. At one time, the timber gave way, and the gallery was nearly closed. When this was repaired and the work was carried forward, the soldiers were obliged to excavate a stratum of marl very hard to manage. Lieutenant Colonel Pleasants then ran an inclined plane rising thirteen and a half feet in a hundred. The timbers to prop the mine were previously prepared and were put up by hand without noise of hammer or tool. The picks were the common army picks straightened for use. The mine was thus built in less than one month after the beginning was made. The whole amount of material excavated was eighteen thousand cubic feet. The magazines were placed exactly underneath the enemy's fort. The enemy had already suspected the existence of the work somewhere in the neighborhood of our operations, and began to countermine. The soldiers below could hear the soldiers above at their daily drill and work.

Everything thus far wore a promising aspect. But just here an omission was made which came nigh being fatal to the whole enterprise. No adequate fuses were supplied. No wires at all were furnished. The fuses that were expected to explode a mine five hundred feet in length were sent in parts and pieces—some of them but ten feet long—and the only materials that could be obtained to splice the pieces were some old blankets. It was evident that the plan was meeting with but little approbation at headquarters, and it might be surmised by an ordinary observer, that a failure of the attempt instead of its success was to be expected, as a justification of the adverse opinion which had already been expressed respecting the undertaking.

During this time, the remainder of the army was not suffered to remain idle. Frequent demonstrations and attacks were made on both sides of the James, with the double purpose of harassing the enemy and of prolonging our lines of circumvallation. General Grant, possibly disturbed from his accustomed equanimity by the enemy's unexpected persistence in defence, and apparently impatient for action, consulted General Meade, early in July, as to the practicability of an assault. General Meade addressed a letter to his corps commanders on the subject. In addressing General Burnside, on the 3d of July, he desired an expression of opinion as to the feasibility of an assault at any point in front of the Ninth Corps, to be made by the second and sixth in conjunction with the Ninth. General Burnside replied on the same day, that if the question was between making an immediate assault and a change of operations, he was in favor of attacking then. If the siege was to continue, he thought it best to wait until the mine was finished. Then he added these words: "If the assault be made now I think we have a fair chance of success, provided my Corps can make the attack, and it is left to me to say when and how the other two corps shall come in to my support." General Meade saw fit to interpret this language as a reflection upon his skill and ability in commanding the Army of the Potomac and replied as follows: "Should it be determined to employ the army under my command in offensive operations on your front, I shall exercise the prerogative of my position to control and direct the same, receiving, gladly, at all times such suggestions as you may think proper to make." Then he added: "I consider these remarks necessary in consequence of certain conditions which you have thought proper to attach to your opinion, acceding to which in advance would not, in my judgment, be consistent with my position as commanding general of this army."

General Burnside was amazed that General Meade should put such a construction upon language so innocent as that which had been used. He accordingly hastened to remove the impression which had been made upon the mind of his commanding officer. On the 4th of July, he wrote to General Meade in the following terms: "I assure you in all candor, that I never dreamed of implying any lack of confidence in your ability to do all that is necessary in any grand movement, which may be undertaken by your army. Were you to personally direct an attack from my front, I would feel the utmost confidence; and were I called upon to support an attack from the front of the second or sixth corps, directed by yourself, or by either of the commanders of these corps, I would do it with confidence and cheerfulness. It is hardly necessary for me to say, that I have had the utmost faith in your ability to handle troops, ever since my acquaintance with you in the Army of the Potomac, and certainly accord to you a much higher position in the art of war than I possess; and I, at the same time, entertain the greatest respect for the skill of the two gentlemen commanding the second and sixth army corps. My duty to the country, to you, and to myself, forbids that I should for a moment assume to embarrass you or them, by an assumption of position or authority. I simply desired to ask the privilege of calling upon them for support at such times, and at such points, as I thought advisable. I would gladly accord to either of them the same support and would be glad to have either of them lead the attack, but it would have been obviously improper for me to have suggested that any other corps than my own should make the attack in my front. What I asked, in reference to calling upon the other corps for support, is only what I have been called upon to do, and have cheerfully done myself, in regard to other corps commanders." Gener al Meade, particularly sensitive in regard to every punctilio of position and rank, could not appreciate the generous nature of the man whom he had thus unjustly suspected; and was not disposed to regard with complete satisfaction the success of General Burnside's operations. Yet he seemed to be somewhat ashamed of the illiberal construction which he had put upon his corps commander's words, and in his reply he wrote: "I am glad to find that there was no intention on your part to ask for any more authority and command than you have a perfect right to expect under existing circumstances. I did not infer that you had any want of confidence in me. I am very grateful for your good opinion as expressed, and shall earnestly try to merit its continuance." Notwithstanding this disclaimer, it became evident, from subsequent events, that General Meade had not forgotten the correspondence.

On the 26th, General Meade called upon General Burnside for a detailed statement of his plan of attack. General Burnsiee immediately submitted it. "My plan would be," he writes, "to explode the mine just before daylight in the morning, or at about five o'clock in the afternoon. Mass the two brigades of the colored division in rear of my first line, in columns of division—'double columns closed in mass,' 'the head of each brigade resting on the front line,'—and as soon as the explosion has taken place, move them forward with instructions for the division to take half-distance. As soon as the leading regiments of the two brigades pass through the gap in the enemy's line, the leading regiment of the right brigade should come into line perpendicular to the enemy's line by the 'right companies on the right into line, wheel,' the 'left companies on the right into line,' and proceed at once down the line of the enemy's works as rapidly as possible; and the leading regiment of the left brigade to execute the reverse movement to the left, moving up the enemy's line. The remainder of the columns to move directly towards the crest in front as rapidly as possible, diverging in such a way as to enable them to deploy into columns of regiments, the right column making as nearly as possible for Cemetery Hill. These columns to be followed by the other divisions of this Corps as soon as they can be thrown in. This would involve the necessity of relieving these divisions by other troops before the movement and of holding columns of other troops in readiness to take our place on the crest in case we gain it and sweep down it. It would, in my opinion, be advisable, if we succeed in gaining the crest, to throw the colored division right into the town. There is a necessity of the coöperation, at least in the way of artillery, of the troops on our right and left. Of the extent of this you will necessarily be the judge."

This plan in brief was, to form two columns and to charge with them through the breach caused by the explosion of the mine, then to sweep along the enemy's line right and left, clearing away the artillery and infantry by attacking in the flank and rear—other columns to make for the crest, and the rest of the Army to coöperate. In accordance with this plan, General Ferrero, in command of the colored division, was instructed, that he would be required to lead the attack when it should be ordered, and he was directed to drill his troops accordingly. He examined the ground and decided upon his methods of advance, which were not to go directly into the crater formed by the explosion, but rather upon one side of it; and then to take the enemy in flank and reverse. He informed his officers and men that they would be called upon to make an important assault and proceeded to drill his division, with a view to familiarizing the troops with the work, which they were expected to perform. For three weeks, in intervals of other duty, they were carefully trained in the various movements, the charging upon earthworks, the wheeling by the right and left, the deployment and other details of the expected operation. The intelligence was received with delight. The drill was performed with alacrity. The soldiers of the colored division, desirous of emulating their brethren of the eighteenth corps in the army of the James, felt that the hour, which they had long expected, had now come, or was fast approaching. They would gain a name and a position in the Army of the Potomac. Selected for the assault, they would show themselves worthy of the honor. They would wipe off whatever reproach an ill-judged prejudice might have cast upon them, and would prove themselves brave men, demanding the respect which brave men deserve.

There were two reasons which influenced General Burnside in his choice of the storming party. He had early expressed his confidence in the soldierly capabilities of colored men, and he now wished to give them an opportunity to justify his good opinion. His white troops moreover had been greatly exposed through the whole campaign, had suffered severely and had been so much under the fire of the sharpshooters, that "it had become a second nature with them to dodge a bullet."* The colored troops had not been so much exposed, and had already shown their steadiness under fire, in one or two pretty severe skirmishes in which they had previously been engaged. General Burnside hoped much from them, and would not have been disappointed had he been allowed to carry out his plan of attack. There was still another reason for the inefficiency of the white troops. They were fairly exhausted with unintermitted marching, fighting and skirmishing. The Ninth Corps had had no rest from the start, but had been subjected to un-

*General Ferrero's testimony before Committee on Conduct of the War.

ceasing labor in most perilous positions. Armies are not mere machines. They are composed of ordinary flesh and blood. General Burnside wished to use his freshest troops.

On the 24th, General Grant again desired that an attempt should be made to assault the enemy's lines at some point, but was finally persuaded by General Meade to wait for a few days for a more favorable opportunity. On the 26th General Burnside's plan of attack was presented. By this time General Meade had come to the conclusion that larger results were to be expected from the mine than he had at first supposed. Now he had cause to think, "that the explosion of the mine and the subsequent assault on the crest would be successful, and would be followed by results, which would have consisted in the capture of the whole of the enemy's artillery and a greater part of his infantry."* All that was necessary for him to do therefore was, to approve General Burnside's plan of attack, to order the coöperation of the other corps, to repair to the front to take command of the entire army in person, and reap the harvest of glory, which his subordinates had so carefully prepared for his ingathering. Yet he did not approve General Burnside's plan, or choose to adopt this plain course. Why he did not it is impossible to say. Was it because he did not wish that the anticipated success might be the result of another's combinations, but rather desired that it should come from some original design of his own? Or did he have some prejudice against the capacity of colored troops? Or was he determined not to allow General Burnside any discretion in the matter, but to make manifest the supreme authority of the commanding general of an army? The reason which General Meade gave before the Committee on the Conduct of the War, for his rejection of General Burnside's plan, was that "as this was an operation which I knew beforehand was one requiring the very best troops, I thought it impolitic to trust it to a division of whose reliability we had no evidence." The commander of an army

*General Meade's Testimony before Committee on Conduct of War, in Attack on Petersburg, p. 52.

must of necessity judge of the reliability of his troops. If he does not consider them able or trustworthy, it is his duty to keep them out of action. Yet the immediate commander of a corps or of a division is presumed to know the capabilities of his soldiers better than an officer further removed from them. If General Burnside was willing to trust his colored division, it would seem like a reflection upon his good judgment to disapprove his opinion. Whatever might have been the motives of General Meade, the fact remains that he did not agree with General Burnside's views upon the subject, and changed the entire plan of operations at so late an hour as to make a remedy for its derangement almost wholly impracticable.

On the 28th General Meade had an interview with General Burnside, in which the whole subject was discussed. General Meade urged that the colored troops were not so reliable for such an assault as was contemplated, as the white troops of the Ninth Corps. The operation was to be a *coup de main*, the assaulting column was to be as a forlorn hope, such as are put in breaches, and the assault ought to be made with the best troops. General Burnside argued—in accordance with what has already been stated—that his white troops were not in proper condition to head an attack of the kind. They had been exposed for forty days to a ceaseless fire and had acquired the habit of sheltering themselves from the enemy's missiles. Moreover, they were worn down by excessive labor, watchings and cares. Their officers had not expected to make an assault—knowing that the colored division had been selected for that purpose—and had not examined the ground. The colored troops on the contrary were fresh and strong, their ranks full, their morale unexceptionable, and their spirits elated by the thought of the approaching conflict. They had been drilled with especial reference to this very movement, and their officers were conversant with all its details, the ground to be traversed, and the work to be done. General Meade could not be turned from his purpose of changing the order of assault, but finally agreed to submit the matter to General Grant. That officer concurred with General Meade, having had no opportunity of hearing the other side of the case presented by General Burnside in person.*

The colored troops were ruled out—very much to the disappointment of themselves, their own commander, and General Burnside. The decision was made known to General Burnside not far from noon on the 29th. General Meade at the same time called at General Burnside's headquarters, where he met the three commanders of the white divisions of the Ninth Corps. On the day previous, he had told General Burnside at an interview which the two officers had at General Meade's headquarters, that he did not approve the order of the formation of the attacking column, "because," as General Burnside testifies, "he was satisfied that we would not be able, in the face of the enemy, to make the movements which were contemplated, to the right and left; and that he was of the opinion that the troops should move directly to the crest without attempting these side movements." On the occasion of the interview with the division commanders on the 29th, General Meade declared, that "there were two things to be done, namely, that we should go up promptly and take the crest." General Meade seemed to have but one plan of action. That was to "rush for the crest." These words he repeated in more than one order on the day of battle. "Don't lose time in making formations," he said, "but rush for the crest."

There seems to have been a little discrepancy in General Meade's recollection of the discussion which took place respecting General Burnside's formation of the assaulting column. As

*General Grant in his testimony before the Committee on the Conduct of the War had the frankness to say, that "General Burnside wanted to put his colored division in front, and *I believe if he had done so it would have been a success*. Still, I agreed with General Meade in his objection to that plan. General Meade said, that if we put the colored troops in front, and it should prove a failure, it would then be said, and very properly, that we were shoving those people ahead to get killed because we did not care anything about them. But that could not be said, if we put white troops in front." It is to be observed, however, that General Meade gave a different reason from that to the Committee, when he was stating why he disapproved General Burnside's plan of attack.

to General Burnside's "tactical formation," he testified before the Committee on the Conduct of the War, "and what he was to do with his troops, I made no objection." "The only objection I intended to make to" his "plan was to the use of the colored troops in advance."* But before the Court of inquiry which, after the battle investigated the whole affair, General Meade testified as follows: "I saw Potter, Ledlie and Willcox and I referred in the presence of those gentlemen to the tactical manœuvres to be made between that crater and the crest—that the only thing to be done was to rush for the crest, and take it immediately after the explosion had taken place; and that they might rest assured that any attempt to take time to form their troops would result in a repulse."† No other conclusion can be reached than that General Meade did object to General Burnside's "tactical formation," and that the entire plan of attack, which had been carefully prepared, was disapproved in all its details. In this situation General Burnside and his division commanders found themselves on the afternoon of the 29th of July.

The decision of General Meade, unexpected as it was, caused no little embarrassment to the officers of the Ninth Corps. The mine was to be exploded at an early hour on the following morning. The colored troops were not to be used in the advance. What division should be selected to take their place? So far as the men were concerned there was little choice between them. There were no special reasons for selecting one in preference to another. Each was as brave as the other. All had been about equally engaged in the very arduous service of the campaign and the siege. General Burnside said to his division commanders: "Gentlemen, there are certain reasons why either one of you should lead the attack. Your division, General Willcox, and yours, General Potter, are both near the point of assault, and it will require less time to put either of them into position, than to bring up General Ledlie's division.

---

*Attack on Petersburg, p. 44. †Attack on Petersburg, pp. 57, 143.

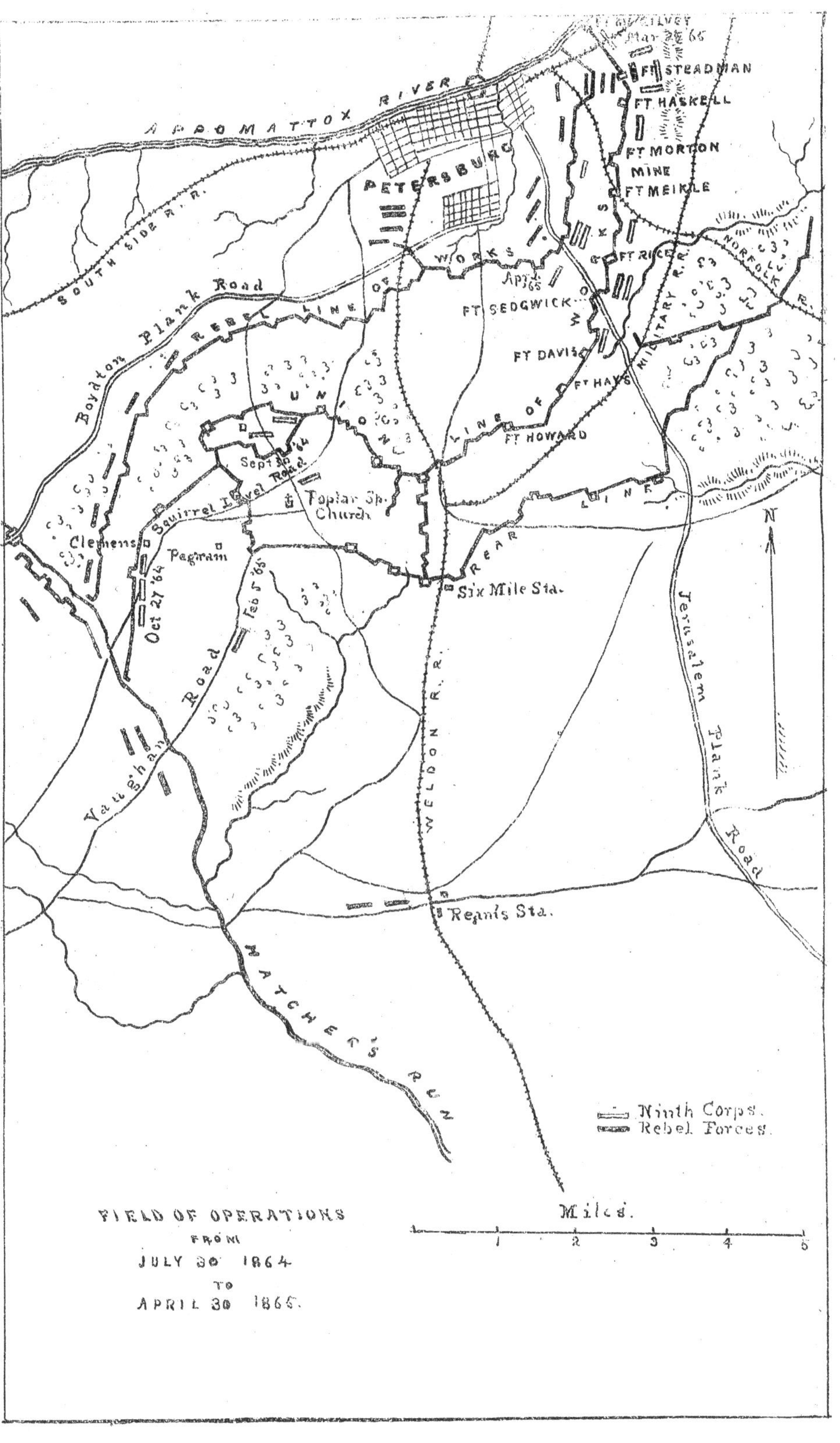
APPOMATTOX RIVER
PETERSBURG
FT STEADMAN
FT HASKELL
FT MORTON
MINE
FT MEIKLE
FT RICE
SOUTH SIDE R.R.
NORFOLK R.R.
MILITARY R.R.
Boydton Plank Road
REBEL LINE OF WORKS
Apr 2 '65
FT SEDGWICK
FT DAVIS
FT HAYS
FT HOWARD
UNION LINE OF WORKS
Sept 30 '64
Squirrel Level Road
Poplar Sp. Church
Clemens
Pegram
Oct 27 '64
Feb 5 '65
REAR LINE
Six Mile Sta.
Vaughan Road
WELDON R.R.
Jerusalem Plank Road
Reams Sta.
HATCHER'S RUN
N
Ninth Corps.
Rebel Forces.
Miles.
1
2
3
4
5
FIELD OF OPERATIONS
FROM
JULY 30 1864
TO
APRIL 30 1865

But, General Ledlie, the men of your division have not been in such close proximity to the enemy as those of the other two, and have not had quite so hard work as they. There is really no overpowering reason why either of you should be selected or excluded. Why not draw lots for the position and thus determine who shall make the assault?" No objection was made, lots were drawn, and the choice fell upon General Ledlie—most unfortunately, as was afterwards thought by General Grant, who considered him an "inefficient" officer. General Ledlie was immediately directed by General Burnside to reconnoitre the ground and prepare for the attack. He afterwards reported, that he had attended to that duty, and only waited for darkness and the relieving troops, to take position for the duties of the coming day.

General Meade issued his battle order: "1. As soon as it is dark, Major General Burnside, commanding Ninth Corps, will withdraw his two brigades under General White,* occupying the intrenchments between the plank and Norfolk roads, and bring them to his front. Care will be taken not to interfere with the troops of the eighteenth corps moving into their position in rear of the Ninth Corps. General Burnside will form his troops for assaulting the enemy's works at daylight of the 30th, prepare his parapets and abatis for the passage of the columns, and have the pioneers equipped for work in opening passages for artillery, destroying enemy's abatis, &c., and the intrenching tools distributed for effecting lodgements, &c.

"8. At half-past three in the morning of the 30th, Major General Burnside will spring his mine, and his assaulting columns will immediately move rapidly upon the breach, seize the crest in the rear, and effect a lodgement there. He will be

---

*General Julius White—favorably known as the commander of a division in the twenty-third corps in East Tennessee—came to General Burnside in July and was assigned to duty in the Ninth Corps. At this time he was in command of the fourth division in the temporary absence of General Ferrero, who was away for a few days on leave General Ferrero returned to camp on the 29th, and General White was appointed Chief of Staff during the day of battle. General Parke was at the time disabled from service by sickness.

followed by Major General Ord, who will support him on the right, directing his movement to the crest indicated, and by Major General Warren, who will support him on the left."

The other corps commanders were directed to move their troops in accordance with the above order. General Warren, of the fifth corps, was to "concentrate all his available forces on his right and hold them prepared to support the attack of the Ninth Corps." General Ord, of the eighteenth corps, was to form his command in the rear of the Ninth Corps and be prepared to support General Burnside. General Hancock, of the second corps, was to move from Deep Bottom, where he had been making a feigned attack "to the rear of the intrenchments held by the eighteenth corps, and be prepared to follow up the assaulting and supporting columns." General Sheridan, with the entire cavalry of the army, was to move against the enemy's right below Petersburg. Engineer officers were to be detailed for each corps, ponton trains were to be prepared, supplies of intrenching materials provided, field artillery to be got in readiness, and all the guns along the line were to open upon those points in the enemy's line that commanded the ground over which our troops were to move. Promptitude, rapidity of execution, and cordial coöperation were commended to the officers and men. Headquarters of the Army of the Potomac for the day were to be established at the headquarters of the Ninth Corps in the rear.

General Burnside issued his battle order:

"1. The mine will be exploded to-morrow morning, at half-past three, by Colonel Pleasants.

"2. General Ledlie will, immediately upon the explosion of the mine, move his division forward as directed by verbal orders, and if possible crown the crest at the point known as Cemetery Hill, occupying, if possible, the cemetery.

"3. General Willcox will move his division forward as soon as possible after General Ledlie has passed through the first line of the enemy's works, bearing off to the left so as to effectually protect the left flank of General Ledlie's column, and make a lodgement, if possible, on the Jerusalem plank road to the left of General Ledlie's division.

"4. General Potter will move his division forward to the right of General Ledlie's division as soon as it is apparent that he will not interfere with the movements of General Willcox's division, and will, as near as possible, protect the right flank of General Ledlie from any attack on that quarter, and establish a line on the crest of a ravine, which seems to run from the Cemetery Hill nearly at right angles to the enemy's main line directly in our front.

"5. General Ferrero will move his division immediately after General Willcox's until he reaches our present advanced line, where he will remain until the ground in his front is entirely cleared by the other three divisions, when he will move forward over the same ground that General Ledlie moved over, will pass through our line, and, if possible, move down and occupy the village to the right."

The formations and movements of the troops had already been explained in personal interviews of General Burnside and his officers. Headquarters of the Ninth Corps for the day were to be at the fourteen gun battery in the centre of our position in front. Such was the state of affairs as the 29th of July closed upon the intrenched camps.

The hours had fled apace. The day was now spent, and but little time remained. General Ord was so slow in coming up to relieve the troops of the Ninth Corps in the trenches, that at nine and three-quarters o'clock in the evening, General Meade ordered the assaulting column to be formed without reference to General Ord's movements, thus leaving the trenches vacant. At half past two o'clock on the morning of the 30th, General Ledlie's division began its formation, and passed on to the designated place of its *débouché* for the attack. It was but an hour and a half to daylight. It was but an hour to the time of action. Certainly it was an anxious night to the commander of the Ninth Corps. All his plans had been frustrated by the superior authority of his commanding general. The mine, which had been constructed under such discouraging circumstances, had finally been regarded, though with evident reluctance, as promising a success. Its explosion would result in a magnificent triumph or a miserable disaster. The one would be for the glory of General Meade. The other would be visited upon the head of the unfortunate corps commander who had taken the enterprise in hand. General Burnside left his headquarters in the rear, repaired to the front of the line and watched for the morning.

At quarter past three o'clock, the fuses were fired. All eyes were turned to the rebel fort opposite, beneath which eight thousand pounds of powder were suddenly to be ignited. In the gray of the morning it was discernible but three hundred feet distant. The garrison was sleeping in fancied security. The sentinels slowly paced their rounds, without a suspicion of the thinness of the crust which lay between them and the awful chasm below. Our own troops, lying upon their arms in unbroken silence, or with an occasional murmur, stilled at once by the whispered word of command, looked for the eventful moment of attack to arrive. A quarter of an hour passed—a half hour, and there was no report. Four o'clock came, and the sky began to brighten in the east. The rebel garrison was bestirring itself. The rebel lines gradually assumed once more the appearance of life. The sharpshooters, prepared for new victims, began to pick off those of our men who came within the range of their deadly aim. Another day of siege was dawning. Still there was no explosion. What could it mean?

The fuses had failed. The dampness had penetrated to the place where the parts had been spliced together, and the powder would not burn. Two men, Lieutenant Jacob Douty and Sergeant, afterwards promoted to Lieutenant, Henry Rees of the 48th Pennsylvania, volunteered to go into the mine to ascertain where the fuses had failed, to put them once again in order, and to relight them. At quarter past four o'clock, they bravely entered the mine, rearranged the fuses and again lighted them. In the meantime, General Meade had arrived at the permanent headquarters of the Ninth Corps, in the grove about a mile in the rear of our main line, had comfortably bestowed himself with General Grant in company, and sent two aides de camp to General Burnside to transmit all necessary information. Not being able to see anything that was going forward, and not hearing any report, General Meade became somewhat impatient. He was not in an amiable mood, and at fifteen minutes past four o'clock, he telegraphed to General Burnside to know what was the cause of the delay. General Burnside was too busy in remedying the failure already incurred to reply immediately—expected, indeed, that before the despatch could be sent the explosion would take place. General Meade ill-naturedly telegraphed the operator to know where General Burnside was. At half past four, the commanding general became still more impatient, and was on the point of ordering an immediate assault upon the enemy's works, without reference to the mine. Five minutes later, he did order the assault.

At precisely sixteen minutes before five o'clock, the mine exploded. Then ensued a scene which beggars description. The ground heaved and trembled. A terrific sound, like the noise of great thunders, burst forth upon the morning air. Huge masses of earth, mingled with cannon, caissons, camp equipage, and human bodies, were thrown up. It seemed like a mountain reversed, enveloped in clouds of smoke, sand and dust, upheaved by the explosion of four tons of powder. A moment more, and all that was left of a six gun battery and its garrison of two hundred men and more, was a great crater, two hundred feet long, fifty wide, and twenty-five deep, with the *debris* of the material of what had been one of the strongest of the enemy's works. The effect upon the rebel forces in the immediate vicinity was wonderful. Some seemed paralyzed with astonishment and fear. Others fled from their works as though they thought that the entire line was mined, and that all would be involved in a common destruction.

Now was the time for action. Forward went General Ledlie's column, with Colonel Marshall's brigade in advance. The parapets were surmounted, the abatis was quickly removed, and the division prepared to pass over the intervening ground and charge through the still smoking ruins to gain the crest beyond. But here the leading brigade made a temporary halt. It was said at the time, that our men suspected a counter mine, and were themselves shocked by the terrible scene which they had witnessed. It was, however, but momentary. The men at once recovered, pushed forward, and in less than a quarter of an hour the entire division was out of its entrenchments, and was advancing gallantly towards the enemy's line. The ground was somewhat difficult to cross over, but the troops pushed steadily on with soldierly bearing, overcoming all the obstacles before them. They reached the edge of the crater, passed down into the chasm, and attempted to make their way through the yielding sand, the broken clay and the masses of rubbish that were scattered everywhere about. The enemy's lines on either side and beyond were found to be very complex, intricate and involved. Many of the enemy's men were lying among the ruins, half buried, and vainly trying to free themselves. They called for mercy and for help. The soldiers stopped to take prisoners, to dig out guns and other materiel. Their division commander was not with them. Of the brigade commanders, General Bartlett, disabled by the loss of a leg in a previous battle in the peninsular campaign, but otherwise a most efficient, brave and meritorious officer, could not move with great facility, and Colonel Marshall was hardly equal to the management of a large command. There was no responsible head. The ranks were broken, the regimental organizations could not be preserved, the troops were becoming confused, the officers stopped to form anew the disordered lines. The 2d Pennsylvania heavy artillery endeavored to extricate itself, and did eventually succeed in advancing a hundred yards beyond the crater, but, finding itself without support, withdrew.

Precious time was passing. The enemy was recovering from his surprise. Our artillery, which had opened along our entire line immediately after the explosion of the mine, began to receive a spirited response. The enemy's men went back to their guns. They gathered on the crest, and soon brought to bear upon our troops a fire in front from the Cemetery hill and an enfilading and cross fire from their guns in battery. Our own artillery could not altogether silence or overcome this fire in flank. Our men in the crater were checked, felt the enemy's fire, sought cover, began to intrench. The movement up and down the enemy's lines had been disapproved and the advance movement could not now be made except with extreme difficulty.

In the mean time, General Potter was doing all that a brave man could to put his division into the action, where it could accomplish the most decisive results. General Griffin's brigade had been massed between the railroad and the advanced line, and in anticipation of the attack, General Griffin was ordered to deploy a line of skirmishers to the right of the crater. In case General Ledlie moved forward successfully, General Griffin was to advance his skirmishers to the right and follow with the main body about parallel with General Ledlie's line of advance. These directions were carefnlly followed. General Griffin pressed forward and struck the enemy's line immediately to the right of the crater. He found that the point at which he entered was difficult of penetration. The line was defended by *chevaux de frise* of pointed stakes, traverses and other appliances, and he was obliged to fight his way along hand to hand. He succeeded, however, in securing about two hundred yards of rifle pits. He advanced even beyond these towards the crest for two hundred yards further, but was there checked. A part of the second brigade under Colonel Z. R. Bliss of the 7th Rhode Island followed the first and, becoming engaged with the enemy, afforded very important aid to General Griffin in his movement. Two regiments passed into the crater, turned to the right and swept down the line for a considerable distance. One of General Potter's regiments even reached a point within twenty or thirty yards of the enemy's battery on the right.

General Willcox on his part directed his column to the left and his second brigade succeeded in occupying about one hundred yards of the enemy's rifle pits in that direction. The greater part of the division, however, followed General Ledlie's troops and became mingled with them amid the confusion that was beginning to prevail. The result which General Burnside had feared now became manifest. The men began to shelter themselves from the fire of the foe instead of pushing boldly forward and overcoming it. Each division had been accompanied by a regiment equipped as engineers, and their intrenching tools came into requisition for protection against the enemy. General Burnside, following General Meade's directions, had urged upon his division commanders the necessity of making for the crest. But in the crowded state of the crater almost any kind of movement became exceedingly difficult. Still the attempt was made. Some of our men struggled through the melee and climbed the crater's side. They stood upon the further edge. There they encountered a severe and destructive fire of shrapnel and canister from a battery which the enemy had posted on the crest.

Such was the condition of things at forty minutes past five o'clock. General Burnside reported to General Meade, that the enemy's first line and the breach were occupied, and that he should "endeavor to push forward to the crest as rapidly as possible." About the same time General Meade intercepted a despatch from Lieutenant Colonel Loring to General Burnside to the effect, that General Ledlie's troops could not be induced to advance. He immediately directed General Burnside to push forward "all his troops to the crest at once," and to call upon General Ord "to move forward his troops at once." The order was short and peremptory. But how could it be executed? General Ord's command—according to General Meade's own order—was massed in the rear of the Ninth Corps. The crater and the space between that and our lines was already filled with men. General Ord found that he could do nothing then; while the troops that had already gone forward and the wounded returning choked the passage, through which he was expected to move.

At six o'clock, General Meade sent an order to General Burnside to push his "men forward at all hazards, white and black," and "not to lose time in making formations, but rush for the crest." At the same hour, he ordered General Ord directly to move forward his "corps rapidly to the crest of the hill, independently of General Burnside's troops and make a lodgement there." General Ord made an attempt to obey this order. General Turner, commanding a division then attached to General Ord's corps, at half past six began his movement. His order was to "to follow Potter's division and move out to the right." He gradually drew his troops out of the lines from the rear, got them to the front by the covered way leading to our advanced line, and sent them forward. At seven o'clock the head of his "column reached the point at which our assaulting column had passed through our lines." He received a second order from General Ord to move out to the right. He found it very difficult so to do owing to the peculiarly broken character of the ground to be passed over. He succeeded after much effort in pushing forward his first brigade, which pressed up to the enemy's lines and occupied a position upon General Potter's right. General Turner's design was to move his first brigade down the enemy's lines while the second brigade marched out of the trenches in support. The second brigade was accordingly formed for that purpose, and the third brigade was massed for attack in case any favorable opportunity should offer or the exigency should demand.*

While these movements were making in the rear, General Potter was endeavoring to remedy the disordered state of affairs in the crater. He felt convinced that there were too many men in that exposed situation, and he knew that their

*General Turner's testimony, Attack on Petersburg, pp. 133, 134, 135.

movements were hampered by their crowded condition. He thought that a diversion should be made upon the right or left. General Burnside, receiving the direct order of General Meade to push forward to the crest, at once transmitted it to General Potter. General Potter in his turn was pressing his division forward and attempted to gain the crest. It was impossible. The enemy's fire was very severe, and told fearfully among our troops. The mortar batteries had now secured the range of our position and were dropping shells into the crater with great accuracy and execution. To send more men in seemed like sending them to certain destruction.

But General Meade's order of six o'clock contemplated no discretion on the part of the commander of the Ninth Corps. Nothing could be more clear. Nothing could be more imperative. "Our chance is now; push your men forward, white and black." Such were the terms. They could not be evaded. General Burnside accordingly directed General Ferrero to put in his division. Lieutenant Colonel Loring, who was standing by General Ferrero at the time the order was received, took the liberty as the senior staff-officer present to countermand the order, until he could consult General Burnside in regard to the matter. But General Burnside had no option but to obey. The order was accordingly repeated, and General Ferrero's division advanced to the attack.

The colored troops charged forward cheering and with great enthusiasm and gallantry. Colonel J. K. Sigfried, commanding the first brigade, led the attacking column. The command moved out in rear of Colonel Humphrey's brigade of the third division, Colonel Sigfried, passing Colonel Humphrey by the flank, crossed the field immediately in front, went down into the crater and attempted to go through. The passage was exceedingly difficult, but, after great exertions, the brigade made its way through the crowded masses in a somewhat broken and disorganized condition, and advanced towards the crest. The 43d United States colored troops moved over the lip of the crater towards the right, made an attack upon the enemy's line of intrenchments and won the chief success of the day—capturing a number of prisoners and a stand of rebel colors, and recapturing a stand of national colors. The other regiments of the brigade were unable to get up on account of white troops in advance of them crowding the line.* The second brigade under the command of Colonel H. G. Thomas, followed the first with equal enthusiasm. The men rushed forward, descended into the crater and attempted to pass through. Colonel Thomas's intention was to go to the right and attack the enemy's rifle pits. He partially succeeded in doing so. But his brigade was much broken up when it came under the enemy's fire. The gallant brigade commander endeavored in person to rally his command and at last formed a storming column of portions of the 29th, 28th, 23d and 19th regiments. These troops made a spirited attack, but lost heavily in officers and became somewhat disheartened. Lieutenant Colonel Bross of the 29th, with the colors in his hand led the charge, was the first man to leap upon the enemy's works, and was instantly killed. Lieutenant Pennell seized the colors, but was shot down riddled through and through. Major Theodore H. Rockwood of the 19th sprang upon the parapet and fell while cheering on his regiment to the attack.† The conduct of these officers and their associates was indeed magnificent. No troops were ever better led to an assault. Had they been allowed the advance at the outset, before the enemy had recovered from his first surprise, General Grant's belief, that their charge " would have been a success," would doubtless have been verified. But it was now too late. The fire to which they were exposed was very hot and very destructive. It came from front and flank. It poured into the faces of the men. It enfiladed their lines. The enemy's rage against the colored troops had its bloody opportunity.

While these movements were making in front, despatches were passing between Generals Burnside and Meade which did

---

*Colonel Sigfried's Report. †Colonel Thomas's Report.

not augur well for the issue of the attack. At twenty minutes past seven o'clock General Burnside sent the following telegram to General Meade: "I am doing all in my power to push the troops forward and if possible we will carry the crest. It is hard work, but we hope to accomplish it. I am fully alive to the importance of it." General Meade at half past seven replied with the following ill-tempered effusion: "What do you mean by hard work to take the crest? I understand not a man has advanced beyond the enemy's line which you occupied immediately after exploding the mine. Do you mean to say your officers and men will not obey your orders to advance? If not, what is the obstacle? I wish to know the truth and desire an immediate answer."

This despatch was carried to General Burnside by Captain Jay, General Meade's aide de camp. Immediately upon its receipt, General Burnside replied: "Your despatch by Captain Jay received. The main body of General Potter's division is beyond the crater. I do not mean to say that my officers and men will not obey my orders to advance. I mean to say that it is very hard to advance to the crest. I have never in any report said anything different from what I conceived to be the truth. Were it not insubordinate, I would say that the latter remark of your note was unofficer-like and ungentlemanly." General Burnside was frank to confess, when examined before the Committee of Congress, that his language was unfortunate. But he felt at the time that General Meade was impugning his veracity, and replied, as a high spirited and truth-loving man would be most likely to do under such aggravating circumstances. General Meade, impatient and petulant before, did not improve in temper on the receipt of this message. His orders became more positive, if possible, than before.

At the extreme front, the condition of affairs did not appear favorable. The colored troops had gone in to the fight manfully. They had lost severely, and their organization was much broken. Colonel Sigfried's brigade had suffered very badly in its loss of officers. Colonel Delavan Bates of the 30th regiment fell shot in the face. Major James C. Lake of the same regiment was severely wounded in the breast. Lieutenant Colonel H. Seymour Hall of the 43d lost his right arm. Lieutenant Colonel Charles J. Wright of the 27th was shot twice and badly wounded. There were no wounds in the back among these brave officers. But all their endeavors and sacrifices did not avail. The work upon which they had been sent could not be accomplished. Colonel Sigfried, in bearing witness to the bravery of his command, believed that "had it not been for the almost impassable crowd of troops in the crater and intrenchments, Cemetery Hill would have been ours without a falter upon the part of my brigade." The attack failed. "A white color bearer with his colors crossed the works in retreat. The troops gave way and sought shelter in the crater where was concentrated a terrific fire."* A panic took place. Many of the men white and black ran to the rear. The enemy gathered about the edge of the crater and along the line of the commanding works, and, with his men in good range and good position, made havoc among our devoted troops. His artillery swept the intervening space between the crater and our line of works, and to retreat was as hazardous as to remain.

Time passes rapidly amid such exciting scenes. At nine o'clock, General Burnside sought an order from General Meade directing General Warren to make an attack upon the enemy in his front. The hostile lines were almost bare of defenders on either flank of the point immediately assailed, and the supporting corps, if they were now to attack, would not only relieve the Ninth Corps, but would also gain a decisive advantage. General Warren commanding the fifth telegraphed to General Meade and suggested that he should come to the front and see for himself the state of the battle. General Meade declined doing so. But at the same time he was unwilling to allow General Burnside any opportunity to exercise command over the corps in his immediate neighborhood. By General Meade's

---

*Colonel Sigfried's Report.

peremptory order, all the troops belonging to the Ninth Corps had been sent into the battle. General Meade now declined to relieve them by ordering an attack to be made by the corps on either side of the position of the Ninth. A marked difference is to be observed, between the character of the orders given to General Burnside and that of those to the other corps commanders. General Burnside was permitted no discretion. Not an order through the entire action was conditional. To Generals Warren, Hancock and Ord obedience to the orders given was to be determined by circumstances. If there was "apparently an opportunity to carry the enemy's works," General Warren was to "take advantage of it and push forward" his troops. When General Warren found the opportunity and was disposed to improve it, he was informed by General Meade that the attack was "suspended." General Hancock was to have his "troops well up to the front prepared to move" as he might be called upon at any moment. "If the enemy are in force and prepared," says General Meade, "you will have to await developments; but if you have reason to believe their condition is such that an effort to dislodge them would be successful, I would like to have it made." General Ord was directed at six o'clock to move forward "independently of General Burnside's troops and make a lodgement" on the crest.* But at eight o'clock, General Ord reported that the topography of the ground was such as to prevent such an attack as General Meade had ordered. Yet notwithstanding this long delay, the commanding general had no word of censure and no reiteration of command. The difference in the orders is so striking as at once to arrest attention.

The men in the crater began to feel that no support was to be given them. Instead of attempting to relieve them by occupying the enemy upon the flank of the crater, General Meade was ordering more men into the confused masses of troops already in the over-crowded position. He had put in the entire

---

*General Meade's orders in Attack on Petersburg, p. 58 and following.

Ninth Corps and one division of the eighteenth. They had all gone into the crater or into positions in its immediate vicinity, since they could go nowhere else. Discouraged by the condition of things, our men felt as though they were sacrificed without sufficient cause and without any good result. The enemy was emboldened to make an attack. But he was effectually repulsed, suffering considerable loss in killed and wounded and even in prisoners. The morning was hot, the men were suffering severely, and many of them in passing to the rear gave the impression that our entire force was on the point of retiring. At nine o'clock, General Burnside telegraphed to General Meade that "many of the Ninth and eighteenth corps" were "retiring before the enemy." He desired that the fifth corps should be then put in promptly. General Meade declares that that was the "first information" that he had received "that there was any collision with the enemy or that there was any enemy present." He was within a mile of the scene of action. He had heard the roar of the battle. One of his aides from the beginning, and two during a greater part of the time had been upon the ground. General Warren and General Hancock had spoken of the enemy's presence in their despatches. Captain Sanders of General Meade's own staff had informed him as early as eight o'clock, that General Griffin had made an attack and had been repulsed. General Grant at six o'clock had gone to the front, had seen that the opportunity of success had passed and then returned to General Meade in the rear. General Burnside's despatches reasonably interpreted would certainly give the impression that the enemy was somewhere present in his front. In the blissful ignorance which prevailed at the headquarters in the shady grove, General Meade knew nothing of any battle or any enemy!

As soon as General Meade had ascertained the fact that any portion of his army was in collision with the enemy, he ordered a withdrawal. General Burnside received the order at half past nine o'clock. General Hancock was informed, at twenty-five minutes past nine, that "offensive operations had been suspended," and that he would hold for the present the line of the eighteenth corps. General Warren, at forty-five minutes past nine, was ordered to resume his original position with his command. General Ord, at the same time, was directed to withdraw his " corps to the rear of the Ninth in some secured place."

General Burnside, immediately upon the reception of the order to retire, visited General Meade at his headquarters and requested that it might be rescinded, as he thought that the crest might still be carried if the supporting corps would relieve the Ninth from the pressure of the enemy. Indeed, while the enemy's troops upon the right and left were allowed to attack the troops in the crater without hindrance, a retreat from the point assailed would be accompanied with great loss, if indeed it could be made at all. General Ferrero had been instructed to dig a covered way from the crater to our lines, in order that the troops, when compelled to withdraw, might retire in comparative security. Could not the order be suspended until this covered way was completed ? General Meade thought not. The order was final. The troops must come back. It was repeated in the most peremptory manner. " The major general commanding," writes the chief of staff, " directs that you withdraw to your own intrenchments."

General Burnside, finding that General Meade could not be moved from his purpose, and would not afford any aid, collected his division commanders at his headquarters in the front and communicated to them the orders of the commanding general. While the deliberation was in progress, other orders came from General Meade to the effect that the troops were to be withdrawn according to the discretion of their commanding officer. This was at ten o'clock. But before this, the order had been sent into the crater. It was returned with the endorsement that it was impossible to retire, " on account of the enfilading fire over the ground between our rifle pits and the crater," and with the request "that our lines should open with artillery and infantry bearing on the right and left of the crater, under which fire," it was thought "every one could get away."*

But there was no fire to open. General Meade's order had suspended all offensive operations and removed the troops on the lines to their former positions. The men in the crater saw that they were not to be aided in any way. The enemy saw it also, and was not slow to take advantage of the opportunity. Still, discouraged as they were, the troops showed a bold front during the entire forenoon. But while waiting for the approval of the endorsement which General Hartranft made, in conjunction with General Griffin, the enemy appeared in greater force for another attack. Our men, worn out by the morning's work and in despair of assistance, could not stand against it. Generals Hartranft and Griffin attempted to draw them off in order, but they were hotly pressed, and those who could made their way in some confusion to their own lines. A considerable number still remained, among whom were General Bartlett, Colonel Marshall, Colonel S. M. Weld, Jr., of the 56th Massachusetts, Lieutenant Colonel Buffum, of the 4th Rhode Island and some officers of the colored division. These officers, unwilling to yield, rallied their men about them and, with great bravery, maintained for a time the unequal contest. They fought with the utmost spirit, but could not withstand the overpowering force of the enemy. A number were killed and wounded, but most of those who thus remained in the crater fell as prisoners into the enemy's hands. The men who retired suffered severely in withdrawing. The entire loss in the Ninth Corps was fifty-two officers and three hundred and seventy-six men killed, one hundred and five officers and one thousand five hundred and fifty-six men wounded, and eighty-seven officers and one thousand six hundred and fifty-two men missing, most of the last being captured at the time of the retreat. The entire loss was three thousand eight hundred and twenty-eight. The eighteenth corps lost about five hundred, and the second

---

* General Hartranft, in Attack on Petersburg, p. 205.

and fifth corps scarcely fifty. General Gregg, with the cavalry, had a smart engagement with the enemy upon our extreme left, but without any decisive result. At eleven o'clock, General Meade returned to the headquarters of the Army of the Potomac. General Burnside, at a later hour, retired to his own headquarters in the rear, sorrow-stricken by the contemplation of the deplorable result. At two o'clock all was over, and such of our men as could withdraw from the crater had returned to the lines. It was especially mortifying to feel that his own plan of action, which had promised a magnificent victory, should have been set aside at the last moment, and another substituted which eventuated in signal disaster and defeat.

NOTE.

General Meade performed an act of justice to Lieutenant Colonel Pleasants by issuing, on the 5th of August, the following general order:

"The commanding general takes great pleasure in acknowledging the valuable services rendered by Lieutenant Colonel Henry Pleasants, 48th regiment Pennsylvania Veteran Volunteers, and the officers and men of his command, in the excavation of the mine which was successfully exploded on the morning of the 30th ult., under one of the enemy's batteries in front of the second division of the Ninth Army Corps. The skill displayed in the laying-out and construction of the mine reflects great credit upon Lieutenant Colonel Pleasants, the officer in charge, and the willing endurance by the officers and men of the regiment of the extraordinary labor and fatigue involved in the prosecution of the work to completion are worthy of the highest praise."

How great an encouragement would have been such a recognition while the mine was in progress! But instead of recognition, Lieutenant Colonel Pleasants had nothing but ridicule at the headquarters of the army.

CHAPTER VI.

INQUIRY AND INVESTIGATION.

THE battle of July 30th naturally caused considerable discussion in and out of the army, and the circumstances of the case demanded a complete investigation of the causes of the disaster. General Meade was highly incensed by the language of General Burnside, in reply to the imperative demand for information respecting the obstacles in the way of gaining the crest. He was also displeased with his silence in regard to the events which took place subsequently to the suspension of hostilities. Accordingly, on the 3d of August, he preferred charges against General Burnside, intending to try him by court martial. He also requested General Grant to relieve the offending officer from duty with the Army of the Potomac. These charges were for "disobedience of orders" and "conduct prejudicial to good order and military discipline." The specifications of the first charge were, for failure in communicating information and neglect in relieving the eighteenth corps. That of the second was, for addressing to General Meade the despatch to which allusion has already been made. General Grant considered these charges so frivolous that he refused to order the court, and thus that matter dropped.

General Meade, however, was not disposed to allow the case to subside. He therefore immediately ordered a court of inquiry to examine the whole subject. The court met and decided that it could not proceed without the authority of the President. The matter was then referred to Washington, and the court was legalized by the authorities there. It was composed of General Hancock, commander of the second corps,

General Ayres, who commanded a division in the fifth corps, and General Miles, who commanded a brigade in the second corps. These gentlemen were officers in the supporting corps on the day of battle. Colonel Schriver, inspector general at General Meade's headquarters, was the judge advocate of the court. This body convened on the 6th of August, and continued in session, at different times, until the 9th of September. General Hancock presided at its deliberations, and is understood to have objected to the character of its composition. General Burnside made a formal protest to the Secretary of War against the constitution of the court, on the ground that the officers composing it held commands in the supporting columns, which were not brought into action on the 30th of July, and that the judge advocate was a member of General Meade's staff. He felt that he had a right to ask that, if an investigation were made, it should be by officers who did not belong to the Army of the Potomac, and were not selected by General Meade. He did not shrink from investigation, but desired that it should be removed from even a suspicion of partiality. Mr. Stanton did not perceive the force of the objection, and assured General Burnside that he might feel entire confidence in the fairness and justice of the President in reviewing the case. "The action of the board of inquiry," said Mr. Stanton, "will be merely to collect facts for the President's information." The court, in accordance with the order, proceeded to investigate the matter, and on the seventeenth day of its session, delivered its decision. It becomes necessary to examine the "finding" and "opinion" which were expressed, and the testimony upon which they were based.

The court declared the causes of failure to be "the injudicious formation of the troops in going forward, the movement being mainly by flank instead of extended front;" "the halting of the troops in the crater instead of going forward to the crest;" "no proper employment of engineer officers and working parties and of materials for their use;" an improper direction of some parts of the assaulting columns, and "the want of a competent common head at the scene of the assault, to direct affairs as occurrences should demand." The opinion of the court was, that the "following named officers were answerable for the want of success: Major General A. E. Burnside, Brigadier General J. H. Ledlie, Brigadier General Edward Ferrero, Colonel Z. R. Bliss, and Brigadier General O. B. Willcox." General Burnside was answerable because he failed to obey the orders of the commanding general. "1. In not giving such formation to his assaulting columns as to insure a reasonable prospect of success; 2. In not preparing his parapets and abatis for the passage of the columns of assault; 3. In not employing engineer officers, who reported to him, to lead the assaulting columns with working parties, and not causing to be provided proper materials necessary for crowning the crest; 4. In neglecting to execute Major General Meade's orders, respecting the prompt advance of General Ledlie's troops from the crater to the crest; or, in default of accomplishing that, not causing those troops to fall back and give place to others, instead of delaying until the opportunity passed away." General Ledlie was answerable because he "failed to push forward his division promptly, according to orders, thereby blocking up the avenue which was designed for the passage of" the supporting troops; and also because, instead of being with his division in the crater, "he was most of the time in a bomb proof ten rods in the rear of the main line of the Ninth Corps." General Ferrero was answerable because his troops were not ready for the attack at the prescribed time, because he did not go with them to the attack, and because he was "habitually in a bomb proof." Colonel Bliss was answerable because "he remained behind with the only regiment of his brigade which did not go forward according to the orders and occupied a position where he could not see what was going on." General Willcox was answerable because he did not exercise sufficient energy in causing his troops to go forward to Cemetery Hill. The court also expressed the opinion in language, the severity of which is but partially disguised in its softness, that "explicit orders should have been given, assigning one officer to the command of all the troops intended to engage in the assault, when the commanding general was not present in person to witness the operations."

To support this finding and opinion, the court examined Generals Grant, Meade, Burnside, Warren, Humphreys, Ord, Hunt, Potter, Willcox, Ferrero, Griffin, Hartranft, Mott, Ames, Ayres, and a number of other inferior officers. But no officers on General Burnside's staff were brought before the court to testify in the case.* It is singular to observe how inconclusively the opinion of the court follows from the testimony adduced.

General Meade, testifying in his own behalf, was strangely inconsistent with himself in the evidence which he offered. He submitted to the court his orders on the day of battle, some of which have already been quoted, and by which it distinctly appears that he directed every moment that was made. The substance of his testimony in other respects was, that he disapproved of the location of the mine and General Burnside's plan of attack; that he had one or more staff officers at General Burnside's headquarters in the front; that he learned, before eight o'clock in the morning, that General Griffin had made an attack on the right of the crater and had been repulsed; that the first positive information which he received that there was any enemy in front or "present" was not before nine o'clock in the morning; that he had ordered the troops withdrawn whenever that could be done with security; that, subsequently to the battle, he remained in "total ignorance of any further transactions until about six or seven o'clock in the evening;" that he did not go forward to the front to witness the action at any time; and that, in fine, he had "been groping in the dark since the commencement of the attack." Comment upon such testimony is wholly needless.

---

* It was stated at the time that the staff officers expected to testify were ill. But they were ready to go before the court previous to its final adjournment.

The testimony of General Burnside and that of his division and brigade commanders, is positive in relation to the fidelity that was manifested by the commander of the Ninth Corps, in his endeavors to execute the commands of General Meade. The formation of his assaulting column must have been determined by the officers having the immediate direction of the attack, and must have been influenced by the condition of the ground. That the troops marched by the flank, instead of an extended front, must have been due to other causes than the failure of General Burnside to obey the orders of General Meade. General Burnside's battle order to his division officers, through whom alone it could be executed, was as clear as General Meade's order to him. Surely, General Burnside was not responsible for the failure of any subordinate officer to obey his orders, any more than General Meade would have been, in case of neglect on the part of any of his corps commanders. A comparison of the two battle orders shows that General Burnside did all that was possible to carry out the wishes of his chief. Indeed, the formation was not altogether by the flank. General Hartranft testified that he "formed his command, which was immediately in rear of the first division, in one or two regiments front." He "put two small regiments together." General Hartranft was a capital officer, and it was General Burnside's misfortune that as good an officer was not in command of the first division.

The second point which the court made, in regard to the preparation for the passage of the assaulting columns, was not well taken. The testimony shows that there was no particular necessity for the leveling of the parapets. The abatis was so much cut up by the enemy's fire as to offer but little obstruction to the advance. General Willcox declared that "what was left of it when his division passed over was no obstacle whatever." The evidence is positive upon that point, and the delay of the troops in passing out of the lines was very brief. Captain Farquhar, the chief engineer of the eighteenth corps, testified that "there seemed to be room enough at" his "salient to pass over, certainly in regimental front," but the passage was not practicable for artillery. Moreover, a greater number of troops passed out of the lines than could be handled upon the ground which they occupied. It is also to be considered that the attack was to be of the nature of a surprise ; that the enemy was immediately in the front, distant but a few hundred feet, and that nothing was to be done before the assault which would give him any intimation of our intentions.

The third point which the Court made against General Burnside in "not causing to be provided the necessary materials for crowning the crest," is entirely discrepant with the testimony. General Burnside testified, that an engineer regiment was detailed for each division of his corps, fully equipped with the necessary tools for intrenching. General Potter testified, that his regiment of engineers was immediately in the neighborhood of the breastwork, prepared with proper tools to level the works for the passage of field batteries, in case the forward movement was successful ; that axes, spades and picks were provided, and the *chevaux de frise* on the enemy's lines for two or three hundred yards was broken down. General Griffin testified, that he had in his brigade a pioneer corps with the proper tools. Major Randall testified, that he thought he saw the 25th Massachusetts near the crater, equipped with shovels and spades. The testimony which it is presumed the Court relied upon for its opinion, was indecisive in its character. The witnesses were Major Duane and Lieutenant Beuyaurd. To the question, whether any working parties accompanied the troops Major Duane answered, that he did not know ; neither did he know, whether or not any arrangements were made "for facilitating the debouch of the troops from our lines, and their passage over the enemy's parapets." Lieutenant Beuyaurd was equally ignorant. He did not know that there were working parties for the assaulting columns, nor that there were any preparations made in the way of collecting gabions, picks, shovels, axes or other tools. These wholly inconclusive statements were allowed to outweigh the positive testimony offered on the other side. It is true, that General Burnside did not employ the engineer officer who was sent to him, for the simple reason that he preferred his own judgment.

The fourth point which the court made, in regard to the alleged neglect in executing General Meade's orders, to push forward General Ledlie's troops from the crater to the crest, is not supported by any testimony that was offered. On the contrary, Surgeon Chubb testified, that General Ledlie received orders in his hearing, "to move his troops forward from where they were then lying," and that General Ledlie "frequently sent up aides to have them moved forward." Surely it could not have been expected, that General Burnside should assume in person the direction of General Ledlie's division. In fact, the court in censuring General Ledlie based its condemnation of that officer upon his neglect to report the condition of affairs to his commander. Thus General Burnside was censured for not sending General Ledlie's troops forward, and General Ledlie was censured for failing to give the information upon which General Burnside was expected to act. Again, General Burnside was considered answerable for the failure, because he did not withdraw General Ledlie's troops in order to give place to others. But it was manifestly impossible to withdraw the troops, while General Meade was continually ordering them forward. The opinion of the court, therefore, so far as General Burnside was concerned, fails in every point to correspond with the testimony.

General Ledlie was undoubtedly in fault for not accompanying his division, and pushing it forward according to orders. He declares, that at the time he was suffering from illness. But, if such were the case he should have asked to be relieved, that some other more efficient officer might direct his troops. No objection, therefore, can be made to the opinion of the court in his case. It is but fair, however, that General Ledlie should be heard in his own defence. In a letter to the Army and Navy Journal of March 18, 1865—after reciting Lieutenant Colonel Loring's evidence before the Committee of Congress, to the effect that the first division moved with promptness, but that the troops in going into the crater could not maintain their organization, and that he reported the fact to the division commander—General Ledlie proceeds: "On receiving the report from Colonel Loring, I immediately issued the proper orders, and took the necessary steps for relieving the confused condition of the division. I am perfectly willing that the record of my conduct should stand upon this sworn statement made by Colonel Loring, with the simple addition of the fact that my life was saved on that occasion only because the ball which struck my person had not force enough to penetrate my watch. I was stunned and temporarily injured by the force of the ball, and then, for the first time, retired to regimental headquarters, which were being used as a hospital. I stayed there but a few minutes, and then returned to my post, where I remained until we received orders to withdraw."

General Ferrero absolutely denied the declaration of the court, that he was in a bomb-proof during the action. Surgeon Chubb's testimony was, that General Ferrero went out of the bomb-proof after he received the order to move his troops forward, and that he returned to it subsequently to their repulse. Surgeon Smith's testimony was, that General Ferrero was in front of the bomb-proof at the time his division charged, that he accompanied his troops to the front when they left, and returned at the time they came back. After the opinion of the court was made public, General Ferrero procured affidavits from Brevet Major Hicks, Captains F. R. Warner, W. W. Tyson and A. F. Walcott and Lieutenant Mowry, members of his staff, who positively swore that General Ferrero was not in a bomb-proof at any time during the action of July 30th, but was on the field, and within ten paces of his command. Lieutenant Colonel Loring, who delivered to General Ferrero the order to advance and who saw him frequently through the day, deposed that he was standing in the front line at the time of the delivery of the order; that he did not see General Ferrero in a bomb-proof at any time, and did not believe that he was in one.

Captain Pell, who was sent by General Burnside to General Ferrero, did not upon any occasion find him in a bomb-proof, and Lieutenant Colonel Ross of the 31st colored troops spoke to General Ferrero on the field and saw him cheering on his men. Surgeon Prince of the 36th Massachusetts and Captain Dimock deposed to the same effect. Whether these affidavits are to be believed, in contradiction to the opinion of the court, must be left to the judgment of the reader. There was but one witness in regard to the conduct of Colonel Bliss, and his testimony was, as expressed in his own words, that "Colonel Bliss remained with the last regiment of his brigade and did not go forward at all to" his "knowledge." The testimony in regard to General Willcox's want of promptness was of the most general character and related to the crowded condition of all the troops in and about the crater—no mention being made of any neglect on the part of General Willcox himself.

From a careful examination of the testimony and a consideration of its *ex parte* character, from the partial constitution of the court, and the circumstances connected with the subject of its inquiry, the fairest conclusion to be reached is, that its "opinion" is of little authority. On one point, indeed, the court may be considered to have formed an equitable judgment. That is its intimation of the want of a competent head upon the immediate scene of action. General Burnside was not permitted to exercise the "prerogative" of the commanding general of the army—had even been rebuked upon the mere suspicion that he had any design to do so—and General Meade fought the battle by telegraph, all the while, to use his own words, "groping in the dark from the commencement of the attack." He might as well have been twenty miles away. When it was suggested by General Warren, he refused to go forward where he could see and know what was doing in the front. His reason for declining was, that his position had been taken and was within telegraphic communication of all the corps, and therefore, there was no necessity for going to the front. Why not then have remained at his own headquarters instead of visiting those of the Ninth Corps? Such a reason could avail in no way to excuse his fighting a battle, without seeing a single soldier who was engaged. Did ever a great captain direct an action so?

The Committee on the Conduct of the War also made an investigation and report concerning this unfortunate transaction. The committee met, at different times, from December 17th, 1864, to January 16th, 1865. The principal witnesses who had been before the court of inquiry were also examined by the committee. Besides these, Lieutenant Colonels Loring and Van Buren, of General Burnside's staff, and Lieutenant Colonel Pleasants added their testimony. The evidence was more complete and clear than that offered before the court. The officers expressed their opinions with greater freedom, and the questions which were put by the committee were more thorough and searching in their character. General Meade's testimony, which has already been commented upon, was somewhat contradictory to itself in different parts. General Grant's evidence contained a very remarkable admission. He said, "I came to the south side of the river before the explosion took place, and remained with General Meade until probably a half or three-quarters of an hour after the springing of the mine. I then rode down to front; that is, I rode down as far as I could on horseback, and went through to the front on foot. I there found that we had lost the opportunity which had been given us." This statement deserves something more than a passing consideration. General Grant, by his own showing, must have been at the front as early as six o'clock. At that time, he considered that the opportunity had passed. He had the supreme control. The query now arises, Why did he not order the troops to be withdrawn? That would seem to have been his imperative duty. Yet the fact remains that the troops were permitted to go forward under General Meade's orders, to crowd into the crater, and to remain there at least three hours subsequent to the time when, in General Grant's judgment, the opportunity of victory was lost. General Grant was especially severe upon General Ledlie, whom he was disposed to consider mostly answerable for the failure. He blamed himself for allowing General Burnside to put General Ledlie in charge of the assaulting column. It is evident from his testimony and from that of General Meade, that the subject of employing the colored troops to lead the attack was not properly presented to his mind. In one breath he approves General Meade's order, and in another he declares that the attack would probably have succeeded, if made by the colored division.

General Warren gave it as his opinion that "there should have been two independent columns, to have rushed in immediately after the explosion of the mine, and to have swept down the enemy's lines right and left, clearing away all his artillery and infantry by attacking in the flank and rear. This would have allowed the main column to have followed on to the main crest rapidly and without molestation." The failure was caused by the delay of the attacking column to advance to the Cemetery hill. The testimony before the committee, as well as that before the court, was positive and clear in regard to General Burnside's repeated directions to his division commanders to send their troops forward to the crest. He evidently did all that could be done, except leading them in person beyond the crater. That was a task which he could hardly have been expected by any one to perform.

The committee, after a review of the testimony, and a careful recital of the facts, express their opinion in decisive terms. "In conclusion," they say, "the cause of the disastrous result of the assault of the 30th of July last is mainly attributable to the fact, that the plans and suggestions of the general who had devoted his attention for so long a time to the subject, who had carried out to so successful completion the project of mining the enemy's works, and who had carefully selected and drilled his troops, for the purpose of securing whatever advantages might be attainable from the explosion of the mine, should have been so entirely disregarded by a general who had evinced no faith in the successful prosecution of that work, had aided it by no countenance or open approval, and had assumed the entire direction and control only when it was completed, and the time had come for reaping any advantage that might be derived from it." This report was submitted to the Senate on the 6th of February, 1865, and was ordered to be printed. With its conclusions, rather than with the opinion of the court of inquiry, a fair and impartial mind will be likely to agree.

CHAPTER VII.

THE BEGINNING OF THE END.

FOR the next few weeks after the explosion of the mine the two opposing armies in front of Petersburg lay in comparative quiet. General Lee had detached a force in the early part of July to make a diversion by way of the Shenandoah valley upon Maryland. To meet and counteract this movement General Grant despatched the sixth corps from the Army of the Potomac to Washington and its neighborhood. The ninteenth corps, opportunely arriving from the South, was also sent in that direction. On the 7th of August, General Sheridan was appointed to the command of the forces in that quarter and soon afterwards inaugurated a very brilliant campaign in the Shenandoah valley, the details of which do not properly come within the province of this narrative.

On the 13th of August General Burnside was granted leave of absence from the Ninth Corps, and immediately left the army for his home in Providence. He was not again called into active service during the continuance of the war. Mr. Lincoln refused to accept his resignation, awaiting some opportunity for sending him again into the field. Immediately before the accession of Mr. Johnson to the presidential chair the resignation was once more tendered and was accepted by the new President on the 15th of April. After the close of the war, General Burnside engaged in business in New York and at the West. In the spring of 1866, the people of Rhode Island demanded an opportunity of expressing their approval of the course of their favorite soldier. On the 30th of March General Burnside was nominated, and on the 4th of April was elected, Governor of Rhode Island. On the 29th of May he was inaugurated into his high office at Newport, amid a more general and enthusiastic expression of public feeling than had ever been observed in the State.

When General Burnside left the Ninth Corps he carried with him the esteem and affection of every officer and soldier in its ranks. It has been a source of extreme gratification to the writer of this volume during its preparation, that all the letters which have been received from the members of the Corps have contained the warmest expressions of affectionate esteem for their former commander. "I hope," writes one, "you will not fail to speak of the love and respect as well as confidence entertained towards General Burnside by all his command. Your book will not be a complete history of the Corps until this is done." This is the uniform tenor of every communication. It is a grateful testimony to the impression which General Burnside's worth of character has made upon all who have been associated with him. There have indeed been those who have attempted to decry and malign him. No man can escape detraction. Professional jealousy will always point the shafts of calumny, but from the true and faithful man, armored with a pure conscience and faithfulness to duty, they fall harmless. He who directs them receives the greatest injury. They always recoil upon the hand from which they were sent. He who wishes to detract from a fair and well earned fame, proves himself to be deficient in true nobility of character, and incapable of appreciating it when manifested by another. A generous nature is never unwilling to acknowledge the merit even of a rival.

General Burnside left the Corps in good hands. General Parke succeeded to the command and retained it until the close of the war, winning for himself great distinction as a brave and able officer. Immediately after the battle of July 30th, General Ledlie was relieved from the command of the first division and General White was appointed in his stead.* Generals Willcox and Potter had earned their brevets of Major General by their faithful service during the campaign, and were accordingly promoted, to date from the 1st of August. General Grant, in his movements to envelope the enemy's defences, threw portions of his army, at one time to the north of the James, at another to the south of Petersburg. Step by step during the subsequent months, he gradually extended his lines in both directions. Every movement met with strenuous resistance, and it was only by dint of hard fighting that any important advantage was gained. The Ninth Corps participated in some of the movements towards the south which had for their object the seizure of the enemy's main line of railroad communication.

On the 18th of August the fifth corps, which was posted in our lines on the left of the Ninth, broke camp and marched towards the Weldon railroad, The Ninth Corps moved to the left and held the vacated position of the fifth. The eighteenth corps moved down to the old lines of the Ninth. The advance of the fifth corps struck the Weldon railroad about eight o'clock in the morning at Six-mile Station, and immediately set to work to destroy the track. The remainder of the corps moved to the right for two or three miles and took position to protect the working parties. At noon the enemy appeared and made a very spirited attack, in which our troops were severely handled. During the night and following day the line was strengthened, but on the 19th the enemy became so menacing in his demonstrations, that reënforcements were needed. General Parke sent the divisions of Generals White, Potter and Willcox to the assistance of General Warren. General Willcox arrived first upon the ground and was posted upon the right of the line. At four o'clock in the afternoon the enemy under General A. P. Hill made a furious charge. General Mahone's division was directed upon General Willcox's command.

*General Ledlie resigned on the 16th of January, 1865. General White resigned November 19, 1864.

General Hartranft's brigade was formed upon the right and Colonel Humphrey's on the left. They steadily held their ground and beat back every attempt to break their lines. The fifth corps, however, was not so fortunate, and General Crawford's division suffered a severe loss. Our centre was in danger of giving way, when General Potter and General White arrived most opportunely on the ground. Their troops had had a most wearisome march, but were immediately formed, charged the enemy and restored the battle. The presence of the Ninth Corps at once decided the conflict in our favor, and the enemy was repulsed. The Corps captured two hundred prisoners and a color. The position was secured and strengthened during the night. The Ninth Corps occupied the line extending from the fifth corps on the Weldon railroad to the left of the second corps near the Jerusalem plank road. The ground thus gallantly wrested from the foe was intrenched and became a part of our defences. But the enemy was unwilling to rest easy under the loss which he had suffered. On the 21st he came down upon our lines and attacked with renewed vigor, charging nearly up to the breastworks. Once and again he advanced only to be repulsed with great slaughter. It was a desperate contest and a decided victory for our troops. General Potter's division participated in this brilliant defence. The losses in the Corps on these two days of fighting amounted to about five hundred, in killed, wounded and missing. On the 27th the fourth division which had been left in the old lines was moved to the left, joined the command and was efficiently engaged in constructing redoubts, slashing timber and otherwise strengthening the works.

The arduous duties which had fallen upon the first division, had reduced the numbers of this gallant body of men to such an extent, as to make a reörganization of the Corps desirable. Scarcely a moiety of the officers and men remained in those regiments which had left Annapolis with full ranks. They had borne an honorable part in every action since the opening of the campaign, and had left on every battle field the evidences of their heroic self-sacrifice. It now became necessary to merge the troops of the first division with those of the second and third. The troops were divided but the name was retained. General White was relieved, and General Willcox was placed in command of the first division and General Potter in command of the second as thus compacted. The colored troops formed the third division and retained their organization.

The month of September passed quietly away. The Ninth Corps had the opportunity of rest. No severer duty was required than the strengthening of the positions already gained. Towards the close of the month there were indications of more active service. A further prolongation of our lines to the left had been determined upon, and the Ninth Corps was destined to take part in the movement. On the 28th the first and second divisions were massed in preparation for the advance, and on the 30th the troops moved out of their encampment. General Parke was to coöperate with General Warren in an endeavor to secure the intersection of the Poplar Spring and Squirrel Level roads. When that point was gained, the command was to open a road across a swamp in the rear to the vicinity of the Pegram estate below the Poplar Spring church. General Warren came in contact with the enemy about noon near Peebles' farm. The rebel forces were posted in a strong position on a ridge of a range of hills. General Charles Griffin's division made a gallant attack, forced the lines and captured one gun and a small number of prisoners.

The enemy retired to an intrenched position about half a mile in the rear of his former line. General Parke moved up to the support of General Warren and pressing beyond the Peebles farm, marched through a belt of timber and came out in a large clearing in which stood the Pegram house. General Potter's division moved beyond the house, entered the timber and attempted to advance up the acclivity upon which the enemy was posted. General S. G. Griffin's brigade made the attack, but was met by a counter charge in superior numbers. The enemy's line overlapped our own, broke in between the Ninth

Corps and the fifth, threw General Potter's line into confusion and swept from the field a thousand prisoners or more. At one time it seemed as though the entire division would be broken in pieces; but the steadiness, with which the 7th Rhode Island, under the command of Brevet Colonel Daniels, held the left flank, prevented such a disaster and aided General Potter in reëstablishing his disordered ranks. General Willcox's division, promptly coming up in support, enabled the first division to rally and reform. At this critical moment, General Charles Griffin's division was hurried forward promptly, attacked and completely stopped the advancing foe. Night coming on put an end to the engagement. The Ninth Corps moved to the line of works which had been captured from the enemy at the Peebles farm. The right connected with the fifth corps; the left was refused covering the Squirrel Level road. This position was intrenched and held. The fruit of the day's operation was an extension of our lines for a distance of about three miles beyond the Weldon railroad. The casualties of the Ninth Corps were sixty-seven killed, four hundred and eighteen wounded, and one thousand five hundred and nine missing—much the larger portion of which fell upon General Potter's division. Towards night a severe rain-storm set in and continued through the subsequent day. In front of the Ninth Corps all was quiet, but the fifth was attacked in the morning and again in the afternoon. In both instances the enemy was signally repulsed with great loss.

On the 2d of October a reconnaissance was made by the second and Ninth Corps. The enemy was found in force covering the Boydton plank road. Our intrenched line was returned running through the Pegram farm. On the 4th General Ferrero's division was moved up and joined the Corps. By the able and willing help of the colored troops the work of intrenchment was pressed with renewed vigor. Two redoubts were thrown up on the front line, three on the flank, and two on the rear with strong infantry parapet connections and heavy slashing in front. Nothing more important than the usual picket firing took place for several days, but on the 8th, a demonstration was made upon the Squirrel Level road by two brigades of the first division, under the personal direction of General Willcox. The enemy was found at all points in front and on the alert. The advanced picket line was established and General Willcox returned. The affair cost the Corps a loss of three killed and thirteen wounded. In these operations, General Parke ascertained that the morale of the command was suffering, and its efficiency was reduced by the presence of conscripts, substitutes and "bounty jumpers." The veterans in every engagement added to their former fame, but many of the new recruits were found sadly deficient in the qualities of the soldier. Notwithstanding this unfavorable circnmstance, the Corps performed a very creditable work in the engagements upon the extreme left of the army.

The month of October was occupied in strengthening the position which we had gained upon the left. The gain was permanent. Our forces could not indeed dislodge the enemy from his strong position along the Boydton plank road, but they established their lines within a mile and a half of it, and within three miles of the South side railroad. The brilliant operations of General Sheridan in the Shenandoah Valley gave fresh encouragement to the army in front of Petersburg. General Grant determined to make another effort against the enemy's works upon our left. It was known that the line of Hatcher's run was fortified, but General Grant hoped that the defences might be turned. The movement by the flank was entrusted to General Hancock. Meanwhile, the Ninth and the fifth corps were to make demonstrations in front. The Ninth Corps was in position on the extreme left of the army, holding the line through the Pegram farm, refusing on the left flank and then returning on the rear. On the 27th, General Willcox moved out his division at three and a half o'clock in the morning. General Ferrero's division followed immediately, and General Potter's brought up the rear. By daylight, the entire corps was marching quickly down the Squirrel Level road.

Colonel Cutcheon's brigade was sent forward in advance, with the design of capturing the enemy's videttes, and, if possible, of surprising the forces covering the Boydton road. Both designs failed; the first by a premature discharge of a musket, which alarmed the enemy's outposts, and the second by the vigilance of the rebel troops.

The works in front of Hatcher's run were found to be strongly constructed, and protected with abatis and slashed timber. The Ninth Corps was deployed, with General Willcox's division on the left, General Ferrero's in the centre, and General Potter on the right and in support. General Willcox formed his division with Colonel Cutcheon's brigade in the centre, and the brigades of Generals Hartranft and McLaughlin on the flank. General Ferrero formed his division with Colonel Bates's brigade on the left and Colonel Russell's on the right. In front, were thick woods, with a heavy undergrowth. Through these General Ferrero advanced, driving in the enemy's skirmishers, until within one hundred yards of the rebel works. There the fallen timber and the abatis were impediments too difficult to overcome. General Ferrero intrenched and held his ground. General Willcox found no opportunity of piercing the enemy's line. Nothing was to be done except to intrench in turn. The object to be accomplished was to occupy the attention of the foe while General Hancock was to make a serious attack; but the enemy made a counter attack, and for a time there was some hard fighting with doubtful results. Both parties finally gave up the contest, with but little advantage to either. A few flags and prisoners were taken on both sides. Our troops held the position through the night of the 27th, but on the morning of the 28th, they received orders from headquarters to withdraw to the former lines. They retired, closely followed by the enemy, without material loss. When within a mile of its encampment, the Ninth Corps formed in line of battle, and the divisions retired in that order, one through the other. The first division formed in line while the second and third passed through. The Corps was all in by six o'clock in the evening, having suffered a loss of eight killed, one hundred and twenty-seven wounded, and fourteen missing.

This movement closed the operations on the left, so far as the Ninth Corps was concerned. Early in December, the troops returned to the front of Petersburg. The Ninth Corps held the right of the line of the army, reaching from the Appomattox to battery twenty-four. General Willcox's division occupied the right, General Griffin's brigade the left of the line, including Fort Sedgwick—called by the soldiers Fort Hell—Forts Davis and Hayes and the battery. Through the winter, the Corps remained in this position, occasionally detaching a brigade or division in support of movements made by other corps. Some changes also took place in the organization. Early in December, it was decided by the military authorities to detach the colored troops from the different corps in which they had previously served, and organize a new corps, the twenty-fifth. The colored division of the Ninth was accordingly separated from the command. It was moved down to Bermuda Hundred, and General Ferrero was placed in charge of the defences of that point. The colored troops had done a faithful service, and would doubtless have accomplished more had they been permitted. But the old army officers did not in all cases take kindly to them. General Burnside had been very favorably disposed to them from the start, and General Parke agreed with his friend and chief. But it has already been seen how chary General Meade had been in giving them any more conspicuous service than the guarding of the trains, the digging of intrenchments, and the hewing down of the forests. But the negroes wrought well, drew commendation even from reluctant lips, and won promotion for their officers. General Ferrero, no less from his own merit than from the good conduct of his command, received the brevet of Major General, to date from the 2d of December, 1864.

A considerable number of Pennsylvania troops, enlisted for one year's service, arrived in camp about the 1st of December, and took the place of the colored soldiers. Six regiments of infantry were organized as the third division, and General Hartranft was assigned to the command. They had the opportunity, before their term of enlistment expired, of seeing some hard and honorable service, and of bearing a distinguished part in the closing scenes of the strife. General Hartranft was too active a soldier to allow his command to remain idle when any work was to be done.

On the 6th of December, General Warren started on a reconnaissance to the Weldon railroad beyond Nottoway Court House, which was effectual in destroying a large portion of the track as far as Hicksford. On the 10th, General Potter's division was sent down to Nottoway Court House to reënforce General Warren and assist his return. The weather was extremely cold, the snow and sleet filled the air and covered the ground, and the troops endured much hardship in marching and bivouacking beneath the inclement skies. General Warren achieved considerable success in his movement, but his command was subjected to great and painful exposure. The appearance of General Potter's division was a welcome sight to the weary men. On the hither side of the Nottoway river the junction was made during the afternoon of the 11th, and on the 12th, the entire force returned to camp.

The routine of the siege was broken by a singular occurrence. During the early part of the winter, several attempts were made to bring the two contending parties together for purposes of negotiation. In these transactions, Mr. F. P. Blair, senior, was prominent, and so successful was he in his representations to the insurgent government, as to induce Mr. Davis to send commissioners from Richmond, to treat with our authorities upon the subject of a cessation of hostilities. On Sunday morning, January 29th, 1865, the pickets in front of the Ninth Corps reported that a flag of truce was flying on the enemy's works. The fact was communicated to Colonel Samuel Harriman, commanding the first brigade of the first division, and by him to General Willcox who was then in command of the Corps. Request was made through the flag for permission to

Messrs. A. H. Stephens, R. M. T. Hunter, and J. A. Campbell to pass through the lines. General Grant at once granted the favor, and sent up an aide to accompany the commissioners to City Point. Colonel Harriman, Major Lydig of General Parke's staff, and Captain Brackett of General Willcox's staff, courteously received the visitors from Richmond, and attended them to General Grant's headquarters. They remained as guests of General Grant until the 30th, when they had a long conference with Mr. Lincoln and Mr. Seward on board a steamboat in Hampton Roads. The interview, however, had but one result, namely:—to assure the rebel authorities that no peace was possible except upon the condition of submission. The commissioners returned as quietly as they came, and made their report. Their visit had the effect upon the soldiers of causing the belief, that the enemy was becoming less sanguine of success, and more disposed to perceive that the defeat of his cause was drawing nigh.

On the 5th of February, 1865, General Hartranft, with the third division, supported a movement made by General Humphreys, with the fifth and sixth corps, towards Hatcher's run. The command left camp at four o'clock in the afternoon, and reached General Humphreys's position on the Vaughan road at eight o'clock, without a straggler. General Hartranft was posted on the right of the second corps, and intrenched in the night, throwing up one thousand yards of rifle pits. On the next day, the 200th Pennsylvania, under the command of Lieutenant Colonel McCall, made a reconnaissance and found the enemy strongly posted. Considerable fighting took place in front of the fifth and sixth corps, but General Hartranft's command was not brought into the action. The operation was designed to dispossess the enemy of his position near the Boydton plank road, and nearly the entire army was engaged in the attempt. General Meade was at one time upon the ground. But the movement failed, and on the 10th, the troops returned to their former positions.

For gallant and meritorious conduct during the stirring scenes

60

through which the Corps had passed, many of its officers were complimented with promotion to brevet rank. Among these were Colonels Christ, Curtin, Humphrey, McLaughlin of the 57th Massachusetts, and Blackman of the 27th colored troops, who were advanced to the grade of brevet Brigadier General. Several gentlemen of the staff were also recognized as worthy of promotion. Captain Roemer, of the artillery, was brevetted Major.

The Ninth Corps retained its place on the right of the army until the final assault. Through the autumn and winter, although it was not called to the severe service in which some other portions of the army were engaged, it yet performed all required duties with promptness and fidelity. Our soldiers were subjected to constant annoyance from the enemy's sharp-shooters, and skirmishing took place almost daily. Artillery duels were also frequent. The neighborhood of "Fort Hell" was especially hot, and appeared to be the object of most spiteful attack. The 7th Rhode Island formed a part of the garrison of the fort, and Colonel Daniels was at one time in command. Up to the 1st of December, 1864, the casualties of the Corps amounted to over sixteen thousand, a sufficient attestation of the bravery and self-sacrifice with which its career was everywhere and always marked. On every scene, the well-tried courage of the officers and men had been conspicuous. As the fate of the rebellion approached, the Corps prepared to take its part in the decisive, final struggle. Faithfully and well had its former work been done. It continued faithful unto the end, and won the illustrious prize of honorable and unwearied service.

CHAPTER VII.

THE CLOSING SCENES.

THE opening of the spring was understood by all to be the signal for entering upon the closing struggle of the war. The rebel government itself had become somewhat discouraged, and General Lee had already intimated his opinion of the hopelessness of continuing the strife. The magnificent campaign of General Sherman had demonstrated the inherent weakness of the "Southern Confederacy." The brilliant operations of General Terry and Admiral Porter, which resulted in the capture of Fort Fisher, on the 15th of January, and the subsequent occupation of Wilmington, had their effect upon the counsels of the insurgent government. The interview of the peace commissioners from Richmond, with the President and Mr. Seward at Hampton Roads, was a virtual confession of weakness. Yet the enemy still showed a resolute front, and, as subsequent events proved, still contemplated desperate measures. But it was evident on all sides that the critical moment was drawing near. There might be other attempts on the part of the enemy to avert the long-threatened blow. Possibly he might deliver some heavy blows himself; but every struggle which he should make was felt to be but the expiring throes of a cause, to which only despair could give a momentary strength, and the certainty of defeat a resolution to die with firmness.

During the month of March, as through the preceding month, the Ninth Corps occupied the right of the intrenchments, extending from the Appomattox to Fort Howard, a distance of seven miles. General Willcox's division occupied the line from the Appomattox to Fort Meikle. General Potter's division extended from Fort Meikle to Fort Howard. General Hartranft's division was posted in the rear, in reserve. The intrenchments held by General Willcox and General Curtin's brigade of General Potter's division were those which had originally been taken from the enemy, and were in very close proximity to the opposing lines. The works were necessarily somewhat defective. Especially was this the case with Fort Stedman. This work was situated at the point where our line crossed Prince George Court House road. It was a small earthwork without bastions, immediately adjoining battery number ten. It was not a compactly built work in the first place, and the frosts and rains of winter had weakened it considerably. Yet the nearness to the enemy prevented even the slightest repairs, except in the most stealthy manner. The ground in the rear of the fort was nearly as high as the parapet itself. The enemy's line was distant only about one hundred and fifty yards. Our own picket line ran about one-third of this distance from the fortified front. This portion of our defences was held by the third brigade of the first division, under General N. B. McLaughlin.

At four o'clock on the morning of the 25th of March, the picket line was visited by the officer on duty. The men were found to be alert, and no signs of an enemy were visible. General Grant, during the winter, had allowed deserters to come into our lines with arms. Squads of men, taking advantage of this permission, appeared soon after the visit of the officer, stole quietly in with the pretence of being deserters, surprised our pickets and gained possession of the picket posts. The line was overpowered in a moment, and almost without resistance. Immediately following these detached parties, was a strong storming force of picked men, and behind these were three heavy columns of the enemy. It was General Gordon's corps, supported by General Bushrod Johnson's division. The guard in the trenches attempted to check the progress of the attacking column, but was overborne at once, and our main line was broken between batteries nine and ten. The assaulting force turned to the right and left, with the intention of sweeping away our troops. The right column soon gained battery ten, which was open in the rear, thus acquiring the great advantage of a close attack on Fort Stedman. The garrison, consisting of a battalion of the 14th New York heavy artillery, under Major Randall, resisted with the utmost spirit, but, being attacked on all sides, was soon overpowered, and most of the men were captured. Forthwith the guns of the battery and fort were turned upon our troops. The enemy pushed on towards Fort Haskell, driving out the troops in battery eleven.

The day had not yet brightened, and it was almost impossible in the dim twilight to distinguish between friend and foe. General McLaughlin, aroused by the tumult, endeavored to rally and form his brigade. Passing on down the line, he ordered mortar battery twelve to open upon the enemy. At the same time, the 59th Massachusetts was formed, made a gallant charge upon battery eleven, and recaptured the work. General McLaughlin went forward to Fort Stedman, and was at once seized by the enemy. General Parke, immediately on receiving intelligence of the enemy's movement, ordered General Willcox to form the remainder of his division for resistance, and General Hartranft to concentrate his right brigade to reënforce the imperilled troops. General Tidball, chief of artillery, was directed to post his batteries on the hills in rear of the point attacked. General Hartranft concentrated his whole division with great promptness, attacked the advancing enemy, and effectually checked his further progress.

The left column proceeded along the line to battery nine, attacked the 57th Massachusetts, and drove the men from the trenches. It next struck the left of the 2d Michigan, and threw it into confusion. The regiment, however, soon rallied, and stoutly resisted the attack till reënforcements came up, when the advance of the enemy was stopped. A line was formed of Colonel Ely's brigade, perpendicular to the intrenchments, the right resting near battery nine. By the assistance of batteries nine and five and Fort McGilvery a heavy assault which the enemy made on battery nine was repulsed, and the attacking column forced back. Foiled in the attempt to sweep our lines in this direction, and to gain possession of the railroad to City Point, the assaulting force withdrew to the rear of Fort Stedman. Here it met once more the column which had gone up to the right, and which had been equally unfortunate. After their temporary surprise, the garrisons of batteries eleven and twelve—the 29th Massachusetts and the 100th Pennsylvania—rallied, and, uniting with Colonel Harriman's brigade of General Willcox's division, formed a second line perpendicular to the intrenchments, its left resting near Fort Haskell, its right connecting with General Hartranft's division.

By this rapid and skilful disposition, the enemy was not only brought to a complete stop in both directions, but was also forced back, enclosed and subjected to a destructive fire in front and on both flanks. The only works which he now held were Fort Stedman and battery ten, but his position there was commanded by our guns from Fort Haskell. He made repeated attempts upon the latter work, in order to secure an uninterrupted line of retreat, but was in every case steadily and bloodily repulsed. "At half-past seven o'clock, the position of affairs was thus: Batteries eleven and twelve had been recaptured, a cordon of troops, consisting of Hartranft's division with regiments belonging to McLaughlin's and Ely's brigades, was formed around Fort Stedman and battery ten, into which the enemy was forced. There he was exposed to a concentrated fire from all the artillery in position bearing on these points and the reserve batteries in the rear."*

General Hartranft was now ordered to advance his troops and retake the line. The 211th Pennsylvania was selected to advance directly upon the fort, in order to occupy the attention of the enemy while the remainder of the command was to rush in on either flank. A large portion of these troops had

---

General Parke's Report.

never before been under fire in a pitched battle, but nothing could exceed the fearless bearing with which they made the assault. At fifteen minutes before eight, the attack was made in the finest style. The enemy's resistance was broken, the troops charged over the works, and, in a moment, Fort Stedman and the battery were recaptured and the enemy compelled to ask for quarter. The cross fire from our batteries prevented retreat, except with great difficulty. A large portion of the entire storming column, which had come out from the opposing lines eager and hopeful of triumph, was now obliged to surrender. One thousand nine hundred and forty-nine prisoners, seventy-one of whom were officers, nine stands of colors, and a large number of small arms were the fruits of this brilliant exploit. Our lines were at once reöccupied, and all damages repaired. Our losses were about one thousand killed, wounded and missing.

General Hartranft, who was in immediate command of the troops engaged, managed the affair with great skill, and won additional renown. "Too much credit," said General Parke, "cannot be given him." By his promptitude and ability in rallying his troops, in making his dispositions, and in conducting the final assault, he changed what threatened to be a great disaster into a glorious success. It was as decisive in its way as General Sheridan's splendid achievement at Cedar Creek. Whatever plan General Lee may have devised for a subsequent movement was completely thwarted. The Army of the Potomac was saved from the danger of entire defeat and ruin. The presence of mind and the rapidity of execution which distinguished General Hartranft in these trying circumstances, won for him the brevet of Major General. Generals Parke, Meade, and Grant, the Secretary of War and the President were equally hearty in the expression of their commendation, and the promotion was immediately made. No honor during the war was more worthily bestowed or more bravely won.

It happened curiously enough, that General Parke was in command of the entire Army of the Potomac at the time of the attack on Fort Stedman, although he was not at first aware of the fact. At half past five o'clock, he reported the intelligence of the enemy's appearance and action to head-quarters. He received no reply to his despatch. Four successive times did he send the communication without a response, until ten minutes past six, when an answer came from the telegraph operator: "General Meade is not here and the command devolves on you." The commanding general had yielded his "prerogative" without intimating to his second in command, that the mantle of authority had fallen from his shoulders. General Meade had given no notice of his absence, and General Parke found himself bearing an unexpected burden of duty. He immediately despatched couriers to City Point and, meanwhile, ordered Generals Wright and Warren to move troops towards the position which the enemy had assailed. He had already received cordial tenders of assistance from his brother officers. The corps commanders were even anxious and eager to attack the enemy, in turn, along the whole line. They would have been glad to have fought a battle under the direction of General Parke, without any intervention of General Meade. There was every prospect of winning a great victory, so far as the judgment of these officers could determine. But General Parke was not willing to take the responsibility of ordering an attack while he was accidentally in command. He had too much self-control to allow himself to be governed by the suggestions of personal ambition, and rejected the opportunity of securing a mere personal glory, through the negligence of his chief. It was an instance of self-command which was very honorable to General Parke. General Wheaton's division of the sixth corps came down to the neighborhood of the points attacked, and stood in readiness to afford any required aid, but General Hartranft was fully competent to do the needed work alone. Immediately after the line was reoccupied, telegraphic communication with head-quarters was renewed. General Meade had now returned to the army and at once sent up orders, that no attack upon the enemy was to be made. The remainder of

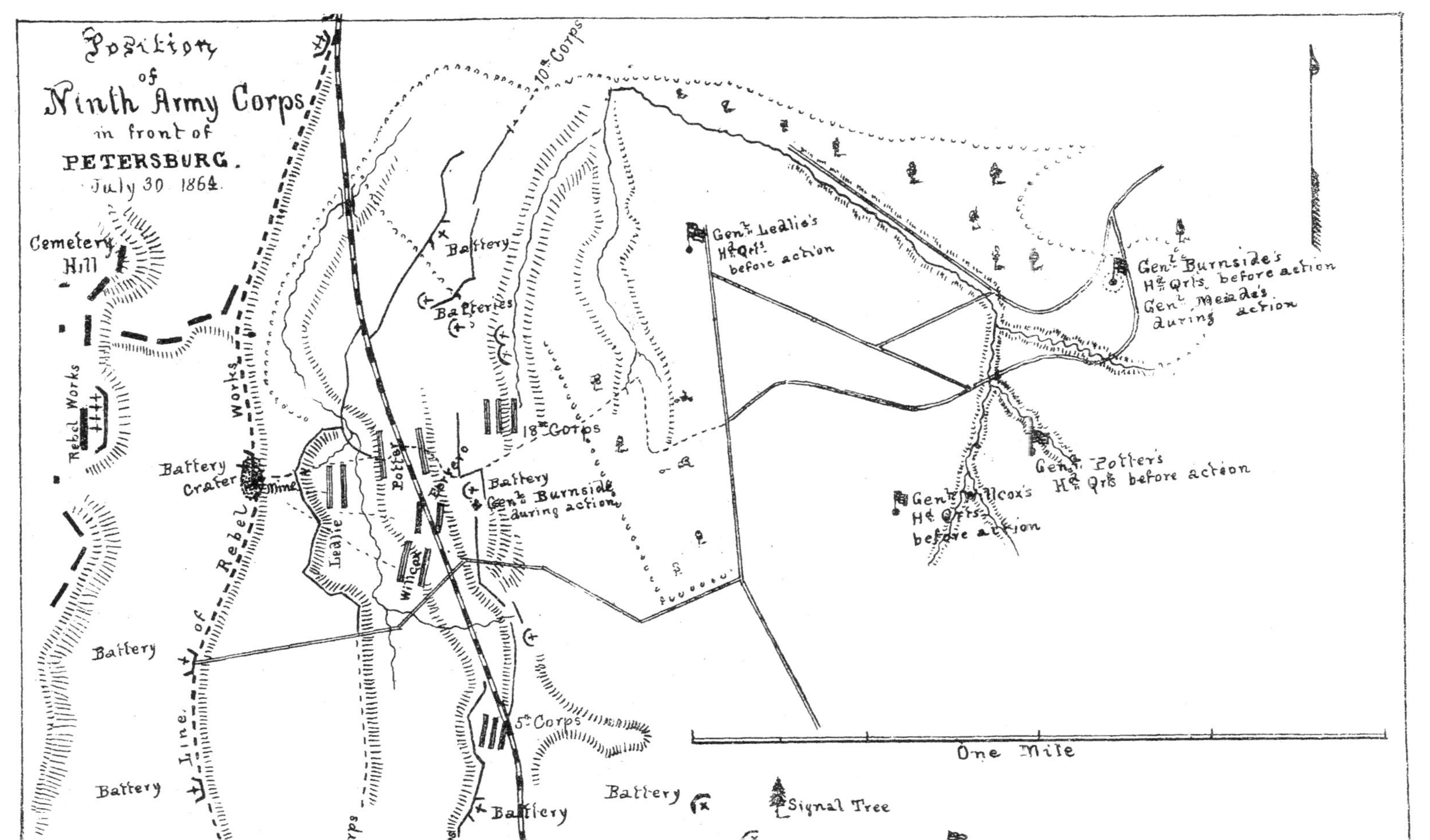

Position of Ninth Army Corps in front of PETERSBURG. July 30 1864.
Cemetery Hill
Rebel Works
Battery
Crater
Mine
Line of Rebel Works
10th Corps
Battery
Batteries
18th Corps
Leadie
Potter
Willcox
Ferrero
Battery
Gen'l Burnside during action
Battery
5th Corps
Battery
Battery
Battery
Battery
Signal Tree
Gen'l Ledlie's Hd Qrts before action
Gen'l Burnside's Hd Qrts before action
Gen'l Meade's during action
Gen'l Potter's Hd Qrts before action
Gen'l Willcox's Hd Qrts before action
One Mile
rps

the day passed in quiet in front of the Ninth Corps. On the left of our line there was some severe fighting, resulting in a loss to the enemy of nearly a thousand prisoners and an equal number of killed and wounded, for which he had previously gained no compensative advantage.

General Meade, on the 27th, issued a congratulatory order, in which he spoke in complimentary terms of the promptness of General Parke, "the firm bearing of the troops of the Ninth Corps in the adjacent positions of the line held by the enemy, and the conspicuous gallantry of the third division, together with the energy and skill displayed by General Hartranft." He had at first reflected severely upon "the want of vigilance of the third brigade of the first division." But on subsequent information, he was convinced that he had spoken wrongly and hastily, and therefore cancelled the order. It was said by some that the enemy contemplated making an attack upon Fort Sedgwick, but our line there was too strongly guarded. He therefore tried the experiment further down towards the river. Whether this was so or not, the movement was skilfully made and nearly proved a success. Under the orders that were given from headquarters, respecting the reception of deserters, it was possible at almost any point, and the wonder is that it was not tried before.

No further opportunity for such a surprise occurred. The enemy had not won the victory which he had hoped. Our troops were put more vigilantly on their guard, and prepared with greater eagerness for the decisive movement which every one felt to be momentarily approaching. Every indication now pointed to General Lee's speedy retreat from Petersburg and Richmond. General Grant prepared his army to strike the final blow before his enemy could escape. General Sheridan, with his cavalry, was hurried to the extreme left, and the entire Army of the Potomac, on the 27th of March, was ordered to be ready to move at a moment's notice. On the 29th, the march commenced. General Sheridan had the advance. General Warren's corps followed, with General

Humphreys in support. The sixth and Ninth Corps held the lines in front of Petersburg, and portions of the Army of the James were brought from the north side of the river to aid in the contemplated attack. It is not needful to follow the magnificent manœuvres and brilliant fighting which, for the next few days, proved to General Lee that the hour of his defeat had come. Still, until the last moment, he tenaciously held upon his fortified positions at Petersburg and Richmond. General Grant found it necessary to attack in front as well as on the flank.

The enemy's line, from the Appomattox to the front of Fort Sedgwick, was the old interior line which had been so often attacked in vain. The line held by the Ninth Corps extended as far as Fort Davis, and fronted the enemy's strong position. On the 30th of March, General Parke received orders to assault on the next morning at four o'clock. The point of attack was left to his discretion. The front of Fort Sedgwick was thought to be the most available for the attempt. The divisions of Generals Potter and Hartranft were concentrated in rear of the fort, ready for the movement. The assault, however, was suspended, by order of General Meade. The operations on the left had not been developed sufficiently to insure success. The troops were therefore ordered back to their old position. At last the time came. On the 1st of April, orders were again issued for attack. About ten o'clock that night our artillery opened and our skirmishers were sent forward. General S. G. Griffin found a weak place in front of his brigade, between Forts Hayes and Howard, rushed in, carried the picket line, and captured two hundred and fifty prisoners; but, finding the enemy's main line fully armed, again withdrew. During the night, the troops were concentrated. General Hartranft's division was massed in front of Fort Sedgwick. Colonel Samuel Harriman's brigade of General Willcox's division, was formed on General Hartranft's right. The 51st Pennsylvania held the brigade line in the works. General Potter's division was massed on General Hartranft's left, to the left of the Jerualem plank road. At three o'clock on the morning of the 2d ›f April, General Parke established his headquarters at Fort Rice. At the same time, Generals Hartranft and Potter formed heir assaulting columns. General Hartranft put the 207th Pennsylvania in advance, and in its immediate rear the 205th, 211th and 208th Pennsylania. The 200th and 209th Pennsylvania were held in reserve. Colonel Harriman's brigade was posted on the right. General Potter formed his column with General Griffin's brigade in advance, immediately supported by General Curtin's. The attacking forces were very kilfully arranged. Storming parties, pioneers with axes, and roops equipped as engineers, and details of artillerists to work any guns that might be captured, accompanied each column. The plan of attack was for General Willcox to make a feint in front of Fort Stedman, while Generals Potter and Hartranft assaulted the enemy's works.

At four o'clock, our artillery opened along the entire line. General Willcox promptly and vigorously pushed out his skirmishers, and was everywhere successful. The 51st Pennsylvania, under Colonel Bolton, captured the enemy's line near the crater. Colonel Ely's brigade carried the picket line and two hundred yards of the main works near the Appomattox. The enemy concentrated a considerable force upon these troops, as was anticipated, and gave an opportunity for the columns on the left. At half-past four, the signal was given, and the troops designed for the main attack sprung away from their place of formation with the greatest alacrity and enthusiasm. Eager to avenge the repulse which they had experienced on almost the same ground, eight months before, they charged the enemy's line with the utmost vigor and resolution. They were received with a storm of grape, canister and musketry, but through the deadly tempest they advanced with an intrepidity which showed that the Ninth had not lost the ancient daring. They plunged through the ditch, tore away the abatis, scaled the walls, swept over the parapets and carried the works. Hartranft's column was successful in capturing twelve guns, a number of colors, and eight hundred prisoners. Harriman's column made a gallant charge upon the right, and carried all that part of the enemy's line which was known as Miller's salient.

General Potter's division advanced upon the left, in the face of a terrific fire, which made dreadful rents in the attacking column. The enemy's line in the part which General Potter assailed was heavily fortified, and it was necessary to drive him from traverse to traverse in a hand to hand conflict. The 6th New Hampshire captured a battery of four guns, and turned them on the enemy. The 56th Massachusetts, assisted by the 5th Massachusetts battery, took and held the line of rebel works on the Jerusalem plank road. The enemy was very tenacious, and fought with great resolution, but was finally obliged to yield before the progress of our troops. For a quarter of a mile, he was borne back into an interior line of works, where he was strongly reënforced, and was enabled to check the advancing columns. A very daring but unsuccessful attempt was made to carry this inner position, in the midst of which General Potter fell, very severely wounded. General Griffin succeeded to the command of the division, and very ably directed its movements for the remainder of its term of service. For his brave and faithful conduct on this day, he was brevetted Major General.

It was now full daylight. The operations thus far had been very successful. The enemy's line, to the distance of four hundred yards on each side of the Jerusalem plank road, including several forts and redans, had been taken by our troops. Meanwhile, the sixth, second, and portions of the twenty-fourth and twenty-fifth corps had attacked from the left, and succeeded in carrying a part of the opposing lines in their front, with two thousand prisoners and at least fifteen pieces of artillery. The enemy resisted strenuously, but, after an obstinate struggle, was compelled to give way, with the loss of his commanding General A. P. Hill. The sixth corps particularly distinguished itself in this day's battle. Trained under Sheridan in the Shenandoah Valley, it had caught the fearless enthusiasm of its leader. It now proved what brave men could do when moving dauntlessly upon a fortified enemy. Before the day had passed, it reached the banks of the Appomattox, on the southwest side of Petersburg. The other assaulting corps were equally fortunate, and, by their courage and perseverance, the city of Petersburg was, for the first time during the siege, effectually invested.

The Ninth Corps, after its first successful assault, received orders to hold on to what it had already gained. General Parke had attacked the enemy's main line, while the other corps had attacked another line, which might be occupied without securing possession of the city. At eight o'clock, General Parke was directed not to advance, unless he saw the way clear to success. He therefore strengthened his position, with a view to holding it against any assaulting force. The enemy seemed disposed to recapture, if possible, the works which he had lost. Just before eleven o'clock, he made a very determined attack, but was repulsed with heavy losses. He continued to attack at intervals until afternoon, gaining some slight advantage. But General Lee evidently considered that his case was hopeless. He telegraphed to Mr. Davis at Richmond, that an evacuation of Petersburg was inevitable.

It was useless to contend against fate. General Lee, beaten on the flank and front, prepared to abandon the position which he had so long and skilfully defended. He still, however, kept up a show of resistance. So threatening at one time were the demonstrations in front of the Ninth Corps, that General Parke was obliged to call for reënforcements. Two brigades were sent up from City Point, and Colonel Hamblin's brigade was ordered down from the sixth corps. At three o'clock in the afternoon, the troops arrived from City Point, and, under the direction of General Griffin, made a spirited attack and forced the enemy back from the immediate front. Between four and five o'clock, Colonel Hamblin arrived upon the ground, and General Parke desired to renew the assault. But upon ascertaining the condition of the men, who were exhausted by twelve hours of hard fighting, he decided simply to make his position entirely secure. He removed the abatis to the front of the reversed line and connected with a cross line to that which he originally held. Some skirmishing occurred until a late hour of the night. The troops were enjoined to exercise the utmost vigilance, that the slightest movement of the enemy might be observed, and advantage taken of any inclination which he might evince to evacuate the position.

At two o'clock on the morning of the 3d the enemy's pickets were still out. They were doubtless withdrawn very soon afterwards, for at four o'clock when our skirmishers advanced they met with no resistance. The troops were immediately put in motion and entered the city at all points. Of the Ninth Corps, Colonel Ely's brigade was the first to pass the enemy's works, and Colonel Ely himself received the formal surrender of the city. At half-past four the 1st Michigan sharpshooters raised their flag upon the Court House and Petersburg at last was ours! General Willcox announced the surrender, and at five o'clock the gratifying intelligence was communicated to General Meade. The enemy in his retreat set fire to the bridge across the Appomattox, but our troops succeeded in saving a portion of the structure. General Willcox at once threw skirmishers over the river, and a few straggling soldiers were captured. General Willcox was placed in command of the city with his division for garrison. General Parke, with the two remaining divisions, was ordered, in connection with the sixth corps, to pursue the retreating foe. The command on the 3rd marched out as far as Sutherland's Station on the Southside railroad, where it encamped for the night. The troops moved at daylight on the next morning, following the sixth corps, pressing on until late in the afternoon, when orders came to move over to the Coxe road, to guard the rear of the pursuing army.

From that time until the surrender of General Lee on the 9th, General Parke was engaged in scouting, and picketing along the railroad and well towards the south, in order to prevent any hostile demonstrations which the enemy might be disposed to make from that direction. At the time of the surrender General Parke's command extended from Farmville to Sutherland's station. The Ninth Corps was not immediately present when the army of Northern Virginia laid down its arms. A few of the officers rode up and witnessed the ceremony. The intelligence was received with the most joyful acclamations. The soldiers were glad to know that their work of carnage and death were finished. Visions of homes and friends rose before their minds. They now awaited the coming of the day when they could lay aside the weapons of war and resume the implements of peace. A citizen soldiery, unaccustomed to scenes of deadly conflict, had learned to face death in its frightfullest forms with calmness, and by heroic deeds and sublime sacrifices, had saved the Republic. The men who had composed the Ninth Corps, drawn from fourteen different States, were faithful representatives of the best portions of our volunteer army. No stain of dishonor ever sullied their fair renown, and no stigma of shame can ever be affixed upon their bright record.

The assassination of Mr. Lincoln caused intense feeling throughout the army and especially among the soldiers of the Ninth Corps to whom the President was like a personal friend. The relations between General Burnside and Mr. Lincoln were particularly intimate and the interest felt in the commander was extended to the troops. By no one more than by the President was the Ninth Corps appreciated for its long and arduous services. The good will was reciprocated, and the Presidential policy was nowhere more firmly supported than among the officers and men of the Corps.

The rest of the story can be quickly told. The Corps remained in the neighborhood of Sutherland's until the 19th, when the troops were ordered to Washington. They embarked at City Point during the week following the 20th, and in due time arrived at Alexandria. General Parke was assigned to the command of the district of Alexandria. On the 22d of May the Corps marched across Long Bridge, bivouacked near the Capitol and on the 23d participated in the grand review. It remained encamped in the neighborhood of Washington for the next four months, gradually disintegrating by the departure of the different regiments which had composed the command. During the trial of the conspirators against the life of the President, General Hartranft was assigned to duty as the guard of the prisoners. The date of final disbandment of the Corps was the 27th of July. General Willcox's division was the last to be mustered out. On the 25th of July General Willcox, who had for a time commanded the district of Washington, issued his last orders. In hearty and affectionate words he bade his soldiers farewell. What he said of his division might well be said of the entire Corps. The story of the command, " various regiments of which have left the bones of their dead to whiten battle fields in seven different States, will form a part of your individual life hereafter," said General Willcox to his troops. " Your families and fellow citizens will welcome your return in peace and victory. You will carry about you in civil life a sense of your own worth, and self-respect will characterize those who have done and deserved so well of their country."

Generals Parke and Potter on the disbandment of the Corps were assigned to duty in the department of the East under General Hooker. General Parke was placed in command of the southern district of New York, and General Potter* of the district of Rhode Island and Connecticut. General Willcox was assigned to duty as the commander of the district of Michigan in the department of the Ohio under General Ord, where he met his former comrade, General Cox. General Hartranft was assigned to the department of Kentucky under General Palmer. The other general officers were mustered out of the service at the time of the final disbandment. On the 1st of

*General Potter was promoted to full Major General September 29, 1865.

January, 1866, General Cox, who had previously been elected Governor of Ohio, resigned his commission in the army. On the 15th of the same month, Generals Parke, Potter, Willcox and Hartranft were "honorably mustered out of the service of the United States."

General Parke returned to the corps of engineers, in which he held the rank of brevet Brigadier General. He was afterwards promoted to brevet Major General in the regular army. The other officers returned to civil life. Generals Potter and Willcox resumed the practice of their profession. General Hartranft was elected in October, 1865, Auditor General of Pennsylvania. Thus with honor to themselves and the country did the men and officers of the Ninth Corps close their term of service. But, though the bonds of army life were severed by the completion of the work, to which they had consecrated their powers, the ties of affection which a community of danger and duty had woven still remain strong as ever. The memory of the noble dead is the common inheritance, and the proud consciousness of duty always well performed the common satisfaction, of those brave men whose names are borne on the rolls of the old NINTH ARMY CORPS!

CHAPTER IX.

CONCLUSION.

ALL history is necessarily imperfect. Even if every detail is told, there still remain many things which cannot be recorded. There are many acts of fidelity, self-sacrifice and heroism of which there can be no chronicle. The more prominent events of a great struggle, the movements of large armies, the battles in which they engage, the shining exploits which win glory for their actors and secure the admiration of the world, stand conspicuously out before the eyes of mankind. But there are many other deeds, less distinguished and less known, which yet have an important influence upon the course and issue of the strife. Much that is borne and done, both in the camp and in the field, cannot be written down or made the object of the public gaze. No one thinks of telling the story except in some choice circle of friendship. The endurance of hardship, the self-discipline and self-control, the spirit of moderation in victory and of steadfastness in defeat, the sense of imperative duty and the love of a great and noble cause—all the qualities of character, in short, which belong to good soldiers and brave men, and make up the morale of an army, belong to that part of history which may well be called unwritten.

Nor is the spirit of a people, which perpetually encourages and reënforces an army in the field, to be disregarded or overlooked. The war of the rebellion was without precedent among the nations of the world. Never was there an army like that which was raised in defence of the Republic. When its numbers, the character of its officers and men for intelligence, faithfulness to duty and patriotic fervor, the spirit of persistrace which animated its action, and wrung the victory of right from the desperation of injustice, and the willingness to suffer and to do all needful things, are considered, the verdict of history must be, that never was a principle more loyally served, and never was its triumph more gloriously won. We have to look beyond the march of armies and the din of battle, to see what it is that carries the day. We have to appreciate the power of invisible forces, the unrecognized virtues and even the unsuccessful heroism, with which every great contest abounds, but which rarely becomes matter of public knowledge, if we wish to understand the greatness of a nation, when struggling for its liberty and its life. There is oftentimes as much heroism in the humblest homes of the people, as on the most famous battle field. Valor in action secures its well-earned meed of honor, but calm and silent endurance also has its exceeding great reward. The trust in God which alleviated the sorrows of bereaved affection, the uncomplaining fortitude, with which the pains of wounds and sickness, and the loneliness of imprisonment were borne, can never be adequately traced by any human pen. But one book—the book of everlasting life—is alone fit to contain such a glorious record.

The soldiers of the Ninth Corps can count many a comrade whose nameless grave lies far away, beneath the turf of southern plain, forest or hill-side. Many were compelled to suffer the rigors and cruelties of southern prisons, and to become familiar with the horrors of Belle Isle, Salisbury and Andersonville. Of the fate of many there is no register and no knowledge, even to this day. They left their homes, they gave up the things which most men think dear, they entered bravely into the struggle, they laid down their lives for their country, and there is no chronicle of their virtues except in the memories of those who mourn their loss. They sank to rest in the silent earth—" unknelled, uncoffined and unknown." It is manifestly impossible to speak the sufficient praise of the unlaurelled heroism of these unnamed martyrs:

"The thousands that, uncheered by praise,
Have made one offering of their days;
For truth, for heaven, for freedom's sake,
Resigned the bitter cup to take;
And silently, in fearless faith,
Bowing their noble souls to death."

In the course of this narrative, notices have been inserted, from time to time, of officers who have fallen in battle. It must not be supposed that these alone are thought to be the subjects of special commendation. Many others, both of officers and men, whose names do not appear in these pages have been equally deserving and equally rich in wealth of duty, courage and self-devotion. Such men require no eulogy. Every life which has thus been given has aided in accomplishing the great result and in making secure the cause, for which it has been sacrificed. There are some officers, however, who are mentioned in the reports of their division commanders and in other documents, and who should not be permitted to pass unnoticed. One such was Major Gilmour of the 48th Pennsylvania, who was mortally wounded on the 31st of May, 1864, in a skirmish near the Tolopotomoy. He is spoken of by General Potter as an invaluable officer. Another was Colonel E. Schall of the 51st Pennsylvania, who was killed at the battle of Cold Harbor. He had gone through all the campaigns of the Corps, occupying different grades and always manifesting a distinguished bravery. He at one time, during the campaign in East Tennessee, commanded the second brigade of the second division, and there proved his fitness for a higher post than the command of a regiment. He was gradually but surely winning his promotion, when death put an end to his honorable career on earth.

The names of Major Byington of the second Michigan, who died of wounds received in the brilliant action before Knoxville on the night of November 24th, 1863; of Adjutant Noble, killed in the same action; of Captain Bradley, mortally wounded June 17th, 1864; of Captain Young of the same regiment, killed in the battle of July 30th; of Lieutenant Colonel Comstock of the 17th Michigan, mortally wounded November 24, 1863: of Lieutenant Colonel Smith of the 20th Michigan, who was killed in front of Knoxville, November 16th, 1863; of Adjutant Seibert who was killed at the battle of Weldon Railroad, September 30th, 1864; of Captain Wiltsie, mortally wounded in front of Knoxville; of Captains Dewey, Carpenter, Blood and McCullom, of the same regiment, who fell during the campaign of 1864; of Major Piper of the 1st Michigan sharpshooters who was killed at Spottsylvania, Major Lewis of the 8th Michigan, killed at Cold Harbor, and Major Moody of the 27th Michigan, mortally wounded in the same battle on the 3d of June; of Zoellner, Billingsly, Galpin, Steadman, Stanley and Clifton Lee, of different regiments, who fell during the siege of Knoxville,* are all names of good and gallant soldiers. Massachusetts, always ready with her offierings, gave her best and noblest. Lientenant Colonel Rice, Captains Frazer, Kelton, Clark, Sampson and Goss of the 21st; Major Chipman, Chaplain Hempstead, Lieutenants Collingwood, Ripley and Pope of the 29th; Major Park, Captains Bartlett, Niles, and White of the 35th; Captains Hastings, Buffum and Holmes, and Lieutenants Holmes, Daniels and Howe of the 36th; Major Putnam of the 56th, Majors Prescott and Doherty of the 57th, Major Ewer, and Captains Upham, McFarland, Johnson and Harley of the 58th, Colonel Gould, Lieutenant Colonel Hodges, and Captains Munroe and Bean of the 59th—are but a few of those who were faithful unto death. Other States have suffered equally with Michigan and Massachusetts. The West and the East have united in a common sacrifice for the salvation of the country which both have served and loved. The roll of honor which the Ninth Corps has made is indeed long, bearing the names of many true, brave and faithful men. A single volume would not suffice to contain the story of their virtue and their valor. Their memory is preserved on the imperishable record which love and friendship keep.

*The batteries around Knoxville received the names of the officers who fell in defence of the town.

Since the war has closed, death has been busy among those who once were connected with General Burnside's command. The members of his own military family have not escaped. A tender and touching interest gathers around the memory of Lieutenant Commander Thomas P. Ives. Of a high social position, the centre of a large circle of friends in the cities of Providence and New York, endowed with the graces of social refinement and a liberal education, a graduate of Brown University of the class of 1854, enjoying the opportunities, comforts and luxuries of great wealth, Captain Ives represented, in the truest manner, that worthy class of our people whom the war for the Union attracted to the field. His honorable career gave the best possible answer to the unjust reproach, which our enemies at home and abroad cast upon the loyal States, that the best of our citizens kept aloof from the conflict. At the breaking out of the rebellion, Mr. Ives promptly tendered the services of himself and his own yacht to the government, and was very diligent in the vigilance which he exercised in patrolling the waters of Chesapeake Bay. When the North Carolina expedition was organized, he was put in command of the gunboat Picket, and his services in that capacity are sufficiently familiar to the readers of this volume. Subsequently to the operations on the North Carolina coast, he was appointed acting Master in the United States Navy, and, in the command of the steamer Yankee, was very effectively employed in the Potomac flotilla. His promotion was rapid.

On the 26th of May, 1863, Mr. Ives was appointed acting volunteer Lieutenant. On the 7th of November, 1864, he was advanced to the grade of Lieutenant Commander, and was assigned to Ordnance duty in the navy yard at Washington. After the close of the war, he was granted leave of absence to recuperate his health, which had been impaired in the service. He visited Europe during the summer of 1865, and was married, on the 19th of October, to Miss Elizabeth Cabot Motley, daughter of the American Minister at Vienna. On the way home, decided symptoms of consumption appeared. The disease was rapidly developed, and he died at Havre, November 17, 1865, at the age of thirty-one. A life of great promise of usefulness was thus early quenched. The unfeigned sorrow of his former companions and of the entire community was freely expressed. It was felt by all that a bright and shining light had been extinguished, and that no greater sacrifice had been made during the war than that of this true and noble life.

The members of General Burnside's staff have been generally fortunate in their freedom from casualty and death. They were exposed in every battle. All won their promotion by their uniform daring and coolness. Some, with great fearlessness, like Loring, Cutting, Richmond, Pell, Goddard, Parke, Lydig and Harris, distinguished themselves on different fields, and gained brevets to higher rank of one, two, and even three grades. But with the exception of the wound of Lieutenant Benjamin and the death of Major Morton, they escaped uninjured. Captain George W. Gowan, who was on General Parke's staff while in front of Petersburg, was transferred to the command of the 48th Pennsylvania, and was killed while serving in that capacity. He was a brave and good officer. Captain Robert A. Hutchins, of General Willcox's staff, a particularly faithful and gallant soldier, was very severely wounded at the battle of the Wilderness. For a time, his life was despaired of, but he recovered, to be of good service afterwards. Captain Brackett, an officer of excellent promise, was wounded in the action on the Tolopotomoy.

The officers of the staff, subjected to the exposure and privations, which they endured in the course of the war, were not free from their influence after its conclusion. Some suffered from illness; no less than three have died. One of the best and most faithful of this company of friends was James Lyman Van Buren, highly esteemed and even dearly beloved by his comrades and his chief. He was born June 21st, 1837, graduated at the New York Free Academy in 1856, remained awhile as resident graduate, and then began the study of law, spending three years in preparation for the profession. He visited Europe in the summer of 1860, and returned in January, 1861. Soon after the outbreak of the war, he was appointed Second Lieutenant in the 53d New York, known as the D'Epineuil Zouaves. At Annapolis, he was transferred to the signal corps, and was assigned to duty on the staff of General Foster. At the battles of Roanoke Island and Newbern, he served as aide de camp, and received the merited commendations of his superior.

On the 23d of March, 1862, Lieutenant Van Buren was transferred to the staff of General Burnside, and acted in the capacity of Judge Advocate. When Governor Stanley arrived in North Carolina, he applied for the services of Lieutenant Van Buren, who was appointed his military secretary. On the 7th of July he was promoted to Major, and was assigned to duty with the Ninth Corps as aide de camp to its commander. On the 1st of December, 1862, Major Van Buren was taken dangerously ill, and thus was unable to participate in the battle of Fredericksburg. Partially recovering, he accompanied General Burnside to Cincinnati, when assigned to the Department of the Ohio. In all the stirring scenes that followed in Ohio, Kentucky and East Tennessee, he was on active and constant duty. Through the arduous campaign of 1864, though physical weakness might well have excused his absence, he was always at hand, attentive and especially faithful in the discharge of every duty. For his services in this campaign, he was promoted to brevet Lieutenant Colonel, and afterwards to brevet Colonel. Subsequently to General Burnside's retirement from the corps, Colonel Van Buren served with General Parke, remaining upon the staff until the close of the war. For his faithfulness in this respect, he received the brevet of Brigadier General. When General Parke was placed in command of the Southern District of New York, General Van Buren was assigned to duty on his staff. While in this position, he was struck down by sickness, in August, 1865, and died, after much suffering and pain, on the 13th of April, 1866. He was a man of singular pure mindedness, modesty and integrity of character. He acquired the entire confidence of all his associates, and was beloved by his friends with a peculiarly strong affection. A man of great gentleness and fearlessness, he was also a man of much practical sagacity. His counsel was always wise, and his rare manliness gave unusual weight to the opinions which he expressed. He devoted the prime of his early manhood to the service of his country, and though he died unwounded, it was as complete a sacrifice as though he had fallen on the field of battle.

There are, in an army, positions and duties, which are not brought prominently into view, but which are especially necessary for the efficiency of all military operations. It is not often that the medical department receives particular notice, or the highest commendation. The glory of war is supposed to belong to illustrious deeds on the field, rather than to patient fidelity in the hospital. Yet whoever rightfully values the character of genuine faithfulness and true heroism, must acknowledge that the medical officer who thoroughly performs his duty, is filling one of the most important positions that can be named. The post of the Surgeon is not always one of great danger. It does not usually require personal exposure to the missiles of death, but it does demand the most watchful care, a wise discretion, and most scrupulous and, at times, laborious fidelity. The preservation of the health of an army while lying in camp, the proper treatment of wounds after a battle, and the recuperation of strength after exhausting labors and marches, are certainly duties of the greatest consequence. The commanding general is indebted for the effectiveness of his military movements, more than he may sometimes think, to the silent and unobtrusive labors of his corps of Surgeons. The health of the soldiers is necessary to their morale, and their morale is an essential element for their achievement of victory. Physical and moral feebleness is the sure condition of defeat.

The Ninth Corps was fortunate in its medical officers. Doctors Church, McDonald, Rivers, Harris and Dalton, were all men who were skilful in their profession and trustworthy in their character. Doctors Rivers and Harris were engaged in the war through almost its entire course. They served under General Burnside when he was Colonel of the First Rhode Island, and they continued with the Ninth Corps during their subsequent terms of service. Doctor Harris was taken prisoner at the first battle of Bull Run, having preferred to stay with the wounded to following the retreating army. He remained a captive until the sick and wounded prisoners of the First and 2d Rhode Island were beyond the need of his services, when he was released on his parole. Having accomplished an exchange, he was appointed Surgeon of the 7th Rhode Island, and in that capacity joined the Ninth Corps. He served with the Corps until the close of the war, passing through the several grades of brigade and division Surgeon, until he became Medical Director. In every position, he exhibited the characteristics of a remarkably diligent and devoted officer. A former experience in the Russian army in the Crimean campaign gave him a great advantage in his profession, and enabled him to be of the utmost service in every position which he filled. He retired to civil life, bearing with him the esteem and confidence of all his associates.

Dr. Rivers served from the commencement of the war until near its close, as Surgeon of the First Rhode Island, of the 4th Rhode Island, of the third brigade in North Carolina, of the third division of the Ninth Corps; as acting Medical Director of the corps, as Surgeon at headquarters of the Army of the Potomac, and of the Department of the Ohio; as Surgeon in chief of Kautz's cavalry division during the campaign of 1864. He proved himself an able and efficient medical officer. After finishing his term of service, he resumed the practice of his profession in Providence.

Dr. Dalton entered the service as Surgeon of a New York regiment, and served in the Peninsular campaign under General McClellan. He continued with the Army of the Potomac, gradually rising in rank and in the confidence of his superior officers, until, in the autumn of 1864, he was assigned to duty in the Ninth Corps as its Medical Director. A gentleman of great skill and wide attainments in his profession, a man of a high and honorable spirit, a genial companion, and a faithful officer, he won largely upon the respect of his brother officers, and left the service with the kindest expressions of interest and friendship from all his companions in duty.

Since the close of the war, Doctors Church and McDonald have fallen victims to disease. William Henry Church was born in Angelica, Alleghany County, New York, June 6, 1826. His father was Hon. Philip Church, and his grandmother was a daughter of General Philip Schuyler. Educated at Canandaigua and Geneva, he chose the profession of medicine, commenced the study in 1846, graduated at the College of Physicians and Surgeons in the spring of 1849, and entered upon practice in the city of New York in the year 1851, with every prospect of abundant success. He was appointed Surgeon of Volunteers August 3, 1861, and, upon the organization of the North Carolina expedition, was assigned to duty as Medical Director of General Burnside's army.

Dr. Church served with General Burnside when in command of the Ninth Corps, of the Army of the Potomac, and of the Department of the Ohio. Highly valued and always trusted, he shared the tent of his commanding general while in the field. In this intimate relation, he became more like a confidential friend and adviser than a subordinate officer. His physical health was never strong, and it was seriously impaired by the hardships and privations to which he had been exposed. On the 26th of October, 1863, he was obliged to resign his commission as Medical Director of the corps. General Burnside's estimate of his character and value of his services can be understood by the language, which he used in accepting Dr. Church's resignation. In an order dated December 5, 1863, the commanding general said, that he could not "part from an officer who has been so long prominently associated with him, without some public expression of his acknowledgment of the laborious and important services, which Dr. Church has performed. Identified with the staff from its earliest organization, he has shared its fortunes in the many scenes of danger and trial through which it has passed, and when the occasion required, has been always ready, in addition to the manifold duties of his department, to perform those of an aide in the field, until impaired health has compelled the tender of his resignation."

In February, 1864, Dr. Church visited New Orleans, and in October, 1865, he went to Europe, with the hope that a change of climate would restore his health; but the hope was vain. He died from hemorrhage from the lungs at Pau, in the south of France, September 27th, 1866, leaving a large circle of friends to mourn his untimely decease. The singular fidelity with which he performed every duty, the manliness of his character, and his engaging and amiable disposition attracted towards him all who came within the range of his influence. The members of the original staff were bound to him by peculiarly strong ties. Not only had he been their comrade in duty and danger, but he had also sustained towards them the tender and close relation of a family physician.

Dr. John E. McDonald succeeded to the position vacated by Dr. Church, and diligently performed its duties during the time of his connection with the corps. Dr. McDonald was of Irish parentage, and exhibited through life those traits of generosity, enthusiasm and adventurous daring, which have at all times distinguished the character of his countrymen. In boyhood, he attracted the attention of Dr. Elliott of New York, who manifested great interest in him, took him into his office, and was instrumental in giving him a medical education. He accordingly graduated in 1854 at the College of Physicians and Surgeons. After his graduation, he devoted himself to the treatment of the eye, became favorably known, secured a very lucrative practice, and excited warm hopes of future distinction in the profession.

Dr. McDonald entered the service as Surgeon of the 79th New York, and went through the campaigns in South Carolina and with the Ninth Corps, in which that regiment bore a distinguished part. He was appointed Surgeon of Volunteers April 13th, 1863, and still continued on duty with the Corps, manifesting a decided skill and effectiveness in the posts of brigade and division Surgeon and Medical Inspector. He came east with the Corps in the spring of 1864, and passed through the campaign of the following summer, making for himself an honorable record. The exposures of the service, and the unwonted labors that fell upon the medical department of the army, wore upon and weakened his health, and in the autumn he felt compelled to seek a less exhausting duty. He was accordingly relieved from active service in the field, and was assigned to the superintendence of a general hospital at Philadelphia. At the close of the war, he returned to the practice of his profession. But having acquired a taste for army life, he decided once more to enter the service. He was examined for the position of Surgeon in the regular army, secured the appointment, and immediately began his work. Assigned to duty at the West, he was stationed at Jefferson barracks, St. Louis. The advent of the cholera in the summer of 1866 put upon him severe burdens, which he took up with his accustomed energy. But his toil overcame him, and he fell a victim himself to the pestilence from which he was endeavoring to save others. He died, leaving behind him the memory of a true, brave and devoted man.

No narrative of military operations during the rebellion would be complete, without notice of the labors of the Sanitary and Christian Commissions. To the former, particularly, not only our own country, but also the entire civilized world is indebted for help in the elucidation of the great problem of alleviating, if not preventing disease among large bodies of men. It is well known that armies are depleted by other causes than casualties in battle. The Sanitary Commission undertook the task at the very outset, of ascertaining and providing for the needs of the soldiers in camp and on the field. The object was to preserve the health and the strength of the armies which were raising, to check the progress of disease, to furnish articles for the hospitals and for the individual sick and wounded, which were not contemplated in the army regulations, to care for soldiers who were *in transitu* from camp to home, or from home to camp, to collect statistics on all the various subjects which pertained to the sanitary condition of the army, and, in short, to do all the work which was requisite for the aid and comfort of the sick, the wounded, the disabled and the bereaved.

The Sanitary Commission was the organized benevolence of the nation, as applied to the army. An appeal was made to the people at the beginning of the war. The people, particularly the women of the nation, responded nobly, generously, ceaselessly. A stream of contributions in supplies and money flowed into the storehouses and treasury of the Commission. For five years it continued. This good will and liberality never gave the slightest indication of exhaustion. When the war ended, the Commission was supplied for a long campaign. The people were not deceived. They did not give in vain. The agents of the Commission were prompt, vigilant and active on every battle field and in every hospital. Sometimes they were the first on the ground with their needed supplies. Often they were among the last to leave. The Ninth Corps, in common with the rest of the army, was the recipient of the bounty which the two Commissions dispensed. Many a poor fellow, far away from home and friends, had them brought to him by the kindness of these benevolent associations and their agents. His loneliness was cheered, his mind soothed, and his dying moments blest, as he was taught to feel that Christian sympathy was freely given him, and Christian love had chosen him for its special object.

There is another class of men, filling a comparatively obscure position, but performing a vast amount of useful labor in the promotion of the effectiveness of an army. The Chaplains, who have served in the hospital or in the field, have rendered an inestimable, though not always recognized service in the cause of the Union. Their names very seldom appeared in official reports, but the duties which they performed, when faithfully discharged, were of the utmost benefit. They have been subject to all the casualties of a soldier's career. Some have suffered imprisonment, others have received wounds, others have contracted disease and died, and others still have lost their lives on the field of battle, while performing the duties of their sacred profession. A Chaplain's status in the army has never been defined. He was an officer, yet he had no rank, and could exercise no authority except that which his personal influence commanded. Most frequently, if he were a man of faithful spirit and of active temperament, he was a servant of all work. It has sometimes been the case, that the Chaplain of a regiment has been called upon to fill the position of postmaster, teacher, amanuensis, private secretary, aide de camp, and even commissary and quarter master, while the Surgeons in the regimental hospitals have at all times felt justified in calling upon him for aid. Left in charge of the wounded after a battle, when the army has been compelled to retreat, Chaplains have not unfrequently fallen into the hands of the enemy. It is true that, in some cases, they have not been retained as prisoners for any long period. "We don't want Yankee Chaplains in the South," said General Stuart to Chaplain Ball of the 21st Massachusetts, after the battle of Chantilly, when he learned the name and position of his prisoner; "I think we will let you go." But all rebel officers were not so lenient as the good-natured cavalry general. Some of the Chaplain's who were captured were treated with great severity, and still bear the marks of their confinement.

The labors of these officers and the influence which they have exerted, belong rather to the unseen and unwritten part of life, than to that which is apparent and well understood. Certainly there was no place where religious teaching was more needed than in the army, and there was no better or more encouraging field to an industrious and faithful man. The influence which a good Chaplain exerted was not altogether temporary. It remains and does its silent work, long after the official connection between him and the soldier has ceased. Men like James of the 25th Massachusetts, who, at the battle of Roanoke Island, personally served the gun of a battery, the men of which had been disabled ; Benton of the 51st New York, who was killed at the battle of Newbern, while in attendance upon the wounded and dying men of his regiment; Ball of the 21st Massachusetts, who, at the battle of Camden, and in the movements of the regiment, performed at different times the duties of every office of the regimental staff; Hunting of the 27th Michigan, who was always active, zealous and efficient in the camp and field ; and others, less known, but not less faithful, have, in the course of the war, done a work the results of which are permanent in their duration. Upon men placed in the circumstances of a soldier's life, if there is any receptivity of good influences, religious services, conducted by a sincere and devoted man, have a wonderful effect. They are a restraint, an encouragement, a help, and an inspiration. The uncertainty of the life in which these men are engaged, the necessity of obeying the commands of a superior at any moment, without any question and in utter ignorance of what may be the issue, and the consequent loss, to a certain extent, of self-confidence, naturally induce a feeling of dependence on a higher Power. It is a time when trust in Divine Providence can be awakened and obedience to Divine laws enforced. The most thoughtless must be affected in some degree, even though no apparent result is produced. In subsequent hours, the words and personal influence of the religious teacher will be remembered, recognized and felt. Or, if death has come upon the field or in the hospital, it is certainly a satisfaction to know that the last hours of many a dying soldier have been solaced, and his pains assuaged by the kindly and gentle ministrations of the devoted Chaplain, who has pointed the struggling spirit to a world of unfading brightness and eternal peace.

There is still another class of men, whom not to mention

would be an act of injustice as well as neglect. These are known as "the rank and file" of our volunteer army. The private soldier does not always receive the attention and the grateful acknowledgment which his services merit. In the great war for the preservation of the Union, the enlisted men of the army have been for the most part especially remarkable for the readiness, with which they first entered upon the duty, the fearlessness which they manifested in the contest, the spirit of self-sacrifice with which they exposed and, by thousands, laid down their lives, and for the facility with which the survivors reëntered upon peaceful occupations and became once more absorbed into the life of the State. In recounting the more distinguished service of officers high in command, the claims of the private soldier to an honorable recognition should not be overlooked.

There were many cases of young men of the best social position, of fine scholarship and even of great wealth, who volunteered to serve as privates in the armies of the Union. Many who enlisted in the three months' regiments at the beginning of the war, served again as officers in regiments subsequently organized for a longer period. Of the members of General Burnside's staff, Messrs. Richmond, Goddard, Pell, French and Cutts were privates in the First Rhode Island. This regiment alone furnished from its private soldiers no less than two hundred and twenty officers of all grades in the army from Second Lieutenant to brevet Brigadier General, and twelve officers in the navy. This is but a single instance. Other regiments could doubtless furnish its parallel. Add to these the promotions which have been made from the ranks, and some estimate can be made of the character of those who have occupied the humble position of the private soldier.

One of the best features of the war has been manifested in the alacrity with which our young men of all classes and conditions undertook the dangerous duty. What a contribution was made by the sturdy yeomanry of the free States! How readily did the laboring men furnish their quota to fill the

64

ranks! All were ready and even eager to participate in the perils and privations of the camp and the field. Accustomed to the free and independent life of northern communities, they yet learned the difficult lesson of obedience and self-abnegation. Wonted to think for themselves, they yet brought themselves to the unquestioning action which the discipline of the army required. Few were the rewards for which their ambition looked. By them, little distinction was to be won. Little glory would gather round their names. Their chief incentive was a spirit of fidelity to the duty which the Republic demanded. That duty they well and thoroughly performed. The State which the fathers founded the sons with equal virtue preserved. They carried their country through the hour of its extreme peril, and proved to all the nations of the world that "the government of the people, by the people and for the people," was not to "perish from the earth." In concluding this narrative of the campaigns through which the NINTH ARMY CORPS passed, let the final word be a grateful tribute to the courage, the fortitude, the loyalty and self-devotion which the private soldiers exhibited on every scene of action, suffering or death!

PROCLAMATION OF THE UNION COMMANDERS

IN

NORTH CAROLINA.

GENERAL BURNSIDE'S STATEMENT

IN THE

VALLANDIGHAM CASE.

ROSTER

OF THE

NINTH CORPS.

PROCLAMATION

OF THE UNION COMMANDERS TO THE PEOPLE OF NORTH CAROLINA.

Roanoke Island, N. C., February 16th, 1862.

The mission of our joint expedition is not to invade any of your rights, but to assert the authority of the United States, and to close with you the desolating war brought upon your State by comparatively a few bad men in the midst of you.

Influenced infinitely more by the worst passions of human nature than by any show of elevated reason, they are still urging you astray to gratify their unholy purposes.

They impose upon your credulity by telling you of wicked and even diabolical intentions on our part—of our desire to destroy your freedom, demolish your property, liberate your slaves, injure your women, and such like enormities—all of which, we assure you, is not only ridiculous, but utterly and wilfully false. Those men are your worst enemies. They, in truth, have drawn you into your present condition, and are the real disturbers of your peace and the happiness of your firesides.

We invite you in the name of the Constitution, and in that of virtuous loyalty and civilization, to separate yourselves at once from their malign influence, to return to your allegiance, and not compel us to resort further to the force under our control.

We are Christians as well as yourselves, and we profess to know full well, and to feel profoundly the sacred obligations of that character. No apprehension need be entertained that the demands of humanity or justice will be disregarded. We shall inflict no injury, unless forced to do so by your own acts, and upon this you may confidently rely.

The Government asks only that its authority may be recognized, and, we repeat, in no manner or way does it desire to interfere with your laws constitutionally established, your institutions of any kind whatever, your property of any sort, your usages in any respect.

L. M. GOLDSBOROUGH,

Flag Officer Commanding North Atlantic Blockading Squadron.

A. E. BURNSIDE,

Brigadier General Commanding Department of North Carolina.

STATEMENT

OF MAJOR GENERAL BURNSIDE, IN THE VALLANDIGHAM CASE, IN ANSWER TO THE PRISONER'S APPLICATION FOR THE WRIT OF HABEAS CORPUS.

HEADQUARTERS DEPARTMENT OF THE OHIO,
Cincinnati, O., May 11, 1863.

To the Honorable the Circuit Court of the United States within and for the Southern District of Ohio:

The undersigned, commanding the Department of the Ohio, having received notice from the Clerk of said Court, thac an application for the allowance of a writ of habeas corpus will be made this morning before your Honor, on behalf of Clement L. Vallandigham, now a prisoner in my custody, asks leave to submit to the Court the following Statement:

If I were to indulge in wholesale criticisms of the policy of the Government, it would demoralize the army under my command, and every friend of his country would call me a traitor. If the officers or soldiers were to indulge in such criticisms, it would weaken the army to the extent of their influence; and if this criticism were universal in the army, it would cause it to be broken to pieces, the Government to be divided, our homes to be invaded, and anarchy to reign. My duty to my Government forbids me to indulge in such criticisms; officers and soldiers are not allowed so to indulge, and this course will be sustained by all honest men. Now I will go further. We are in a state of civil war. One of the States of this Department is at this moment invaded, and three others have been threatened. I command the Department, and it is my duty to my country and to this army, to keep it in the best possible condition; to see that it is fed, clad, armed, and, as far as possible, to see that it is encouraged. If it is my duty and the duty of the troops to avoid saying anything that would weaken the army, by preventing a single recruit from joining the ranks, by bringing the laws of Congress into disrepute, or by causing dissatisfaction in the ranks, it is equally the duty of every citizen in the Department to avoid the same evil. If it is my duty to prevent the propagation of this evil in the army, or in a portion of my Department, it is equally my duty in all portions of it; and it is my duty to use all the force in my power to stop it. If I were to find a man from the enemy's country distributing in my camps speeches of their public men, that tended to demoralize the troops, or to destroy their confidence in the constituted authorities of the Government, I would have him tried, and hung, if found guilty, and all the rules of modern warfare would sustain me. Why should such speeches from our own public men be allowed? The press and public men, in a great emergency like the present, should avoid the use of party epithets and bitter invectives, and discourage the organization of secret political societies, which are always undignified and disgraceful to a free people, but which now are absolutely wrong and injurious;—creating dissensions and discord, which just now amount to treason. The simple names "Patriot" and "Traitor" are comprehensive enough. As I before said, we are in a state of civil war, and an emergency is upon us which requires the operations of some power, that moves more quickly than the civil. There never was a war carried on successfully without the exercise of that power. It is said that the speeches which are condemned have been made in the presence of large bodies of citizens, who, if they thought them wrong, would have then and there condemned them. That is no argument. These citizens do not realize the effect upon the armies of our country, who are its defenders. They have never been in the field; never faced the enemies of their country; never undergone the privations of our soldiers in the field: and, besides, they have been in the habit of hearing their public men speak, and, as a general thing, of approving of what they say. Therefore, the greater responsibility rests upon the public men and upon the public press, and it behooves them to be careful as to what they say. They must not use license and plead that they are exercising liberty. In this Department, it cannot be done. I shall use all the power I have to break down such license, and I am sure I will be sustained in this course by all honest men. At all events, I will have the consciousness, before God, of having done my duty to my country; and when I am swerved from the performance of that duty by any pressure, public or private, or by any prejudice, I will no longer be a man or a patriot. I again assert, that every power I possess on earth, or that is given me from above, will be used in defence of my Government, on all occasions, at all times, and in all places within this Department. There is no party—no community—no State Government—no State Legislative body—no corporation or body of men that have the power to inaugurate a war policy that has the validity of law and power, but the constituted authorities of the Government of the United States; and I am determined to support their policy. If the people do not approve that policy, they can change the constitutional authorities of that Government at the proper time and by the proper method. Let them freely discuss the policy in a proper tone; but my duty requires me to stop license and intemperate discussion, which tend to weaken the authority of the Government and army. Whilst the latter is in the presence of the enemy, it is cowardly so to weaken it. This license could not be used in our camps—the man would be torn in pieces who would attempt it. There is no fear of the people losing their liberties; we all know that to be the cry of demagogues, and none but the ignorant will listen to it. All intelligent men know that our people are too for advanced in the scale of religion, civilization, education and freedom to allow any power on earth to interfere with their liberties; but the same advancement in these great characteristics of our people teaches them to make all necessary sacrifices for their country when an emergency requires. They will support the constituted authorities of the Government, whether they agree with them or not. Indeed, the army itself is a part of the people, and is so thoroughly educated in the love of civil liberty, which is the best guarantee for the permanence of our republican institutions, that it would itself be the first to oppose any attempt to continue the exercise of military authority after the establishment of peace by the overthrow of the rebellion. No man on earth can lead our citizen soldiery to the establishment of a military despotism, and no man living would have the folly to attempt it. To do so, would be to seal his own doom. On this point, there can be no ground for apprehension on the part of the people. It is said that we can have peace if we lay down our arms. All sensible men know this to be untrue. Were it so, ought we to be so cowardly as to lay them down until the authority of the Government is acknowledged? I beg to call upon the fathers, mothers, brothers, sisters, sons, daughters, relatives, friends and neighbors of the soldiers in the field to aid me in stopping this license and intemperate discussion, which is discouraging our armies, weakening the hands of the Government, and thereby strengthening the enemy. If we use our honest efforts, God will bless us with a glorious peace and a united country. Men of every shade of opinion have the same vital interest in the suppression of this rebellion; for, should we fail in the task, the dread horrors of a ruined and distracted nation will fall alike on all, whether patriots or traitors. These are substantially my reasons for issuing "General Order No. 38," my reasons for the determination to enforce it, and also my reasons for the arrest of Hon. C. L. Vallandigham, for a supposed violation of that Order, for which he has been tried. The result of that trial is now in my hands. In enforcing this Order, I can be unanimously sustained by the people, or I can be opposed by factious, bad men. In the former event, quietness will prevail; in the latter event, the responsibility and retribution will attach to the men who resist the authority, and the neighborhoods that allow it.

All of which is respectfully submitted.

A. E. BURNSIDE,
Major General Commanding Department of the Ohio.

ROSTER OF THE NINTH CORPS.

CORPS COMMANDERS.

AMBROSE E. BURNSIDE: Brevet Second Lieutenant, 2d Artillery, U. S. A., July 1, 1847; Second Lieutenant, 3d Artillery, Sept. 8, 1847; First Lieutenant, Nov., 1851; resigned Nov. 1, 1853; Colonel 1st Rhode Island infantry (mustered into service) May 2, 1861; Brigadier General of Volunteers Aug. 6, 1861: Major General of Volunteers, Mar. 18, 1862; resigned April 15, 1865; Governor of Rhode Island May 29, 1866.

JESSE L. RENO: Brevet Second Lieutenant, ordnance department, U. S. A., July 1, 1846; Second Lieutenant Mar. 3, 1847; brevet First Lieutenant, Apr. 18, 1847; brevet Captain, Sept. 13, 1847; First Lieutenant, Mar. 3, 1853; Captain, July 1, 1860; Brigadier General Vols., Nov. 12, 1861; Major General Vols., Apr. 26, 1862; killed at South Mountain, Sept. 14, 1862.

JACOB D. COX: Brigadier General Vols., May 7, 1861; Major General Vols., Dec. 7, 1864; resigned Jan. 1, 1866; Governor of Ohio, Jan., 1866.

ORLANDO B. WILLCOX: Second Lieutenant 4th Artillery, U. S. A., July 1, 1847; First Lieutenant Apr. 30, 1850; resigned Sept. 10, 1857; Colonel 1st Michigan infantry, (mustered into service) May 1, 1861; wounded and taken prisoner at Bull Run, July 21, 1861; released Aug, 1862; Brigadier General Vols., July 21, 1861; brevet Major General Vols., Aug. 1, 1864; mustered out, Jan. 15, 1866.

JOHN SEDGWICK: Second Lieutenant 2d Artillery, U. S. A. July 1, 1837; First Lieutenant Apr. 19, 1839; brevet Captain, Aug. 20, 1847; brevet Major, Sept 13, 1847; Captain, Jan 29, 1849; Major 1st Cavalry, Mar. 8, 1855; Lieutenant Colonel 2d Cavalry, Mar. 16, 1861; Colonel 4th Cavalry, Apr. 25, 1861; Brigadier General Vols., Aug. 13, 1861; brevet Brigadier General, U. S. A., May 31, 1862; Major General Vols. July 4, 1862; killed at Spottsylvania May 9, 1864.

WILLIAM F. SMITH: Brevet Second Lieutenant, topographical Engineers, U. S. A., July 1, 1845; Second Lieutenant, July 14, 1849; Captain, July 1, 1859; Brigadier General Vols., Aug. 13, 1861; Major, Mar. 3, 1863; Major General Vols., Mar. 9, 1864; Mustered out Jan. 15, 1866; brevet Lieut. Colonel, brevet Colonel, brevet Brigadier General, U. S. A., Mar. 13, 1865.

JOHN G. PARKE : Second Lieutenant, topographical Engineers, U. S. A., July 1, 1849 ; First Lieutenant, July 1, 1856 ; Captain, Sept. 9, 1861 ; Brigadier General Vols., Nov. 23, 1861 ; Major General Vols., July 18, 1862 ; Major of Engineers, June 17, 1864 ; brevet Lieutenant Colonel, April 26, 1862 ; brevet Colonel, July 12, 1863 ; brevet Brigadier General, Mar. 13, 1865 ; brevet Major General, U. S. A., Mar. 13, 1865 ; mustered out Major General Vols., Jan'y 15, 1866.

ROBERT B. POTTER : Major 51st New York infantry Oct. 14, 1861 ; Lieutenant Colonel Oct. 29, 1861 ; Colonel, Sept. 10, 1862 ; Brigadier General Vols. Mar. 13, 1863 ; brevet Major General Vols. Aug. 1, 1864 ; Major General Vols. Sept. 29, 1865. Mustered out Jan. 15, 1866.

ASSISTANT ADJUTANTS GENERAL.

LEWIS RICHMOND : Captain, Assistant Adjutant General Vols., Sept. 13, 1861 ; Major, Apr. 28, 1862 ; Lieutenant Colonel, July 22, 1862 ; brevet Colonel, Aug. 1, 1864 ; brevet Brigadier General, Mar. 13 1865.

WILLIAM P. ANDERSON : Second Lieutenant 5th infantry, U. S. A., Aug. 5, 1861 ; First Lieutenant, Sept. 25, 1861 ; Captain Assistant Adjutant General, Sept. 15, 1862 ; resigned Mar. 18, 1864 ; brevet Major, Mar. 15, 1865.

EDWARD M. NEILL : Major, Assistant Adjutant General Vols., Mar. 11, 1863 ; resigned, Oct. 22, 1864 : brevet Lieutenant Colonel, Aug. 1, 1864 ; brevet Colonel, Mar. 13, 1865.

GUSTAVUS M. BASCOM : Captain, Assistant Adjutant General Vols. Aug. 20, 1861 ; Major, Oct. 7, 1862 ; brevet Lieutenant Colonel ; brevet Colonel, Nov. 4, 1865. With Gen. Cox.

ROBERT A. HUTCHINS : Captain, Assistant Adjutant General Vols. Sept. 7, 1862 ; wounded in the Wilderness May 6, 1864 ; brevet Major, Aug. 1, 1864. With Gen. Willcox.

DANIEL R. LARNED : Private Secretary to Gen. Burnside, Dec. 1, 1861 ; Captain, Assistant Adjutant General Vols., Mar. 13, 1863. brevet Major, Aug. 1, 1864 ; brevet Lieutenant Colonel, Mar. 13, 1865.

PHILIP M. LYDIG : Captain, Assistant Adjutant General Vols., Jan. 9, 1862 ; Major, Mar. 18, 1864 ; brevet Lieutenant Colonel, Dec. 2, 1864 ; brevet Colonel.

JOHN C. YOUNGMAN : Captain, Assistant Adjutant General Vols., July 25, 1864 ; brevet Major.

CHARLES E. MALLAM : Captain, Assistant Adjutant General Vols., Nov. 25, 1864 ; brevet Major.

NICOLAS BOWEN : Second Lieutenant, topographical Engineers, U. S. A., July 1, 1860 ; First Lieutenant, Aug. 6, 1861 ; Captain, Mar. 3, 1863 ; Lieutenant Colonel Vols., Jan. 23, 1863 ; brevet Major, brevet Colonel. With Gen. Potter.

SAMUEL WRIGHT: Captain, June 4, 1863; brevet Major, Dec. 2, 1864. With Gen. Potter.

ASSISTANT INSPECTORS GENERAL.

CHARES G. LORING, JR.: Captain, Assistant Quartermaster, Feb. 3, 1862; Lieutenant Colonel, Assistant Inspector General, July 22, 1862; brevet Colonel, Aug. 1, 1864; brevet Brigadier General Vols., Aug. 1, 1864; brevet Major General Vols., July 17, 1865. With the Ninth Corps through its entire term of service.

JACOB F. KENT: Second Lieutenant, 3d infantry, U. S. A., May 6, 1861; First Lieutenant, July 31, 1861, Captain, January 8, 1864; Lieutenant Colonel Vols., Assistant Inspector General, Jan. 1, 1863; brevet Colonel Vols., Oct. 19, 1864; brevet Major, brevet Lieutenant Colonel, U. S. A., Mar. 13, 1865. With Gen. Willcox.

ORVILLE E. BABCOCK: Second Lieutenant, Engineers, U. S. A., May 6, 1861; First Lieutenant, Nov. 17, 1861; Captain, June 1, 1863; Lieutenant Colonel Vols., Assistant Inspector General, Jan. 23, 1863; brevet Colonel Vols., Feb. 24, 1865; brevet Major, brevet Lieutenant Colonel, U. S. A., Mar. 13, 1865. Detailed as Engineer with Gen. Potter.

ROBERT H. I. GODDARD: Lieutenant Volunteer Aide de Camp, Sept. 20, 1862; Captain, Mar. 11, 1863; brevet Major, Aug. 4, 1864; brevet Lieutenant Colonel, April 2, 1865. Assistant Inspector General in last campaign.

MEDICAL DIRECTORS.

WILLIAM H. CHURCH: Surgeon Vols., Aug. 3, 1861; Medical Director, Department of North Carolina, Feb., 1862; Medical Director of Ninth Corps, July 22, 1862; resigned Oct. 26, 1863; brevet Lieutenant Colonel, Aug. 1, 1864; died Sept. 26, 1866.

JOHN E. McDONALD: Surgeon 79th New York, Jan. 22, 1862; Surgeon Vols., Apr. 13, 1863; Medical Director of Ninth Corps, Oct. 26, 1863; brevet Lieutenant Colonel, Aug. 1, 1864; resigned and appointed Surgeon in the regular army; died, 1866.

EDWARD B. DALTON: Surgeon 36th New York Infantry, Oct. 31, 1861; Surgeon Vols., Mar. 26, 1863; brevet Lieutenant Colonel, Mar. 13, 1865; brevet Colonel, Aug. 15, 1865.

HENRY W. RIVERS: Surgeon 1st Rhode Island, May 2, 1861; Surgeon 4th Rhode Island, Oct. 30, 1861; Brigade Surgeon, Mar. 8, 1862; Division Surgeon, July 25, 1862; Acting Medical Director Ninth Corps, Oct. 8, 1862; Medical Director Army of the Defences of Harper's Ferry, Oct. 17, 1862; Surgeon to Headquarters, Army of the Potomac, Nov. 22, 1862; Headquarters Department of the Ohio, Mar. 25, 1863; Division Medical Inspector, Ninth Corps, July 1, 1863; Surgeon in Chief to Kautz's Cavalry Division, May 2, 1864; brevet Lieutenant Colonel, Mar. 13, 1865.

JAMES HARRIS: Assistant Surgeon 1st Rhode Island infantry, May 2, 1861; taken prisoner at Bull Run, July 21, 1861; Surgeon 7th Rhode Island Infantry, Sept. 6, 1862; brigade surgeon, division surgeon, medical inspector, medical director; brevet Lieutenant Colonel; mustered out of service June 9, 1865.

PATRICK A. O'CONNELL: Surgeon 28th Massachusetts infantry, Oct. 25, 1861; Surgeon of Vols., June 13. 1863; brevet Lieutenant Colonel; medical director. With Gen. Willcox.

W. W. HOLMES: Surgeon of Volunteers, Apr. 4, 1862; discharged Oct. 22, 1863. Medical director with Gen. Cox.

ENGINEERS.

ROBERT S. WILLIAMSON: Second Lieutenant of Engineers, U. S. A., July 1, 1848; First Lieutenant, Apr. 30, 1856; Captain, August 6, 1861; brevet Major; Major, May 7, 1863.

ORLANDO M. POE: brevet Second Lieutenant of Engineers, U. S. A., July 1, 1856; Second Lieutenant, Oct. 7, 1856; First Lieutenant, July 1, 1861; Colonel 2d Michigan, Sept. 16, 1861; resigned Feb. 16, 1863; Captain, Mar. 3, 1863; brevet Colonel, Dec. 21, 1864; brevet Brigadier General, Mar. 13, 1865.

JAMES ST. CLAIR MORTON: Second Lieutenant Corps of Engineers, U. S. A., July 1, 1851; First Lieutenant; Captain, Aug. 6, 1861; Major, July 3, 1863; Brigadier General Vols., Nov. 29, 1862; discharged B. G., Nov. 7, 1863; killed in front of Petersburg, June 17, 1864. Engineer in chief Army of the Cumberland, May, 1862; Engineer in chief of Ninth Corps, May 18, 1864.

ORDNANCE OFFICERS.

DANIEL W. FLAGLER: Second Lieutenant, Ordnance, U. S. A., June 24, 1861; First Lieutenant Aug. 3, 1861; Captain, Mar. 3, 1863; brevet Major; brevet Lieutenant Colonel.

WILLIAM H. HARRIS: Brevet Second Lieutenant, Ordnance, U. S. A., June 24, 1861; Second Lieutenant, Aug. 3, 1861; First Lieutenant, Sept. 14, 1862; Captain, June 1, 1863; brevet Major, brevet Lieutenant Colonel, U. S. A.; brevet Colonel, Aug. 1, 1864.

ORRIN M. DEARBORN: Second Lieutenant, 3d New Hampshire, Aug. 22, 1861; First Lieutenant, June 27, 1862; Captain, Dec. 15, 1863.

CHIEF OF CAVALRY.

WILLIAM P. SANDERS: Brevet Second Lieutenant, 1st Dragoons, U. S. A., July 1, 1856; Second Lieutenant, May 27, 1857; First Lieutenant, May 10, 1861; Captain, May 14, 1861; Colonel 5th Kentucky Cavalry, 1863; Brigadier General Vols.; mortally wounded in front of Knoxville, Nov. 18, 1863.

CHIEFS OF ARTILLERY.

JOHN EDWARDS, Jr.: Second Lieutenant 3d artillery U. S. A., July 1, 1851; First Lieutenant; Captain July 23, 1861; brevet Major, brevet Lieutenant Colonel, brevet Colonel, Mar. 13, 1865.

SAMUEL N. BENJAMIN: Second Lieutenant, 2d artillery U. S. A., May 6, 1861; First Lieutenant, May 15, 1861; Captain, June 13, 1864; brevet Major, Aug. 1, 1864; brevet Lieutenant Colonel, brevet Colonel, Mar. 13, 1865.

JOHN C. TIDBALL; Second Lieutenant, 2d artillery, U. S. A., July 1, 1848; First Lieutenant; Captain May 14, 1861; Colonel 4th New York heavy artillery; brevet Brigadier General Vols., Aug. 1, 1864; brevet Major, brevet Lieutenant Colonel U. S. A., Mar. 13, 1865; brevet Major General Vols., Apr. 2, 1865.

AIDES DE CAMP.

JAMES LYMAN VAN BUREN: Second Lieutenant 53d New York, Oct. 26, 1861; Signal Corps, Jan, 1, 1862; Judge Advocate, Mar. 23, 1862; Major, Aide de Camp, July 7, 1862; brevet Lieutenant Colonel; brevet Colonel, Aug. 1, 1864; Brevet Brigadier General Vols., Apr. 2, 1865; died April 18, 1866. With the Corps throughout.

WILLIAM CUTTING: Captain, Assistant Quartermaster, Nov. 16, 1861; Major, Aide de Camp, July 22, 1862; Brevet Colonel, Aug. 1, 1864; brevet Brigadier General Vols., Mar. 13, 1865. With the Corps throughout.

GEORGE R. FEARING: Lieutenant Volunteer Aide de Camp, Dec. 1, 1861; Captain, Apr. 4, 1862; resigned Feb. 1, 1864; brevet Major, Aug. 1, 1864.

DUNCAN A. PELL; Lieutenant Volunteer Aide de Camp, Dec. 1, 1861; Captain Apr. 4, 1862; brevet Major, Dec. 2, 1864; brevet Lieutenant Colonel, Mar. 13, 1865; brevet Colonel, Apr. 2, 1865. With the Corps throughout.

JOHN B. PARKE: First Lieutenant 17th infantry, U. S. A., May 14, 1861; Captain, July 14, 1864; brevet Major, Aug. 1, 1864.

GEORGE W. GOWEN: First Lieutenant 48th Pennsylvania infantry, Aug. 20, 1861; Captain, Sept. 20, 1862; brevet Major, Dec. 2, 1864; Lieutenant Colonel, Oct. 6, 1864; Colonel, Jan. 2, 1865; killed in assault on Petersburg, Apr, 2, 1865.

SAMUEL S. SUMNER: Second Lieutenant of 5th Cavalry, U. S. A., June 11, 1861; First Lieutenant, July 17, 1862; Captain, Aide de Camp, Aug. 20, 1862; discharged A. D. C., Aug. 15, 1863; Captain 5th Cavalry, Mar. 30, 1864; brevet Major Mar. 13, 1865.

FREDERIC VAN VLIET: Second Lieutenant 3d Cavalry, U. S. A., Aug. 5,

1861; Adjutant July 12, 1862; First Lieutenant July 17, 1862; Brevet Captain Aug. 1, 1864; brevet Major Mar. 13, 1865.

GILES W. SHURTLIFF; Captain 7th Ohio infantry, June 17, 1861. With Gen. Willcox.

CHARLES A. MCKNIGHT: Second Lieutenant 7th Michigan infantry, July 1, 1861: First Lieutenant May 10, 1862; Captain May 26, 1863. With Gen. Willcox.

HENRY H. HOLBROOK: Captain 51st New York infantry, Mar. 19, 1862; brevet Major. With Gen. Potter.

CLIFFORD CODDINGTON: Second Lieutenant 51st New York infantry, Dec. 21, 1861; First Lieutenant July 21, 1862; Captain July 26, 1862. With Gen. Potter.

SAMUEL L. CHRISTIE: First Lieutenant 1st Kentucky infantry, Jan. 22, 1862: Captain Oct. 19, 1862. With Gen. Cox.

JAMES W. CONINE: First Lieutenant 1st Kentucky infantry. With Gen. Cox.

CHALES G. HUTTON: Captain Aide de Camp, Mar. 11, 1863; brevet Major Aug. 1, 1864.

WILLIAM V. RICHARDS: Fiist Lieutenant 17th Michigan infantry, July 2, 1862; Captain, July 19, 1864; brevet Major Dec. 2, 1864. With Gen. Willcox.

LEVI CURTIS BRACKETT: Second Lieutenant 28th Massachusetts, Apr. 4, 1862; First Lieutenant, Sept. 24, 1862; brevet Captain Aug. 1, 1864; Captain 57th, Nov. 5, 1864; brevet Major July 6, 1865. With Gen. Willcox

JAMES ROMEYN: Lieutenant 7th Michigan. With Gen. Willcox.

ROBERT S. SHILLINGLAW: Captain 79th New York infantry May 27, 1861.

CHARLES A. WHITTIER: Major Aide de Camp Apr. 25, 1863; Lieutenant Colonel; brevet Colonel, brevet Brigadier General Vols., April 9, 1865.

CHARLES HOWE: Second Lieutenant 33d New York infantry Dec. 27, 1861; Captain Aide de Camp.

S. CAREY: First Lieutenant 33d New York infantry.

J. A. SCRYMER: Second Lieutenant, 43d New York infantry, Nov. 28, 1861.

MATTHEW BERRY: Second Lieutenant 5th Pennsylvania cavalry, Dec. 12, 1861; First Lieutenant Dec. 11, 1863.

CAMPBELL TUCKER: Second Lieutenant 49th Pennsylvania infantry Nov. 19, 1862.

GEORGE S. WILLIAMS: Second Lieutenant 2d Michigan infantry, Aug. 17, 1862; First Lieutenant Dec. 1, 1862; mortally wounded at Cold Harbor June 3, 1864.

QUARTER MASTERS.

HERMAN BIGGS: Brevet Second Lieutenant 10th infantry, U. S. A., July 1, 1856; First Lieutenant 1st infantry, May 10, 1861; Captain, Quartermaster's Department, Aug. 3, 1861; Lieutenant Colonel Vols., July 22, 1862. Detached from Ninth Corps Aug., 1862; brevet Major, brevet Lieutenant Colonel, brevet Colonel, brevet Brigadier General Mar. 13, 1865.

RICHARD N. B. BATCHELDER: Captain, Assistant Quartermaster, Aug. 3, 1861; Lieutenant Colonel, Jan. 1, 1863; brevet Colonel, brevet Brigadier General Vols., Mar. 13, 1865.

LUTHER H. PIERCE; Captain, Assistant Quartermaster, Nov. 16, 1861; Lieutenant Colonel, June 15, 1864; brevet Colonel; Captain, Quartermaster's Department, U. S. A., May 18, 1864.

THERON E. HALL; First Lieutenant 21st Massachusetts, Sept. 18, 1861; Captain Assistant Quartermaster, July 22, 1862; resigned Dec. 5, 1864; brevet Major, Mar. 13, 1865.

JOHN A. MORRIS: Captain Assistant Quartermaster, Mar. 16, 1863; brevet Major, Mar. 13, 1865.

ENOCH P. FITCH: Captain Assistant Quartermaster, Aug. 3, 1861. With Gen. Cox.

H. S. CHAMBLOS: Captain, Assistant Quartermaster.

THOMAS B. MARSH: Second Lieutenant, 51st New York, Oct. 18, 1861; First Lieutenant, Mar. 14, 1862; Captain, Sept. 30, 1862; Major, Dec. 31, 1864; Lieutenant Colonel, Apr. 29, 1865. Chief Ambulance Corps

WILLIAM W. VAN NESS: Lieutenant, Quartermaster 67th New York infantry, June 24, 1861; Captain Assistant Quartermaster, Feb. 19, 1862.

SAMUEL B. TOBEY, JR.: Second Lieutenant 3d New York artillery, Mar. 5, 1862; First Lieutenant, Apr. 10, 1863; Captain Assistant Quartermaster, May 24, 1864; resigned September, 1864.

JACOB WAGNER: Lieutenant Quartermaster 48th Pennsylvania infantry, Dec. 21, 1862; Assistant Quartermaster.

DANIEL S. REMINGTON: First Lieutenant 7th Rhode Island infantry; Captain June 8, 1865.

COMMISSARIES OF SUBSISTENCE.

EDWIN R. GOODRICH; First Lieutenant and Quartermaster, 2d New Hampshire infantry, June 20, 1861; Captain, Commissary of Subsistence, Oct. 31, 1861; Lieutenant Colonel, July 22, 1862: brevet Colonel, Mar. 13, 1865.

JAMES F. DEWOLF; Captain Commissary of Subsistence, Nov. 16, 1861; resigned Dec. 3, 1864; brevet Major Aug. 1, 1864.

RICHARD B. TREAT; Captain, Commissary of Subsistence, Aug. 26, 1862.

JOHN H. COALE; Captain, Commissary of Subsistence, Aug. 30, 1862; Lieutenant Colonel, Jan. 1, 1863; brevet Colonel.

WILLIAM H. FRENCH; Secretary, Dec. 1, 1861; Captain Commissary of Subsistence, Feb. 19, 1863: resigned, Sept. 28, 1864; brevet Major, Mar. 13, 1865.

M. A. PARK: Captain, Commissary of Subsistence.

JUDGES ADVOCATE.

JAMES M. CUTTS; Captain 11th infantry, U. S. A., May 14, 1861; detatched from Staff, Sept. 28, 1863; brevet Major; brevet Lieutenant Colonel, Aug. 1, 1864.

HENRY L. BURNETT; Major Judge Advocate, Aug. 10, 1863; brevet Lieutenant Colonel, Aug. 1, 1864; brevet Colonel, Mar. 8, 1865; brevet Brigadier General Vols., Mar. 13, 1865.

COMMISSARIES OF MUSTERS.

HENRY R. RATHBONE; Captain 12th infantry, U. S. A., May 14, 1861; brevet Major, Aug. 1, 1864.

MORGAN L. OGDEN; First Lieutenant 18th infantry, U. S. A., May 14, 1861; Captain Aug. 12, 1863.

JAMES S. CASEY; Second Lieutenant, 5th infantry, U. S. A., Aug. 5, 1861; First Lieutenant, Sept. 25, 1861: Captain, Dec. 1, 1863; brevet Major, Apr. 2, 1865.

DIVISION COMMANDERS.

JESSE L. RENO; See above. In command of Corps, Aug. 1, 1862.

JACOB D. COX: See above. In command of Corps, Sept. 14, 1862.

ELIAKIM P. SCAMMON: Colonel 23d Ohio infantry, June 14, 1861; Brigadier General Vols., Oct. 15, 1862.

GEORGE CROOK: Brevet Second Lieutenant, 4th infantry, U. S. A., July 1, 1852; Second Lieutenant, July 1, 1852; First Lieutenant, Mar. 11, 1856; Captain, May 14, 1861; Colonel 36th Ohio infantry, Sept. 12, 1861; Brigadier General Vols., Sept. 7, 1862; brevet Major General Vols., July 18, 1862; Major General Vols., Oct. 21, 1864; brevet Major, brevet Lieutenant Colonel, brevet Colonel, brevet Brigadier General, U. S. A., Mar. 13, 1865.

ORLANDO B. WILLCOX: See above. In command of Corps, Oct. 8, 1862, to Jan. 1863.

JOHN G. PARKE: See above. In command of Corps, Mar. 1, 1863; Aug. 13, 1864, to July, 1865.

ISAAC I. STEVENS: Second Lieutenant, Corps of Engineers, U. S. A. July 1, 1839; First Lieutenant July 1, 1840; brevet Captain Aug. 20, 1847; brevet

Major Sept. 13, 1847; resigned 1853; Governor of Washington Territory; Colonel 79th New York infantry; Brigadier General Vols., Sept. 28, 1861; Major General Vols.; killed at Chantilly, Sept. 1, 1862.

ISAAC P. RODMAN: Captain 2d Rhode Island infantry, June 1, 1861; Lieutenant Colonel 4th Rhode Island infantry Oct. 19, 1861; Colonel, Oct. 30, 1861; Brigadier General Vols., Apr. 28, 1862; mortally wounded at Antietam, Sept. 17, 1862.

SAMUEL D. STURGIS: Brevet Second Lieutenant 2d Dragoons, U. S. A., July 1, 1846; Second Lieutenant 1st Dragoons, Feb. 16, 1847; First Lieutenant July, 1853; Captain, March 3, 1855; Major 4th Cavalry May 3, 1861; Brigadier General Vols., Aug. 10, 1861; Lieutenant Colonel 6th Cavalry, U. S. A., Oct. 27, 1863.

GEORGE W. GETTY: Second Lieutenant 4th artillery, U. S. A., July 1, 1840; First Lieutenant, Oct. 31, 1845; brevet Captain, Aug. 20, 1847; Captain 5th artillery, Nov. 4, 1853; Lieutenant Colonel Vols., A. D. C., Sept. 28, 1861; Brigadier General Vols., Sept. 25, 1862; Major 5th artillery, Aug. 1, 1863; brevet Major General Vols., Aug. 1, 1864; brevet Lieutenant Colonel, U. S. A., March 13, 1865.

WILLIAM W. BURNS: Brevet Second Lieutenant 3d infantry, U. S. A., July 1, 1847; Second Lieutenant 5th infantry, Sept. 8, 1847; First Lieutenant, Aug. 12, 1850; Captain Commissary of Subsistence, Nov. 3, 1858; Major Commissary of Subsistence, Aug. 3, 1861: Brigadier General Vols.; brevet Lieutenant Colonel, U. S. A.

RUSH C. HAWKINS: Colonel 9th New York infantry, May 13, 1861.

EDWARD HARLAND: Colonel 8th Connecticut infantry, Sept. 4, 1861; Brigadier General Vols., Nov. 29, 1862.

ROBERT B. POTTER: See above. In command of Corps, Sept. 1, 1863, to Jan. 1, 1864.

THOMAS WELSH: Colonel 45th Pennsylvania infantry, July 22, 1861; Brigadier General Vols., Mar. 13, 1863; died Aug. 14, 1863.

EDWARD FERRERO: Colonel 51st New York infantry, Oct. 14, 1861; Brigadier General Vols., May 6, 1863; brevet Major General, Dec. 2, 1864.

THOMAS G. STEVENSON: Major 4th Battalion Massachusetts infantry, May 4, 1861; Colonel 24th Massachusetts infantry, Aug. 31, 1861; Brigadier General Vols., Mar. 14, 1863; killed near Spottsylvania, May 10, 1864.

THOMAS L. CRITTENDEN: Brigadier General Vols., Sept. 27, 1861; Major General Vols., July 17, 1862; resigned Dec. 13, 1864.

JAMES H. LEDLIE: Colonel 3d New York artillery, Nov. 18, 1861; Brigadier General Vols., Oct. 27, 1863; resigned Jan. 16, 1865.

JULIUS WHITE: Brigadier General Vols., June 9, 1862; resigned Nov. 19, 1864.

66

John F. Hartranft: Colonel 51st Pennsylvania, July 27, 1861; Brigadier General Vols., May 12, 1864; brevet Major General, Mar. 25, 1865.

Simon G. Griffin: Captain 2d New Hampshire infantry, June 4, 1861; Lieutenant Colonel 6th New Hampshire infantry, Oct. 26, 1861; Colonel Apr. 22, 1862; Brigadier General Vols., May 12, 1864; brevet Major General, Apr. 2, 1865.

John I. Curtin; Major 45th Pennsylvania infantry, July 30, 1862; Lieutenant Colonel, Sept. 4, 1862; Colonel, Mar. 1, 1863; brevet Brigadier General Vols., Oct. 12, 1864; brevet Major General Vols., Apr. 2, 1865.

BRIGADE COMMANDERS.

Isaac P. Rodman: See above.

James Nagle: Colonel 6th Pennsylvania infantry. Apr. 15, 1861; Colonel 48th Pennsylvania, Aug. 14, 1861; Brigadier General Vols., Mar. 13, 1863; resigned May 9, 1863. Colonel 194th Pennsylvania, July 21, 1864.

Thomas Welsh: See above.

Edward Ferrero: See above.

Eliakim P. Scammon: See above.

George Crook: See above.

Rush C. Hawkins: brevet Brig. Gen. Vols., Mar. 13, 1865. See above.

Harrison S. Fairchild: Colonel 89th New York infantry, Dec. 4, 1861; brevet Brigadier General Vols., Mar. 13, 1865.

Edward Harland: See above.

B. C. Christ: Lieutenant Colonel 5th Pennsylvania infantry, Apr. 15, 1861; Colonel 50th Pennsylvania, July 27, 1861; brevet Brigadier General Vols., Aug. 1, 1864.

Hugh Ewing: Colonel 30th Ohio, Aug. 15, 1861; Brigadier General Vols., Nov. 29, 1862.

Augustus Moor; Colonel 28th Ohio, June 10, 1861.

William M. Fenton; Colonel 8th Michigan infantry, Aug. 7, 1861; resigned Mar. 15, 1863.

Francis Beach: Colonel 16th Connecticut infantry, Aug. 7, 1862.

Robert B. Potter: See above.

John F. Hartranft: Colonel 4th Pennsylvania infantry, Apr. 15, 1861. See above.

Simon G. Griffin: See above.

William Humphrey: Captain 2d Michigan infantry, May 25, 1861; Colonel, Feb. 16, 1863; mustered out (term expired) Sept. 30, 1864; brevet Brigadier General Vols., Mar. 13, 1865.

Henry Bowman: Captain 15th Massachusetts infantry, Aug. 1, 1861; Major 34th Massachusetts, Aug. 6, 1862; Colonel 36th Massachusetts, Aug. 22, 1862.

DAVID MORRISON: Lieutenant Colonel 79th New York infantry, Dec. 3, 1861; Colonel, Feb. 17, 1863; brevet Brig. General Vols., Mar. 13, 1865.

DANIEL LEASURE: Adjutant 12th Pennsylvania infantry, Apr. 15, 1861; Colonel 100th Pennsylvania, Aug. 28, 1861.

JOSHUA K. SIGFREID: Major 48th Pennsylvania infantry, Aug, 20, 1861; Lieutenant Colonel, Nov. 30, 1861; Colonel, Sept. 20, 1862; brevet Brigadier General Vols., Mar. 13, 1865.

EDWIN SCHALL: Major 4th Pennsylvania infantry, Apr. 15, 1861; Major 51st Pennsylvania, July 27, 1861; Lieutenant Colonel, Sept. 17, 1862; Colonel, May 13, 1864; killed in battle.

WILSON C. LEMERT: Major 86th Ohio, June 10, 1862; Colonel, July 14, 1863.

EBENEZER W. PIERCE: Brigadier General Massachusetts detached militia, Apr. 15, 1861; Colonel 29th Massachusetts, Dec. 13, 1861; discharged Nov. 8, 1864.

JAMES H. LEDLIE: See above.

JOHN I. CURTIN: See above.

HENRY G. THOMAS: Captain 11th infantry, U. S. A., Aug. 5, 1861; Colonel 19th United States Colored Troops; Brigadier General Vols., Nov. 30, 1864; brevet Major, Lieutenant Colonel, Colonel, U. S. A., Mar. 13, 1865.

ZENAS R. BLISS: Brevet Second Lieutenant 1st infantry, U. S. A., July 1, 1854; Second Lieutenant, 8th infantry, Mar. 3, 1855; First Lieutenant, Oct. 17, 1860; Captain, May 14, 1861; Colonel 9th Rhode Island infantry, May 26, 1862; Colonel 7th Rhode Island, Sept. 6, 1862; brevet Major, brevet Lieutenant Colonel, U. S. A., Mar. 13, 1865.

HENRY PLEASANTS: Captain 48th Pennsylvania infantry, Aug. 20, 1861; Lieutenant Colonel, Sept. 20, 1862; Colonel, Oct. 6, 1864; brevet Brigadier General Vols., Mar. 13, 1865.

ELISHA G. MARSHALL: Brevet Second Lieutenant 4th infantry, U. S. A., July 1, 1850; Second Lieutenant, July 1, 1850; First Lieutenant 6th infantry, Mar. 26, 1855; Captain, May 14, 1861; Colonel 13th New York infantry, Apr. 6, 1862; Colonel 14th New York heavy artillery, May 23, 1863; brevet Major, brevet Lieutenant Colonel, U. S. A., brevet Brigadier General Vols. Mar. 13, 1865.

CHARLES E. GRISWOLD: Major 22d Massachusetts infantry, Sept. 12, 1861; Lieutenant Colonel, Oct. 4, 1861; Colonel, June 28, 1862; Colonel 56th Massachusetts, July 14, 1863; killed at the battle of the Wilderness, May 6, 1864.

SUMNER CARRUTH: Captain 1st Massachusetts infantry May 22, 1861; Major 35th Massachusetts, Aug. 20, 1862; Lieutenant Colonel, Aug. 27, 1862; Colonel, April 25, 1863; brevet Brigadier General Vols., Mar. 13, 1865.

Stephen M. Weld, Jr.: Second Lieutenant 18th Massachusetts infantry, Jan. 24, 1862; First Lieutenant, Oct. 24, 1862; Captain, May 4, 1863; Lieutenant Colonel 56th Massachusetts, July 22, 1863; Colonel, May 6, 1864; Brevet Brigadier General Vols., Mar. 13, 1865.

Jacob Parker Gould: Major 13th Massachusetts infantry, July 16, 1861; Colonel 59th Massachusetts, Apr. 25, 1864; died of wounds, Aug. 22, 1864.

Ralph Ely; Captain 8th Michigan infantry, Aug. 12, 1861; Major, Sept. 10, 1862; Lieutenant Colonel, Feb. 1, 1863; brevet Colonel, July 6, 1864; Colonel, May 7, 1864; brevet Brigadier General Vols., Apr. 2, 1865.

Samuel Harriman: Captain 30th Wisconsin infantry, Aug. 25, 1862; Colonel 37th, Mar. 7, 1864; brevet Brigadier General Vols., Apr. 2, 1865.

William F. Bartlett: Captain 20th Massachusetts infantry, July 10, 1861; Colonel 49th Massachusetts, Nov. 12, 1862; Colonel 57th Massachusetts, Aug. 17, 1863; Brigadier General Vols., June 20, 1864; brevet Major General, Mar. 13, 1865.

Napoleon B. McLaughlin: Second Lieutenant 4th cavalry, U. S. A., Mar. 27, 1861; First Lieutenant, May 3, 1861; Captain, July 17, 1862; Colonel 1st Massachusetts infantry, Oct. 1, 1862; Colonel 57th Massachusetts, July 21, 1864; brevet Brigadier General Vols., Sept. 30, 1864; brevet Major, brevet Lieutenant Colonel, U. S. A., Mar. 13, 1865.

Byron C. Cutcheon: Captain 20th Michigan infantry, July 29, 1862; Major, Oct. 14, 1862; Colonel, Nov. 21, 1864; brevet Brigadier General Vols., Mar. 13, 1865.

Herbert B. Titus: Major 9th New Hampshire, June 14, 1862; Colonel, Nov. 22, 1862; discharged Sept. 27, 1864; reappointed, Nov. 1, 1864.

Joseph H. Barnes: Captain 29th Massachusetts infantry, Apr. 25, 1861; Lieutenant Colonel, Dec., 13, 1861.

Walter Harriman: Colonel 11th New Hampshire infantry, Aug. 26, 1862; resigned Aug. 15, 1863; re-appointed Jan. 26, 1864; brevet Brigadier General, Vols., Mar. 13, 1865.

Joseph A. Mathews; Colonel 205th Pennsylvania infantry, Sept. 2, 1864; brevet Brigadier General Vols., Mar. 13, 1865.

Delavan Bates: Colonel 30th United States colored troops; brevet Brigadier General Vols., July 30, 1864.

Charles S. Russell; Captain 11th infantry, U. S. A.; Colonel 28th United States Colored Troops; brevet Brigadier General Vols., July 30, 1864.

Alfred B. McCalmont: Colonel 208th Pennsylvania infantry, Sept. 12, 1864; brevet Brigadier General Vols., Mar. 13, 1865.

CHIEF OF ARTILLERY.

JOHN A. MONROE*: First Lieutenant 1st Rhode Island light artillery, June 6, 1861; Captain, Sept. 7, 1861; Lieutenant Colonel, Dec. 4, 1862.

REGIMENTS COMPOSING THE NINTH CORPS.

MAINE. *31st infantry*: Colonel Thomas Hight. Apr. 29, 1864; resigned July 2, 1864. Colonel Daniel White, July 8, 1864. Joined the Corps April, 1864.

32d infantry: Colonel Mark F. Wentworth, May 6, 1864; resigned Oct. 18, 1864. Lieutenant Colonel James L. Hunt, Oct. 18. 1864, Consolidated with 31st, Dec. 1, 1864. Joined the Corps April, 1864.

2d battery of light artillery: Captain Albert F. Thomas, Nov. 30, 1861; discharged Jan. 22, 1865. Captain Charles E. Stubbs. Joined the Corps April, 1864.

7th battery of light artillery: Captain Adelbert B. Twitchell, Dec. 29, 1863; wounded Jan. 2, 1865. Captain William B. Lapham, Mar. 8, 1865. Joined the Corps April, 1864.

VERMONT. *17th infantry:* Colonel Francis V. Randall, Feb. 10, 1864. Joined the Corps April, 1864.

3d battery of light artillery: Captain Romeo H. Start, Nov. 23, 1863. In reserve artillery.

NEW HAMPSHIRE. *6th infantry:* Colonel Simon G. Griffin. See above. Lieutenant Colonel Henry H. Pearson, Oct. 15, 1862; killed at the North Anna, May 26, 1864. Lieutenant Colonel Phineas P. Bixby, July 28, 1864. In North Carolina. With the Corps throughout.

9th infantry: Colonel E. Q. Fellows, June 14, 1862; Colonel Henry B. Titus. See above. Major George H. Chandler. Joined the Corps, September, 1862.

10th infantry: Colonel Michael T. Donahoe, Aug. 1862; brevet Brigadier General Vols., Mar. 13, 1865. With the Corps from October, 1862, to March, 1863.

11th infantry: Colonel Walter Harriman; taken prisoner in the Wilderness, May 6, 1864; discharged in November, 1864. See above. Lieutenant Colonel Leander W. Cogswell, Aug. 20, 1864. Joined the Corps October, 1862.

13th infantry: Colonel Aaron F. Stevens, Aug. 26, 1862; brevet Brigadier General. With the Corps from December, 1862, to March, 1863.

MASSACHUSETTS. *21st infantry:* Colonel William S. Clark, May 16. 1862; resigned Apr. 22, 1863. Lieutenant Colonel George P. Hawkes, Dec.

---

*Omitted above.

18, 1862. Major H. H. Richardson, Dec. 18, 1862. Veterans re-enlisted January, 1864, and transferred to 36th. In North Carolina. With the Corps throughout.

28th infantry: Colonel William Monteith, Nov. 25, 1861; Colonel Richard Byrnes, Sept. 29, 1862; Colonel George W. Cartwright, July 21, 1864. Joined the Corps Aug., 1862; transferred to Second Corps, November, 1862.

29th infantry: Colonel E. W. Pierce. See above. Colonel Thomas W. Clarke, Nov. 8, 1864. Lieutenant Colonel Charles D. Browne, from June 18, 1865, to Aug. 11, 1865.

35th infantry: Colonel Edward A. Wild, Apr. 24, 1863. Brigadier General Vols., Apr. 24, 1863. Colonel Sumner Carruth. See above. Lieutenant Colonel William S. King, Apr. 25, 1863. Lieutenant Colonel John W. Hudson, Nov. 14, 1864. Joined the Corps, September, 1862.

36th infantry: Colonel Henry Bowman. See above. Lieutenant Colonels Arthur A. Goodell, William F. Draper. Colonel Thaddeus L. Barker, Nov. 13, 1864. Joined the Corps September, 1862.

56th infantry: Colonels Charles E. Griswold, Stephen M. Weld, Jr. See above. Lieutenant Colonel Horatio D. Jarvis, May 7, 1864. Joined the Corps, April, 1864.

57th infantry: Colonels William F. Bartlett, Napoleon B. McLaughlin. See above. Lieutenant Colonel Charles L. Chandler, Apr. 20, 1864; killed May 24, 1864; Lieutenant Colonel Julius M. Tucker. Joined the Corps, April, 1864.

58th infantry: Colonel John C. Whiton, Aug. 31, 1864. Joined the Corps, April, 1864.

59th infantry: Colonel Jacob P. Gould. See above. Lieutenant Colonel Joseph Colburn, from August, 1864. Major Ezra P. Gould, from February, 1865. Consolidated with 57th, July 1, 1865. Joined the Corps, Apr., 1864.

8th light battery of artillery: Captain Asa M. Cook, July 1, 1862. Joined the Corps, August, 1862. A six months battery.

11th light battery of artillery: Captain Edward J. Jones, Aug. 25, 1862; brevet Major. Joined the Corps, April, 1864.

14th light battery of artillery: Captain Joseph W. B. Wright, Feb. 3, 1864. Joined the Corps, April, 1864.

RHODE ISLAND. *4th infantry:* Colonel William H. P. Steere, June 12, 1862; wounded Sept. 17, 1862. Lieutenant Colonel Joseph B. Curtis, from Sept. 17 to Dec. 13, 1862, killed Dec. 13, 1862. Lieutenant Colonel M. P. Buffum, from Dec. 13, 1862, to June, 1864; brevet Colonel, Mar. 13, 1865. Consolidated with 7th, Oct. 21, 1864. In North Carolina. With the Corps until March, 1863. Rejoined, June, 1864.

7th infantry: Colonel Zenas R. Bliss. See above. Captain Theodore

Winn, from May 18 to June 15, 1864. Lieutenant Colonel and brevet Colonel Percy Daniels, from June 29, 1864. Joined the Corps, October, 1862.

12*th infantry:* Colonel George H. Browne, Oct. 13, 1862. Nine months. Joined the Corps, December, 1862.

7*th battalion of infantry:* Captain Caleb T. Bowen, July 22, 1863; from June 6, 1865, to July 13, 1865.

Battery D, 1*st light artillery:* Captain W. W. Buckley, Oct. 30, 1862; resigned Sept. 20, 1864. Captain Elmer L. Corthell, Nov. 2, 1864. Joined the Corps, December, 1862.

Battery H., 1*st light artillery:* Captain Crawford Allen, Jr., Oct. 1, 1863; brevet Major, Apr. 2, 1865; brevet Lieutenant Colonel. In reserve artillery.

CONNECTICUT. 8*th infantry:* Colonel Edward Harland. See above. Lieutenant Colonels Hiram Appelman, John E. Ward. In North Carolina. With the Corps till March, 1863.

11*th infantry*: Colonel Henry W. Kingsbury, April 25, 1862; killed at Antietam, Sept. 17, 1862. Colonel Griffin A. Stedman, Jr., Sept. 17, 1862. In North Carolina. With the Corps till March, 1863.

15*th infantry:* Colonel Dexter R. Wright, July 22, 1862; resigned Feb. 17, 1863. Colonel Charles L. Upham, April 6, 1863. With the Corps from November, 1862, till March, 1863.

16*th infantry:* Colonel Francis Beach. See above. With the Corps from September, till March, 1863.

21*st infantry:* Colonel Arthur H. Dutton, Aug. 19, 1862. With the Corps from October, 1862, till March, 1863.

NEW YORK: 9*th infantry:* Colonel Rush C. Hawkins. See above. Lieutenant Colonel Edgar A. Kimball, Feb. 14, 1862. In North Carolina. With the Corps until March, 1863.

46*th infantry:* Colonel Rudolph Rosa, September 16, 1861; Colonel Joseph Gerhardt, Dec. 17, 1862; Colonel George W. Travers, Nov. 8, 1863. Joined the Corps July, 1862.

51*st infantry:* Colonels Edward Ferrero, Robert B. Potter. See above. Colonel Charles W. Le Gendre, Mar. 14, 1863; bvt. Brig. Gen. Vols. Colonel Gilbert McKibben, Dec. 9, 1864. Colonel John G. Wright, Apr. 29, 1865; bvt. Brig. Gen. Vols. In North Carolina. With the Corps throughout.

79*th infantry:* Colonel Addison Farnsworth, Dec. 17, 1861; brevet Brigadier General Vols., Sept. 17, 1865. Colonel David Morrison. See above. Lieutenant Colonel Henry G. Heffron, Jan. 26, 1865. Joined the Corps, July, 1862, and remained throughout.

89*th infantry:* Colonel Harrison S. Fairchild. See above. In North Carolina. With the Corps from July, 1862, to March, 1863.

103*d infantry:* Colonel F. W. Von Egloffstein, Feb. 20, 1862. Colonel Benjamin Ringgold, Sept. 15, 1862. Colonel William Heine, May 15, 1863. In North Carolina. With the Corps throughout.

109th infantry: Colonel Benjamin F. Tracy, Aug. 20, 1862; Colonel Isaac S. Catlin, May 17, 1864. Joined the Corps, April, 1864.

179th infantry: Colonel William M. Gregg, Sept. 8, 1864; brevet Brigadier General Vols., Mar. 13, 1865. Joined the Corps, September, 1864.

186th infantry: Colonel Bradley Winslow, Sept. 21, 1864; brevet Brigadier General Vols., Apr. 2, 1865. Joined the Corps, October, 1864.

2d Mounted Rifles (serving on foot): Colonel John Fisk, Feb. 3, 1864; Colonel Louis Siebert, Dec. 31, 1864. Joined the Corps, April, 1864.

5th cavalry: Colonel Othneib De Forest, Jan. 31, 1863; Colonel John Hammond, Mar. 29, 1864; Colonel Amos H. White, Nov. 14, 1864. With the Corps from April, 1864, till June, 1864.

6th cavalry: Colonel Thomas C. Devin, Nov. 18, 1861; brevet Brigadier General Vols. With the Corps from September, 1862, to February, 1863.

24th cavalry, dismounted: Colonel George F. Raulston, Jan. 26, 1864. Killed in front of Petersburg, June 18, 1864. Colonel Walter C. Newberry, Dec. 15, 1864; brevet Brigadier General Vols., Mar. 13, 1865.

1st light artillery, Battery D.: Captain Thomas W. Osborne, Oct. 25, 1861. With the Corps from November, 1862, to February, 1863.

2d light artillery, Battery L.: Captain Jacob Roemer, Mar. 4, 1862; brevet Major, Aug. 1, 1864; transferred to command of 34th independent battery. With the Corps throughout.

4th light artillery battery: Captain W. B. Barnes, Jan. 2, 1862. Joined the Corps, April, 1864.

6th independent battery of light artillery: Captain Walter M. Bramhall, Jan. 23, 1862. Captain Joseph B. Martin, Feb. 16, 1863. Captain Moses P. Clark, February 18, 1865.

9th infantry's battery of howitzers: Captain James R. Whiting, Aug. 18, 1861. In North Carolina. With the Corps until March, 1863.

19th independent battery of light artillery: Captain Edward W. Rogers, Sept. 16, 1863. Joined the Corps, April, 1864.

27th independent battery of light artillery: Captain John B. Eaton, Nov. 29, 1862. Joined the Corps, April, 1864.

34th independent battery of light artillery: Captain Jacob Roemer. See above. Joined the Corps, April, 1864.

14th heavy artillery: Colonel Elisha G. Marshall. See above. Lieutenant Colonel Clarence H. Corning, Sept. 4, 1863. Lieutenant Colonel William H. Reynolds, Mar. 8, 1865. Joined the Corps, May, 1864.

NEW JERSEY. *25th infantry:* Colonel Andrew J. Morrison, Sept. 6, 1862. With the Corps from December, 1862, to March, 1863.

27th infantry: Colonel George W. Mindil, Oct. 3, 1863; brevet Brigadier General Vols., Mar. 13, 1865. A nine months regiment. With the Corps from December, 1862, to July, 1863.

3d cavalry: Colonel Andrew J. Morrison, Nov. 4, 1863. With the Corps from April, 1864, to June, 1864.

PENNSYLVANIA. *45th infantry:* Colonels Thomas Welsh, John I. Curtin. See above. Lieutenant Colonel Francis M. Hill, Mar. 1, 1863; resigned Sept. 16, 1864. Lieutenant Colonel Theodore Gregg, Sept. 15, 1864: brevet Colonel, July 30, 1862. Joined the Corps, September, 1864.

48th infantry: Colonels James Nagle, Joshua K. Sigfried, Henry Pleasants, George W. Gowen. See above. Brevet Colonel Isaac F. Brannon, Apr. 2, 1865; Colonel, Apr. 3, 1865. In North Carolina. With the Corps throughout.

50th infantry: Colonel Benjamin C. Christ. See above. Major Edward Overton, Jr., Sept. 30, 1861; Lieutenant Colonel, Aug. 20, 1863. With the Corps throughout.

51st infantry: Colonels John F. Hartranft, Edwin Schall. See above. Lieutenant Colonel Thomas S. Bell; killed at Antietam, Sept. 17, 1862. Colonel William J. Bolton, June 8, 1864; brevet Brigadier General, Mar. 13, 1865. In North Carolina. With the Corps throughout.

75th infantry: Colonel Francis Mahler, July 30, 1862. With the Corps from September, 1862, to December, 1862.

100th infantry: Colonel Daniel Leasure. See above. Lieutenant Colonel David A. Lecky, July 12, 1862; resigned Dec. 30, 1862. Colonel Norman J. Maxwell, April 8, 1865. Lieutenant Colonel Matthew M. Dawson; died June 30, 1864. With the Corps throughout.

200th infantry: Colonel Charles W. Diven, Sept. 3, 1865; brevet Brigadier General Vols., Mar. 25, 1865. Lieutenant Colonel W. H. McCall; brevet Colonel, Mar. 25, 1865; brevet Brigadier General Vols., Apr. 2, 1865. Joined the Corps, December, 1864.

205th infantry: Colonel Joseph A. Matthews. See above. Lieutenant Colonel William F. Walter. Joined the Corps, December, 1864.

207th infantry: Colonel Robert C. Cox, Sept. 8, 1864; brevet Brigadier General Vols., Apr. 2, 1865. Joined the Corps, December, 1864.

208th infantry: Colonel Alfred B. McCalmont. See above. Brevet Brigadier General Vols., Mar. 13, 1865. Lieutenant Colonel M. T. Heintzelman; brevet Colonel, Apr. 2, 1865. Joined the Corps, December, 1864.

209th infantry: Colonel Tobias B. Kaufman, Sept. 16, 1864; brevet Colonel George W. Frederick, April 2, 1865. Joined the Corps, Dec., 1864.

211th infantry: Colonel James H. Trimble, Sept. 16, 1864; honorably discharged Mar. 18, 1865. Colonel Levi A. Dodd, Mar. 19, 1865; brevet Brigadier General, July 8, 1865. Joined the Corps, December, 1864.

13th cavalry: Colonel Michael Kerwin, Oct. 7, 1863. Transferred to Cavalry Corps, June, 1864. Joined the Corps, May, 1864.

2d heavy artillery: Colonel James L. Anderson, July 23, 1864; killed in battle. Colonel William M. McClure, Sept. 30, 1864; honorably discharged

67

Mar. 7, 1865. Colonel S. D. Strawbridge, Mar. 8, 1865. Joined the Corps, May, 1864.

Battery B, independent volunteer artillery: Captain Charles F. Muller, Sept. 1, 1861; resigned Nov. 12, 1862. Captain Alanson J. Stevens, Dec. 6, 1852.

Battery D, independent volunteer artillery: Captain George W. Durell, Sept. 24, 1861; discharged Sept. 23, 1864. Captain Samuel H. Rhoads, Sept. 24, 1864. With the Corps throughout.

MARYLAND. *2d infantry:* Colonel T. B. Allard. Lieutenant Colonel J. E. Duryea, Sept. 21, 1861. Major H. Howard.

3d infantry (veterans): Lieutenant Colonel Gilbert P. Robinson; brevet Colonel, Aug. 18, 1864.

OHIO. *11th infantry:* Colonel Charles A. DeVilliers, July 6, 1861. Major Lyman J. Jackson. With the Corps from September, 1862, to October, 1862.

12th infantry; Colonel Carr B. White, Sept. 10, 1861. Joined the Corps September, 1862; transferred to West Virginia, October, 1862.

14th infantry: Colonel George P. Este, July 17, 1862. Joined the Corps, May, 1864.

23d infantry: Colonel Eliakim P. Scammon. See above. Lieutenant Colonel R. B. Hayes. Major J. N. Cornly. Joined the Corps September, 1862; transferred to West Virginia, October, 1862.

28th infantry: Colonel Augustus Moor; taken prisoner Sept. 12, 1862. See above. Lieutenant Colonel G. Becker; resigned Sept. 24, 1862. Major A. Bohlender. Joined the Corps, September, 1862; transferred to West Virginia, October, 1862.

30th infantry: Colonel Hugh Ewing. See above. Lieutenant Colonel Theodore Jones. Major George H. Hildt. Joined the Corps, September, 1862; transferred to West Virginia, October, 1862.

36th infantry: Colonel George Crook. See above. Lieutenant Colonel Melvin Clark, Major E. B. Andrews. Joined the Corps, September, 1862; transferred to West Virginia, October, 1862.

60th infantry: Lieutenant Colonel James N. McElroy, April 6, 1864; resigned. Lieutenant Colonel Martin P. Avery, Aug. 16, 1864. Joined the Corps, May, 1864.

86th infantry: Colonel Wilson C. Lemert, July 14, 1863. See above. Lieutenant Colonel Robert W. McFarland, July 8, 1863. Major William Krauss. Company K as artillery. A six months regiment. With the Corps in Kentucky and East Tennessee.

129th infantry: Colonel Howard D. John, Aug. 10, 1863. Company K as artillery. A six months regiment. With the Corps in Kentucky and East Tennessee.

1st battery of light artillery: Captain James R. McMullen, July 31, 1861.

Joined the Corps, September, 1862; transferred to West Virginia, October, 1862.

22d battery of light artillery: Captain Henry M. Neil, July 14, 1863. Formed from 86th and 129th infantry. See above.

23d battery of light artillery: Captain Simmons. Originally a company of the 1st Kentucky infantry, composed of Ohio men. Joined the Corps, September, 1862; transferred to West Virginia, October, 1862.

2d cavalry: Colonel George A. Purinton, May 9, 1864; mustered out, Oct. 28, 1864. Colonel Dudley Seward, Nov. 4, 1864. Joined the Corps, April, 1864.

Independent company of volunteer cavalry: Captain Frank Smith. Joined the Corps, September, 1862; transferred to West Virginia, October, 1862.

4th independent battalion of volunteer cavalry: Major J. T. Wheeler, Aug. 20, 1863. With the Corps in Kentucky and East Tennessee.

ILLINOIS. *Company of volunteer dragoons:* Captain F. Schambeck. Joined the Corps, September, 1862; transferred to West Virginia, October, 1862.

INDIANA. *71st infantry, (mounted):* Colonel James Biddle, Nov. 11, 1862; brevet Brigadier General, Mar. 13, 1865. With the Corps in Kentucky and East Tennessee.

3d cavalry: Colonel Scott Carter, Oct. 21, 1861. With the Corps from August, 1862, to November, 1862.

MICHIGAN. *2d infantry:* Colonel Orlando M. Poe. See above. Colonel William Humphrey. See above. Colonel Edwin J. March, Sept. 30, 1864. Joined the Corps, October, 1862.

8th infantry: Colonel William M. Fenton. See above. Colonel Frank Graves, May 1, 1863; killed at the battle of the Wilderness, May 6, 1864. Colonel Ralph Ely. See above. Lieutenant Colonel Richard N. Doyle. Joined the Corps, July, 1862.

15th infantry: Colonel John M. Oliver, Jan. 15, 1862. With the Corps in Mississippi only.

17th infantry: Colonel William H. Withington, Aug. 11, 1862; resigned Mar. 21, 1863. Colonel Constant Luce, Mar. 21, 1863. Joined the Corps, September, 1862.

20th infantry: Colonel Adolphus W. Williams, July 26, 1862. Colonel Byron M. Cutcheon. See above. Major Claudius B. Grant, June 20, 1864. Joined the Corps, September, 1862.

27th infantry: Colonel Dorus M. Fox, Dec. 31, 1862; resigned, Oct. 3, 1864. Colonel William B. Wright, Oct. 3, 1864. Colonel Charles Waite, brevet Brigadier General Vols., March 13, 1865. Joined the Corps, April, 1863.

1st sharp shooters: Colonel Charles V. Deland, Jan. 1, 1863. Joined the Corps, March, 1864.

VIRGINIA. *1st cavalry:* One company, Captain D. Deland. Joined the Corps September, 1862; transferred to West Virginia, October, 1862.

1st artillery: Companies B and D.

WISCONSIN. *37th infantry:* Colonel Samuel Harriman. See above. Lieutenant Colonel Anson O. Doolittle, Apr. 2, 1864; resigned Sept. 7. 1864. Lieutenant Colonel William J. Kershaw, Sept. 27, 1864; resigned Oct. 18, 1864. Lieutenant Colonel John Green, Dec. 15, 1864. Joined the Corps, April, 1864.

38th infantry: Colonel James Bintliff, Mar. 8, 1864; brevet Brigadier General Vols., Apr. 2, 1865. Joined the Corps, April, 1864.

UNITED STATES. *4th infantry:* First Lieutenant Robert P. McKibbin, Aug. 1, 1862. First Lieutenant George M. Randall, Nov. 6, 1862. With the Corps, from April, 1864, to July, 1864.

10th infantry: With the Corps, from April, 1864, to July, 1864.

2d artillery, battery D: First Lieutenant Edward B. Williston, Sept. 27, 1861.

2d artillery, battery E: Captain Samuel N. Benjamin. See above. Lieutenant James S. Dudley, May 23, 1863. With the Corps throughout.

2d artillery, battery M: First Lieutenant Carle A. Woodruff, July 24, 1862.

2d artillery, battery B and L: First Lieutenant John McGilvery, May 6, 1864.

3d *artillery, battery C:* Captain Dunbar R. Ransom, Nov. 1, 1861.

3d artillery, battery G: First Lieutenant Edmund Pendleton, Oct. 26, 1861; dismissed Oct. 14, 1864.

3d artillery, battery L and M: Captain John Edwards, Jr. See above.

4th artillery battery: Captain Joseph C. Clark, Jr., May 14, 1861.

4th artillery, battery E: First Lieutenant George Dickenson, Nov. 29, 1861; killed at Fredericksburg, Dec. 13, 1864. Battery C added; Captain Marcus P. Miller, May 11, 1864.

5th artillery, battery A: First Lieutenant Charles P. Muhlenburg, May 14, 1861.

5th artillery, battery L: First Lieutenant Wallace F. Randolph, Mar. 1, 1862.

The Artillery Brigade was under the command of Captain JAMES M. ROBERTSON, May 14, 1861; brevet Brigadier General Vols., Mar. 13, 1865.

UNITED STATES COLORED TROOPS. *19th infantry:* Colonel Henry G. Thomas. See above.

23d infantry: Colonel Cleveland J. Campbell; brevet Brigadier General Vols., Mar. 13, 1865.

27th infantry: Colonel A. M. Blackman; brevet Brigadier General Vols., Oct. 27, 1864.

28th infantry: Colonel Charles S. Russeli; died at Cincinnati, Nov. 2, 1866. See above.

29th infantry: Lieutenant Colonel Bross; killed in the Crater, July 30, 1864.

30th infantry: Colonel Delavan Bates. See above. Lieutenant Colonel H. A. Oakman; brevet Colonel, Mar. 13, 1865.

31st infantry: Colonel Henry C. Ward; brevet Brigadier General Vols., Nov. 9, 1865.

39th infantry: Colonel C. J. Wright; brevet Brigadier General Vols.

43d infantry: Colonel L. B. Yeoman; brevet Brigadier General Vols., Mar. 13, 1865.

Troops in North Carolina, under the command of General Burnside, not enumerated above:

MASSACHUSETTS. *17th infantry:* Colonel Thomas J. C. Amory, Sept. 2, 1861; brevet Brigadier General Vols.; died Oct. 7, 1864.

23d infantry: Colonel John Kurtz, Oct. 23, 1861.

24th infantry: Colonel Thomas G. Stevenson. See above. Lieutenant Colonel Francis A. Osborn, Aug. 31, 1861; brevet Brigadier General Vols., Mar. 13, 1865.

25th infantry: Colonel Edwin Upton, Sept. 9, 1861.

27th infantry: Colonel Horace C. Lee, Sept. 3, 1861.

RHODE ISLAND. *Battery F. 1st light artillery:* Captain James Belger, Oct. 17, 1861.

5th battalion infantry: Major John Wright, Dec. 16, 1861.

CONNECTICUT. *10th infantry:* Colonel Charles L. Russell, Oct. 24, 1861; killed at Roanoke Island, Feb. 8, 1862. Colonel Albert W. Drake, Feb. 8, 1862; died June 5, 1862. Colonel Ira W. Pettibone, June 5, 1862.

NEW YORK. *3d battery of light artillery*; Captain Thaddeus P. Mott, Nov. 2, 1861.

3d cavalry: Colonel James H. Van Alen, Aug. 28, 1861. Colonel Simon H. Mix, April 8, 1862.

Marine Artillery: Colonel William A. Howard, Sept. 1, 1861.

Rocket battalion of volunteer artillery: Major Thomas M. Lyon, Dec. 7, 1861.

NEW JERSEY. *9th infantry:* Colonel Joseph W. Allen; drowned Jan. 15, 1862. Lieutenant Colonel James Wilson.

UNITED STATES. 1st artillery, Company C. Captain L. O. Morris, Apr. 21, 1861.

VOLUNTEER AIDES AT THE BATTLE OF FREDERICKSBURG.

LLOYD ASPINWALL; Colonel by special order, Dec. 11, 1862.

WILLIAM GODDARD; Major 1st Rhode Island, June 27, 1861; Major by special order, Dec. 11, 1862.

Ulric Dahlgren: Captain, A. D. C., May 29, 1862.
Brock Cutting: Captain by special order, Dec. 11, 1862.

Note.—The division and brigade staffs changed so often as to make it impossible to give them with accuracy.

GENERAL INDEX.

ADDENDA.

PHILIP M. LYDIG, (p. 514.): With the Corps throughout.

MEDICAL DIRECTOR.

GEORGE TAYLOR: assistant Surgeon, U S. A., Apr. 1, 1856; Surgeon, Aug. 27, 1862. Succeeded Dr. McDonald and continued with the Corps till Mar. 11, 1865.

JAMES HARRIS, (p. 16,): brigade Surgeon, Mar. 27, 1864; medical inspector, June 19, 1864; division surgeon, Oct. 19, 1864; acting medical director, May 20 1865.

BRIGADE COMMANDER.

GEORGE F. RAULSTON: Colonel 24th New York dismounted cavalry, Jan. 26, 1864.

NEW YORK. *79th infantry*, (p. 527); Lieutenant Colonel John More, Feb. 17, 1863.

INDEX.

www.ingramcontent.com/pod-product-compliance
Lightning Source LLC
LaVergne TN
LVHW021224110826
845150LV00002B/236

9781425564117